FUN DANCE RHYTHMS

FUN DANCE RHYTHMS

ALMA HEATON

Brigham Young University Press
Provo, Utah

Library of Congress Cataloging in Publication Data

Heaton, Alma
  Fun dance rhythms.

  Bibliography: p.
  1. Dancing. I. Title
GV1751.H386   793.3   76-15242
ISBN 0-8425-0478-8

Library of Congress Catalog Card Number: 76-15242
International Standard Book Number: 0-8425-0478-8
Brigham Young University Press, Provo, Utah 84602
ⓒ 1976 by Brigham Young University Press. All rights reserved
Printed in the United States of America
11-76   2.5M   7042

This book contains dances for all ages and occasions, including round, social, folk, square, tap, elementary, and creative dances in all formations.

This book is dedicated to all who enjoy fun dancing, but especially to amateur groups with amateur leaders, who can find herein all that is necessary for an exciting evening of the kind of dance of their choice.

CONTENTS

FOREWORD

Lloyd Shaw, square dance teacher and promoter, said in <u>The Round Dance Book</u>, "Of course you can't dance . . . alone. You'll have to have a partner. . . . Then, to have any fun, you'll have to invite over to your house one or two other couples, and you'll show them how. But that, brother, is teaching."

It is for this kind of teacher, as well as for the professional, that this book is written. It is for the person who wants to have fun dancing and recognizes that he cannot do so alone. It is for those who find themselves in charge of an evening's fun and who want some specifics on what to do and how to do it. It contains a wealth of information gleaned and adapted by the author during a quarter of a century as a successful and beloved teacher of dancing at the university level. It is a useful tool for all who share Alma Heaton's enthusiasm for dancing.

--The Editors

Alma Heaton, Professor of Recreation
Brigham Young University

ACKNOWLEDGMENTS

I acknowledge a debt of gratitude to Dr. Israel C. Heaton for his constructive criticism, his encouragement to me in presenting the manuscript of this book for publication, and his permission to use excerpts from his book Planning for Social Recreation. I am indebted also to the students at Brigham Young University who encouraged me and provided me with the opportunity to teach recreation dances in an educational situation.

I am grateful to Robert Oliphant and Mary Bee Jensen for their help with the folk dances; to Bruce Elm and Earl Beck for their assistance on the square dance chapter; to Ben DeHoyos for his help with the ballroom dance chapter; to Christine Walton Ollerton for the section on children's creative dance; to Margaret Greenwood Blake for the article on rope jumping; and to Wayne Turley, Burton Olsen, Roy Mavor, and Stewart Glazer for their suggestions. Diane Chatwin, Nina Booth, Kay Seamonson, Carolyn Rasmus, Gayle Blackmore, Jeanne Probert, Emerson and LeGene Lyman, Tom Zimmerman, Davitt and Betty Kasdan, Sally Edmonds, and Susanne Davis also contributed significantly to this volume.

Acknowledgment and sincere thanks are due Everett Chaffer, associate superintendent of the Los Angeles city schools, for excerpts from the book Rhythmic Activities, and to the Folk Dance Federation of California for their help.

Although the dances described in this book have come from countless sources, a considerable number of the dances and mixers are original. My thanks to my students for their help in developing many of these. Also, I am deeply indebted to the various authors and publishers who granted permission to include dances published in their books, and to the following record companies for permission to use their dances: Black Mountain Records, MacGregor Records, Old Timer Records, Lloyd Shaw Records, Western Jubilee Records, Windsor Records, Ed Gilmore, Aqua Records, Balance Records, Hoedown Records, Longhorn Records, Morrison Records, Tempo Recording and Record Co., Radio Corporation of America, and MGM Records.

INTRODUCTION

Few recreational activities are more popular than dance. Yet often this activity is neglected in recreational programs. Many children are not acquainted with dance. By the time they become teenagers few of them can fully enjoy the possibilities of dance unless they have had some previous training. They are far too interested in what their peers will think to let themselves learn dancing skills.

Proper dance training develops a person by--

- Increasing coordination, cooperation, and powers of attention
- Developing the ability to follow directions
- Increasing mental alertness
- Developing creativity
- Bringing the family closer together
- Developing an understanding of other cultures and customs

A BRIEF HISTORY OF DANCE

Movement is universal, both internally in our physiological mechanisms and externally in our conduct. Anyone hearing a loud sudden noise will jump. Most people express joy with some movement of delight, such as skipping or jumping for joy. Worry universally calls forth a certain pattern of nervous movements, such as uncontrollably pacing the floor.

Thus emotions are expressed in movements which, though sometimes not intentional, are always revealing. Dance is the conscious artistry of communicating feelings, sometimes by imitating, often by exaggerating, the involuntary movements of people seized by powerful emotions. Dance is observable in most cultures of the world and its form is modified by geography, climate, race, religion, social environment, and cultural traditions. The history of dance is a history of man's efforts to communicate, first with his own kind, and then with powers greater than himself.

Primitive man especially found expression for his feelings in dancing. With dance he displayed his valor as hunter or warrior; pled with his gods for rain, sunshine, bountiful crops, good hunting, children, or victory in battle; exulted in his manhood; courted his woman; and expressed his feelings for his tribe, his traditions, or his religion. Unlike his modern counterpart, primitive man did not dance for amusement; dancing was a continuous part of his hard-working life.

The movements of the primitive dances were simple; the rhythm was intricate and syncopated. The men, who did the dancing, danced close to the ground in crouching positions to establish a close relationship with the earth. The women participated by hand-clapping or drum-beating or merely by watching.

The Egyptians were among the ancient peoples noted for their dance. The people danced, the priests danced, and professional dancers entertained the rich and the royal. An ancient form of Egyptian dance which persists today is a type of astral ballet which imitates the rhythm of the stars of the universe.

Among the ancient Greeks dance was highly esteemed and was recognized as having aesthetic value. There were special dances for religious events;

soldiers danced as part of their training for battle; leaders were recognized for their skill in dance as well as in affairs of state; philosophers taught their followers to dance for the effect it had on mind and body; poets were dancers, and one of their number, Sophocles, was celebrated for his special dancing ability. At banquets dancers replaced after-dinner speakers on many occasions. The Greek writer Lucian stated in his Dialogues (A.D. 162-65):

> Dance is not one of the facile arts that can be plied without pains, but reaches to the very summit of all culture, not only in music but in rhythm and metre, and especially in philosophy, but also in physics and ethics. Then too, all the rest are activities of one or the other of the two elements in man, some of them are activities of the soul, some of the body; but in dancing, both are combined, and there is a display of mind in the performance as well as expression of bodily development, and the most important part of it is the wisdom that controls the action and the fact that nothing is irrational.

When the Romans in their conquests came into contact with Greek culture, they were impressed with the dance. Lacking the Greek sense of the aesthetic, however, they cheapened the dance, replacing its dignity with sensationalism and obscenity.

With the deterioration of Rome and the rise of Christianity, dance as an art form faded from the scene. Although dance was generally not forbidden by the Christian fathers, they recognized the dangers inherent in pagan pageantry and in Roman licentiousness. Dancing was supervised by the church and permitted in western Europe among the village folk only in celebration of certain festivals.

There are few records left of the way of life in Europe during the Dark Ages, but in church writings some mention is made of dancing. Saint Basil, for example, told his hearers that since dancing would be their chief occupation in heaven they would do well to practice it on earth.

As the Renaissance dawned with its rich appreciation for all art forms, dance experienced a rebirth. The wild, crude dances of the peasants were brought into the newly developing towns and into the courts of Europe, where they were refined and subdued. Ballet, combined with song, poetry, and acting, became popular in court circles. In 1661 Louis XIV of France, a dancer himself, founded the Royal Academy of Music and the Dance in Paris, and instruction in dance became an essential part of the education and training of a gentleman. In an age which stressed elegance and refinement, dancing once again became dignified but moved on to become stilted and artificial, lacking spirit and spontaneity. In the country the peasants continued to dance with wild abandon and to develop what have become the folk dances of the world. An outgrowth of the stylized dancing among the royalty and nobility was professional ballet, and a whole series of ballerinas undertook the arduous task of acquiring the skills of classical ballet which eventually lifted them onto their toes and carried dance into the modern period.

So restricted was dance in the 1800s that a rebellion was early in the making against its repression and lack of spirit. Among the innovators were Russian Michel Fokine, who worked his revolution within the framework of the ballet. But Isadora Duncan, an American who made Europe her home, turned to classical Greece for her inspiration. She rejected ballet and built a free form of dance based on natural body movements. A magnificent performer, she endowed dance with new concepts that have endured to enrich the art.

Her contemporary Ruth St. Denis lived and danced and taught in the United States. She married Ted Shawn, also a dancer, teacher, and pioneer in new dance forms. Together they formed the Denishawn Dancers, who toured the United States and Europe in the 1930s with richly staged productions. From the Denishawn Dancers developed a group who called themselves the modern dancers and who helped pioneer and stabilize modern dance in this country. Among them were Martha Graham, Doris Humphrey, and Charles Weidman.

The dance scene today is a conglomerate. Ballet continues to enjoy a popular performance spotlight, having been rescued from its stilted and heavily stylized form in the nineteenth century. It has influenced and been influenced by modern dance, which is also popular today in many milieus from college campus to television stage.

Social dancing, which had its beginnings in the peasant dances of Europe and was toned down by the minuets and quadrilles of the eighteenth and nineteenth centuries, greatly increased its momentum with the waltz and the polka in the 1800s. Since the turn of the century in the United States there has been an intermittent waxing and waning of enthusiasm for social dancing, as well as a geographical diversity of dance forms. Square dancing has never lost its popularity in such widely dispersed places as South Dakota ranches and New England halls. Ethnic groups cling to their native folk dances, which are imitated and sometimes embellished by university or professional dance groups. Television has encouraged a rebirth of tap dancing and the old soft-shoe routines of vaudeville days. After several years of hard and soft rock music and independent dancing, Americans are showing signs of a returning interest in ballroom dancing: waltz and foxtrot, with perhaps an admixture of Latin rhythms--rumba, tango, cha-cha, and conga.

Dancing is a normal, natural expression of the fundamental instinct for rhythm and social contact. It also offers opportunities for the development of grace, refinement, manners, and poise.

I believe that dancing can help promote world understanding and should be taught to every person attending school. I believe the educational value in dance rates along with all other academic subjects and that students of dance will gain skills that will be of benefit and enjoyment to them throughout their lives.

FUN DANCE RHYTHMS

HOW TO USE THE BOOK

Each dance in this book is written in two columns, with calls in one column and instructions in the other. The name of each step is underlined both in the call column and in the instruction column. Thus at a glance the reader can find the instruction for any step. The calls are written so that the direction for the next step is given on the last count of the preceding measure. This helps the caller call the step in time with the music and ahead of the dancers.

Examples of the calls are as follows: instead of calling, "Forward,two, three, four," calls are written, "One, two, three, back," eliminating the "four" count. Following this pattern, the dancers have time to hear the call and respond in rhythm to the music, thus increasing their enjoyment of the performance. This method of not calling the step during the exact time the dancers should be executing it requires a little study and practice but in the long run reduces teaching time considerably.

The measures in each line in the call column have been numbered consecutively, allowing the teacher to find quickly the line he wants to refer to and call.

Capital letters indicate a SLOW movement (two beats), and lowercase letters indicate a quick movement (one beat). The apostrophe (') following a word or number indicates a double-quick movement (one-half beat). Also, commas are used to break the call into measures where there is more than one measure for each line in the call. The rhythm is thus included in the directions for each dance, giving the caller an idea of the time allotted for each movement--and thus for each word called. Following this method, the beginning teacher is able to call correctly and thus keep the dancers in rhythm.

The words quick and SLOW also indicate a change of weight. Every direction, word, or count should indicate a change of weight or foot movement. The name of the step is mentioned regardless of the type of call used.

The key word to be called on the last of each measure (to introduce the next step) is underlined.

In the call column, numerals with no intervening punctuation indicate a count of one beat. A different count, when necessary, is indicated by an apostrophe (one-half beat) or a dividing comma (a full measure of two or more beats).

Because the male partner traditionally maintains the lead position in dancing, the dances in this book are written for the man, indicating the direction in which he moves and the steps he takes. In all cases where the footwork is described as opposite (and in some cases--especially in social dancing--where no indication is given), the lady must do exactly the opposite of what is written. Although at first this may be difficult, it becomes easier with practice.

Other difficulties can be avoided by remembering that in round dance mixers for couples the man always goes back to find a new partner and the lady goes forward. In a threesome formation the man goes forward and the ladies back for new partners.

Although specific music is suggested for most dances, the suggestion is made only for the convenience of the uninitiated and need not be binding.

3

In fact, each group leader is encouraged to select current tunes popular with the group, provided the rhythm is right for the dance involved.

For the sake of brevity, instructions and calls for long round dances and mixers are limited to one sequence where this is possible.

The final organization of this material, its use, and its presentation are, of course, individual matters, depending upon the needs, interests, and abilities of a particular group.

A B B R E V I A T I O N S

The following abbreviations are used generally throughout the book in the dance instructions.

a--quarter beat
agLOD--against line of dance
ccw--counterclockwise
cnt--contact
ct--count
çw--clockwise
diag--diagonally
fwd--forward
L--left and/or left foot
LOD--line of dance
meas--measure
q--quick (one beat)
R--right and/or right foot
S--slow (two beats)
'--half beat

Action round: Steps danced while singing a round.

Against line of dance: Clockwise around the dance floor.

And: (a) The indication of a second quick count. (b) An advance count used as a preparatory signal for starting.

Arch: A movement for which partners join hands and raise them so that one or both of them (see Dishrag, below) or other dancers may go under the raised arms. Four hand contacts are possible: left-right, right-left, right-right, left-left. The arch may be executed while the feet are moving through any of the basic steps.

Axial movements: Movements on a stationary base.

Backward: A term referring to walking or otherwise moving a foot or feet backward.

Balance: A hesitation with no change of weight; a step (followed by a touch, swing, brush, point, draw, lift, hold, dot, heel, toe, flick, stomp, kick, dig, or ball turn), holding at least one beat.

Ball-change: A quick change of weight from the ball of the left foot to the ball of the right foot and back to the left foot, or vice versa.

Ballroom dance: A particular style of step danced to a given piece of music. Examples: foxtrot, rumba, waltz. It can involve repetition of the same sequence of steps as in fun dances, round dances, and sequence dances.

Ballroom dancing: The style of dancing which may be done in large ballrooms.

Ballroom mixer: An activity requiring a change of partners while engaged in ballroom dancing.

Ballroom round dance: Ballroom steps danced in a set routine.

Ballroom round dance mixer: Ballroom steps danced in a set routine and accompanied by a change of partners.

Ball-turn: A turn accomplished by crossing one foot over or behind the other foot and turning on the balls of the feet.

Basic: Fundamental, preparatory, or introductory movement or step.

Basket: A dance formation in which the men join hands to form one circle (inside) and the ladies join hands to form another (outside). Keeping hands joined, the ladies walk under the men's raised arms to make a single circle. Without releasing hands, the men lower their hands until their arms are around the backs of the ladies and the two circles are intertwined.

Break: A change of direction, rhythm, or position. This applies primarily

5

to rhythm dances.

Brush: A movement accomplished by lightly touching the floor with the free foot, then "brushing" the inside edge of the supporting foot with the inside edge of the free foot and following through with the free foot before moving it to the side for the weight change.

Buzz step: A step in which partners assume a swing or right-side position with the two right feet placed inside and close to each other forming a pivot point and with the upper body leaning away. The left feet are used to push the dancers around the pivot in a manner similar to pushing a child's scooter.

Calls: Verbally given name of or instructions for a dance step. All calls are for the men, except sometimes in square dancing. Some dances will have to be called completely through the record, but most of them just two or three times; this depends on the caller, the group, the record, the rhythm, the difficulty of the dance, and whether or not the caller calls ahead on the preceding measure.

Calling ahead: The calling of the name of the step on the measure preceding its execution.

Canter: Two weight changes to one measure of waltz time.

Center of hall: A movement where dancers dance in to the center of the floor or dancing area, either sideward, forward, backward, or rotating.

Change: (a) A shifting of weight, (b) an altering of direction or position, or (c) a changing of partners.

Chanting call: A call that assists only in keeping the dancers in rhythm.

Chassé: A step and a close which may be forward or backward but is usually sideward. The free foot never passes the supporting foot. It is generally used in a series.

Chorus girl line (see Basket): A formation the same as a basket except that the dancers are in a line.

Chug: A step accomplished by stepping left with the left foot, then closing the right toe to it and changing weight just long enough to move the left foot left again. This is repeated three more times, then reversed to the right.

Close: The act of bringing the feet together and changing weight. The free foot should be placed flat alongside the supporting foot, as in international style competition dancing.

Combination of units: The act of beginning with the left unit of one step and completing with the right unit of another step. (Most steps are completed in two units; a unit is half of a step.)

Contact: Connection of hands between partners. In indicating contact, the

6

man's hand is mentioned first.

Contra-body movement: A movement executed by turning one side of the body in the direction opposite that of the moving foot; for example, moving the left foot forward and the left shoulder backward.

Controlled practice: The second part of a lesson. Dancers have some freedom in that the instructor tells them (a) what to do but not when to do it, or (b) when but not what. For example, the instructor may call, (a) "Do four basic foxtrot rhythms during this number. Go"; or (b) "Change position six times. One, two, change, one, two, change, one, two, change. . . ."

Corte: A step where the man dips back, bending the left knee, as the lady steps forward, bending the right knee. Dancers are usually in closed position.

Count: (a) The number of weight changes, or (b) musical or dance count.

Counterpart: An instruction to the lady indicating that though she may turn opposite from the man she does the same footwork on the opposite foot and travels in the same directions.

Counting call: A call that counts the music beats or weight changes.

Couple dance: A dance requiring a partner.

Cross: A step accomplished by moving one foot over the other foot either forward or backward.

Cross ball-change (back pas de basque): A step executed by leaping to the left, crossing the right foot behind the left for a momentary weight change, then shifting the weight back to the left foot to reverse the movement to the right.

Dance count: A call used to count out the rhythm of the foot movements and weight changes (not the music beats). For example, 1, 2, 3 and 4 is the count for one unit of a cha-cha step.

Dance mixer: A dance that requires a change of partners.

Dance rhythm: (a) A repetition of the same sequence of slow and quick movements. For instance, the foxtrot contains several well-known rhythms: walk (SSSS), two-step (qqS), chassé (qqqqqqS), box (Sqq), magic (SSqq). (b) A call used to indicate weight changes and used to keep the dancers changing weight rhythmically. Example: SLOW, SLOW, quick, quick.

Demonstration: (a) A teaching technique in which the leader shows the dance routine while calling the steps in rhythm. (b) A pantomime or walk-through of a step or figure not in rhythm.

Diagonal: A change of direction achieved by making a forty-five-degree turn right from the line of dance (known as a diagonal out), or a forty-five-degree turn left from the line of dance (a diagonal in).

Different: An instruction indicating that the lady's foot pattern differs from her partner's.

7

HAND CONTACTS

Left-right

Right-left

Left-left

Right-right

Right-left, left-right

Right-right, left-left

Shine (no contact)

Dig: A movement executed by touching the ball of the free foot on the floor and to the side of the supporting foot with a strong emphasis.

Direct teaching: The first part of instruction of each lesson, in which the instructor directs and calls every movement. There is no controlled practice or free practice in this part.

Directional call: The calling of the step pattern. Used to indicate to the dancer the direction of the foot movement. Example: FORWARD, FORWARD, side, together.

Dishrag: A movement in which partners join hands in two-hand position to form a double arch, then turn together under the arch, keeping hands joined.

Docey: Another term for do-si-do.

Do-si-do: A movement executed by passing right shoulders to circle around partner, and backing into place passing left shoulders.

Dot: A touch of the right or left toe behind the supporting foot.

Double: An instruction indicating that both man and lady do the same step on opposite feet. Double does not mean to dance the step twice.

Double circle: Two concentric circles of partners opposite each other.

Draw: A movement following a sideward step in which the free foot is brought slowly to the side of the supporting foot without changing weight. It is held for at least one beat of music.

Face-to-face: A position in which partners stand facing each other. Hands may not be joined.

Fall-away: A step in which the couple moves backward in semi-open position.

Flick: A quick lift of the foot to the side and back, leg bending at the knee.

Follow-through: A continuation of foot and body movement to anticipate the next step, as in international style competition dancing.

Foot movement: Locomotor movement. A foot movement may or may not entail a change of weight. For example, a walking step is a movement with a weight change, while a swing or dot of the foot is a movement without a change of weight.

Footwork: An instruction telling the dancer which foot to start on and when to change weight. For example, in left footwork both the man and the lady start on the left foot; in right footwork both start on the right foot; in opposite footwork the man starts on the left foot and the lady on the right foot.

Formation: The orientation of dancers on the dance floor--e.g., in lines, a single circle, a double circle, a threesome circle, a square, and so on.

Formations:
    Double circle: Two single circles, one inside the other, of partners opposite each other.
    Line: A continuous row of dancers.
    Mass: Dancers scattered around the floor (with partners).
    Single circle: A single circle of dancers with or without partners.
    Square: Groups of four couples facing each other, each couple forming one side of a square.
    Team dancing: Groups of two couples facing in the line of dance or facing each other, or two threesomes facing each other.
    Threesome circle: Threesomes (a man between two ladies or a lady between two men) in a circle, either facing in the line of dance or facing each other in teams.

Free practice: The third part of teaching, in which the dancers are free to dance any step in the lesson or routine. Music is playing, but the instructor does not call.

Full turn: A turn in which the dancers make one complete revolution.

Grand right-and-left: A step executed in circle formation in which partners join right hands and walk passing right shoulders, with ladies advancing clockwise and men counterclockwise. Men join left hands with the ladies now facing them and pass left shoulders with them. Dancers continue on around the circle, alternating right and left hands. Men usually pick up the fifth lady for the next partner. The most common basic step is a walk, but any of the basic steps may be used.

Grapevine: A step executed by stepping to the left with the left foot, crossing the right foot behind it, stepping left again, and crossing the right foot in front of the left.

Hands: Contact between partners.

Hash: A chanting call, mainly associated with square dancing, where the caller makes up calls that are appropriate for the dance.

Heel: (a) Heel (wrist) of the hand, referring to the man's hand lead. (b) Heel of the foot, referring to the touching of the heel of the foot to the floor.

Heel-toe: A movement executed by placing one heel forward, then the toe of the same foot back. No weight change.

Hesitation: A balance step holding at least one count. See also Balance.

Hold: (a) A wait of a designated length of time before another step is taken. (b) In English dance terminology, the carriage of the arms, head, and body in relation to one's partner. Also known as dance position.

Hop: A momentary weight change executed by hopping on the supporting foot.

Host couple: The couple or threesome facing against the line of dance in team or square formation in a circle.

Individual turn: A right or left turn executed by both man and lady in shine position.

In place: A shift of weight without moving the feet.

Instructor's calls: The directions called out by the instructor to cue students. Below is an example of the different types of calls for the magic step.

Dance footwork	L	R	l	r
Dance direction	FORWARD	FORWARD	side	together
Dance rhythm	SLOW	SLOW	quick	quick
Dance count	1	2	3	and
Dance chant	STEP	STEP	step	step
Music count	1 2	3 4	5	6
Prompting call	NOW	THE	magic	step
Movement count	1	2	3	4
Weight change count	1	2	3	4

Jump: A movement executed by pushing off the floor with one or both feet and landing on the opposite foot or on both feet.

Junior: The combining of semi-open and reverse positions or the change from one to the other.

Junior step: Any step that requires a semi-open to reverse position and where the lady's footwork or direction is the same as the man's.

Kick: A raise of the free foot forward, backward, sideward, or crosswise after bending the knee.

Lady same (opposite, different): A term indicating the lady's position and footwork in relation to the man's.

Latin ballroom round dance mixer: Latin ballroom steps danced in a set routine and accompanied by a change of partners.

Lead: (a) The pressure of the man's hand, shoulder, or body to indicate the direction, position, and beginning and end of step movement. The proper lead gets dancers into, through, and out of the step. (b) Starting ("leading") with the left or right foot.

Leap: A movement executed by springing lightly from one foot to the other.

Left: A directional call referring to foot, hand, or side.

Left-left contact: The joining of the man's left hand with the lady's left hand.

Left side: (a) A dance position or (b) a direction of movement.

Leverage: A body lead indicating a change from a quick to a slow movement or from a slow to a quick movement without changing direction.

Lift: A movement in which the free foot points in the direction opposite to which the body is moving.

Line: A continuous row of dancers.

Line of dance: An imaginary line of direction of movement counterclockwise around the outside of the room.

Lock (closed-cross): A tight cross of the feet or ankles backward or forward.

Locomotor movement: Progressive dance movements of the feet.

Loop, loop turn: A movement in which the lady turns to her left under an arch, opposite from the direction in which she would turn for an ordinary arch turn.

Mass: A formation in which the dancers are scattered around the floor (with partners).

Measure: A grouping of musical beats containing an equal amount of time in any given piece of music. The portion of music between two bars.

Mixer: (a) An activity for changing partners or getting acquainted while engaged in a dance or game. (b) A type of dance or party that allows dancers to mix together and get acquainted.

Movement: A change of foot position, or the manner (axial and/or locomotive) of transferring or not transferring weight.

Movement count: The count of every foot movement and weight change. For example, the conga step has eight movements and six weight changes: 1-2-3-kick, 1-2-3-kick.

Music rhythm: Music count or time, indicating the music beats, such as 3/4, 4/4, 2/4.

Musical mixer: A game played to music (not a dance).

Opposite: An instruction indicating that the lady's footwork is opposite from that of her partner (may or may not be written).

Paddle: A chug step executed in swing position, which moves the dancer in a tight turn instead of a line. See Chug.

Pantomime: A demonstration or walk-through of a step not in rhythm.

Parallel position: A dance position in which the man stands directly behind his partner. They may or may not be holding hands.

Pas de basque: A step executed exactly like the cross ball-change, except that the right foot crosses in front of the left. See Cross ball-change (back pas de basque).

Patter call: A chanting call that serves as a rhythmical background in order for the dancers to keep in rhythm.

Pick-up: A change of partners in which a dancer on the floor goes to the side of the hall and joins hands with another person, bringing him or her onto the floor.

Pivot: A movement executed by spinning or turning with a partner in closed position without bringing the feet together.

Point: A movement of the free foot forward, backward, sideward, or crosswise without changing weight.

Polka: A fast-moving dance performed as a two-step and hop, or hop and two-step.

Preparation: Basic or introductory steps which prepare dancers for more advanced steps.

Progressive step (progression): A step which does not end in the same place it starts, thus moving dancers around the hall.

Progressive dance program: Dance lessons which advance the student from a beginning class to a more advanced class.

Promenade position: A position in which two dancers stand side by side in two-hand position--R-R and L-L contact. Both are facing forward, and the man's right hand is over the lady's left hand.

Prompting call: A call that gives only the name of the step.

Quick: An instruction indicating a change of weight distinguished by how long the weight is on the foot. Two quick steps take the same length of time as one slow step, regardless of the tempo of the music.

Recreational dance: Folk, social, square, and round dance steps placed together in short routines, with a change of partner after each sequence.

Reel: A dance in which the man turns his own partner, then also turns each lady within the formation. (a) Circle reel: The man turns his partner one full turn with an elbow lead, then turns the next lady with left elbows hooked. He continues turning each lady all the way around the circle. (b) Line reel: The man turns his own partner before turning each lady down the line. The lady also turns each man after having turned her own partner.

Reverse: A change of direction in order to dance the same step or unit in the opposite direction.

Rhythm: (a) In dance: the regularity of flow of movement. (b) In music: the pattern of recurring light and heavy accents.

Rhythm dances: Dances in which there is dancing on the spot, as opposed to progressing around the dance hall.

Right: A directional call referring to foot, hand, or side.

Right-left contact: A position in which the man's right hand is joined with the lady's left hand.

Right-right contact: A hand position in which partners' right hands are joined.

Ripple: A forward movement of the knees, hips, stomach, shoulders, and head, in this order.

Rise-and-fall: A controlled raising and lowering of the body while dancing.

Rock: A movement executed by moving back and forth or turning while shifting weight but without changing foot positions.

Rock dancing: A term for fad, modern, or popular dance.

Roll: A movement in which the lady makes one complete turn in front of her partner, traveling from his right side to his left side.

Rotate: An instruction indicating (a) a turn to left or right, or (b) a change of partners.

Round dance (sequence dance): A dance with a set routine. It can be composed of social, folk, or square dance steps and is not necessarily danced in a circle.

Round dance mixer: A dance with a set routine which requires a change of partners.

Routine: One or more figures in a set pattern comprising an entire dance. A routine is the largest subdivision of a dance. (It might help to remember these terms if you were to think of them in the following manner: The dance is a completed report, while the routine is a paragraph of the report. The figure is a sentence and the step is a word in the sentence. The unit is a syllable and the change of weight (or movement) is a letter in the syllable or word.)

Run: A fast, alternating transfer of weight from one foot to another with a slight elevation.

Same: A term indicating that the lady's footwork is the same as her partner's, usually on the opposite foot from the man's. The call is the same as the man's.

Schottische: (a) A schottische dance. (b) A step executed by progressing with three forward steps L-R-L and hopping on the L foot, then repeating R-L-R and hopping on the R foot.

School figure: A figure or step known and given the same name in all schools of dance.

Senior: The combining of right- and left-side positions or the change from one to the other.

Senior step: Any step that requires a left- to right-side position, with the lady dancing opposite footwork.

Shine, or challenge, position: An individual position with no contact between partners.

Shoulder-waist position: A position in which the man places his hands on the lady's waist and the lady places her hands on the man's shoulders.

Shuffle: (a) Short walking steps used in square dancing while promenading or swinging a partner. The feet brush the floor. (b) A movement accomplished by placing the left foot forward and changing foot positions by placing the left foot back and the right foot forward.

Side ball-change: A movement executed by stepping left with the left foot, closing the right foot to it for a momentary weight change.

Sideward left: A move to the man's left with a chassé, cross, slide, etc.

Single circle: A single circle of dancers around the room, with or without partners.

Skip: A combination of a step and a hop to a series of long-short rhythms.

Slide: A movement executed by stepping to the side with one foot, closing the other foot, changing weight, and repeating.

Slow: The count for a step, equaling two quick steps and indicating a change of weight.

Spin: A rapid turn without any weight change while in shine position.

Spot: The area required for a step not progressing in any direction.

Square dance: A dance in which four couples face each other, each couple forming one side of a square, dancing as directed.

Star: A figure in which three or more dancers place the left or right hands together and walk forward or backward.

Step: One or more movements, weight changes, or units which carry a name for identification. Basic ballroom steps are the walk, rock, cross, arch, wheel, pivot, chassé, and hesitation. Basic round dance steps include the hesitation, chug, grapevine, paddle, pas de basque, side ball-change, cross ball-change, walk, slide, two-step, and swing partner.

Step combination: The placing together of two or more basic steps or step variations.

Step swing: The act of stepping on one foot and swinging the free foot. No weight change is involved.

Step variation: Variation from the basic step.

Stomp: A movement executed by placing the flat of one foot on the floor with a heavy accent without changing weight.

Style: The appearance and technique of a couple while in motion.

Sweetheart position (varsouvienne position): A position in which the man places his right hand over his partner's right shoulder, holding her right hand. Left hands are joined and held out to the side at shoulder height. There are four variations of this position: the man's position relative to the lady's may be before, behind, to the left, or to the right.

Swing: A lift of the free foot forward, backward, sideward, or crosswise.

6 Swing partner (buzz swing): A step executed by pushing or paddling with the left or outside foot while in right-side position with the right foot touching the partner's right foot. The left foot must be kept behind the right foot. The lady may get back onto the correct foot or change to the opposite foot by holding for a beat of music or stepping twice to a beat of music. The following are seven ways in which a man may swing his partner.
   Backhand swing: A swing, starting in right-side position, in which both man and lady place the left arm behind their own back and interlock right elbows. They then take their partner's left hand in their own right and swing to the right.
   Elbow swing: A shuffle, walk, or paddle swing to left or right with left or right elbows linked, respectively.
   Shoulder swing: A swing to the right in which both man and lady place the right hand on their partner's right shoulder, join left hands, place the right foot forward, and paddle.
   Two-hand swing: A swing to the right or left in which partners join hands in two-hand position, place one foot forward, and bend back slightly to swing.
   Waist swing: A swing to the right with both man and lady holding the left arm up and placing the right arm around the partner's waist.
   Irish swing: A swing executed with right hands joined and left hand holding the partner's right elbow.
   Neck swing: A swing in which partners stand in right-side position, holding hands in right-left, left-right contact. With hands still joined, partners raise the clasped left hand behind their own neck and their clasped right hand behind their partner's neck. The swing is to the right.

Team dance, team dancing: A dance in which two couples stand facing each other with the lady to the man's right side. Three dancers may also form a team by facing another set of three. One team faces the line of dance and the other faces against the line of dance.

Tap: A touch of the ball of the free foot to the floor.

Threesome: A team formation of one man between two ladies or one lady between two men.

Threesome circle: Threesomes in a circle (a man between two ladies or a lady between two men).

Toe-heel: A movement executed by placing the free foot back touching the

TYPES OF SWINGS

Backhand

Elbow

Shoulder

Two-hand

Waist

Irish

Neck

One-hand
(not described)

Shoulder-waist
(not described)

toe to the floor, then placing the heel of the same foot forward touching the floor.

Together: An instruction to close the feet and change weight unless otherwise designated.

Touch: A movement executed by bringing feet together and touching the free foot to the supporting foot without changing weight.

Turn: A rotation of the body.

Twirl: A movement in which the lady makes one complete turn in front of the man.

Two-step: A step accomplished by stepping forward with the left foot, closing the right foot to the left, then stepping forward again with the left foot. Then the process is repeated, starting with the right foot.

Types of dances: The types of dances are listed below.
     Action round: Steps danced while singing a round.
     Ballroom mixer: An activity requiring a change of partners while engaged in ballroom dancing.
     Ballroom round dance: Ballroom steps danced in a set routine.
     Ballroom round dance mixer: Ballroom steps danced in a set routine and accompanied by the changing of partners.
     Couple dance: A dance requiring partners.
     Dance mixer: A dance that requires a change of partner.
     Latin ballroom round dance mixer: Latin ballroom steps danced in a set routine, with the changing of partners.
     Round dance: A dance with a set routine (can be in any formation).
     Round dance mixer: A dance with a set routine which requires a change of partners.
     Square dance: A dance in which four couples face each other, each couple forming one side of a square, dancing as directed.

Unit: One or more movements or changes of weight used to comprise a step. A unit is the smallest segment into which a step can be broken down and still retain the rhythm pattern. For example, the waltz box contains two units: unit 1--forward side close; unit 2--back side close. In this example each unit is started on a different foot. In the foxtrot, senior walk, magic rhythm, a step consists of two units, both starting on the left foot: unit 1--FORWARD FORWARD side close; unit 2--BACK BACK side close.

Variation: A figure in any dance which is not known as a basic figure.

Varsouvienne position: See Sweetheart position.

Vine: A shortened term for grapevine. "Vine" takes one beat to say and helps in calling dance steps.

Visiting couple: The couple or threesome facing the line of dance when in team formation. Those facing the line of dance travel in the line of dance to dance with a couple or threesome facing against the line of dance (host couple).

Walk: A progressive alternate transfer of weight from one foot to the other during which one foot remains in contact with the floor.

Walk-through: A practice session without music in which the group practices the routine as the leader calls the steps in rhythm.

Weight change: The transfer of weight from the supporting foot to the free foot.
    One weight change to a beat: SLOW.
    Two weight changes to a beat: quick.
    No weight change: hold.

    The following terms are used to indicate weight changes:

Slow	Together	Step
Quick	Close	In place

    The following terms may or may not indicate weight changes:

Forward	Sideward	Right (or left) turn
Backward	Close	Cross

    The following terms are used to indicate foot movements with no change of weight (also referred to as hesitation or balance steps):

Ball turn	Brush	Dig
Dot	Draw	Flick
Heel	Heel-toe	Hold
Hop	Jump	Kick
Lift	Point	Ripple
Stomp	Swing	Touch

Wheel: A turn on the spot in positions other than closed, conversation, or shine.

Zigzag: Diagonal movement in and out or out and in, i.e. to right and left of the line of dance.

Dishrag

Allemande right

TECHNIQUES OF TEACHING

ONE STEP AT A TIME

It is important for a teacher to teach only one thing at a time. If more than one technique is presented, the learning dancer becomes confused. The teacher should instruct from known to unknown, from simple to complex-- for example, first the movement, then the weight-change unit, the step, the rhythm, and finally the dance routine. The teacher should put it all together only after the fundamental and preparatory techniques have been learned.

With the basics mastered, the student is free to concentrate on the formations and is able to pay attention to his partner. With a knowledge of basic steps, positions, and leads, both teacher and student are free to learn the style and the order of steps in the various dance routines.

SUGGESTIONS FOR THE TEACHER

Dances written in this book employ several techniques not commonly used in writing dances. By mastering the suggestions given, you will save considerable time and will be more efficient in teaching. The following instructions will help prepare you.

- Be enthusiastic about the dance. If necessary, be a good actor.
- Know the dance thoroughly.
- Think it through step by step before facing the group. Ask yourself, "Where shall I stand?" "Where and how will the group be standing?" "What shall I say first?" "What will the participants do first? Next?" and so on.
- Keep the attention of the group at all times. Remember, if the music is not playing you should be talking; otherwise you may lose them.
- Demonstrate while explaining the dance. This is important. People learn best by seeing; often, teachers talk too much and demonstrate too little. Use students for demonstrations whenever possible.
- Dance for fun. Have fun even if mistakes are made. Dancers often have as much fun making mistakes as dancing correctly, provided it does not cause embarrassment. Strive for excellence only as long as it is enjoyable.
- Ask the students to save their questions, since many of the answers will become apparent during the dancing.
- It is a good rule to call the same words in the demonstration as in the walk-through; then play the music and call the dance just long enough to insure success.
- Stop before interest lags; stop when the group wants more. Dance through a record just once. See that dancers do not stand or sit too long or get too hot, thirsty, or dizzy.
- Always make a group correction, never an individual one. Laughter is the best corrective. Laugh with the group, not at them.
- Analyze the class for the distribution of sexes and skills; then choose your dances accordingly (single, couple, or threesome dances; easy or hard dances).
- Use the "whole concept" of teaching when possible by demonstrating the entire step rather than instructing one part of it at a time.
- Teach in lines with less than twenty students and in circles with more than twenty students.

21

●For a warm-up use a dance the class knows.
　●Use stories, brief patterns, and steps to help the students remember the dance.
　　●Refrain from teaching a difficult dance or step to a beginning group.
　●Use visual aids.

C A L L I N G   D A N C E   S T E P S

The practice of using calls while teaching a dance is a valuable aid to both learner and teacher. Calls help establish a rhythmical framework for the dancers and add interest and variety to the learning process.
There are five types of calls. All except the prompting call can be used with or without music. All calls should be metrical so that the dancer will keep in time while learning and be able to make a smooth transition from dancing without music to dancing with music. To keep the dancers in rhythm, use one of the following types of calls.

Directional call--example: FORWARD FORWARD side together

Rhythm call--example: SLOW SLOW quick quick

Counting call--examples:
　　Dance counting call: 1 2 3' and' 4
　　Music counting call: 1 2 3 4

Chanting call--examples: cha' cha' cha, turn' turn' turn, rock' rock' rock, step' step' step

Prompting call--example: now box step (Just the name of the step is called on the preceding measure. The music will keep the dancer in rhythm.)

Keep the dancers in rhythm even when the music is not playing. Be able to use any one of the five types of calls during the demonstration and walk-through. Variety is desirable; however, there are specific calls that work better with specific steps. For example, a counting call is most effective for a chug. The following is a detailed description of each of the different calls.
　The directional call is the best rhythmical call with which to start.
　　a.　It tells the dancers the direction in which to go.
　　b.　It keeps them in rhythm, since every word or syllable is equal to a beat of music.
　　c.　Every word or syllable usually means a change of weight.
　The rhythm call is used (a) for keeping dancers in rhythm, and (b) in controlled practice periods.
　　a.　The dance rhythm should not be confused with the music count.
　　b.　Each word means a change of weight.
　　c.　The words used to indicate a dance rhythm are SLOW and quick.
　In the counting call, the instructor may count changes of weight, move-ment, dance rhythm, or music rhythm. Counting can be the poorest method of keeping dancers in rhythm if the instructor is not consistent. He should use the same count throughout the dance. If instructors use and for a quick count and make each count equal a change of weight and beat of music, the counting call can be just as useful as a rhythm call. Counting does not tell

dancers in which direction to go.

a. For a weight-change count, teachers may count the weight changes by using the words SLOW and quick, by using any other words, or even by imitating musical instruments.

b. A movement count calls the number of slows and quicks in any given step, plus any hesitation movement where there is not a change of weight. For example, the movement count call for the conga would be 1 2 3 kick.

c. A dance count may be like the music count except for the important difference that the dance count indicates the slows and quicks in any given step. In the box step, for example, the movement count and the dance count are the same, but for the count to show a quick tempo, the count reads 1 2' and'. The and is always equal to a "quick" count, thus breaking up the music count to fit the dance rhythm.

d. A music count gives the actual count of beats in a measure which corresponds to a complete step, figure, or routine. Counting the music beat may be used (a) to start dances; (b) during controlled practice periods, where it keeps the dancers moving and allows freedom of movements, steps, position, leading, and following; and (c) in teaching steps in which the lady does not execute the same movements as the man. A good example is the cha-cha danced in shine position. In this case counting the music does not tell dancers where to put their feet or whether a movement is quick or slow; however, it does show them the beginning of a new measure, thus helping them to stay in rhythm and eventually to get back to the basic step pattern.

In a chanting call the name of the step, such as rock, may be used to keep the dancers in rhythm if it is called on the exact beat upon which the movement is executed. It may also be called ahead and used as a prompting call.

The prompting call is used only when music is playing. The key word (name of the step, position, direction--in other words, the call) should always be called in the measure preceding its execution. This key word can be called on any beat in that measure, but wherever it is called, it should be called in rhythm. The teacher may call one, two, three, or four beats ahead of the dancers but should be consistent. Examples of calls on each of the four beats in the measure preceding are:

Beginning elementary dancers	swing	step	right	now
Beginning junior high dancers	let's	swing	right	now
Intermediate dancers	one	two	swing	now
Advanced dancers	one	two	now	swing

When the instructor has the class so far advanced that he does not have to call to keep dancers in rhythm, he may use only a prompting call.

T H E   I M P O R T A N C E   O F   C A L L I N G   A H E A D

Calling the dance step during the measure just preceding its execution is one of the most important techniques to be employed in teaching fun dances. In this book, the key word to be called on the last of each measure (to introduce the next step) is underlined. While the group is dancing the last step, the teacher is calling the next step. This procedure takes a little practice, but it is essential for effective teaching.

EXAMPLE OF CALLING AHEAD

Four basic directions: Forward, backward, turn left, turn right. Notice the difference between the dancer's actions and the caller's words.

Formation: Double circle
Position: Closed
Footwork: Opposite (man L, lady R)

Music: Stay As Sweet As You Are
Record: Daz 51319
Rhythm: 4/4

MEAS	CALL	INSTRUCTIONS

[Before dance begins, call:]

Forward walk: Walk 4 steps in LOD.

mark time ready and

Backward walk: Walk 4 steps agLOD.

1 [Caller] 1 2 forward walk
   [Dancer] left right left right

Left turn: In 4 steps, turn 1 full turn L to end with man facing LOD.

2 [Caller] forward forward backward walk
   [Dancer] forward forward forward forward

Right turn: In 4 steps, turn 1 full turn R to end with man facing LOD.

3 [Caller] back back left turn
   [Dancer] back back back back

4 [Caller] turn turn right turn
   [Dancer] turn turn turn turn

C L A S S R O O M   P R O C E D U R E

1. Place the record on a warmed-up machine and have a microphone ready.
2. Call the name, formation, position, and footwork of the dance.
3. After the dancers are in the formation you have called, move to a place where all the dancers can see you. If needed, take a partner. If it is a circle dance, for example, step inside the circle facing in the same direction and in the same relative position as the other dancers.
4. Call, "Watch the demonstration." The dancers should stand and watch while you demonstrate the dance.
5. Call either the direction ("Ready, forward") or the name of the step ("Ready, walk"). Demonstrate while calling the instructions.
6. Call, "Take position for a walk-through." The dancers should take the correct position and go through the dance as you--
   (a) call the name of the step on the preceding measure, and
   (b) call the direction, rhythm, step, or count on each beat in the rhythm and tempo the music will play.
   Before the music is started, remember to give these introductory items of information:

1. The name of the dance--example: Nola.
2. The formation--example: Single circle.
3. The position--example: Hands joined.
4. The footwork--example: Left foot.

5. The demonstration.
6. The positioning and the walk-through.
   Only now are you ready for the music.

   Always get the group into the correct formation for the demonstration.
It is not necessary, however, for the learners to take the position while they
are watching the demonstration. Nearly all dances require the mention of the
footwork. The call for the walk-through should be the same as for the demonstration. It is very important to stand in plain sight of all in order to be
seen and heard by the entire group. Do not stand directly in the center of a
circle. This makes it difficult for those behind you to hear or to determine
in which direction you are dancing.

   If the dance calls for changing partners, explain that the man will
always go back and the lady ahead for a new partner, and much confusion will
be avoided.

   Avoid long explanations; dancers are not interested in learning the
breakdown of all the steps. They are there to have fun. "Put your left foot
forward" is the best way to start a dance. If a leader knows the call well,
the walk-through can frequently be eliminated.

   When the music is started you can help the dancers get in rhythm by
counting the beats in the music. Know ahead of time how many introductory
measures are on the record. The following sample call is for four introductory measures:

1	2	3	4
2	2	3	4
now	let's	walk	forward
READY		WALK	

P O S I T I O N S   A N D   F O R M A T I O N S

P O S I T I O N S

   Dance positions refer to the relative positions of dancers' bodies, feet,
hands, and arms. There may be as much fun in a change of position as there
is in a change of steps or partners. The following descriptions are of ballroom and social dance positions, but they are commonly used in other types of
dancing also.

Closed: Partners stand directly in front of each other with the leader facing
in the line of dance. Heads are turned left slightly to look over each other's
right shoulder, and shoulders are parallel. The leader's right hand is on
the small of the follower's back with fingertips just over and on the right
side of the vertebrae. The leader's left hand holds his partner's right hand
just above elbow height, while the fingertips of the follower's left hand rest
lightly on the leader's right shoulder. Partners' elbows are matched, and the
follower's feet are in line with the leader's. The lead is the palm of the
right hand.

Conversation: From closed position both the leader and the follower turn one-
fourth turn to the right. The leader's left shoulder and follower's right
shoulder are in the line of dance. The lead is the heel of the right hand.

25

BASIC BALLROOM DANCE POSITIONS

Closed   Conversation   Semi-open

Right-side   Left-side   Reverse

Open   Full-open   Back-to-back

<u>Semi-open</u>: From conversation position the leader turns one-fourth turn to the left while the follower turns one-fourth turn to the right. The leader's left hand and the follower's right hand are still joined. The lead is the heel of the right hand.

<u>Right-side</u>: From conversation position both turn one-fourth turn to their own left with right sides together. The lead is the fingers of the right hand.

<u>Left-side</u>: From conversation position both turn one-fourth turn to their own right with left sides together. The lead is the heel of the right hand.

<u>Reverse</u>: Standing in conversation position and retaining hand contacts, the leader turns one-fourth turn to the right while the follower turns one-fourth turn to the left. Both face against the line of dance. The leader's left and the follower's right sides are together. The lead is the fingers of the right hand and a simultaneous lowering or raising of the left hand.

<u>Open</u>: From conversation position the leader turns one-fourth turn to the left and the follower turns one-fourth turn to the right. The leader's left and the follower's right hands drop to their sides. The lead is the heel of the right hand.

<u>Full-open</u>: From conversation position partners step away from each other and stand with hands joined. The lead is a gentle push with the right hand. Hand contact may be left-right, right-left, right-right, or left-left.

<u>Back-to-back</u>: From conversation position the leader turns one-half turn to the left and the follower turns one-half turn to the right. Partners stand back to back with the leader's right and follower's left hands joined. The lead is the right hand moved in the line of dance and the left handclasp dropped.

<u>Two-hand</u>: From conversation position partners step back from each other one step, both hands joined at arm's length. The leader's left hand holds the follower's right hand, and his right hand holds her left hand. The lead is a gentle push with the left hand.

<u>Cuddle</u>: From two-hand position the leader crosses his left arm high over his partner's head without letting go of hands, turning the follower left and bringing her left side against his right side, both facing the same direction. The lead is the left hand high and the right hand low.

<u>Backhand promenade, or twist</u>: From conversation position both face in the line of dance and each holds both his partner's hands behind his back as though shaking hands. The leader's right arm is around the follower's waist and the follower's left arm is around the leader's waist. The lead is the left hand held behind the back.

<u>Skaters'</u>: From backhand promenade position the leader lets go with his left hand and holds the follower's left hand extended in front of him; the leader's right hand continues holding the follower's right hand on her waist. The leader stands slightly behind the follower, facing the same way. The lead is the left handclasp dropped.

BASIC ROUND DANCE POSITIONS

Two-hand

Cuddle

Backhand promenade

Skaters'

Varsouvienne (sweetheart)

Parallel

Crossed-hands

Promenade

Shine

Varsouvienne, or sweetheart: From skaters' position partners join right hands above the follower's right shoulder while retaining left handclasp in front. The lead is the right hand raised high.

Parallel: From closed position the follower turns one-half turn to the right so that both face in the line of dance. The leader ends standing directly behind the follower with hands joined and extended. The lead is the left hand raised over the follower's head and a change of hands to turn her.

Crossed-hands: From two-hand position, partners cross hands, with the contact right-right and left-left. The lead is the right hand over the left.

Promenade: From crossed-hands position the leader turns one-fourth turn to the left and the follower turns one-fourth turn to the right so that they stand side by side facing in the line of dance. The lead is both hands moved forward.

Individual, shine, or challenge: From any other position, partners drop hands so that there is no contact.

F O R M A T I O N S

Dance formations refer to the patterns formed by the dancers as they stand to begin dancing. The following formations are most commonly used.

Line dances with or without partners are appealing to young people. They may be used to start an evening of fun. As the crowd arrives, a conga line may be an enticement to hook on and join the dance. Many line dances are adapted from circle and couple dances.

Single circle dances without partners will help solve the problem of getting people active as soon as they are on the floor, expecially when there is some reluctance to dance with the opposite sex or in a closed positon. By starting the music, calling the dance, and shortening the teaching process, anyone can use this formation to get a group dancing quickly. After the dancers are having fun, it is easier to get them into couples, where they will use the same steps and much the same routines in other formations.

Single circle dances with partners usually call for a change of partners. The lady on a man's right is always his partner.

Double circle (couple) dances are the most common type of round and folk dances. Though there are difficulties involved in getting dancers paired off and in keeping the extra dancers happy, couple dances are popular because there can be a change of partners. Many believe it is ten times as much fun to dance with ten partners as it is to dance with one.

Threesome dances are designed to take care of a group that contains twice as many ladies as men or vice versa.

Team dances are those in which two couples or two threesomes face each other to dance, usually in a circle.

Mass formation is that in which the dancers or couples are scattered at random around the floor. This formation is usually used in ballroom dancing, but other types of dances can be danced in it too.

STARTING FORMATIONS

Key: ▲ man ⬤ lady

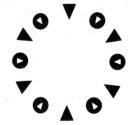

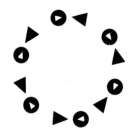

Single circle, all facing
center, ladies to R of
partners

Single circle, all facing
ccw, one partner behind
other

Single circle, partners
facing each other, men
facing ccw, ladies cw

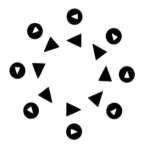

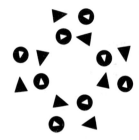

Double circle, couples
facing ccw, ladies outside

Double circle, partners
facing each other, ladies
outside

Double circle, every two
couples facing each other
around circle (team)

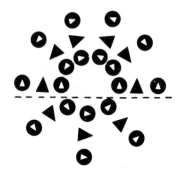

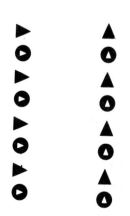

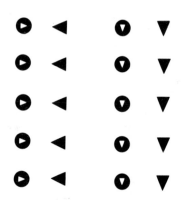

Triple circle, all three-
somes face ccw; or every
two threesomes face each
other (threesome team)

Single line
Chorus-girl   Conga

Double line
Lines   Columns

Using a line to start the dance class or party generally proves to be successful. The leader can end the line dance in a single circle and, after a few single circle dances, get the group into a double circle or threesome with a grand march.

If there are more of one sex, threesomes are the best formation. All dances that can be danced in a double circle can be danced in a threesome circle. A man can dance the same steps with two ladies that he can dance with one.

CHANGING PARTNERS

There are several ways to change partners. Partners may go to another couple and ask them if they would like to change partners for one dance. During a round dance couples often dance together for eight or sixteen measures and then change partners by moving around the circle to the next person. It is the usual practice for the men to travel to the new partners while the ladies dance in place, either turning or dancing on the spot.

There are several ways to change partners in a round dance mixer without losing the rhythm of the dance.

In lines: (a) The man may hop ahead or back to a new partner. (b) With the man holding the lady's waist, each couple jumps and turns halfway around. The man then releases his hold and the lady places her hands on the waist of the man in front of her. Each new couple jumps and turns back to the line of dance. (c) Men may move sideward to the left with a chug or slide, then slide between two different ladies in the line when they return on the second unit of the step.

In a single circle: (a) The man may walk to the center, then back to a new partner. (b) The man can swing his partner and leave her on his right to be swung by the next man ahead. He then swings the lady on his left, who becomes his new partner.

In a double circle: (a) The most common way is for the ladies to go ahead counterclockwise, and the men back clockwise around the circle while dancing any of the basic steps. (b) The dancers can turn individually or walk straight forward or back to a new partner. (c) From closed or conversation position, the couple may wheel or do a two-step turn and the man arch the lady before releasing her to a new partner.

In a team formation: (a) Couples can move on to new couples by dropping hands and moving forward through each other, passing right shoulders, or one couple can arch as the other couple goes under the arch. (b) A couple may also promenade around the other couple to face a new couple and form a new team. Dancers may dance any of the basic steps when changing partners.

In a threesome formation: (a) With a man between two ladies, the most common method of changing partners is for the man to move ahead while the ladies move back or circle in place, dancing any of the basic steps. (b) The man may go back and the ladies ahead when changing partners, but either way the routine should be consistent throughout the evening.

PICK-UP

There are several ways to pick up dancers from the sidelines.

In a chain line: The person on the end can pick up a person from the side with his free hand. The leader must keep the line close to the edge of the hall and the dancers that are to be picked up.

In a double circle: Each partner on the outside may pick up a person from the side to make a threesome circle.

T H E   B A S I C   D A N C E   S T E P S

The following steps are the basis for all round, social, folk, and square dance steps. If would-be dancers learn these steps before attempting the dance routines they will find dancing easier and more fun.

These basic dance steps are:

1.	hesitation	5.	slide	9.	side ball-change
2.	pas de basque	6.	chug	10.	cross ball-change
3.	two-step	7.	paddle	11.	swing partner
4.	walk	8.	grapevine		

Most fun dances include some of these steps. The hesitation step and the swing step have several variations. All the steps but the walk and the swing consist of two units, one to the left and one to the right. Between the two units there is usually a change in direction, and any one of the hesitation variations may be used to execute this change. All steps start on the left foot for the man and the right foot for the lady unless otherwise designated.

Detailed descriptions of these steps with diagrams of their execution are given below. Also included are examples of counts and calls for them, set in columns for easy comprehension of the rhythm. In the diagrams, the left foot is black and the right foot white. Foot movements are indicated by arrows and are numbered to show the order of their execution. The letters Q and S mean quick and slow and indicate the relative speed of the foot movement. Where just half the foot is shown there is no weight change. The free foot is touched to the side of supporting foot without changing weight.

Hesitation: The movement of a foot without a weight change, usually taking one or two beats of music. This can be done in many ways and each is given a specific name. Listed below are the kinds of hesitation steps. They are described in the list of terms at the beginning of the book.

1.	Ball-turn	7.	Heel	13.	Lift
2.	Brush	8.	Heel-toe	14.	Point
3.	Dig	9.	Hold	15.	Ripple
4.	Dot	10.	Hop	16.	Stomp
5.	Draw	11.	Jump	17.	Swing (not swing partner)
6.	Flick	12.	Kick	18.	Touch

Directional call:	side' touch'	side' touch'	side' touch'	side' touch'
Rhythm call:	quick' hold'	quick' hold'	quick' hold'	quick' hold'
Chanting call:	step' hold'	step' hold'	step' hold'	step' hold'
Dance count:	1' and'	2' and'	3' and'	4' and'
Music count:	1	2	3	4

Note

Any of the steps listed above may be done quickly or slowly, depending on the rhythm and tempo of the specific dance.

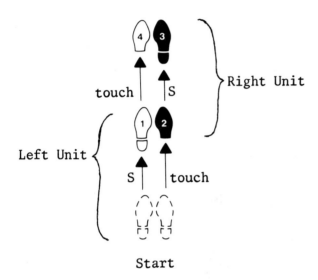

Progressive Forward

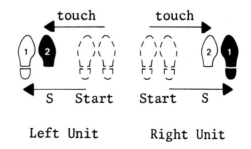

Sideward

Pas de basque: A step executed by leaping to the side with the left foot, crossing the right foot over the left foot for a momentary weight change, and dropping back on the left foot, this comprising the left unit. The right unit is executed by repeating all the above to the right.

Directional call:	side' ball'	- change	side' ball	- change
Rhythm call:	quick' quick'	slow	quick' quick'	slow
Chanting call:	leap' ball'	- change	leap' ball'	- change
Dance count:	1'	a' 2	3'	a' 4
Music count:	1	2	3	4

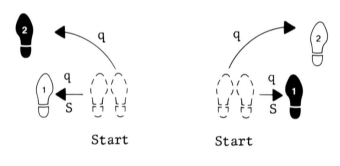

Start   Start

Left Unit   Right Unit

34

Two-step: A step executed by stepping forward with the left foot, closing the right foot to the left foot, and stepping forward with the left foot to comprise the left unit. The right unit is executed by repeating all the above, starting with the right foot.

Directional call:	forward	close	FORWARD,		forward	close	FORWARD	
Rhythm call:	quick	quick	SLOW,		quick	quick	SLOW	
Chanting call:	step	close	STEP,		step	close	STEP	
Dance count:	1	and	TWO,		3	and	FOUR	
Music count:	1	2	3	4,	1	2	3	4

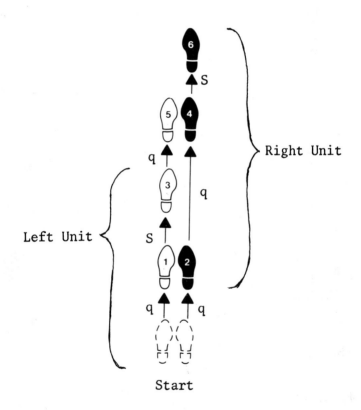

35

<u>Walk</u>: Four walking steps in any direction, changing weight on each count,
including the fourth. If just three walking steps are taken, any of the hesitation steps can be danced in place on the fourth count.

Directional call:	forward	forward	forward	forward
Rhythm call:	quick	quick	quick	quick
Chanting call:	walk	walk	walk	walk
Dance count:	1	2	3	4
Music count:	1	2	3	4

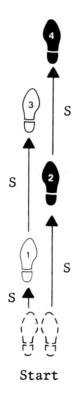

Start

Forward

Backward

Start

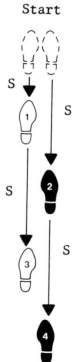

<u>Slide</u>: A step to the side with the left foot, closing the right foot to the left, repeated three times to comprise the left unit. The right unit is executed by repeating all the above to the right.

Directional call:	side'	close'	side'	close'	side'	close'	reverse,
	side'	close'	side'	close'	side'	close'	side

Rhythm call:	quick'	quick'	quick'	quick'	quick'	quick'	slow,
	quick'	quick'	quick'	quick'	quick'	quick'	slow

Chanting call:	slide		slide		slide		slide,
	slide		slide		slide		slide

Dance count:	1'	and'	2'	and'	3'	and'	4,
	1'	and'	2'	and'	3'	and'	4

Music count:	1		2		3		4,
	1		2		3		4

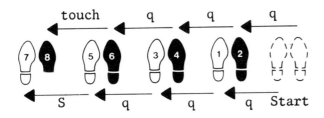

Left Unit

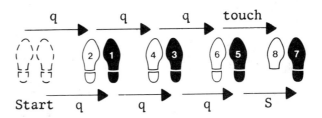

Right Unit

Chug: A step executed by stepping to the side with the left foot with all the weight on the left foot, the right foot closing to the left foot and touching the floor just long enough to push the body sideward. As the weight is dropped on the left foot, the right foot should flick out from its own pushing action. This is repeated three more times to comprise the left unit. The right unit is executed by repeating all the above to the right.

| Directional call: | side' | close' | side' | close' | side | | reverse, |
| | side' | close' | side' | close' | side' | close' | side |

| Rhythm call: | quick' | quick' | quick' | quick' | quick' | quick' | slow, |
| | quick' | quick' | quick' | quick' | quick' | quick' | slow |

| Chanting call: | step' | ball' - change' | ball' - change | | reverse, |
| | step' | ball' - change' | ball' - change' | ball' - change |

| Dance count: | 1' | a'2' | a'3' | a'4, |
| | 1' | a'2' | a'3' | a'4 |

| Music count: | 1 | 2 | 3 | 4, |
| | 1 | 2 | 3 | 4 |

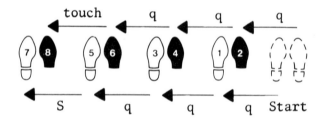

Left Unit

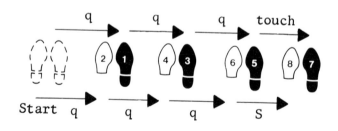

Right Unit

<u>Paddle</u>: A step executed the same as the chug except that dancers are turning left and right instead of dancing sideward to the left and right. The first unit takes the dancer one full turn around to the left and the second unit takes him one full turn to the right. The calls are the same as for the chug.

| Directional call: | turn' | close' | turn' | close' | turn | | reverse, |
| | turn' | close' | turn' | close' | turn' | close' | turn |

| Rhythm call: | quick' | quick' | quick' | quick' | quick' | quick' | slow, |
| | quick' | quick' | quick' | quick' | quick' | quick' | slow |

| Chanting call: | step' | ball' - change' | ball' - change | | reverse, |
| | step' | ball' - change' | ball' - change' | ball' - change |

| Dance count: | 1' | a'2' | a'3' | a'4, |
| | 1' | a'2' | a'3' | a'4 |

| Music count: | 1 | 2 | 3 | 4, |
| | 1 | 2 | 3 | 4 |

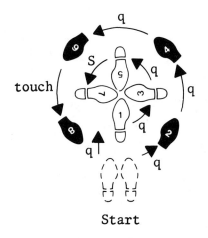

Start

Left Unit

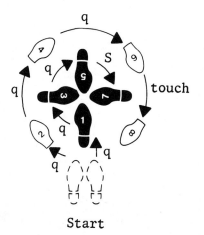

Start

Right Unit

Grapevine: A step executed by stepping to the side with the left foot, stepping the right foot behind the left foot, stepping to the side with the left foot, and swinging the right foot over the left foot. (Other hesitation steps may be used on the fourth beat instead of the swing.) This comprises the left unit; the right unit is executed by repeating all the above to the right.

Directional call:	side	behind	side	swing,	side	behind	side	swing
Rhythm call:	quick	quick	SLOW,		quick	quick	SLOW	
Chanting call:	step	step	step	reverse,	step	step	step	swing
Dance count:	1	and	TWO,		3	and	FOUR	
Music count:	1	2	3	4,	1	2	3	4

touch or swing

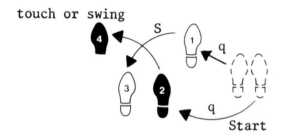

Left Unit

touch or swing

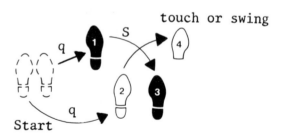

Right Unit

40

<u>Side ball-change</u>: A step executed the same as the pas de basque except that the feet come together instead of crossing over. The left unit is executed by stepping to the side on the left foot, closing the right foot to the left, and changing weight momentarily (right left). The right unit is executed by repeating the above, starting with the right foot.

Directional call:	side'	close'	change	side'	close'	change
Rhythm call:	quick'	quick'	slow	quick'	quick'	slow
Chanting call:	step'	close'	step	step'	close'	step
Dance count:	1'		a'2	3'		a'4
Music count:	1		2	3		4

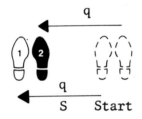

Left Unit

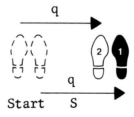

Right Unit

41

Cross ball-change: A step executed like the pas de basque except that the free foot crosses behind the supporting foot for the ball-change. The left unit is executed by leaping to the side on the left foot, crossing the right foot behind the left foot, changing weight momentarily, and dropping the weight back on the left foot. The right unit is executed by repeating the above, starting on the right foot.

```
Directional call:   side'   cross'  change  side'   cross'  change
Rhythm call:        quick'  quick'  slow    quick'  quick'  slow
Chanting call:      leap'   ball' - change  leap'   ball' - change
Dance count:        1'              a'2     3'              a'4
Music count:        1               2       3               4
```

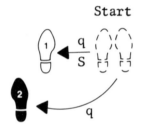

Left Unit

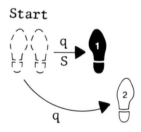

Right Unit

Swing partner: A variation of the walk, paddle, or slide step. There are many ways to swing one's partner, but the basic footwork remains the same through them all. For various holds for a swing, see the list of terms under "swing partner."

When using a two-hand swing hold, the footwork should always be the chassé swing. For children, this is a slide step that wheels the partners around a central point as they face each other. For adults, the footwork is something between a slide and a paddle step, with the right foot forward and the left foot pushing to the side.

Other swing holds may use either chassé, shuffle, or buzz footwork. A shuffle is a walk where the feet brush the floor, and a buzz is exactly the same as a paddle, except that it usually takes twice as long to complete a full turn.

Directional call:	forward	close	forward	close,	forward	close	forward	close
Rhythm call:	quick	quick	quick	quick,	quick	quick	quick	quick
Chanting call:	step	close	step	close,	step	close	step	close
Dance count:	1	and	2	and,	3	and	4	and
Music count:	1	2	3	4,	1	2	3	4

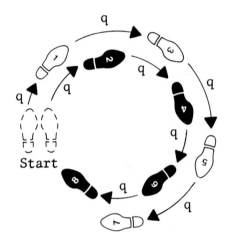

Shuffle

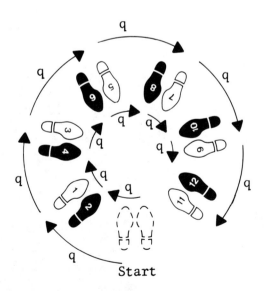

Chassé

43

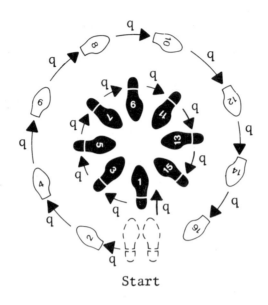

Start

Buzz or Paddle

Buzz swing

44

A COUNTING CALL FOR TEACHING THE BASIC DANCE STEPS

This is an instructional practice routine for teachers. As such, it may be practiced in any formation or position to any music of 4/4 rhythm. Footwork is same or opposite, depending on the position of the dancers. The call is a dance counting call.

MEAS	CALL					INSTRUCTIONS
	walk forward and back					Instructions for these steps are as detailed above.
	READY		WALK			
1	1	2	3		back	
2	now	let's	SLIDE			
3	1' and'	2' and'	3		reverse	
4	now	let's	PADDLE			
5	1'	a'2'	a'3		reverse	
6	now	let's	GRAPEVINE			
7	1	2	3		reverse	
8	now	let's	pas' de'	basque		
9	1'	a'2	3'	a'4		
10	now	let's	two	- step		
11	1' and'	2	3' and'	back		
12	now	let's	CHUG			
13	1'	a'2'	a'3		reverse	
14	now	let's	side' ball'-change			
15	1'	a'2	3'	a'4		
16	now	let's	HESITATE			
17	1	2	3	4		
18	now	let's	cross' ball'-change			
19	1'	a'2	3'	a'4		
20	now	swing	your	partner		

MEAS	CALL				INSTRUCTIONS
21	1	2	3	4	
22	5	6	walk	forward	

PRACTICE SEQUENCE FOR THE BASIC DANCE STEPS

The following steps may be danced in any sequence. For younger students two or four steps should be used together in a short routine. Four or eight steps will always match the phrases of the music. The call is a directional chanting call.

Formation: Single circle
Position: Hands joined
Footwork: All start L

Music: Own choice
Record: Own choice
Rhythm: 4/4, 24 meas

MEAS	CALL
	walk forward and back
	READY WALK
1	forward forward walk back
2	back back slide left
3	slide slide slide reverse
4	slide slide paddle left
5	paddle paddle paddle right
6	paddle paddle GRAPEVINE
7	side behind side reverse
8	side behind pas' de' basque
9	front' ball'-change front' ball'-change
10	front' ball'-change two-step
11	step' close' step back now
12	step' close' step chug left
13	chug chug chug right
14	chug chug side' ball'-change

INSTRUCTIONS

Instructions for the steps are as detailed above.

Note

Teachers or dancers may create their own original dances by putting any four of these steps in a routine and setting it to 4/4-rhythm music of their choice.

MEAS	CALL	INSTRUCTIONS

15   side' ball'-change side'
            ball'-change

16   side' ball'-change <u>side touch</u>

17   side touch side touch

18   side touch <u>cross' ball'-change</u>

19   cross' ball'-change cross'
            ball'-change

20   cross' ball'-change <u>walk</u> now

21   forward forward <u>swing' your'</u>
            <u>partner</u>

22   1 2 3 4

23   1 2 3 4

24   now <u>start OVER</u>

V E R S A T I L I T Y   I N   T E A C H I N G   D A N C E S

Most dances can be danced in several different formations and can be adapted to almost all age groups. Use the formation best adapted to the group involved and make the instructions simple or sophisticated according to the age of the dancers.

On the following pages the round dance Nola and several simple schottisches are presented to demonstrate how these dances can be danced in different formations and positions. Nola is given first as a line dance, then in five other formations, showing the necessary changes in the calls. The schottisches incorporate a number of different sequences and movements to the same basic step in different formations and positions. In studying this presentation, the would-be dancer or dance leader can begin to master the technique of calling ahead and can gain an appreciation for the versatility and adaptability of these dances.

Following the schottisches is the bunny hop, with adaptations making it suitable for age groups ranging from first- and second-graders to adults. From these examples, it should be possible to adapt succeeding dances to fit any situation.

N O L A
(Line dance, with or without partners)

This version and the single circle version of this dance are written to demonstrate the technique of calling ahead. In the call column, the line headed "Caller" indicates his spoken directions. The line headed "Dancer" indicates the dancer's actions at the same moment.

Formation: Conga line
Position: Hands on waist of person ahead
Footwork: All start L

Music: Nola
Record: Windsor 7602
Rhythm: 4/4, 8 meas

MEAS CALL

point and SLIDE

READY POINT

INSTRUCTIONS

Point: Point L foot to side, touch L to R, repeat.

Slide: Take 4 slides to L, starting on L.

Reverse: Repeat point and slide to R.

Swing: Step on L foot, swing R foot across in front of L, reverse to R.

Dot: Step L, touch R toe behind L foot, reverse to R.

Two-step forward: Take 4 two-steps fwd, starting on L foot. (Avoid dancing backward in a line.)

Point: Repeat entire dance. "Start over" may also be called.

1 [Caller] point touch point slide
  [Dancer] point touch point touch

2 [Caller] slide slide slide reverse
  [Dancer] slide slide slide slide

3 [Caller] point touch point slide
  [Dancer] point touch point touch

4 [Caller] slide slide now swing
  [Dancer] slide slide slide slide

5 [Caller] step swing now dot
  [Dancer] step swing step swing

6 [Caller] step dot two'-step' forward
  [Dancer] step dot step dot

7 [Caller] step' close' step now repeat
  [Dancer] step' close' step step' close' step

8 [Caller] step' close' step now point
  [Dancer] step' close' step step' close' step

N O L A
(Single circle without partners)

Formation: Single circle
Position: Hands joined, facing center
Footwork: All start L

Music: Nola
Record: Blue Star 1588
Rhythm: 4/4, 8 meas

MEAS CALL

INSTRUCTIONS

Calls for meas 1-6 are the same as for preceding line dance. Meas 7 and

8 for single circle dance are as follows.

7	[Caller] step' close' step now back	Back: Take 2 two-steps back to place.
	[Dancer] step' close' step step' close' step	Repeat entire dance.
8	[Caller] step' close' step now point	
	[Dancer] step' close' step step' close' step	

N O L A
(Double circle)

Formation:	Double circle	Music:	Nola
Position:	Two-hand	Record:	Windsor 4637
Footwork:	Opposite (man L, lady R)	Rhythm:	4/4, 8 meas

MEAS   CALL   INSTRUCTIONS

Calls for meas 1-5 are same as for preceding line and single-circle dances. Meas 6-8 for double circle dance are as follows.

6	step dot individual turn	Individual turn: Man turns L, lady R in 4 two-steps. (Individual turns are easier than closed-position turns and are not embarrassing even with different age groups dancing together.)
7	step' close' step change partners	
8	step' close' step start over	

Change partners: Lady two-steps in small circle as man moves fwd to new partner.

Repeat entire dance.

N O L A
(Team formation)

To change to team formation, couples number off. All odd-numbered couples turn against the line of dance to face the even-numbered couples.

Formation:	Double circle, team formation	Music:	Nola
Position:	Full-open	Record:	Windsor 7602
Footwork:	Opposite (man L, lady R)	Rhythm:	4/4, 8 meas

MEAS	CALL	INSTRUCTIONS

point and OVER

READY POINT

MEAS	CALL	
1	point touch OVER	
2	slide slide slide reverse	
3	point touch UNDER	
4	slide slide step swing	
5	step swing now dot	
6	couples change couples arch	
7	step' close' step step' close' step	
8	full-open start over	

Point: Point L foot to side, touch L to R, repeat.

Over: Couple facing LOD (visiting couple) raises hands in R-L contact high and stands still while host couple joins both hands and slides under arch in 4 slides.

Reverse: Repeat point to R.

Under: Reverse over sequence such that visiting couple slides under host couple's joined hands.

Step swing: Step L, swing R foot across in front of L, reverse to R.

Dot: Step L, touch R toe behind L foot, reverse to R.

Couples change: Host couple takes full-open position and raises joined inside hands. Visiting couple takes skaters' position and two-steps under arch to new couple in 4 two-steps, taking full-open position on 4th two-step.

Repeat entire dance.

N O L A
(Threesomes)

To change to threesome formation, extra ladies move to the center of the floor. All couples two-step around the floor, picking up an extra lady with the man's free hand to form threesomes.

Formation:	Threesome circle, man between two ladies, all facing LOD	Music:	Nola
Position:	Full-open	Record:	Blue Star 1588
Footwork:	All start L	Rhythm:	4/4, 8 meas

MEAS   CALL   INSTRUCTIONS

Calls for meas 1-5 are same as for preceding line and single-circle dances. Meas 6-8 for threesome dance are as follows.

6	step dot change partners	Change partners: Man dances

MEAS	CALL	INSTRUCTIONS
7	step' close' step step' close' step	fwd in 4 two-steps to new partners; lady on L turns L and lady on R turns R to circle back in 4 two-steps to new partner.
8	join hands <u>start over</u>	

Repeat entire dance.

N O L A
(Threesome teams)

To create a threesome team formation, threesomes number off. All men with odd numbers turn their threesomes around against the line of dance to face the even-numbered threesomes, forming teams.

Formation:	Threesome circle, man between two ladies, threesomes facing	Music: Nola
		Record: Windsor 4637
		Rhythm: 4/4, 8 meas
Position:	Full-open	
Footwork:	All start L	

MEAS	CALL	INSTRUCTIONS

Calls for meas 1-5 are same as for preceding line and single-circle dances. Meas 6-8 for threesome team dance are as follows.

MEAS	CALL	INSTRUCTIONS
6	step dot <u>pass-through</u>	<u>Pass-through</u>: Dancers drop hands and each passes R shoulders with person he is facing, dancing 4 two-steps fwd to face new threesome.
7	step' close' step step' close' step	
8	face three <u>start over</u>	Repeat entire dance.

S C H O T T I S C H E

Formation:	Single circle, facing center	Music: Frontier Schottische
		Record: MacGregor 5005-B
		Rhythm: 4/4, 12 meas
Position:	Hands joined	
Footwork:	All start L	

MEAS	CALL	INSTRUCTIONS
	basic step in' and' out	<u>Forward and hop (basic step)</u>: Step to center L,R,L, hop L.
	ready <u>forward and hop</u>	
1	1 2 3 <u>back</u>	<u>Back</u>: Return to place, back R,L, R, hop R.
2	1 2 <u>circle left</u>	<u>Circle left</u>: Circle ccw, starting L, in 4 step-hops.
3	step-hop step-hop	

MEAS	CALL	INSTRUCTIONS
4	now forward and hop	Ladies arch and turn: In 4 step-hops, lady turns under partner's arm (L-R contact) while he step-hops in place.
5	1 2 3 back	
6	ladies arch and turn	
7	step-hop step-hop	Step-hop back: Back to place in 4 step-hops.
8	now forward and hop	Repeat entire dance.
9	1 2 3 hop	
10	1 2 step'-hop' back	
11	step-hop step-hop	
12	now start OVER	

S C H O T T I S C H E

Formation: Double circle
Position: Full-open, R-L contact, facing LOD
Footwork: Opposite (man L, lady R)

Music: Frontier Schottische
Record: MacGregor 5005-B
Rhythm: 4/4, 12 meas

MEAS	CALL	INSTRUCTIONS
	BASIC STEP	Forward and hop (basic step): Step L,R,L, hop L in LOD. Continue R, L,R, hop R.
	ready forward and hop	
1	1 2 3 hop	Step-hop: Take 4 step-hops fwd.
2	1 2 step-hop	Ladies arch: Man, moving fwd in 4 step-hops, raises R arm in arch. Lady turns R under arch (hands still joined) in 4 step-hops. (Lady may turn once or twice.)
3	step-hop step-hop	
4	now forward and hop	
5	1 2 3 hop	
6	1 2 ladies arch	Individual turn: Drop hands, turn individually on the step-hops, lady R, man L, progressing as couple in LOD, lady's hands on skirt, man's hands behind back.
7	step-hop step-hop	
8	now forward and hop	Repeat entire dance.
9	1 2 3 hop	Variation
10	1 2 individual turn	For mixer, lady may turn fwd on individual turn to new partner.

MEAS	CALL	INSTRUCTIONS
11	step-hop step-hop	
12	now start OVER	

S C H O T T I S C H E

Formation: Team, both couples facing LOD
Position: Full-open, outside hands joined with other couple
Footwork: Opposite (man L, lady R)

Music: Frontier Schottische
Record: MacGregor 5005-B
Rhythm: 4/4, 16 meas

MEAS	CALL	INSTRUCTIONS
	ready forward and hop	Forward and hop (basic step): Fwd L,R,L, hop L. Repeat, starting R.
1	1 2 3 hop	
2	1 2 step-hop	Step-hop: Fwd 4 step-hops in LOD.
3	step-hop step-hop	
4	now forward and hop	Break-step: Front couple drops inside hands and dances around behind other couple on step-hops, maintaining outside handholds, to rejoin inside hands as new back couple.
5	1 2 3 hop	
6	1 2 break-step	
7	step-hop step-hop	
8	now forward and hop	Dishrag: Back couple raises inside hands to form arch; front couple backs under arch in 2 step-hops as back couple takes 2 step-hops fwd to front. Couple in back then takes 2 step-hops in place while couple in front, maintaining all handholds, turns inward under own arms in 2 step-hops. On 2nd dishrag couples change back to original position.
9	1 2 3 hop	
10	1 2 DISHRAG	
11	step-hop step-hop	
12	now forward and hop	Repeat entire dance.
13	1 2 3 hop	
14	1 2 DISHRAG	Variation
15	step-hop step-hop	This dance could be made 24 meas long by repeating meas 1-4 and meas 5-8 immediately after they are performed.
16	now start OVER	

SCHOTTISCHE

Formation:	Threesome circle, facing LOD`
Position:	Full-open, man between two ladies
Footwork:	Opposite (man L, ladies R)

Music:	Frontier Schottische
Record:	MacGregor 5005-B
Rhythm:	4/4, 16 meas

MEAS	CALL
	ready forward and hop
1	1 2 3 back
2	1 2 ladies arch
3	step-hop step-hop
4	now forward and hop
5	1 2 3 back
6	1 2 bow knot
7	step-hop step-hop
8	now forward and hop
9	1 2 3 back
10	1 2 3 wheel
11	step-hop step-hop
12	now go FORWARD
13	1 2 3 hop
14	1 2 3 wheel
15	step-hop step-hop
16	now start OVER

INSTRUCTIONS

Forward and hop (basic step): Fwd L,R,L, hop L.

Back: Return to place, back R,L, R, hop к.

Ladies arch: Man raises both arms and ladies turn under arch in 4 step-hops. (R lady turns R, L lady turns L, free hands on skirts.) Man step-hops in place.

Bow knot: As man takes 4 step-hops in place, ladies take 8 running steps around man, keeping hands joined. R lady crosses in front of man (going ccw) and under arch made by man and L lady; L lady travels cw. Ladies pass each other behind man with R lady making arch and L lady going under.

Wheel: In 4 step-hops, L lady wheels fwd, R lady wheels back, and man wheels in place, so that entire threesome wheels 1/2 turn R.

Go forward: Dance basic step agLOD, once fwd and back.

Repeat entire dance.

B U N N Y   H O P
(First and second grades)

Formation:	Single circle
Position:	Hands joined
Footwork:	All start R

Music:	Bunny Hop
Record:	MacGregor 6995-B
Rhythm:	4/4, 8 meas

MEAS	CALL	INSTRUCTIONS

kick right foot out

READY KICK

Kick: Kick R fwd twice, kick L fwd twice.

| 1-2 | RIGHT RIGHT, NOW JUMP |

Jump: Feet together, jump once fwd, once back, then 3 jumps fwd.

| 3 | FORWARD BACK |

| 4 | forward forward KICK |

Jump back: Feet together, jump once fwd, once back, then 3 jumps back.

| 5-6 | RIGHT RIGHT, now let's jump back |

Repeat entire dance as often as desired.

| 7 | FORWARD BACK |

| 8 | back back now kick |

B U N N Y   H O P
(Third and fourth grades)

Formation: Single circle
Position: Hands joined
Footwork: All start R

Music: Bunny Hop
Record: MacGregor 6995-B
Rhythm: 4/4, 12 meas

MEAS   CALL   INSTRUCTIONS

Calls for meas 1-7 are same as for preceding dance. Meas 8-12 are as follows.

| 8 | back back back clap |

Clap: Clap hands above head twice, clap hips twice.

| 9 | hands hands hips stomp |

| 10 | stomp stomp stomp clap |

Stomp: With L hand on L hip, raise R hand and stomp L,R,L,R.

| 11 | hands hands hips stomp |

Repeat entire dance.

| 12 | stomp stomp stomp kick |

B U N N Y   H O P
(Fifth and sixth grades)

Formation: Double circle
Position: Two-hand
Footwork: All start R

Music: Bunny Hop
Record: MacGregor 6995-B
Rhythm: 4/4, 16 meas

MEAS   CALL   INSTRUCTIONS

kick right foot out

READY KICK

Kick: Both kick R foot across L twice, then kick L foot across R twice.

MEAS	CALL	INSTRUCTIONS

MEAS	CALL
1-2	KICK KICK, NOW jump back
3	JUMP BACK
4	back back now kick
5-6	KICK KICK, NOW jump forward
7	FORWARD JUMP
8	jump jump now walk
9-10	1 2 3 hop, 1 2 now clap
11	hands hands now hips
12	left right now walk
13-14	1 2 3 hop, 1 2 now clap
15	hands hands now hips
16	hold hands and kick

INSTRUCTIONS

Jump back: Jump once fwd and once back, then 3 jumps back away from partner, dropping hands. On last jump turn 1/4 turn R to face new partner.

Jump forward: Jump once fwd and once back, then 3 jumps toward new partner.

Walk: Partners face LOD and join inside hands. Boy starts L, girl R, walk L,R,L, hop L, then R,L,R, hop R.

Clap: Partners face and clap hands above head twice, clap own hips twice.

Hips: Put L hand on L hip, raise R hand, move hips L,R,L,R.

Repeat entire dance.

B U N N Y   H O P
(Adults)

Formation: Double circle
Position: Two-hand
Footwork: All start R

Music: Bunny Hop
Record: MacGregor 6995-B
Rhythm: 4/4, 16 meas

MEAS	CALL
	kick right foot forward
	READY KICK
1-2	KICK KICK, SIDE JUMP
3	LEFT RIGHT
4	left left now kick
5-6	KICK KICK, SIDE RIGHT
7	RIGHT LEFT
8	right right now kick
9-10	KICK KICK, NOW DOCEY

INSTRUCTIONS

Kick: Kick R foot to side twice, then L foot to side twice.

Side jump: Jump L,R, 3 jumps L to stand opposite next person on L.

Side right: Jump R,L, 3 jumps R to original partner.

Docey: Both man and lady jump toward each other and back, then exchange places by passing back to back in 3 jumps while turning 1/2 turn. Man is now facing center, lady facing wall. On return docey, dancers jump back to face new partner on right.

Repeat entire dance.

MEAS	CALL	INSTRUCTIONS
11	TOGETHER BACK	
12	let's _kick_ AGAIN	
13-14	KICK KICK, NOW _DOCEY_	
15	TOGETHER BACK	
16	change partners and _kick_	

D A N C E   F E S T I V A L   O R G A N I Z A T I O N*

Each year many schools include folk and contemporary dances and other rhythmic activities in programs to which the public is invited. These programs are especially suitable because they provide a convenient means of demonstrating to the parents and community a very important part of the physical education program. However, to make certain that the rhythmic activities represent to the public the high quality of work the schools are doing, and at the same time give the pupils maximum educational benefits, it is advisable for the principal to supervise the planning and to evaluate the activities that are to be presented.

G E N E R A L   S U G G E S T I O N S

ACTIVITIES

If pupils are to get acceptable educational experiences, activities included in the program should be the culmination or outcome of regular class activities. They should be educationally justifiable and sound in content, methods, and performance.

LONG-RANGE PLANNING

The principal should be involved in long-range planning with a festival chairman. The festival chairman, in turn, plans with each teacher his or her part in the program. A theme should be selected. This planning should take place long enough in advance to insure adequate and unhurried preparation.

APPROVAL BY PRINCIPAL

Activities considered for presentation, other than those suggested in the basic and supplementary sections in this teaching guide, should have the approval of the principal. This is to prevent the selection of a dance which a teacher believes will fit the general program but which may be too difficult for the skill and maturity of the pupils.

* Permission to use this material granted by Los Angeles City Schools.

PARTICIPATION IN FESTIVAL

As far as possible, every pupil should be given an opportunity to participate. The program would probably be better if given by a selected few, but much of the educational benefit would be lost. The opportunity to participate should be granted to all pupils, for each has some contribution to make.

TEACHER PLANNING

The teacher, when planning for a presentation, should--
1. select simple material which all the children can do well;
2. consider the weekly rhythmic period sufficient preparation for the program, thus keeping the time spent in preparation to a minimum and keeping the children from becoming too tired;
3. grant all children an equal opportunity to participate in the presentation;
4. give less proficient children additional help by allowing for split or double sessions in rehearsal;
5. order materials needed for simple costumes.

COMBINATION OF CLASSES

In large schools grades of the same level may dance together so that the program will be of a more suitable length than if each class performed separately.

SCHOOL PLANNING MEETINGS

Early in the spring semester, the principal, general festival chairman, and school faculty should meet to consider the following aspects of their spring dance festival.

Theme: A timely, meaningful, and appropriate theme in relation to the various rhythmic activities should be chosen. A general festival title, covering rhythmic activities already familiar to the children, is preferable to a specific theme for which new or special rhythmic activities must be prepared.

Date and hour: When scheduling the festival, the committee should--
1. consult the calendar of school events to avoid scheduling conflicts;
2. consider weather and possible emergencies (choose an alternate date or location in case of rain);
3. consider the school enrollment in relation to the timing and length of the program;
4. discuss the possibility of holding the festival on the final day of school.

Responsibilities: Responsibilities should be defined, and assignments for arranging materials, equipment, invitations, programs, and costumes should be made at this time.

Many people at one time or another have wished for either the ability or the opportunity to create a dance. In order to be able to create a fun dance, become familiar with the basic formations, positions, and steps that comprise fun dancing. Then you will be able to feel the rhythm and pick the step that should go with each phrase of music.

In writing a fun dance, decide whether the music is to be chosen first and the dance made to fit the music, or the dance written and music chosen later to fit the dance. You may wish to use a certain combination of dance steps and then have a good musician write music to accompany the dance, or simply choose suitable music already written.

Before beginning to write the dance, consider and answer as completely as possible the following questions. (More answers may turn up as you work with it.)

1. What formation shall I use? (line, single or double circle, team, threesome, or mass)

2. At a party, when would this dance be used? (opener, get-acquainted mixer, socializer, floor-show number, finale)

3. What type of group will it be for? (all one sex, uneven distribution, children, teenagers, adults, senior citizens)

4. How adaptable can I make it?

5. Shall I confine myself to round or square dance steps, or include some social dance steps too?

Follow these rules in writing fun dances.

1. Name the dance
2. Give the formation, position, and footwork.
3. Decide on the music, record (name of the company and number of the record), and rhythm.
4. Make three columns: one each for measures, calls, and instructions.
5. Make each line equal to one or more measures, but don't split a measure between two lines.
6. Write instructions for movements or calls two beats long in capital letters; for movements or calls one beat long, use lowercase letters. Indicate half-beat lengths by an apostrophe (') and quarter-beat lengths, if necessary, by the filler count <u>a</u>. (This is the same notation system used throughout this book--see the call column of any dance description for an example.)
7. Name each step in the dance.
8. Make each call word equal to a change of weight or movement.
9. Underline in the call column and at the beginning of each instruction the key words (usually the name of the step) called ahead. Detail the instruction for that step in the instruction column.
10. Make the dance phrase with the music (usually in phrases of eight or sixteen measures).
11. Make the dance short and easy enough to teach with one demonstration and walk-through.

Note: For examples of other dance-writing methods, see Appendix.

The following is a list of dance steps which should help you make the dance figure phrase with the music.

Two-unit steps completed in four counts. Left and right units each require two counts.

1. Balance
2. Ball-change
3. Two-step
4. Pas de basque

Two-unit steps completed in eight counts. Left and right units each require four counts.

5. Chug
6. Grapevine
7. Paddle
8. Slide
9. Walk and balance

One-unit steps completed in four counts.

10. Buzz swing
11. Walk
12. Jump
13. Hop

One-unit step completed in three counts.

14. Canter

Step in any number of counts and units.

15. Arch

When two units are required to complete a step, they are referred to as left and right units. A balance step or a slow movement separates the two units. The left unit starts with the left foot and is first, except in folk dances when the dance often starts on the right foot. Two-count units of steps should be combined with other two-count units of steps and four-count units with other four-count units, rather than mixing units of different lengths.

Wedging means placing one step between two units of another step. It is tricky and probably should not be used by the novice dance writer. Amalgamation means the order of placement of the foot patterns; these should be kept simple for beginning dancers and dance writers.

The following is a list of some of the things that make dancing difficult. Avoid them if possible when writing a dance.

1. Incompetent instructions
2. Changing rhythms
3. Steps that have no lead
4. Records that have no definite beat
5. Routines that repeat the same steps in a different sequence
6. Figures and steps not repeated in succession
7. Steps, turns, and figures too similar to each other
8. Needless introductions, interludes, and endings
9. Steps and figures that do not phrase with the music
10. Inconsistent style in writing
11. Wedging
12. Tricky or difficult amalgamations
13. Poorly composed calls (remember to call the name of the step ahead and to give verbal directions to keep dancers in rhythm after the step has been called)
14. Steps that do not flow freely
15. Abrupt changes of directions, positions, or steps

The method used to change partners in the fun dance will depend on the formation. Dancers in a fun dance party should always change partners moving in the same direction. The following are suggestions for changing partners in various formations.

Single circle formation, all facing center: The man takes the lady on the left for a new partner.

Single circle, closed position: The man moves ahead to a new partner.

Double circle formation: (a) If the dance ends in two-hand or conversation position, the man takes the lady on the right for a new partner. (b) If the dance ends in full-open, semi-open, reverse, or right-side position, the man takes the lady behind for his new partner.

Threesome formation: The inside member goes forward and the outside members go back to find new partners.

CHANGING TEAMS

Arch-couples

Turn back-threesomes

Dive under-teams

Pass-through-threesome
teams

ROUND DANCING

A round dance is a dance in which a set routine is repeated over and over again. It need not be danced in a circle; it can be danced in any formation, as long as the steps are in a set routine and follow the same sequence. Most round dances are simple enough to teach in a short time. They are used for dance parties, for all grades in school--indeed, for people of all ages who want to enjoy themselves dancing.

T R A D I T I O N A L   R O U N D   D A N C E S

Perennial favorites among round dances are the minuet, the gavotte, the varsouvienne, the waltz, the polka, the conga, the bunny hop, la raspa, and the schottische. Some of these dances are so well known that the moment the music starts dancers fill the floor without being asked, and little or no instruction is needed. Brief historical information on each of these dances follows.

The <u>minuet</u> (4/4 time) flourished in the days of the powdered wigs and elaborately full, long skirts, the days of white stockings and knee breeches and heavy, colorful coats. Led by the all-important dancing master, the minuet was danced at arm's length and was composed of many intricate patterns of stately dance. It was an exhibition dance performed by only the most practiced dancers--couples moving in a circle, circling each other, advancing and retreating, and bowing deeply to each other in a set pattern.

The minuet was danced by the kings and courtiers of Europe for many decades and came to America with the colonists of more aristocratic descent. George Washington danced the minuet and was once paid a great compliment by a French visitor who said, after observing Washington's grace and dignity, "A Parisian education could not have rendered his execution more admirable."

Although the minuet yielded to the waltz in popularity, it is still danced in modified versions. The basic steps include the walk, the balance, the pointing of the toe, and the bow. One sequence might consist of step side left, point the right foot over the left, step forward right, left, right, point the left foot forward, and bow. A modernized version is found in the Oxford Minuet.

The <u>gavotte</u> (4/4 time), another dance of roughly the same period, originated among and was named after the peasants in the province of Dauphiné in southeastern France, ebullient native dancers called <u>Gavots</u>. However, they would scarcely have recognized their lively, jumping dance as it was later performed in court circles. When the gavotte left the mountain country, it became first formal and stately, and finally stiff and artificial. Like the minuet, it became part of the ballet repertoire and was danced at grand balls throughout Europe and the United States in the seventeenth and eighteenth centuries. Also like the minuet, the gavotte was complicated by intricate steps perpetuated by dancing masters. It is characterized by raising the feet rather than sliding them, and the basic step is three walking steps followed by pointing the toe.

Probably originating in Poland near the middle of the nineteenth century, the varsouvienne or mazurka (3/4 time) perhaps derives its name from that of Poland's capital city, Warsaw, where the dance found its greatest popularity. It evolved from one of the simpler steps of the original mazurka, now practically extinct. The Texans, however, also claim its origin; and in Texas the varsouvienne is usually called "Little Foot" or "Put Your Little Foot" after the song by the same name to which it is often danced.

The characteristic series of steps for the varsouvienne is as follows: sweep the left foot back, around, and over the right instep; glide forward on the same foot; and close right to left. Often this series is followed by walking three steps and pointing the toe ("your little foot"). It is usually danced in the varsouvienne position--the man, standing behind the lady slightly to her left side, places his right arm over her right shoulder and takes her right hand. The left hands are also joined at shoulder height.

The waltz (3/4 time) of the twentieth century descends from the Weller, an Austrian and Bavarian peasant dance with wide, wild steps in rapid turning movement, and from the Styrian Ländler, a turning dance with separate figures, such as handclapping or spinning the ladies under the upraised arms of their stomping partners. The sliding, gliding steps of these sixteenth- and seventeenth-century country dances became the Waltzer of the middle 1800s in German and Austrian cities. An expression of a new era for the emerging bourgeois society, this dance spread to France by 1790. The English, scandalized at first at the thought of giving up their orderly quadrilles and having men and women dance in such close proximity, failed to accept it until about 1812. In spite of the protests of the dancing masters, the waltz conquered the world, overcoming all objections with its universal appeal.

The classical or Viennese waltz developed in Vienna when the tempo increased to about two hundred quarter notes to the minute. Viennese composers Johann Strauss the Younger, Eduard Strauss, Franz Lehár, and Oscar Strauss set it to unforgettable music. Today the fast, staccato Viennese waltz, requiring great agility, has given way to the smoother, slower American version, a gliding dance with graceful movements.

The waltz transcends the barriers between round dancing and social or ballroom dancing. It is well known and accepted as part of both. Included in this chapter as round dances are several waltzes. The waltz is also presented later as a social dance.

Three rhythms should be mastered by those interested in the waltz as a round dance. All, of course, are in three-quarter time.
   ●Box or walk rhythm, in which the weight is changed on every beat of music.
   ●Canter rhythm, in which a weight change occurs twice in a three-beat measure.
   ●Hesitation or balance rhythm, in which the dancer changes weight once

The polka (2/4 time) is a dance of Bohemian origin. It is said to have been invented by a farm servant named Anna Slazak near Prague, Czechoslovakia, in 1830. From Prague, where it became popular within the decade, it was introduced to Vienna, where both the music and dance met with enthusiastic acceptance. In 1840 at the Odéon Theatre in Paris it was received with great applause and soon became a favorite dance in both private and public halls there. It spread to every country in Europe, as well as the United States, and is now common in every part of the civilized world.

The polka has many variations. Young people like the vigorous type, in which the dancing couple turns halfway around on each step unit and progresses rapidly around the floor. Older dancers prefer the businessman's polka, which resembles a smooth, slow samba. The basic polka step may be described as a hop and a two-step.

Beginning couples should start learning the polka in an open position until they have mastered the basic step. As they advance to the polka turn, the man places his hands on the lady's waist, and she places hers on the man's shoulders. They start dancing the polka in place, then move a little to the right and to the left, turning slightly on each step and increasing the size of the turn until they can turn halfway around on each step unit. It is best to learn by turning to the right. Arches, crosses, wheels, and individual turns are also fun in dancing the polka.

The conga (4/4 time) beat came from Africa by way of Cuba. Introduced into the United States early in the twentieth century, the conga consists mainly of three steps and a kick and is usually, but not always, danced in a line, with each person holding the waist or shoulders of the person ahead. Variations may be added in the form of snapping the fingers, clapping the hands, stomping the foot, changing direction, and the like.

The bunny hop (4/4 time) is an American dance of recent origin--if, indeed, it can be called a dance. Basically, it is a series of jumps, interspersed with kicks and walking steps. Popular with all age groups, it is often done in a conga line.

La Raspa (4/4 time) is a delightful circle dance that comes from Mexico. This dance is not to be confused with the Mexican hat dance although it is often called the Mexican clap dance.

There are several variations to this dance but the basic unit consists of three kick-shuffle steps interspersed with clapping. The feet remain lightly in contact with the floor as they change in forward and backward movements. When the foot is forward, the heel is placed on the floor. On the backward movement the toe carries the weight of the body.

The schottische (4/4 time) originated in Germany as a variation of the waltz. The name is derived from the German word "Schotte," meaning Scotsman. The basic unit of the schottische is three walking steps and a hop.

Note

For certain of the following round dances, the usual call system has been discarded in favor of a patter call (such as those in the chapter on square dancing) or a verse to be sung while dancing. In the latter case, the leader must be sure that the dancers know the sequence of steps thoroughly before they attempt the dance to music, as there are no calls to cue them.

There are several types of lines; the lines referred to here are conga lines, in which dancers hold the waist or shoulders of the person ahead.

Line dances are used to move dancers from one building to another, from one room to another, and to start a party. When a line is started it is easy for those dancers coming late to hook on and join the line, and partners are not needed.

B E G I N N E R ' S   D A N C E

This dance is simplified for young beginners.

Formation: Line
Position: All holding hands
Footwork: All start L

Music: Anything popular with youth
Record: Own choice
Rhythm: 4/4, 4 meas

MEAS   CALL

WALK FORWARD

READY WALK

1   forward forward slide' and' touch

2   slide slide walk back

3   back back slide right

4   slide slide walk forward

INSTRUCTIONS

Walk: Walk fwd 4 steps L,R,L,R.

Slide and touch: Slide L 4 slides, and touch R foot to L.

Walk back: Walk back 4 steps starting R,L,R,L.

Slide right: Slide 4 slides R, and touch L foot to R.

Repeat entire dance.

Variation

Sliding steps may be either quick or slow.

B U N N Y   H O P

Formation: Conga line
Position: Hands on shoulders of person ahead
Footwork: All start L

Music: Bunny Hop
Record: MacGregor 6995B
Rhythm: 4/4, 32 meas

MEAS   CALL

forward and CLAP

READY FORWARD

INSTRUCTIONS

Forward and clap: Walk fwd 3 steps, hop L. Repeat. Clap hands above head twice, clap hips twice. Put L hand on

1-2	1 2 3 hop, 1 2 3 clap	L hip, raise forefinger of R hand, move hips L,R,L,R. Repeat all above, moving fwd.
3	hands hands hips hips
4	<u>forward</u> once MORE	Kick: Kick R twice, kick L twice.
5-6	1 2 3 hop, 1 2 3 clap	Jump: Jump fwd and back, 3 jumps fwd.
7	hands hands hips hips	Side jump: Jump L,R, and 3 jumps L.
8	now let's KICK	Jump right: Jump R,L, and 3 jumps R.
9-10	RIGHT RIGHT, now <u>jump</u> FORWARD	Kick and turn: Kick R twice, kick L twice, jump fwd and back, make 1 individual turn to L in 3 jumps. Kick R twice, kick L twice, jump fwd and back, make 1 individual turn to R in 3 jumps.
11-12	FORWARD BACK, let's <u>kick</u> AGAIN
13-14	RIGHT RIGHT, NOW <u>JUMP</u>	Repeat entire dance.
15-16	FORWARD BACK, let's <u>kick</u> AGAIN	Suggestion
17-18	RIGHT RIGHT, <u>SIDE JUMP</u>	Any two of the above steps make a good dance routine.
19-20	LEFT RIGHT, left left <u>KICK</u>
21-22	RIGHT RIGHT, <u>JUMP RIGHT</u>
23-24	RIGHT LEFT, let's <u>kick and turn</u>
25-26	RIGHT RIGHT, LEFT LEFT
27-28	FORWARD BACK, turn turn TURN
29-30	RIGHT RIGHT, LEFT LEFT
31-32	JUMP TURN, now go <u>FORWARD</u>

C O N G A

Formation: Conga line
Position: Hands on waist of person ahead
Footwork: All start L

Music: Conga
Record: Yates 731
Rhythm: 4/4, 16 meas

MEAS	CALL	INSTRUCTIONS
	FORWARD BASIC	Forward (basic step): Walk fwd 3 steps (L,R,L) and kick R foot to R side.
	READY <u>FORWARD</u>	Walk fwd 3 steps (R,L,R) and kick L foot

1-2	1 2 3 kick, 1 2 3 kick	to L side. Repeat.
3-4	1 2 3 kick, now it's to' the' <u>side</u>	<u>Side</u>: Step side L, cross R foot over L, step side L, kick R foot to R side. Step side R, cross L foot over R, step side R, kick L foot to L side. Repeat.
5-6	side cross side kick, side cross side kick	
7-8	side cross side kick, <u>forward and CROSS</u>	<u>Cross</u>: Basic step fwd and kick R foot over L. Basic step fwd, kick L foot over R. Repeat.
9-10	1 2 3 cross, 1 2 3 cross	<u>Center</u>: All drop hands and take 3 steps to center of hall L,R,L; turn, kick R foot toward wall while snapping fingers. Take 3 steps toward wall, R,L,R; turn, and kick L foot toward center of hall, snapping fingers. Repeat
11-12	1 2 3 cross, now it's to' the' <u>center</u>	
13-14	1 2 turn snap, 1 2 turn snap	
15-16	1 2 turn snap, let's go <u>FORWARD</u>	Repeat entire dance.

E I G H T E E N   N I N E T Y - E I G H T

Formation: Conga line
Position: Hands on waist of person ahead
Footwork: All start L

Music: Eighteen Ninety-Eight or medium foxtrot
Record: Windsor 7613 or own choice
Rhythm: 4/4, 8 meas

MEAS	CALL		INSTRUCTIONS
	<u>tap and SLIDE</u>		<u>Tap and slide</u>: Brush L foot fwd. Tap and cross L foot over R as foot comes back; brush fwd, tap back to place. Step side L, close, step side L, touch R foot to L. Repeat brush and slide to R.
	READY TAP		
1-2	tap tap tap tap, side together side touch		
3-4	tap tap tap tap, side together <u>two-step</u>		<u>Two-step</u>: Starting L, take 4 two-steps fwd.
5	step' close' step step' close' step		<u>Side ball-change</u>: Step side L, close and change weight momentarily. Repeat to R. Repeat for total of 4 ball-changes.
6	step' close' step <u>side' ball'-change</u>		
7	side' ball'-change side' ball'-change		Repeat entire dance.
8	side' ball'-change <u>start over</u>		<u>Variation</u>

Substitute grapevine for slide: After tap step, step side L, cross R foot behind L, step side L, touch R foot to L. Repeat tap step and grapevine to R.

G L O W W O R M

Formation: Conga line
Position: Hands on waist of per-
son ahead
Footwork: All start L

Music: Glowworm
Record: Windsor 4613, MacGregor 3105B
Rhythm: 4/4, 8 meas

MEAS	CALL
	walk and POINT
	READY WALK
1-2	1 2 3 point, 1 2 GRAPEVINE
3	step behind step reverse
4	center left turn point
5-6	1 2 turn point, 1 2 two-step
7	step' close' step step' close' step
8	step' close' step walk' and' point

INSTRUCTIONS

Walk and point: Walk fwd 3 steps (L,R, L), point R foot fwd. Walk fwd 3 steps (R,L,R), point L foot fwd.

Grapevine: Step side L, cross R foot behind L, step side L, swing R foot over L.

Reverse: Repeat grapevine to R.

Center and point sequence: Walk 3 steps toward center of hall, turn, and point R foot to wall. Walk 3 steps toward wall, turn, and point L foot to center.

Two-step: Take 4 two-steps fwd.

Repeat entire dance.

H I T C H H I K E

Formation: Conga line
Position: Hands on shoulders of person ahead
Footwork: Jump with both feet together

Music: Tennessee Saturday Night
Record: Decca 4613
Rhythm: 4/4, 12 meas

MEAS	CALL
	jump and HITCH
	READY JUMP
1-2	BACK BACK, RIGHT RIGHT
3-4	BACK BACK, LEFT LEFT
5-6	BACK BACK, RIGHT LEFT
7-8	BACK BACK, BOTH two-step
9	step' close' step step' close' step

INSTRUCTIONS

Jump and hitch sequence: Take 2 jumps back; swing R toe out, at same time pointing R thumb over R shoulder, then repeat. Take 2 jumps back; repeat hitch with L foot and thumb. Take 2 jumps back, hitch once to R and once to L. Take 2 jumps back, repeat hitch with both thumbs and feet simultaneously. (Rock on both heels as toes go out.)

Two-step: Starting L, dance 8 two-steps fwd.

10	step' close' step step' close' step	Repeat entire dance.
11	step' close' step step' close' step	
12	step' close' step jump back	

P A T T Y - C A K E   P O L K A

Formation: Conga line
Position: Hands on shoulders of person ahead
Footwork: All start L

Music: Patty-cake Polka
Record: Windsor 4624
Rhythm: 4/4, 8 meas

MEAS	CALL	INSTRUCTIONS
	heel-toe and slide	Heel-toe: L heel fwd, L toe back, repeat.
	READY heel-toe	
1	heel-toe heel slide	Slide: Take 4 slides to L.
2	slide slide slide reverse	Reverse: Starting R, repeat heel-toe and slide to R.
3	heel-toe heel slide	Clap: Clap R shoulder of person ahead 3 times, clap L shoulder 3 times, clap both shoulders 3 times, clap hands 3 times.
4	slide slide now clap	
5	right' 2' 3 left' 2' 3	
6	both' 2' 3 two'-step' forward	Two-step: Starting L, take 4 two-steps fwd.
7	step' close' step step' close' step	Repeat entire dance.
8	step' close' step heel-toe	

S H A K E   A   L E G

Formation: Conga line
Position: Hands on shoulders of person ahead
Footwork: All start L

Music: Secondhand Store
Record: Windsor 4671B
Rhythm: 4/4, 8 meas

MEAS	CALL	INSTRUCTIONS
	heel and STOMP	Heel and stomp: Tap L heel on floor twice, then stomp L,R,L. Repeat heel and stomp starting R.
	READY HEEL	

70

1	heel heel stomp' stomp' right	Shake a leg: Stand on R foot, lean R, raise L leg in line with body, shake it. Stomp L,R,L. Repeat, standing on L foot.
2	heel heel shake' a' leg	
3	shake shake now' shake' right	Walk and two-step: Walk 2 steps, one two-step. Repeat twice more.
4	shake walk' and' two-step	Jumping jack: Jump with both feet together, bending knees on landing to go down into full squat; jump up again.
5	walk walk step' close' step	
6	walk walk step' close' step	Repeat entire dance.
7	walk walk jumping jack	
8	down up start over	

THE STROLL

Formation:	Two lines, 1 of men, 1 of ladies, facing, six feet apart	Music:	The Stroll
		Record:	Corral 9-61930
		Rhythm:	4/4
Position:	Full-open, R-L cnt (active couple)		
Footwork:	Opposite (man L, lady R)		

MEAS   CALL

INSTRUCTIONS

READY STROLL

Stroll: Head couple moves between lines by stepping fwd L,R (ct 1-2), and crossing L foot behind R to stand back to back (ct 3). Partners then step fwd R,L in LOD (ct 4,1), and cross R foot behind L to stand face to face (ct 2). Repeat, moving to foot of set, always maintaining R-L cnt. When head couple reaches foot, they take places in lines.

1	forward forward back forward
2	forward back forward forward
3	back forward forward back
4	forward forward back forward

. . .

Meanwhile, dancers in lines step side L (ct 1), touch R foot beside L (ct 2); step side R (ct 3), touch L foot beside R (ct 4); step side L (ct 1), touch R foot beside L (ct 2); step side R (ct 3), cross L foot behind R (ct 4), step side R (ct 1), touch L foot beside R (ct 2). (Pattern is 3 step-touches, 1 grapevine R.) Repeat continually so that lines progress slowly sideways agLOD of active couple.

Repeat entire dance with new head couple,
until every couple has strolled down
set.

T H E   T W O - S T E P

Formation: Conga line
Position: Hands on waist of per-
son ahead
Footwork: All start L

Music: Polka
Record: MacGregor 5005 A
Rhythm: 4/4, 4 meas

MEAS	CALL	INSTRUCTIONS
	heel-toe' and' two-step	Heel-toe and two-step: L heel fwd, L toe back; take 1 two-step fwd. Repeat, starting R.
	READY heel-toe	
1	heel-toe step' close' step	Side ball-change: Step side L, close R foot to L, changing weight momentarily; repeat to R.
2	heel-toe side' ball'-change	
3	side' ball'-change brush' and' stomp	Brush and stomp: Step side L, swing R foot across L brushing floor. Stomp feet, R,L,R.
4	step brush heel-toe	

Repeat entire dance.

V I R G I N I A   R E E L

Formation: Two lines, 1 of men, 1
of ladies, facing
Position: Shine
Footwork: Opposite (man L, lady R)

Music: Virginia Reel
Record: RCA Victor 41-6180, Victor EPA
4138
Rhythm: 4/4, 16 meas

MEAS	CALL	INSTRUCTIONS
	walk forward and bow	Walk and bow: Take 4 steps toward partner, bow, 4 steps back.
	READY WALK	
1	forward forward BOW	Right hands around: Take 4 steps to partner, join R hands, walk around once and back to place.
2	back back right' hands' around	
3	1 2 3 around	Left hands around: Repeat right hands around sequence but join L hands for turn.
4	back back left' hands' around	
5	1 2 3 around	Both hands around: Repeat right hands around sequence but join both hands and circle to R.

6	back back <u>both' hands'</u> <u>around</u>	Do-si-do: In 4 steps fwd and 4 back, partners pass R shoulders, pass back to back, pass L shoulders, and back into place.
7	1 2 3 around	
8	back back <u>do'-si'-do</u>	Down the center: Head couple joins hands, slides down aisle between lines and back to place in 8 slides.
9	1 2 3 around	
10	head couple <u>down' the'</u> <u>center</u>	March around: In 8 walking steps partners in head couple lead lines in opposite directions around outside of set and back to where foot of set **was**.
11	slide slide slide <u>reverse</u>	
12	slide slide <u>march around</u>	Arch: Head couple makes 2-hand arch; all other couples pass under in 8 walking steps to reform set, with second couple as new head couple.
13	1 2 3 4	
14	head couple <u>ARCH</u>	
15	1 2 3 4	Repeat entire dance until all couples have been head couple.
16	now <u>start OVER</u>	

S I N G L E   C I R C L E   D A N C E S

Single circle dances are used when there are more of one sex than the other and when there are tall ladies and short men. It is easier for a dancer to join the crowd when he does not need a partner and all are in a single circle facing the center of the hall. There is seldom a change of partners in a single circle dance.

When learning a dance in a single circle, dancers should all start on the left foot. Ladies can easily switch to the right foot when the formation changes to a double circle.

C I R C A S S I A N   C I R C L E

Formation: Single circle
Position: Hands joined
Footwork: All start L

Music: Circassian Circle
Record: Windsor A7S3
Rhythm: 4/4, 16 meas

MEAS   CALL

          walk to CENTER

          READY <u>WALK</u>

INSTRUCTIONS

Walk: Take 4 walking steps to center, <u>4 walking steps back.</u>

1-2	forward 2 3 back, back now <u>ladies in</u>
3-4	forward 2 3 back, back now <u>men in</u>

Ladies in: Ladies walk 4 steps to center and 4 back.

Men in: Men walk 4 steps to center.

5	forward 2 turn left	Turn left: Men turn around L and take 4 steps to lady formerly on L.
6	new partner shoulder swing	
7-8	1 2 3 4, now all PROMENADE	Shoulder swing: Join L hands, place R hand on R shoulder of new partner, swing twice around in total of 8 ct.
9-16	1 2 3 4, 2 2 3 4 3 2 3 4, 4 2 3 4 5 2 3 4, 6 2 3 4 7 2 3 4, now start OVER	Promenade: Promenade with new partner 8 meas, then rejoin hands into single circle.

Repeat entire dance.

C O N G A   M I X E R

Formation:	Single circle, men facing LOD, ladies agLOD	Music:	Rock-A-Conga
Position:	Hands joined	Record:	Cameo C155-A
Footwork:	Opposite (man L, lady R)	Rhythm:	4/4, 8 meas

MEAS	CALL	INSTRUCTIONS
	grand right-and-left	Grand right-and-left (basic step): Grand right-and-left fwd 3 walking steps to next dancer and kick R foot back. Repeat 3 more times.
	READY GRAND	
1	forward 2 3 kick	
2	forward 2 3 kick	Wheel: Join R hands with 5th dancer, (counting original partner as 1st). Wheel fwd twice around in 2 basic steps.
3	forward 2 3 kick	
4	right-hand WHEEL	Repeat entire dance.
5	forward 2 3 kick	
6	go around AGAIN	## Variation
7	forward 2 3 kick	Take R-side position on wheel. Back away from partner on last step and join R hands for grand right-and-left.
8	grand right-and-left	

Suggestion

On grand right-and-left, circle should be joined (i.e., all holding hands) for kick.

H O M E T O W N   P O L K A

Formation:	Single circle	Music:	Hometown Polka
Position:	Hands joined	Record:	Windsor 4624-B
Footwork:	All start L	Rhythm:	4/4, 8 meas

74

| MEAS | CALL | INSTRUCTIONS |

MEAS   CALL

heel-toe and slide

READY heel-toe

MEAS	CALL
	heel-toe and slide
	READY heel-toe
1	heel-toe heel slide
2	slide slide slide reverse
3	heel-toe heel slide
4	slide slide slide clap
5	right' 2' 3 left' 2' 3
6	hands' 2' 3 knees' and' two'-step'
7	step' close' step now back
8	step' close' step now' heel'-toe

INSTRUCTIONS

Heel-toe and slide: Put L heel fwd, L toe back, repeat; slide L 4 slides. Repeat to R.

Clap: Clap R knee 3 times, clap L knee 3 times, clap hands 3 times, clap both knees 3 times.

Two-step: Take 2 two-steps fwd and 2 two-steps back.

Repeat entire dance.

IRISH WALTZ

Formation: Single circle
Position: Varsouvienne
Footwork: All start L

Music: Irish Waltz
Record: Windsor 4695-A
Rhythm: 3/4, 24 meas

MEAS	CALL
	swing your foot
	ready SWING
1-2	STEP, CANTER
3-4	BACK close, now FORWARD
5-6	forward TOUCH, forward TURN
7-8	1 2 3, now SWING
9-10	STEP, CANTER
11-12	BACK close, now FORWARD
13-14	forward TOUCH, forward TURN
15-16	1 2 3, slide and brush
17-18	SIDE close, side BRUSH

INSTRUCTIONS

Note

In CALL column capital letters represent either two beats or three, as needed to complete measure. (End of measure is indicated by comma or by end of line.)

Swing: Step fwd L (ct 1); swing R foot fwd (ct 2-3); swing R foot back while pivoting R 1/2 turn on L foot to lift R foot fwd (ct 1-3). Retain handclasp so that man's L arm is now around lady's shoulder.

Canter: Step back on R (ct 1-2), close L to R (ct 3), step back on R (ct 1-3).

Forward: Step fwd on L foot (ct 1) and touch R toe behind L (ct 2-3). Repeat, starting R.

19-20	SIDE close, side BRUSH
21-22	SIDE close, side BRUSH
23-24	change PARTNERS, start OVER

Turn: In 3 short steps (L,R,L), turn L ½ turn back to LOD while retaining handclasp (ct 1-3), step on R again (ct 1), and hold (ct 2-3). Repeat meas 1-8.

Slide and brush: Step side L (ct 1-2), close R foot to L (ct 3), step side L (ct 1), brush R foot fwd and back (ct 2-3); step on R turning ¼ turn to R (ct 1-2), close L to R (ct 3), step R (ct 1), brush L (ct 2-3); change from R varsouvienne position to L and back while sliding and brushing. Repeat meas 17-20. On last meas (24), man takes 3 steps to new partner on his R.

Repeat entire dance.

J E S S I E   P O L K A

Formation: Single circle
Position: Hands joined
Footwork: All start L

Music: Jessie Polka
Record: Old Timer 8210
Rhythm: 4/4, 4 meas

MEAS	CALL	INSTRUCTIONS
	heel-stand and touch	Heel-stand (basic step): L heel fwd; close L foot to R and change weight to it. Touch R toe back, touch R foot to side of L, kick R foot fwd, close R foot to L and change weight. Point side L, point L foot in front of R.
	READY heel-stand	
1	heel-stand back touch	
2	kick stand two'-step' forward	Two-step: Take 2 two-steps fwd, 2 back.
3	step' close' step now back	Repeat entire dance.
4	step' close' step heel-stand	

J I N G L E   B E L L S

Formation: Single circle
Position: Shine
Footwork: Opposite (man L, lady R)

Music: Jingle Bells
Record: MacGregor 1003
Rhythm: 4/4

MEAS	CALL	INSTRUCTIONS
	swing your PARTNER	Swing: Lady gives R forearm or elbow to partner, swings once around (meas 1-2). Lady then gives L forearm or elbow to
	READY SWING	

1	right arm to partner	man on her R and swings him (meas 3-4), swings partner with R-arm grip as he walks ahead to meet her (meas 5-6). Lady alternates around circle between her partner and each man, continuing to place in circle where they were originally and taking that place.
2	swing once AROUND	
3	lady's left' arm' to' next' man	
4	SWING AROUND	
5	right arm to partner	
6	SWING AROUND	
	. . .	Second couple start: Couple to R of 1st couple's place in circle starts swing sequence around circle after 1st couple has passed 3 couples.
15	ALTERNATE and now	Repeat entire dance until each couple has had turn to swing around circle.
16	second couple START	

. . .

Variation

In large circle, have several couples start at different places. When active couple comes to break in circle, they take that place.

M E   A N D   M Y   S H A D O W

Formation: Single circle
Position: Parallel, hands joined
            high, facing LOD
Footwork: All start L

Music: Me and My Shadow
Record: Windsor 4828
Rhythm: 4/4, 8 meas

MEAS	CALL	INSTRUCTIONS
	heel-toe' and' two-step	Heel-toe and two-step: L heel fwd, L toe back, and take 1 two-step fwd. Repeat heel-toe and two-step, starting R.
	READY heel-toe	
1	heel-toe step' close' step	Two-step: Two-step 2 more times.
2	heel-toe two-step	Walk: Starting L, take 4 steps fwd.
3	step' close' step now walk	Side two-step: Take 1 two-step L, changing weight on balls of feet and moving arms (retaining handholds) to L high over head. Repeat to R. Repeat once again to L and R.
4	1 2 side' two'-step	
5	step' close' step step' close' step	
6	step' close' step now walk	Change partners: Partners drop hands; lady moves back, man fwd 4 steps to new partner.
7	1 2 change partners	
8	1 2 heel-toe	Repeat entire dance.

77

MEXICAN SHUFFLE

Formation: Single circle	Music: El Molino	
Position: Hands joined	Record: Windsor A-7S1-B	
Footwork: All start L	Rhythm: 4/4, 16 meas	

MEAS	CALL	INSTRUCTIONS
	READY SHUFFLE	Shuffle: Point L toe fwd (slow). Change feet to stand on L and point R toe fwd (slow). Change to stand on R foot and point L toe (quick). Change to stand on L and point R (quick), and to stand on R and point L (slow). Repeat meas 1-2, pointing R toe fwd first. Repeat meas 1-4.
1-2	LEFT RIGHT, left right LEFT	
3-4	RIGHT LEFT, right left RIGHT	
5-6	LEFT RIGHT, left right LEFT	
7-8	RIGHT LEFT, now slide LEFT	
9-10	1 2 3 4, 5 6 slide right	Slide: Join hands and slide 8 slides L; reverse for 8 slides R.
11-12	1 2 3 4, two-step to center	Two-step: Take 4 two-steps to center and 4 two-steps back.
13	step' close' step step' close' step	Repeat entire dance.
14	step' close' step two'-step' back	
15	step' close' step step' close' step	
16	step' close' step shuffle now	

OLD SOFT SHOE

Formation: Single circle	Music: Old Soft Shoe or any foxtrot	
Position: Hands joined	Record: Windsor 7610 or own choice	
Footwork: All start L	Rhythm: 4/4, 8 meas	

MEAS	CALL	INSTRUCTIONS
	GRAPEVINE LEFT	Grapevine left: Step side L, step R foot behind L, step L, swing R foot over L. Reverse to R.
	READY GRAPEVINE	
1	side behind side reverse	Balance left: Step fwd L, touch R foot beside L, step back R, touch L foot beside R, swinging arms fwd and back with steps.
2	balance forward left foot	
3	forward touch paddle left	

4	1 2 _grapevine right_	**Paddle left:** Dropping hands, lean to L, putting weight on ball of L foot, and push with R toe 4 times to make 1 complete L turn. Rejoin hands.
5	step behind step reverse	
6	_balance_ forward _right_ foot	
7	forward touch _paddle right_	**Grapevine right:** Repeat _grapevine left_ sequence, starting to R.
8	1 2 _grapevine left_	**Balance right:** Repeat _balance left_ sequence, starting on R foot.

Paddle right: Repeat _paddle left_ sequence to R for 1 complete R turn.

Repeat entire dance.

O X F O R D   M I N U E T

Formation: Single circle
Position: Hands joined
Footwork: All start L

Music: Oxford Minuet
Record: Windsor 4606
Rhythm: 4/4, 8 meas

MEAS	CALL	INSTRUCTIONS
	walk to center' and' point	**Walk and point sequence:** Walk fwd 3 steps and point R toe fwd.
	READY WALK	
1	forward 2 3 _back_	**Back:** Walk back 3 steps, starting R, and point L toe fwd.
2	back 2 _step-point_	**Step-point:** Step side L, point R toe across L; step side R, point L toe across R. Repeat to L and R.
3	step point step point	
4	step point _walk' and' point_	**Slide:** Take 8 slides L, reverse for 8 slides R.
5	1 2 3 _back_	
6	back 2 _step point_	Repeat entire dance.
7	step point step point	**Variation**
8	_slide_ 8 slides' to' left	Instead of 8 slides L and R, take 4 two-steps to center and 4 back.
9-10	1 2 3 4, 5 6 now right	
11-12	1 2 3 4, 5 6 _walk' and' point_	

P O P   G O E S   T H E   W E A S E L

Formation: Single circle
Position: Hands joined

Music: Pop Goes the Weasel
Record: Windsor A7S3

79

Footwork: All start L

Rhythm: 4/4, 12 meas

MEAS	CALL	INSTRUCTIONS
	READY chug left	Chug left: With weight on L foot, push 4 steps to L with R foot.
1	1 2 chug right	
2	1 2 balance left	Chug right: Repeat chug left sequence to R.
3	FORWARD paddle left	Balance left: Fwd on L foot, touch R to L, back on R foot, touch L to R.
4	1 2 chug right	
5	1 2 chug left	Paddle left, right: Leaning in direction of turn and pushing with opposite foot 4 times, turn individually 1 full turn.
6	1 2 balance right	
7	FORWARD paddle right	Balance right: Repeat balance left sequence, starting with R foot.
8	grand right-and-left	
9	step' close' step step' close' step	Grand right-and-left: In 4 two-steps grand right-and-left to 5th person.
10	wheel now turn' and' spin	Turn and spin: Hold R forearms, walk once around in 4 steps. Man then spins lady 1 turn to R.
11	1 2 spin now	
12	START OVER	Repeat entire dance.

S U S A N ' S   G A V O T T E

Formation: Single circle, facing agLOD
Position: Hands joined
Footwork: All start L

Music: Lili Marlene
Record: MacGregor 3105 A
Rhythm: 4/4, 12 meas

MEAS	CALL	INSTRUCTIONS
	walk left' and' slide left	Walk and slide sequence: Walk 4 steps fwd agLOD around circle. Face center and take 4 slides L. Repeat walk and slide to R.
	READY WALK	
1-2	1 2 3 slide, 1 2 3 reverse	
3-4	1 2 3 slide, 1 2 step-swing	Step-swing: Step L, swing R foot across L. Step R, swing L foot across R. Repeat for total of 4 step-swings, 2 each side.
5	step swing step swing	
6	walk left turn' and' point	Walk and point sequence: Walk 3 steps

7-8	1 2 turn point, 1 2 <u>two-step</u>	L, then turn 1/2 turn R and point R foot on 4th step. Walk 3 steps R, then
9	step' close' step step' close' step	turn 1/4 to face center of circle and point L foot to center.
10	step' close' step two'-step' back	<u>Two-step:</u> Starting L, take 4 two-steps to center, 4 two-steps back.
11	step' close' step step' close' step	Repeat entire dance.
12	step' close' step <u>walk'</u> <u>and'</u> <u>slide</u>	

S W I N G I N' T H E B L U E S

Formation:	**Single** circle	Music:	Third Man Theme
Position:	Hands joined	Record:	MacGregor 644
Footwork:	All start L	Rhythm:	4/4, 8 meas

MEAS	CALL	INSTRUCTIONS
	slide and CLAP	<u>Slide:</u> Slide L 3 slides (slow). In place of 4th slide clap hands. Repeat, starting to R.
	READY SLIDE	
1-2	ONE TWO, THREE REVERSE	<u>Clap and turn sequence:</u> Clap R knee with R hand (ct 1), clap hands (ct 2),
3-4	ONE TWO, THREE <u>CLAP</u>	clap L knee with L hand (ct 3), clap hands (ct 4), clap R knee with R hand
5	right together left together	(ct 1), clap hands (ct 2), clap both knees with both hands (ct 3), and hold
6	right together TURN	(ct 4). Turn L 1 full turn in 4 steps. On meas 8, clap both knees (ct 1), both
7	1 2 now clap	hips (ct 2), hands (ct 3), then hold (ct 4).
8	knees hips now <u>slide</u>	

Repeat entire dance.

<u>Variation</u>

Repeat dance as above, except on slide have group take turns mimicking some animal, musical instrument, etc.

V A R S O U V I E N N E

Formation:	Single circle, facing agLOD	Music:	Varsouvienne
Position:	Hands joined	Record:	Windsor 7615
Footwork:	All start L	Rhythm:	3/4, 16 meas

MEAS	CALL	INSTRUCTIONS

MEAS	CALL
	circle LEFT
	ready CIRCLE
1-2	raise step close, turn and point
3-4	raise step step, now circle right
5-6	raise step close, raise step close
7-8	walk and point, 4 TIMES
9-10	raise step step, turn POINT
11-12	raise step step, turn POINT
13-14	raise step step, turn POINT
15-16	and NOW, circle LEFT

INSTRUCTIONS

Circle left (basic step): Starting with weight on R foot, sweep L foot up across R (ct 1), step fwd with L (ct 2), slide R foot up to L (ct 3). Repeat, moving L around circle.

Turn and point: Sweep L foot up across R (ct 1), then walk 3 steps to L starting on L foot (ct 2,3,1); turn and point R on 4th step (ct 2-3).

Circle right: Repeat basic step to R by starting with weight on L foot (meas 5-6), then repeat turn and point sequence to R by sweeping R foot up across L, and so on (meas 7-8).

Walk and point: Repeat turn and point sequence 4 times; to L, then to R, then to L, then to R.

Repeat entire dance.

Variation

For walk and point sequence, drop hands and make complete L turn in 2 turning steps in place of 2nd and 3rd walking steps. (When repeating to R, make complete R turn.)

W A L K   M I X E R

Formation:	Single circle
Position:	Hands joined
Footwork:	All start L

Music:	Any popular tune
Record:	Own choice
Rhythm:	4/4, 4 meas

MEAS	CALL
	walk to CENTER
	READY FORWARD
1	forward forward now back
2	back back circle left
3	forward forward circle right
4	forward forward walk' to' center

INSTRUCTIONS

Walk to center: Starting on L foot, walk 4 steps to center of hall.

Back: Walk 4 steps back.

Circle left: Take 4 walking steps circling to L, retaining handclasp.

Circle right: Take 4 walking steps to R.

Repeat entire dance.

D O U B L E   C I R C L E   D A N C E S

Double circles are used when there are the same number of men and ladies. The men usually form the inside circle and ladies the outside circle. When changing partners, men go back against the line of dance and the ladies go forward in the line of dance to the next man.

A L L - A M E R I C A N   P R O M E N A D E

Formation: Double circle
Position: Full-open, R-L cnt
Footwork: Opposite (man L, lady R)

Music: All-American Promenade
Record: Windsor 7605
Rhythm: 4/4, 8 meas

MEAS	CALL
	walk and TURN
	READY WALK
1	1 2 turn back
2	back back forward again
3	1 2 turn back
4	back back away-together
5	AWAY now roll
6	1 2 together-away
7	TOGETHER now arch
8	now walk and turn

INSTRUCTIONS

Walk and turn: Walk fwd 4 steps; on 4th step turn in toward partner ½ turn to face agLOD, L-R cnt, and walk back 4 steps. Walk fwd 4 steps agLOD; on 4th step turn ½ turn and walk 4 steps back, facing LOD, R-L cnt.

Away-together: Both facing fwd, step apart with side ball-change, and then together with side ball-change.

Roll: In 4 steps, lady rolls 1 full turn L, crossing in front of man to full-open position, L-R cnt.

Together-away: Repeat side ball-change together, then apart.

Arch: Change partners, lady arching under partner's L arm to outside of circle and to man ahead.

Repeat entire dance.

B I N G O

Formation: Double circle
Position: Promenade
Footwork: All start L

Music: Bingo
Record: Windsor A7S2
Rhythm: 4/4, 12 meas

MEAS	CALL
	walk and SING
	READY WALK

INSTRUCTIONS

Walk 8 steps fwd; retaining handclasps, turn 1/2 turn on 8th step to face agLOD (meas 1-2). Walk 8 steps agLOD, then

1	A farmer's black dog sat on his back porch,
2	And Bingo was his name.
3	A farmer's black dog sat on his back porch,
4	And Bingo was his name.
5-6	B-I-N-G-O, B-I-N-G-O,
7	B-I-N-G-O,
8	And Bingo was his name.
9-12	B---I---N---G---O.

drop hands and turn ¼ turn to face partner (meas 3-4). Take 2 slides L (meas 5), 2 slides R (meas 6), 2 slides L (meas 7), and bow to partner (meas 8).

Partners take R hands and grand right-and-left, facing new partner with each letter of "BINGO" (meas 9-12). On "O," man hugs lady (5th from beginning position), swings her, and takes her as new partner.

Repeat entire dance.

B O S T O N   T W O - S T E P

Formation: Double circle
Position: Full-open, R-L cnt
Footwork: Opposite (man L, lady R)

Music: Boston Two-step
Record: MacGregor 309
Rhythm: 4/4, 8 meas

MEAS	CALL	INSTRUCTIONS
	side' ball'-change and cross	Side ball-change: Step away from partner with side ball-change, then together with side ball-change. (On 2nd time, step together first, then away.)
	READY side' ball'-change	
1	out' close' step now cross	Cross: Lady crosses over in front of partner with L turn in 4 steps, to full-open position, L-R cnt.
2	1 2 side' ball'-change	
3	in' close' step walk back	Walk back: Walk back agLOD 4 steps, coming gradually into two-hand position facing partner.
4	face partner step-swing	
5	step swing now arch	Step-swing: Step L, swing R foot over L; step R, swing L foot over R.
6	1 2 two'-step' turn	Arch: Change places with partner, lady arching under man's R arm in 4 walking steps. Take closed position for two-step R turn in 2 two-steps. Man then walks to new partner as lady arches under his L arm to new partner ahead.
7	step' close' step under' the' arm	
8	new partner side' ball'-change	

Repeat entire dance.

B U M P T Y   B U M P

Formation: Double circle
Position: Full-open, R-L cnt
Footwork: Opposite (man L, lady R)

Music: Bumpty Bump
Record: Mercury 70444
Rhythm: 4/4, 8 meas

MEAS	CALL	INSTRUCTIONS
	pas' de' basque and grape-vine	Pas de basque and grapevine sequence: Step side L, cross R foot over L, change weight momentarily. Repeat to R. Drop hands and grapevine apart (step L, cross R foot behind L, step L, swing R foot over L). Repeat pas de basque to R first, then L; grapevine together (starting R).
	READY pas' de' basque	
1	pas' de' basque GRAPEVINE	
2	side behind pas' de' basque	
3	pas' de' basque GRAPEVINE	Two-step: Take 2 two-steps fwd in full-open position.
4	side behind two-step	
5	step' close' step individual turn	Individual turn: In 4 steps turn 1/2 turn L, man turning back, lady ahead to new partner.
6	1 2 now' two'-step	Repeat entire dance.
7	step' close' step individual turn	
8	1 2 pas' de' basque	

B U S Y B O D Y

Formation: Double circle
Position: Full-open, R-L cnt
Footwork: Opposite (man L, lady R)

Music: Busybody
Record: Windsor 7612
Rhythm: 4/4, 8 meas

MEAS	CALL	INSTRUCTIONS
	pas' de' basque and turn	Pas de basque: Step L, cross R foot over L, changing weight momentarily. Repeat to R.
	READY pas' de' basque	
1	pas de' basque' out now' walk'	Walk: Walk 4 steps fwd.
2	forward forward turn' and' brush	Turn and brush: Drop hands and turn away from partner by stepping with outside foot, brushing free foot; repeat 3 more times, making 3/4 individual turn to end facing partner. Take two-hand position for next call.
3	step brush step brush	

85

| 4 | join hands and <u>grapevine</u> | Grapevine: Step side L, cross R foot |
| 5 | step behind step reverse | behind, step side L, swing R foot over L. Repeat to R. |

6	now <u>two-step turn</u>	Two-step turn: In closed position,
7	step' close' step under' the' arm	partners turn in 2 two-steps; man arches lady, who walks 4 steps to new partner as man walks 4 steps back to new part-
8	change partners <u>pas' de' basque</u>	ner.

Repeat entire dance.

B Y   T H E   S E A

Formation:	Double circle	Music:	By the Sea
Position:	Full-open, R-L cnt	Record:	Broadcast Record 475
Footwork:	Opposite (man L, lady R)	Rhythm:	4/4, 8 meas

MEAS   CALL

INSTRUCTIONS

<u>two-step and slide</u>

READY two-step

Two-step and slide: Take 2 two-steps in LOD, 1 face to face with partner and 1 back to back with partner. Take two-hand position, slide 4 slides agLOD. Repeat meas 1-2, starting agLOD.

1	face' to' face back' to' back
2	slide slide slide reverse
3	face' to' face back' to' back

Individual paddle: Paddle once around, man L, lady R, in 4 ct. Repeat in opposite direction.

| 4 | slide slide <u>individual paddle</u> |
| 5 | 1 2 paddle right |

Two-step turn: In closed position, take 2 two-steps, turning R. Lady arches under man's arm and walks 4 steps fwd to new partner. Man moves back 4 steps to new partner.

| 6 | 1 2 <u>two'-step' turn</u> |
| 7 | step' close' step arch' and' walk |

Repeat entire dance.

| 8 | change partners <u>two'-step' forward</u> |

C A L I F O R N I A   S C H O T T I S C H E

Formation:	Double circle	Music:	California Schottische
Position:	Varsouvienne	Record:	Imperial 1046
Footwork:	All start L	Rhythm:	4/4, 16 meas

MEAS   CALL

INSTRUCTIONS

point left over right

READY POINT

1-2	CROSS SIDE, back side FORWARD
3-4	CROSS SIDE, back side FORWARD
5-6	CROSS SIDE, back side FORWARD
7-8	CROSS SIDE, walk and TURN
9-10	SLOW SLOW, turn go BACK
11-12	BACK BACK, turn go FORWARD
13-14	FORWARD FORWARD, now go BACK
15-16	CHANGE PARTNERS, NOW POINT

Point (basic step): Point L foot over R, point L to side. Cross L foot behind R, step side R, step fwd L (meas 1-2). Repeat, starting by pointing R foot (meas 3-4). Repeat meas 1-4.

Walk and turn: Walk fwd (slow, slow, quick, quick, slow), turning back R on quick steps to L varsouvienne position (meas 9-10). Walk back 5 steps in same rhythm, turning L on quick steps to R varsouvienne position (meas 11-12). Repeat meas 9-12. To change partners on meas 12, man arches lady ahead under L arm on quick steps and takes new partner from behind.

Repeat entire dance.

Hint

When couple is walking fwd man's R arm is over lady's shoulder; when walking back, man's L arm is over lady's shoulder.

CANADIAN   BARN   DANCE

Formation: Double circle
Position: Full-open, R-L cnt
Footwork: Opposite (man L, lady R)

Music: Canadian Barn Dance
Record: MacGregor 631
Rhythm: 4/4, 8 meas

MEAS   CALL

walk forward and tap

READY WALK

1-2	1 2 3 back, 1 2 3 away
3-4	1 2 3 together, 1 2 3 forward
5-6	1 2 3 reverse, 1 2 two'-step' turn
7	step' close' step under' the' arm
8	now forward and tap

INSTRUCTIONS

Forward and tap: Walk fwd 3 steps and tap inside foot in front.

Back: Walk back 3 steps agLOD and tap.

Away: Drop hands, move apart with 3 walking steps, turning on 3rd step (ct 1-3); tap free foot (ct 4).

Together: Move together with 3 steps (ct 1-3); take semi-open position and tap free foot on ct 4.

Forward: In semi-open position, walk fwd 3 steps, taking reverse position on ct 4.

Reverse: In reverse position walk 3 steps agLOD. Turn and point outside foot fwd on ct 4.

Two-step turn: Turn in 2 two-steps (meas 7). Man then arches lady, who walks 4 steps ahead to new partner; man walks back 4 steps to new partner.

Repeat entire dance.

C L A P   D A N C E

Formation: Double circle
Position: Skaters'
Footwork: Opposite (man L, lady R)

Music: Back Home in Indiana
Record: Windsor, Album No. 4 (3-04)
Rhythm: 4/4, 8 meas

MEAS	CALL	INSTRUCTIONS
	two-step and turn	Two-step: Take 2 two-steps fwd.
	READY two-step	Individual turn: In 2 two-steps man turns L, lady R 1 complete turn.
1	step' close' step individual turn	
2	step' close' step clap' your' hands	Clap: Clap own hands 3 times (ct 1-2), partner's hands 3 times (ct 3-4).
3	now' your' partners now' back' away	Back away: Walk back 4 steps (man to center, lady to wall), as group counts to 4 aloud.
4	back back move right	Move right: Turn 1/4 turn R to new partner, walk 4 steps fwd to face each other. On 2nd time, take skaters' position to start over. (Man dances with every 2nd lady.)
5	1 2 clap' your' hands	
6	now' your' partner's now' back' up	Repeat entire dance.
7	back back move right	Variation
8	take' this' girl two'-step' forward	Instead of clapping partner's hands, man claps hands behind lady's back, lady claps hands behind man's neck.

C L A P   Y O U R   H A N D S

Formation: Double circle
Position: Two-hand
Footwork: Opposite (man L, lady R)

Music: Third Man Theme
Record: MacGregor 644
Rhythm: 4/4, 8 meas

MEAS	CALL	INSTRUCTIONS

slide and CLAP	Slide and clap: Facing partner with palms of hands together, fingertips up, slide L 3 slides, moving hands L and R with music. Clap own hands on 4th slide. Repeat to R.
READY SLIDE	
1-2 SLIDE SLIDE, SLIDE REVERSE	
3-4 SLIDE SLIDE, SLIDE CLAP	Clap: Clap each other's hands as follows: R and own and L and own (meas 5), R and own and both hands of partner (meas 6).
5 right together left together	
6 right together individual turn	Individual turn: Bending over, take 4 steps, turning L 1 full turn; face new partner on R (meas 7). Clap hips, own hands, and hands of new partner while straightening up (meas 8).
7-8 1 2 3 clap, hips hands SLIDE	

Repeat entire dance.

C O N G R E S S   M I X E R

Formation: Double circle	Music: Five Foot Two
Position: Two-hand	Record: Windsor 4619
Footwork: Opposite (man L, lady R)	Rhythm: 4/4, 8 meas

MEAS	CALL	INSTRUCTIONS
	step swing and turn	Swing: Step L, swing R foot, step R, swing L foot.
	READY SWING	
1	step swing step turn	Turn: Wheel R 4 steps, retaining handclasp, so that men end facing in. (On 2nd turn, couple returns to original position.)
2	let's swing AGAIN	
3	step swing step turn	Walk: Couple takes full-open position and walks 4 steps fwd.
4	now forward WALK	
5	1 2 3 slide	Slide: Couple resumes two-hand position and slides L 4 slides.
6	1 2 do'-si'-do	Do-si-do: In 4 steps fwd and 4 back, partners pass R shoulders, returning to face new partner on R.
7	take a new partner	
8	now let's SWING	Repeat entire dance.

D A I S Y

Formation: Double circle	Music: Daisy
Position: Full-open, R-L cnt	Record: All sing
Footwork: Opposite (man L, lady R)	Rhythm: 6/8, 8 meas

MEAS	CALL	INSTRUCTIONS

	walk and sing	Walk 8 steps fwd (meas 1-4).
	ready WALK	Reverse direction to L-R cnt, walk 8 steps agLOD (meas 5-8).
1-4	Daisy, Daisy, give me your promise, do.	Partners face, shaking forefinger at each other (meas 9-10).
5-8	I'm half crazy, all for the love of you.	Fold arms, shake head, and look sad (meas 11-12).
9-10	It won't be a stylish marriage	Point finger at new partner on R and swing this new partner, increasing tempo on swing (meas 13-16).
11-12	For I can't afford a carriage,	Repeat entire dance.
13-14	But you'll look sweet upon the seat	
15-16	Of a bicycle built for two.	

D E C I S I O N

Formation:	Double circle	Music:	Glowworm or March Time
Position:	Full-open, R-L cnt	Record:	MacGregor 3105B, Windsor 7613,
Footwork:	Opposite (man L, lady R)		Old Timer 8004, Folk 1365
		Rhythm:	4/4

MEAS	CALL	INSTRUCTIONS

	WALK FORWARD	Forward: March fwd 4 steps in LOD.
	READY WALK	Back: Face partner, march back 4 steps (man toward center of circle, lady toward outside). Face diag R, march 4 steps fwd to new partner.
1-2	1 2 3 back, 1 2 3 turn	
3-4	1 2 3 around, 1 2 3 forward	Right-side turn, right hands around, left hands around, do-si-do, balance, dishrag, shake hands, tap your foot: In 8 ct, perform each of these fundamentals as called with new partner.
5-6	1 2 3 back, right hands AROUND	
7-8	1 2 3 around, 1 2 3 forward	Decision: Man gives lead for one of above or any other dance fundamental that keeps in time and step with music and does not interfere with other dancers.
9-10	1 2 3 back, left hands AROUND	
11-12	1 2 3 around, 1 2 3 forward	Leads

Turn: Arms out, L hand high, R hand low.

MEAS	CALL	INSTRUCTIONS
13-14	1 2 3 back, 1 2 do'-si'-do	Right hands around; R hand forward.
15-16	1 2 3 around, 1 2 3 forward	Left hands around: L hand forward.
17-18	1 2 3 back, 1 2 3 balance	Do-si-do: Fold arms.
19-20	1 2 hold hands, 1 2 3 forward	Balance: Both hands low.
21-22	1 2 3 back, 1 2 DISHRAG	Dishrag: Both hands high.
23-24	1 2 3 under, 1 2 3 forward	Shake hands: R hand low.
25-26	1 2 3 back, 1 2 shake hands	Tap your foot: Both hands low, L foot forward.
27-28	1 2 3 shake, 1 2 3 forward	Continue dance as long as desired.
29-30	1 2 3 back, 1 2 tap' your' foot	
31-32	1 2 now tap, 1 2 3 forward	
33-34	1 2 3 back, 1 2 3 decision	
35-36	1 2 3 around, 1 2 3 forward	
37-38	1 2 3 back, 1 2 3 decision	
39-40	1 2 3 around, 1 2 3 forward	

. . .

D E S E R T   S T O M P

Formation: Double circle
Position: Two-hand
Footwork: Opposite (man L, lady R)

Music: Desert Stomp
Record: Western Jubilee 705
Rhythm: 4/4, 4 meas

MEAS	CALL	INSTRUCTIONS
	slide and STOMP	Slide: Step L, close R foot to L; step L, close R foot to L. Repeat, starting R.
	READY SLIDE	
1	slide together slide reverse	Step-stomp twice: Step side L, stomp R foot, step R, stomp L foot.
2	step-stomp TWICE	Change partners: In 4 walking steps turn individually, man L, lady R. Take new partner on R.
3	step stomp change partners	

MEAS	CALL	INSTRUCTIONS
4	turn now SLIDE	Repeat entire dance.

H E L L O   A N D   G O O D B Y E

Formation: Double circle   Music: Five Foot Two
Position: Full-open, R-L cnt   Record: Windsor 4619-B
Footwork: Opposite (man L, lady R)   Rhythm: 4/4, 16 meas

MEAS	CALL	INSTRUCTIONS
	FORWARD WALK	Forward: In full-open position, walk fwd 4 steps in LOD.
	READY FORWARD	
1	forward forward back away	Back away: Face partner, walk back 4 steps (man toward center, lady toward wall).
2	back back new partner	
3	both hands AROUND	New partner: Face diag R, walk 4 steps fwd to new partner.
4	around around forward now	Both hands around: Take two-hand position, wheel new partner once around to R in 4 steps.
5-6	1 2 back away, 1 2 new partner	
7-8	do-si-do around, 1 2 forward now	Do-si-do: Fold arms, walk fwd around partner passing R shoulders, walk back passing L shoulders, all in 8 steps.
9-10	1 2 back away, 1 2 new partner	Right hands around: Take partner's R hand, wheel 1 full turn in 4 steps.
11-12	right hands AROUND, 1 2 forward walk	Shake hands: Shake R hands with new partner (may turn 1 full R-hand turn if desired), then assume full-open position, R-L cnt.
13-14	1 2 back away, 1 2 new partner	
15	shake hands say hello	Repeat entire dance.
16	1 2 forward now	

H I   H O P

Formation: Double circle   Music: Wrangler's Two-step
Position: Full-open, R-L cnt   Record: MacGregor 711, Windsor 7612
Footwork: Opposite (man L, lady R)   Rhythm: 4/4, 8 meas

MEAS	CALL	INSTRUCTIONS
	walk and SLIDE	Walk and slide sequence: Walk 4 steps

MEAS	CALL	INSTRUCTIONS

MEAS	CALL
	READY WALK
1-2	1 2 3 slide, 1 2 3 reverse
3-4	1 2 3 slide, 1 2 3 <u>clap</u>
5	knees hands partner thumbs
6	<u>INDIVIDUAL TURN</u>
7	step-hop step-hop
8	step-hop now <u>walk</u>

INSTRUCTIONS

in LOD (meas 1), then assume two-hand position and slide 4 slides to man's L (meas 2). Repeat meas 1-2 agLOD.

<u>Clap</u>: Facing partner, slap knees (ct 1), clap own hands (ct 2), partner's hands (ct 3), point R thumb over R shoulder while saying "Hi!" (ct 4). Repeat, pointing L thumb over L shoulder while saying "Goodbye."

<u>Individual turn</u>: Man turns L and lady R 1 full turn in 4 step-hops to new partner on R. While turning, wave R forefinger over head and hold L hand on stomach. On ct 4 of meas 8, new partners yell, "Hi!"

Repeat entire dance.

H I T C H H I K E

Formation: Double circle
Position: Two-hand
Footwork: Opposite (man L, lady R)

Music: Tennessee Saturday Night
Record: Decca 46136, Jubilee 707
Rhythm: 4/4, 12 meas

MEAS	CALL
	<u>jump and HITCH</u>
	READY JUMP
1-2	BACK BACK, RIGHT RIGHT
3-4	BACK BACK, LEFT LEFT
5-6	BACK BACK, RIGHT LEFT
7-8	CHANGE PARTNERS, <u>TWO-STEP</u>
9	step' close' step step' close' step
10	step' close' step now <u>wheel</u>
11-12	1 2 3 4, 5 6 7 <u>jump</u>

INSTRUCTIONS

<u>Jump and hitch sequence</u>: Releasing hands, jump back away from partner twice; then swing R toe to R side twice (heel resting in place on floor) while pointing R thumb over R shoulder twice (meas 1-2). Repeat jump back and hitch to L (meas 3-4). Repeat jump and hitch to R and then L (meas 5-6), then repeat jump and hitch to both sides at once, standing on heels as both toes point out (meas 7-8).

<u>Two-step</u>: Take 4 two-steps fwd to new partner on R.

<u>Wheel</u>: Take new partner with R elbow lock or R forearm grip and turn twice around in 8 steps.

Repeat entire dance.

I MISS MY SWISS

Formation: Double circle
Position: Full-open, R-L cnt
Footwork: Opposite (man L, lady R)

Music: I Miss My Swiss
Record: MacGregor 722
Rhythm: 4/4, 8 meas

MEAS	CALL	INSTRUCTIONS
	walk and ball-change	Walk: Walk fwd 4 steps.
	READY WALK	Ball-change: Step fwd L, close R, change weight momentarily. Step back R, close L, change weight momentarily.
1	1 2 3' ball'-change	
2	step' close' step forward again	Forward again: Repeat walk and ball-change. On 2nd ball-change, turn to face partner and take two-hand position.
3	1 2 3' ball'-change	
4	join hands and grapevine	Grapevine: Step side L, cross R foot behind L, step side L, swing R foot over L. Repeat to R.
5	step behind step reverse	
6	now two-step turn	Two-step turn: In closed position, take 2 two-steps, turning 1 complete turn R. Man arches lady R under L-R arch; she walks fwd as man walks back 4 steps to new partner.
7	step' close' step under' the' arm	
8	change partners and walk	Repeat entire dance.

JA DA JUMP

Formation: Double circle
Position: Two-hand
Footwork: Opposite (man L, lady R)

Music: Ja Da
Record: Windsor 4-504
Rhythm: 4/4, 16 meas

MEAS	CALL	INSTRUCTIONS
	jump away and clap	Jump away: Drop hands and jump 4 slow jumps away from partner, clapping hands on each jump. On 4th jump face 1/4 R to new partner.
	READY JUMP	
1-2	BACK BACK, jump and WALK	Jump and walk: Jump fwd and back, take 2 slow steps fwd.
3-4	FORWARD BACK, WALK WALK	
5-6	TOGETHER CUDDLE, SLOW RUN	Jump and cuddle: Resuming two-hand position, jump fwd, jump back, walk 2 slow steps fwd into cuddle position (man crosses L arm above partner's head, and lady makes 1/2 turn L under arch to cuddle position with both facing out).
7-8	1 2 3 4, spin girl' and' jump away	

MEAS	CALL	INSTRUCTIONS

Run and spin sequence: Wheel twice around in cuddle position, man running fwd and lady running back 6 steps. On ct 7-8, man lets go with L hand and pulls with R hand, spinning lady out to two-hand position.

Repeat entire dance.

J A M B A L A Y A

Formation:	Double circle	Music:	Jambalaya
Position:	Full-open, R-L cnt	Record:	Jubilee 712
Footwork:	Opposite (man L, lady R)	Rhythm:	4/4, 8 meas

MEAS	CALL	INSTRUCTIONS
	walk and BRUSH	Walk and brush: Walk fwd 3 steps and brush. Repeat, beginning on inside foot.
	READY WALK	
1	1 2 3 brush	Grapevine and clap: Partners, still facing fwd, grapevine away from each other, lady to R, man to L, clapping hands on swing.
2	GRAPEVINE and clap	
3	step behind step reverse	
4	now heel-toe turn	Reverse: Repeat meas 3, moving back together.
5-6	HEEL-TOE, turn 2 THREE	Heel-toe turn: Make 1 slow heel-toe with outside foot and turn individually 1/2 turn in 3 steps. Repeat meas 5-6, starting with other foot; ladies turn in place, men move back while turning to take new partner.
7	HEEL-TOE	
8	change partners and walk	

Repeat entire dance.

K E N T U C K Y   B A B E

Formation:	Single circle	Music:	Kentucky Babe or medium foxtrot
Position:	Closed	Record:	Windsor 7637-A or own choice
Footwork:	Opposite (man L, lady R)	Rhythm:	4/4, 8 meas

MEAS	CALL	INSTRUCTIONS
	walk and BRUSH	Walk and brush: Walk 3 steps in LOD in closed position, both face outside circle and brush outside foot once.
	READY WALK	

1	forward forward forward brush	Walk 3 steps in LOD in closed position, face inside circle and brush inside foot once.
2	now ladies arch' and' dot	
3	step dot chug behind	Arch and dot: Man steps L, dots R toe behind L, steps R, dots L toe behind R. Lady step-dots twice, arching under L-R cnt toward center of circle to full-open position, arms fully extended.
4	chug chug step-dot	
5	step dot chug back	
6	chug chug step-dot	Chug: Chug 4 times, man R, lady L, to parallel position with man's hands on lady's waist.
7	step dot change partners	
8	closed position walk' and' brush	Step-dot: Step-dot twice (man starting L, lady R) with lady looking at partner as though flirting.

Chug back: Chug 4 times, man L, lady R, to full-open position.

Change partners: Lady walks 4 steps ahead to new partner, while man takes 4 steps in place. Assume closed position.

Repeat entire dance.

M O C K I N G B I R D   W A L T Z

Formation: Double circle
Position: Full-open, R-L cnt
Footwork: Opposite (man L, lady R)

Music: Mockingbird Waltz
Record: Capitol 45015
Rhythm: 3/4, 16 meas

MEAS	CALL	INSTRUCTIONS
	brush and run	Brush and run: Step L, brush R, take 3 running steps. Repeat, starting R.
	ready BRUSH	
1-2	step BRUSH, 1 2 3	Grapevine: Partners face and take two-hand position, then step side L (ct 1), cross R foot behind L (ct 2-3), step side L (ct 1), swing R foot over L (ct 2-3). Reverse, starting R.
3-4	step BRUSH, now GRAPEVINE	
5-6	step BEHIND, step REVERSE	
7-8	step BEHIND, balance and arch	Balance and arch: Step fwd L (ct 1), touch R foot beside L (ct 2-3), step back R (ct 1), touch L foot beside R (ct 2-3). Man raises L arm, lady goes under, turning ½ turn and changing places with partner in 4 steps (ct 1-3, 1); point toe and hold (ct 2-3). Re-
9-10	TOGETHER and, arch NOW	
11-12	under 2 3, BALANCE and	

| 13-14 | TOGETHER and, arch NOW | peat meas 9-10. Man arches lady under R arm in 6 steps; lady moves fwd and |
| 15-16 | change PARTNERS, now BRUSH | man moves back to new partners. |

Repeat entire dance.

N A R C I S S U S

Formation:	Double circle	Music:	Narcissus
Position:	Two-hand	Record:	Windsor Record 7601
Footwork:	Opposite (man L, lady R)	Rhythm:	4/4, 8 meas

MEAS	CALL	INSTRUCTIONS
	slide to the left	Slide: Take 2 slow and 3 quick slides L, dot R foot behind L. Repeat, moving R.
	READY SLIDE	
1-2	SLIDE SLIDE, 1 2 3 reverse	Dot: Step L, dot R toe behind L. Repeat to R.
3-4	SLIDE SLIDE, 1 2 3 dot	
5	step dot now swing	Swing: Step L, swing R foot over L. Repeat to R.
6	step swing individual turn	Individual turn: In 4 two-steps, lady circles R in place as man turns L in small circle to take new partner on R.
7	step' close' step step' close' step	
8	new partner now slide	Repeat entire dance.

O K L A H O M A   M I X E R

Formation:	Double circle	Music:	Schottische
Position:	Varsouvienne	Record:	Jubilee #700
Footwork:	All start L	Rhythm:	4/4, 8 meas

MEAS	CALL	INSTRUCTIONS
	two-step and swagger	Two-step: Take 4 two-steps fwd.
	READY two-step	Swagger: Starting L, walk fwd 4 slow steps, crossing L foot over R, R foot over L, L foot over R, R foot over L.
1	step' close' step step' close' step	
2	step' close' step now swagger	Heel-toe: Put L heel fwd, L toe back. With man's L hand holding lady's L hand, lady turns 3 steps toward center of circle to end facing agLOD. Put R heel fwd, R toe back. Lady arches in 3 steps to next partner, turning to varsouvienne position under his R arm, while man backs up 3 steps and raises R
3-4	CROSS CROSS, now heel-TOE	
5-6	ladies to the center, 1 2 THREE	

| 7-8 | CHANGE PARTNERS, two-step
NOW | arm for new partner to come under. |
| | | Repeat entire dance. |

O V E R   T H E   T O P

Formation: Double circle
Position: Full-open, R-L cnt
Footwork: Opposite (man L, lady R)

Music: Over the Top
Record: Decca 28887
Rhythm: 4/4, 4 meas

MEAS	CALL	INSTRUCTIONS
	heel-toe and' two'-step	Heel-toe and two-step sequence: Put L heel fwd, L toe back, take 1 two-step fwd. Repeat, starting R.
	READY HEEL	
1	heel-toe step' close' step	Cross ball-change: Step side L, cross R foot behind L, change weight momentarily. Repeat to R.
2	heel-toe cross' ball'-change	
3	cross' ball'-change now' let's' turn	Turn: Partners turn individually in 4 walking steps, man L, lady R. Man takes lady behind for new partner.
4	change partners heel-toe	Repeat entire dance.

O X F O R D   M I N U E T

Formation: Double circle
Position: Full-open, R-L cnt
Footwork: Opposite (man L, lady R)

Music: Oxford Minuet
Record: Windsor 7606 (78 rpm) or 4606 (45 rpm)
Rhythm: 4/4, 12 meas

MEAS	CALL	INSTRUCTIONS
	walk and POINT	Walk and point: Walk 3 steps fwd, point R toe fwd, and immediately swing R foot back, pivoting R ½ turn and changing hands to L-R cnt.
	READY WALK	
1	walk 2 3 reverse	Reverse: Repeat meas 1 agLOD, except pivot 1/4 turn to take two-hand position.
2	1 2 step-point	
3	step point step point	Step-point: In two-hand position, step L, point R foot over L, step R, point L foot over R. Repeat.
4	step point forward again	
5	1 2 3 reverse	Forward again: Repeat meas 1-4, bowing to partner on ct 4 of meas 8.
6	1 2 step-point	
7	step point step point	Two-step turn: In closed position, partners take 6 fast two-steps in LOD.

| 8 | closed position two'-step' turn | On meas 12, lady arches ahead to new partner in 2 two-steps. |
| 9 | step' close' step step' close' step | Repeat entire dance. |

Variation

10	step' close' step step' close' step	For nonmixer, formation is mass. On two-step turn, couples take 8 two-steps, progressing anywhere around room.
11	step' close' step arch' and' walk	
12	new partner <u>walk' and' point</u>	

P E G   O'   M Y   H E A R T

Formation:	Double circle	Music:	Peg o' My Heart
Position:	Full-open, R-L cnt	Record:	Windsor 6599-A
Footwork:	Opposite (man L, lady R)	Rhythm:	4/4, 8 meas

MEAS	CALL	INSTRUCTIONS
	walk forward ball-change	**Walk (basic step):** Step fwd L,R,L, close R foot to L and change weight momentarily (R,L) in Balboa rhythm (slow, slow, quick, quick, slow). Step
	READY <u>WALK</u>	
1	forward forward forward back	back R,L,R, then turn individual ½ turn R on ball-change. Repeat meas 1-2
2	back back reverse direction	agLOD, turning L on ½ turn.
3	forward forward forward back	**Grapevine:** Dropping hands and moving away from partner, step side L, step R
4	back <u>GRAPEVINE</u> away	foot behind L, step side L, ball-change. Repeat to R, coming into closed posi-
5	side behind side reverse	tion.
6	closed position <u>two'-step' turn</u>	**Two-step turn:** Turn 1 full turn R in 2 two-steps. Lady arches R under L-R arch and walks ahead in 4 steps as man
7	step' close' step under' the' arm	walks back in 4 steps to new partner.
		Repeat entire dance.
8	change partners <u>walk forward</u>	

P I C K   'E M   U P   A N D   L A Y   'E M   D O W N

Formation:	Double circle	Music:	Little Brown Jug
Position:	Promenade	Record:	Rondo U-919, Old Timer 8077
Footwork:	Opposite (man L, lady R)	Rhythm:	4/4, 8 meas

MEAS	CALL	INSTRUCTIONS

MEAS	CALL
	READY PROMENADE
1	Pick 'em up and lay 'em down,
2	Everybody goes to town.
3	Back away and say adieu,
4	Balance to the right of you.
5	Do-si-do and watch her smile,
6	Step right up and swing awhile.
7	Step right back and watch her grin,
8	Step right up and swing again.

INSTRUCTIONS

Promenade: Walk 8 steps fwd. Turn to face partner and back away 4 steps.

Balance: Step side L, swing R foot over L; step R, swing L foot over R. End facing new partner on R.

Do-si-do: Pass R shoulders to circle around new partner and walk back to place.

Swing: Swing new partner once around. Back away 1 step, then swing again. Man turns lady under L arm to promenade position.

Repeat entire dance.

P R E T T Y   B A B Y

Formation:	Double circle	Music:	Pretty Baby
Position:	Two-hand	Record:	Windsor 7618-B
Footwork:	Opposite (man L, lady R)	Rhythm:	4/4, 8 meas

MEAS	CALL
	side ball-CHANGE
	READY SIDE
1	side' ball'-change side' ball'-change
2	side' ball'-change individual turn
3	turn 2 3 touch
4	join hands two-step
5	face' to' face back' to' back
6	a mountain do'-si'-do
7	men go BACK

INSTRUCTIONS

Side ball-change: Leap to side with L foot, touch R foot beside L, change weight momentarily. Repeat to R. Repeat meas 1.

Individual turn and touch sequence: Turn individually in 3 steps, man L, lady R, and touch R foot to L, also touching hands momentarily. Repeat to end in face-to-face position, R-L cnt.

Two-step: Starting face to face, two-step starting L, turning out to back-to-back position; then two-step, starting R, back to back in LOD. Repeat.

Mountain do-si-do: Man steps 4 times in place; lady crosses in front of him to place her R shoulder against his L shoulder and roll back to back, all in

| 8 | change partners <u>side'</u> <u>ball'-change</u> | 4 steps, to end with her L shoulder against his R shoulder, facing in LOD. Man then walks back, lady ahead 4 steps to new partners. |

Repeat entire dance.

P R O G R E S S I V E   T W O - S T E P

Formation:	Double circle	Music:	Left-footer's One-step
Position:	Full-open, R-L cnt	Record:	Windsor 4650-A
Footwork:	Opposite (man L, lady R)	Rhythm:	4/4, 8 meas

MEAS	CALL	INSTRUCTIONS
	WALK FORWARD	<u>Walk</u>: Take 4 walking steps fwd.
	READY <u>WALK</u>	<u>Back</u>: Walk 4 steps back.
1	1 2 3 <u>back</u>	<u>Pas de basque</u>: Step side L, cross R foot over L and change weight momentarily. Repeat to R.
2	1 2 <u>pas' de' basque</u>	
3	pas' de' basque <u>brush' and'</u> <u>stomp</u>	<u>Brush and stomp</u>: Step on L foot, brush R, stomp in place, R,L,R.
4	step brush now' <u>heel'-toe</u>	<u>Heel-toe</u>: Put L heel fwd, L toe back, 1 two-step fwd. Repeat, starting on R foot.
5	heel-toe step' close' step	
6	heel-toe <u>individual turn</u>	<u>Individual turn</u>: Make 1 full turn in 4 two-steps. Man takes lady behind him for new partner.
7	step' close' step step' close' step	
		Repeat entire dance.
8	change partners now <u>walk</u>	

P U R P L E   P E O P L E - E A T E R

Formation:	Double circle	Music:	Purple People-eater
Position:	Full-open, R-L cnt, face-to-face	Record:	MGM KGC-147
		Rhythm:	4/4, 8 meas
Footwork:	Opposite (man L, lady R)		

MEAS	CALL	INSTRUCTIONS
	grapevine left and right	<u>Grapevine</u>: Step side L, cross R foot behind L, step side L, swing R foot over L. Repeat to R.
	READY <u>GRAPEVINE</u>	
1	side behind side reverse	<u>Back away and clap</u>: Dropping hands,

2	back away and clap	walk 4 steps back while clapping hands, man toward center, lady toward wall.
3	back 2 3 forward	
4	grand right-and-left	Forward: Walk fwd 4 steps and join R hands.
5	forward 2 3 brush	Grand right-and-left: Walk in grand right-and-left to 3rd lady agLOD.
6	right 2 3 brush	
7	under the right arm	Under the right arm: Join R hands, turning lady fwd under arch, and change to R-L cnt.
8	now let's GRAPEVINE	Repeat entire dance.

ROCKING WALTZ

Formation: Double circle   Music: Rocking Waltz
Position: Full-open, R-L cnt   Record: Folk Dancer MH-3003-B
Footwork: Opposite (man L, lady R)   Rhythm: 3/4, 16 meas

MEAS	CALL	INSTRUCTIONS
	forward and point	Forward and point: In full-open position, run fwd L,R,L,R, then point L toe and hold as partners face. Repeat.
	ready POINT	
1-2	1 2 3, step POINT	Balance: Take two-hand position, balance fwd on L foot, back on R.
3-4	forward 2 3, step BALANCE	
5-6	TOGETHER and, now ARCH	Arch: Partners change places with R-L cnt arch in 4 steps, and hold.
7-8	1 2 3, grapevine CANTER	Grapevine canter: Partners face in and take two-hand position. Step side L (ct 1-2), step R foot behind L (ct 3), step side L (ct 1), swing R foot over L (ct 2-3). Repeat to R.
9-10	STEP behind, step SWING	
11-12	STEP behind, now BALANCE	
13-14	TOGETHER and, change PARTNERS	Change partners: Man arches lady under R-L arch; both run 4 steps (L,R,L,R), lady fwd, man in place. Man takes lady behind him for next partner.
15-16	1 2 3, forward and point	

Repeat entire dance.

ROUND AND ROUND

Formation: Double circle   Music: Round and Round
Position: Full-open, R-L cnt   Record: RCA H2PW0965
Footwork: Opposite (man L, lady R)   Rhythm: 4/4, 8 meas

102

MEAS	CALL	INSTRUCTIONS

walk forward and brush

READY WALK

Forward and brush: Walk fwd 3 steps, brush R fwd.

Back now: Walk back 3 steps, touch L to R.

1 forward forward back now

2 back back turn' and' clap

Turn and clap: In 3 steps, turn individually 1 complete turn, man L toward center, lady R toward wall (ct 1-3) and clap own hands (ct 4).

3 turn turn reverse turn

Reverse turn: In 3 steps, man turns R, lady L to come back together and take two-hand position.

4 turn turn DISHRAG

Dishrag: Both man and lady turn (man L, lady R) to roll back to back under arch formed by their joined hands.

5 under under reverse dishrag

Reverse dishrag: Man turns R, lady L to arch back to place.

6 closed position two'-step' turn

7 step' close' step under' the' arm

Two-step turn: Assuming closed position, turn in 2 two-steps. Man turns lady ahead under L-R cnt arch to new partner in 4 steps.

8 change partner forward' and' brush

Repeat entire dance.

S E N T I M E N T A L   J O U R N E Y

Formation:	Double circle
Position:	Varsouvienne
Footwork:	All start L

Music:	Sentimental Journey
Record:	Windsor 7601, MacGregor 642, Lloyd Shaw 113
Rhythm:	4/4, 16 meas

MEAS	CALL	INSTRUCTIONS

cross and POINT

READY CROSS

Cross and point: Cross L foot over R (ct 1-2), then point L toe to L side (ct 3-4). Place L foot behind R foot and shift weight to L (ct 1), step side R (ct 2), step fwd on L (ct 3), point R toe fwd (ct 4). Repeat, starting R.

1-2 CROSS SIDE, back side FORWARD

3-4 CROSS SIDE, let's do it again

Two-step: Take series of 14 two-steps: 2 two-steps fwd, then lady makes 1 complete R turn in 2 two-steps under her own and man's R arms. Resume varsouvienne position; 2 two-steps fwd,

5-6 CROSS SIDE, back side FORWARD

7-8	CROSS SIDE, now let's <u>two-step</u>	then man makes 1 complete L turn under his and lady's R arms with 2 two-steps. Resume varsouvienne position; 2 two-steps fwd, then partners release both hands, both make 1 complete individual turn in 4 two-steps.
9	step' close' step ladies turn	
10	step' close' step forward again	Change partners: In 2 two-steps, man takes lady behind as new partner.
11	step' close' step men turn	Repeat entire dance.
12	step' close' step forward again	
13	step' close' step both turn	
14	step' close' step step' close' step	
15	step' close' step <u>change partners</u>	
16	start over <u>cross' and' point</u>	

S I D E   B Y   S I D E

Formation: Double circle
Position: Backhand promenade
Footwork: All start L

Music: Side by Side
Record: MacGregor 677
Rhythm: 4/4, 16 meas

MEAS	CALL	INSTRUCTIONS
	heel-toe and walk	Heel-toe and walk: Place L heel fwd, L toe back, walk fwd 3 steps. Repeat, starting with R foot.
	READY <u>heel-toe</u>	
1-2	HEEL-TOE, forward 2 THREE	Swagger: Walk fwd 4 steps by crossing L foot over R, R foot over L.
3-4	HEEL-TOE, now let's <u>SWAGGER</u>	
5-6	ONE TWO, THREE <u>TWIST</u>	Twist: Bend over at waist and turn in 4 steps without letting go of hands; look partner in eye, then straighten up. Repeat in reverse. After 2nd twist, man walks back agLOD to new partner.
7-8	ONE TWO, other way BACK	
9-10	HEEL-TOE, 1 2 THREE	
11-12	HEEL-TOE, now let's <u>SWAGGER</u>	Repeat entire dance.
13-14	ONE TWO, NOW <u>TWIST</u>	
15-16	CHANGE PARTNERS, <u>HEEL-TOE</u>	

T E A   F O R   T W O

Formation:	Double circle
Position:	Two-hand
Footwork:	Opposite (man L, lady R)

Music:	Tea for Two
Record:	Windsor 7606
Rhythm:	4/4, 8 meas

MEAS	CALL	INSTRUCTIONS
	grapevine and SLIDE	Grapevine and slide: Progressing in LOD, step side L, R foot behind L, step side L, swing L foot over R. Slide L 3 times, swing R foot over L in LOD. Repeat meas 1-2 agLOD.
	READY GRAPEVINE	
1	step behind step forward	
2	slide slide slide reverse	Butterfly: In two-hand position take 1 diag fwd ball-change to R-side position, take 1 ball-change back to starting position. Repeat ball-change diag fwd to L-side position and back.
3	step behind step forward	
4	slide slide BUTTERFLY	
5	forward' close' step left side	Do-si-do: Starting with L foot, partners do-si-do around each other in 4 two-steps and 2 individual turns L. End facing person on R of partner; take this person as new partner.
6	forward' close' step' and' do'-si'-do	
7	step' close' step step' close' step	Repeat entire dance.
8	change partners grapevine slide	

T E N N E S S E E   W I G   W A L K

Formation:	Double circle
Position:	Full-open, R-R cnt, lady facing agLOD
Footwork:	Opposite (man L, lady R)

Music:	Tennessee Wig Walk
Record:	Decca 28846
Rhythm:	4/4, 8 meas

MEAS	CALL	INSTRUCTIONS
	heel-toe cross over	Heel-toe: Place L heel fwd, L toe back. Repeat.
	READY heel-toe	
1	heel-toe cross over	Cross over, cross back: Man grapevines toward wall (step L foot behind R, step side R, swing L foot over R, close L foot to R) and lady grapevines toward center of circle (step side R, step L foot behind R, step side R, touch L
2	side behind heel-toe	
3	heel-toe cross back	

105

4	right-hand <u>WHEEL</u>	foot beside R); join L hands. After repeat of meas 1 reverse to original place, joining R hands.
5	1 2 3 brush	
6	now <u>change PARTNERS</u>	<u>Wheel</u>: Retaining R handclasp, make 1 complete wheel to R by taking 3 steps fwd (L,R,L), brushing R foot fwd, and repeating, starting on R foot.
7	JUMP JUMP	
8	now <u>heel-TOE</u>	

<u>Change partners</u>: Drop hands and jump back 2 jumps to new partner (ct 1-4), pause (ct 1), then stomp twice, L,R (ct 2-3), and join R hands (ct 4).

Repeat entire dance.

T E T O N   M O U N T A I N   S T O M P

Formation:	Double circle	Music:	Teton Mountain Stomp
Position:	Conversation	Record:	Windsor 7615
Footwork:	Opposite (man L, lady R)	Rhythm:	4/4, 8 meas

MEAS	CALL	INSTRUCTIONS
	<u>slide and STOMP</u>	<u>Slide and stomp</u>: Step side L, close R to L, step side L, stomp R foot; repeat to R.
	READY SLIDE	
1	slide together slide stomp	<u>Stomp</u>: Step L, stomp R, step R, stomp L. Repeat.
2	now <u>stomp</u> 4 times	
3	step stomp step stomp	<u>Right-side</u>: Turn to R-side position, man facing LOD, and walk 4 steps in LOD.
4	step stomp <u>right-side</u>	
5	forward forward <u>left-side</u>	<u>Left-side</u>: Turn to L-side position, walk 4 steps back in LOD (ladies walk fwd).
6	back back now <u>arch</u>	
7	forward forward under' the' arm	<u>Arch</u>: Walk fwd 4 steps while turning lady under L arm. Take lady behind for new partner.
8	change partners <u>slide' and' stomp</u>	Repeat entire dance.

Variation

Men may lead their partners in any position they desire in place of R- and L-side positions.

THE VARSOUVIENNE

Formation: Double circle
Position: Varsouvienne
Footwork: All start L

Music: Varsouvienne
Record: MacGregor 398
Rhythm: 3/4, 16 meas

MEAS	CALL	INSTRUCTIONS

forward cross behind

ready FORWARD

Forward, cross behind, point sequence (basic step): Starting with weight on R foot, sweep L foot up across R, step fwd with L, glide R foot up to L. Repeat (meas 1-2). Both raise L foot, man crosses behind partner to L varsouvienne position in 3 walking steps as lady steps in place; both point R foot and hold (meas 3-4). Repeat meas 1-4, starting with weight on L foot.

1-2 raise step close, raise step close

3-4 cross BEHIND, and POINT

5-6 raise step close, raise step close

7-8 cross BEHIND, grand right'-and'-left

Grand right-and-left: Releasing R handclasp, lady swings ½ turn toward center, joining R hands with man behind. All grand right-and-left with 3 basic steps bowing to 1st dancer, smiling at 2nd, winking at 3rd. Man arches 3rd lady under R arm, keeping her for new partner.

9-10 raise step step, and BOW

11-12 raise step step, and SMILE

13-14 raise step step, and WINK

15-16 VARSOUVIENNE step, forward NOW

Repeat entire dance.

VIRGINIA REEL

Formation: Double circle
Position: Shine, six feet apart
Footwork: Opposite (man L, lady R)

Music: Turkey in the Straw
Record: Folkraft F1067-A, Jubilee 704 Wc, Old Timer 8006, MacGregor 735 Nc, 734Wc
Rhythm: 4/4, 16 meas

MEAS	CALL	INSTRUCTIONS

walk forward and bow

READY WALK

Walk: Take 4 short walking steps toward partner, bow on 4th step, and walk 4 steps back to place.

1 Walk to your partner,

2 And back you go.

Right hand up: For 8 ct, walk once around partner with R hands joined and return to place.

3 Right hand up and around your own

Left hand up: For 8 ct, with L hands joined, walk once around partner and return to place.

4 And back to place.

5	Left hand up and around again;	Both hands up: For 8 ct, holding both hands, turn 1 full turn to R with partner and return to place.
6	Back to place.	
7	Both hands up and around you go;	Do-si-do: Walk around partner passing R shoulders, backing up passing L shoulders, and link R elbows for reel, all in 4 ct.
8	Back to place.	
9	Now do-si-do and ready to reel,	Reel: For 3 meas do usual elbow or forearm grip reel, using R arms. Move to next dancer as in grand right-and-left and reel with L arms; then to next and reel with R arms. Turn each partner 1 full turn in 4 ct.
10	Reel your own and on to the next.	
11-12	[Fill in with 8 more ct patter.]	Promenade: With new partner, promenade for 4 meas, then drop hands and step about 6 feet apart to double circle formation.
13	Take your gal and promenade the hall.	
14-16	[Fill in with 12 more ct promenade patter.]	Repeat entire dance.

Hint

Young people like to two-step on promenade; older people prefer shuffle step.

W A L T Z   O F   T H E   B E L L S

Formation: Double circle
Position: Full-open, R-L cnt
Footwork: Opposite (man L, lady R)

Music: Waltz of the Bells
Record: MacGregor 611
Rhythm: 3/4, 32 meas

MEAS	CALL	INSTRUCTIONS
	forward and back	Note
	ready BALANCE	In CALL column capital letters represent either two beats or three, as needed to complete measure. (End of measure is indicated by comma or by end of line.)
1-2	forward SWING, back TOUCH	
3-4	forward SWING, INDIVIDUAL turn	
5-6	turn 2 3, now DRAW	Balance: Step fwd L, swing R foot fwd. Step back R, touch L toe to floor beside R foot. Repeat.
7-8	DRAW, REVERSE	
9-10	forward SWING, back TOUCH	Individual turn: Man turns L in 6 steps while lady turns R in 6 steps. End with partners facing in two-hand position.
11-12	forward SWING, INDIVIDUAL turn	

| 13-14 | turn 2 3, now DRAW | Draw: Take 2 draw steps to man's L. |

| 15-16 | DRAW, draw and arch | Reverse: Repeat meas 1-8, turning and drawing in opposite direction. |

| 17-20 | DRAW, DRAW, ARCH, REVERSE | Draw and arch: With both hands joined, partners take 2 slides to man's L, swinging arms to "ring the bell" (meas 17-18). Man releases his R hand from lady's L and takes 1 slide-step to his L while she arches R under her R and man's L arms in 3 steps (meas 19). Partners assume two-hand position and take 1 slide to man's L (meas 20). Repeat meas 17-20 to R, lady arching L. |

| 21-24 | DRAW, DRAW, girls ARCH, balance AWAY | |

| 25-28 | AWAY, TOGETHER, AWAY, TURN | |

| 29-30 | turn 2 3, under the arm | |

| 31-32 | change PARTNERS, now BALANCE | |

13-14   turn 2 3, now DRAW

15-16   DRAW, draw and arch

17-20   DRAW, DRAW, ARCH, REVERSE

21-24   DRAW, DRAW, girls ARCH, balance AWAY

25-28   AWAY, TOGETHER, AWAY, TURN

29-30   turn 2 3, under the arm

31-32   change PARTNERS, now BALANCE

Draw: Take 2 draw steps to man's L.

Reverse: Repeat meas 1-8, turning and drawing in opposite direction.

Draw and arch: With both hands joined, partners take 2 slides to man's L, swinging arms to "ring the bell" (meas 17-18). Man releases his R hand from lady's L and takes 1 slide-step to his L while she arches R under her R and man's L arms in 3 steps (meas 19). Partners assume two-hand position and take 1 slide to man's L (meas 20). Repeat meas 17-20 to R, lady arching L.

Balance: With inside hands joined, balance back and fwd. Repeat.

Turn: In closed position make L waltz turn; lady arches fwd under man's L arm; man takes lady behind him for new partner.

Repeat entire dance.

W R A N G L E R ' S   T W O - S T E P

Formation:	Double circle	Music:	Wrangler's Two-Step
Position:	Full-open, R-L cnt	Record:	Windsor 7621-B
Footwork:	Opposite (man L, lady R)	Rhythm:	4/4, 8 meas

MEAS   CALL

INSTRUCTIONS

walk touch and twirl

READY WALK

1	1 2 3 twirl
2	twirl twirl side' ball'-change
3	in close' step' twirl back
4	twirl twirl face' and' chug
5	1 2 3 reverse
6	closed position two'-step' turn

Walk touch and twirl: Walk fwd 3 steps, touch R foot to L. Man turns 1 full turn R behind lady in 3 steps, touches L foot to R; lady turns L 1 full turn in front of him in 3 steps, touches L foot to R.

Side ball-change: Join hands in L-R cnt; side ball-change 1 in, 1 out.

Twirl back: Man turns 1 full turn L behind lady in 4 steps; lady turns 1 full turn R in front of man in 4 steps.

Face and chug: Face partner, join hands, extending arms to sides at shoulder height, and take 4 chug steps

| 7 | step' close' step under' the' arm | to L and 4 to R. |
| 8 | change partners <u>start over</u> | Two-step turn: Take closed position and make two-step turn to R; lady turns fwd under L-R arch, man walks back to new partner in 4 steps. |

Repeat entire dance.

T E A M D A N C I N G

Changing formations, positions, or directions can be as much fun as changing steps. Included here are a few team dances that should prove interesting. All that is necessary to make a team is to turn every other couple halfway around to face another couple. If couples are numbered, the odd couples can turn around. One couple faces counterclockwise while the other faces clockwise. The lady should be standing on the right side of the man.

T H E B E A R W E N T O V E R T H E M O U N T A I N

Formation:	Team	Music:	The Bear Went over the Mountain
Position:	Full-open		
Footwork:	Opposite (man L, lady R)	Record:	All sing
		Rhythm:	4/4, 8 meas

MEAS	CALL	INSTRUCTIONS
	right-hand STAR	All join R hands in center of set and walk 8 steps cw, then turn ½ turn R to join L hands in center and walk 8 steps back to place (meas 1-4).
	READY STAR	
1	Oh, the bear went over the mountain,	
2	The bear went over the mountain,	Clap own hands twice and partner's once with both hands. Repeat (meas 5-6).
3	The bear went over the mountain	Bow to other couple, turn, and bow to partner (meas 7).
4	To see what he could see.	Couples face and slide sideways to new couple, with visiting couple sliding through other couple; face new couple (meas 8).
5	To see what he could see,	
6	To see what he could see.	Repeat entire dance.
7	Oh, the bear went over the mountain	
8	To see what he could see.	

G R A N D   S W I N G

Formation:	Team	
Position:	Full-open	
Footwork:	All start L	

Music: Wabash Rambler
Record: Windsor 7639-A
Rhythm: 4/4, 16 meas

MEAS   CALL

            INSTRUCTIONS

            GRAPEVINE LEFT

            READY VINE

Grapevine: Dance 2 grapevines to L (8 ct). On ct 8 swing R foot over L. Repeat grapevines to R (8 ct).

MEAS	CALL
1	side back side forward
2	side back vine right
3	side back side forward
4	side back grand square
5	1 2 back' to' sides
6	1 2 swing now
7	1 2 3 4
8	5 6 center now
9	1 2 back now
10	1 2 swing' your' own
11	1 2 3 4
12	right-and-left through
13	across from YOU
14	1 2 pass-through
15	1 2 3 4
16	to' the' next start over

Grand square: Couples walk 4 steps together (meas 5). On ct 4, turn ¼ turn to face partner and back away 4 steps (meas 6). Face new partner and swing 6 ct; on ct 7-8, man puts lady on his R and couples face each other (meas 7-8). Walk together 4 steps, change ladies, walk back 4 steps (meas 9-10). Swing for meas 11-12. (Couples are now halfway around with original partner.)

Right-and-left through: Give R hand to person opposite and pass R shoulders, releasing handclasp when past. Give L hand to own partner, and turn ½ turn around as couple to face other couple. (Couples are now in original place.)

Pass-through: Couples drop hands and pass R shoulders, moving to next couple in 8 steps.

Repeat entire dance.

H U L A   M I X E R

Formation:	Team	
Position:	Full-open	
Footwork:	All start L	

Music: Hula Mixer
Record: Sets in Order, S-1-0-300
Rhythm: 4/4, 8 meas

MEAS	CALL	INSTRUCTIONS

<table>
<tr><td></td><td>forward ball-CHANGE</td><td>Ball-change: Step fwd L, close R foot to L, change weight momentarily on</td></tr>
<tr><td></td><td>READY FORWARD</td><td>balls of feet; repeat, stepping back R (meas 1). Repeat meas 1.</td></tr>
<tr><td>1</td><td>forward' ball'-change back' ball'-change</td><td>Grapevine: Step side L, step R foot</td></tr>
<tr><td>2</td><td>forward' ball'-change GRAPEVINE</td><td>behind L, step side L, swing R foot over L. Repeat to R.</td></tr>
<tr><td>3</td><td>side behind side swing</td><td>Brush: Turn individually, stepping L and brushing R, then stepping R and</td></tr>
<tr><td>4</td><td>INDIVIDUAL BRUSH</td><td>brushing L, for total of 4 step-brushes, 2 each foot.</td></tr>
<tr><td>5</td><td>step brush step brush</td><td>Pass-through: Drop hands and walk</td></tr>
<tr><td>6</td><td>PASS-THROUGH</td><td>through to next couple, passing R shoulders.</td></tr>
<tr><td>7</td><td>walk 2 3 4</td><td>Repeat entire dance.</td></tr>
<tr><td>8</td><td>and forward ball-change</td><td></td></tr>
</table>

S P A N I S H   C I R C L E

Formation:	Team	Music:	Hi-Lili, Hi-Lo
Position:	Full-open	Record:	Decca 9-28745
Footwork:	Opposite (man L, lady R)	Rhythm:	3/4, 32 meas

MEAS	CALL	INSTRUCTIONS

<table>
<tr><td></td><td>BALANCE and, ARCH</td><td>Note</td></tr>
<tr><td></td><td>READY, BALANCE</td><td>In CALL column capital letters repre-</td></tr>
<tr><td>1-2</td><td>FORWARD, ARCH</td><td>sent either two beats or three, as needed to complete measure. (End of</td></tr>
<tr><td>3-4</td><td>1 2 3, now BALANCE</td><td>measure is indicated by comma or by end of line.)</td></tr>
<tr><td>5-6</td><td>TOGETHER, ARCH</td><td>Balance and arch: Step fwd on L foot</td></tr>
<tr><td>7-8</td><td>1 2 3, BALANCE</td><td>and back on R. Let go of partner's hand and take opposite lady by hand</td></tr>
<tr><td>9-10</td><td>TOGETHER, ARCH</td><td>with R-L cnt. This lady moves and turns ¼ turn L under man's R arm as</td></tr>
<tr><td>11-12</td><td>1 2 3, BALANCE</td><td>man moves fwd and turns ¼ turn R, both in 3 running steps and 1 balance.</td></tr>
<tr><td>13-14</td><td>TOGETHER, ARCH</td><td>Repeat 3 more times to end in original place.</td></tr>
<tr><td>15-16</td><td>RIGHT-hand, STAR</td><td>Star: All join R hands and waltz fwd in LOD 12 steps. All turn ½ turn L to</td></tr>
<tr><td>17-20</td><td>1 2 3, 4 5 6, LEFT-hand, STAR</td><td>reverse direction, join L hands, and</td></tr>
</table>

21-24	1 2 3, 4 5 6, NOW, BALANCE	waltz fwd 12 steps agLOD back to place. Partners take full-open position and
25-26	TOGETHER, arch and point	balance fwd and back.
27-28	forward POINT, forward POINT	Arch and point: Visiting couple goes under arch made by host couple to new
29-30	forward POINT, and BOW	couple in 4 step-points.
31-32	BALANCE and, ARCH	Bow: Bow to new couple in 2-meas balance.

Repeat entire dance.

T I N G - A - L I N G   W A L T Z

Formation:	Team	Music:	Ting-a-ling
Position:	Full-open	Record:	Windsor 4605-B
Footwork:	Opposite (man L, lady R)	Rhythm:	3/4, 32 meas

MEAS	CALL	INSTRUCTIONS
	swing FORWARD	Swing: Step fwd L (ct 1), swing R fwd (ct 2-3). Step back R (ct 1), point L
	ready SWING	foot over R (ct 2-3). Repeat.
1-2	forward SWING, back POINT	Right-hand star: All join R hands and circle 12 waltz steps fwd to end in
3-4	forward SWING, right-hand star	original place.
5-8	1 2 3, 4 5 6, 7 8 9, now swing again	Left-hand star: All join L hands and circle 12 waltz steps fwd to end in original place.
9-10	forward SWING, back POINT	Side draw: Step L (ct 1), draw R foot up to L (ct 2-3), repeat 3 more times.
11-12	forward SWING, left-hand star	Repeat to R 4 times.
13-16	1 2 3, 4 5 6, 7 8 9, now side draw	Balance: Partners take two-hand position and balance fwd and back. Repeat.
17-18	side draw close, side draw close	Walk-point: Step fwd L, point R foot, step fwd R, point L foot; repeat.
19-20	side draw close, now REVERSE	Visiting couple goes under arch of host couple to meet new couple.
21-22	side draw close, side draw close	
23-24	side draw close, now BALANCE	Repeat entire dance.
25-28	now TOGETHER, now AWAY, drop HANDS, walk-POINT	

29-30	forward POINT, forward POINT
31-32	forward POINT, step SWING

M A S S   F O R M A T I O N   D A N C E S

Mass formation means that dancers are scattered around the dance floor and is used when there are too many to form circles. Social dancing is usually in mass formation; however, the leader might call for dancers to form sets of four and to circle or star and change partners.

When dancing round dances in mass formation, the group faces the center and dances forward to the center of the hall and then back to the wall. They are often in individual or shine position and dance the steps alone. The Hitchhike and Bunny Hop are good dances for a crowd in mass formation.

Mass formation dances do not usually lend themselves to the changing of partners, as the following dances show. However, some mass formation dances can become mixers for more advanced groups.

T H E   C A R L Y L E   P O L K A

Formation: Mass (couples)   Music: Any polka
Position : Closed   Record: Own choice
Footwork: Opposite (man L, lady R) Rhythm: 4/4, 4 meas

MEAS	CALL	INSTRUCTIONS
	left foot to side	Basic step: Stand on R foot, point L foot to side. (This makes it easier to get started correctly.) Close L foot and swing R out to side, placing L foot where R was; close R foot (placing it where L foot was) and swing L to side. Close L foot (placing it where R foot was) and swing R to side. Change weight momentarily while feet are apart, R,L. Repeat, using opposite footwork.
	basic step ready and	
1	swing swing swing' ball'-change	
2	swing swing two'-step' turn	
3	step' close' step now' slide'-leap	
4	slide slide start over	Two-step turn: Starting L, take 2 two-steps, turning R 1 complete turn.

Slide-leap: Take 3 slides L (ct 1-3); leap and cross R foot in front of L, stepping on R and turning ¼ turn to face partner. Take closed position.

Repeat entire dance.

THE RACE IS ON

Formation:	Mass	Music:	Any good rock number
Position:	Shine	Record:	Own choice
Footwork:	All start L	Rhythm:	4/4, 8 meas

MEAS	CALL	INSTRUCTIONS
	face left two-step	Scoot: Step diag fwd with L foot, close R, step fwd L, and turn ½ turn R. Step fwd R foot, close L, step fwd R, and turn ½ turn L. Repeat meas 1-2.
	READY SCOOT	
1	side together side turn	
2	side together side turn	
3	side together side turn	Clap: Clap both knees (ct 1) and hold (ct 2), clap own hands (ct 3) and hold (ct 4). Raise R hand above head, twirling forefinger in circle, at same time moving hips L,R,L,R with L hand on hip. Repeat meas 5, then meas 6 with L hand in the air.
4	now let's CLAP	
5	KNEES HANDS	
6	right twirl twirl twirl	
7	KNEES HANDS	Repeat entire dance.
8	left twirl start over	

SALTY DOG RAG

Formation:	Mass (couples)	Music:	Salty Dog Rag
Position:	Promenade	Record:	Decca 27981
Footwork:	All start R	Rhythm:	4/4, 16 meas

MEAS	CALL	INSTRUCTIONS
	grapevine and HOP	Grapevine: Step side R, step L foot behind R, step side R, swing L foot over R. Repeat, starting L.
	READY GRAPEVINE	
1	side behind side swing	Step-hop: Step L, hop L; step R, hop R. Repeat.
2	step-hop FORWARD	
3	step-hop step-hop	Cross over: Drop R hands. Man crosses behind lady toward wall, lady in front of man toward center of circle, both in 3 steps (R,L,R). Retain L hand-clasp.
4	now let's GRAPEVINE	
5	side behind side swing	
6	now step-HOP	Twirl: Both pull with L hand and twirl behind partner, making 1 individual L

7-8	step-hop step-hop, now cross OVER	turn back to back. Man twirls toward center, lady toward wall; join R hands.
9-10	now let's TWIRL, now let's WHEEL	Wheel: Make 1 full R-hand wheel in 4 step-hops. Man spins lady to end facing LOD.
11-12	step-hop step-hop, now cross OVER	Repeat entire dance.
13-14	now let's TWIRL, now let's WHEEL	
15-16	step-hop step-hop, now let's GRAPEVINE	

W H O L E H E A R T E D   H O P

Formation:	Mass (couples)	Music:	Soft Shoe Shuffle
Position:	Parallel, man holding partner's waist	Record:	Capitol 3531
		Rhythm:	4/4, 8 meas
Footwork:	All start L		

MEAS	CALL	INSTRUCTIONS
	step-hop around lady	Hop: Man hops to L and fwd around lady to stand in front of her, while she hops in place (meas 1-2). Then lady hops to L and fwd around man to stand in front of him while he hops in place, so that they regain their original positions (meas 3-4). Man holds partner's waist.
	READY HOP	
1	step-hop step-hop	
2	ladies go AROUND	
3	step-hop step-hop	
4	now let's BRUSH	Brush: Both step fwd with L and brush R foot to side, then step fwd on R and brush L foot to side. Repeat.
5	step brush step brush	
6	now turn and jump	Turn and jump: With man still holding lady's waist, couple turns 1 full turn R in 2 slow, 2 quick, and 1 slow jump.
7	TURN TURN	
8	now men HOP	Repeat entire dance.

Suggestion

For mixer, each could jump to new partner, but do not attempt this until dance is thoroughly learned.

T H R E E S O M E   D A N C E S

Too many ladies and not enough men to have a dance; some of the men don't know how to dance--these situations are likely to present themselves at any social gathering. How can dance leaders provide interesting programs of dances and other rhythmic social activities for groups where men and ladies are unequally distributed? "Two's company, three's a crowd," doesn't need to be true. Three can be just enough if the round dances described in this section are used.

If there are a few men without a second lady it is of no concern, since every step that can be danced with two partners can be danced with one. When changing partners, men go ahead to a new threesome as the ladies dance back to a new partner.

T H R E E S O M E   R O U N D

This dance is a simple beginning routine to help dancers learn about three-somes.

Formation: Threesome
Position: Full-open
Footwork: Opposite (man L, ladies R)

Music: It's a Small World
Record: Activity Records 527
Rhythm: 4/4, 8 meas

MEAS	CALL

INSTRUCTIONS

SIDE-TOUCH

READY SIDE

Side-touch: Step side L, touch R foot to L; step side R, touch L foot to R. Repeat.

1   side touch side touch

2   side touch slide left

Slide: Step side L, close R foot to L; step side L, touch R foot to L. Step side R, close L foot to R; step side R, touch L foot to R.

3   side close slide right

4   side close walk forward

Walk: Walk fwd 4 steps, L,R,L,R.

5   walk walk chug left

Chug: Chug L 4 times, touching R foot to L on 4th chug. Repeat to R.

6   chug chug chug right

7   chug chug change partners

Change partners: In 2 two-steps, man dances fwd to new partners, L lady turns L and R lady R in circle back to new partner.

8   step' close' step start over

Repeat entire dance.

BAY PATH SCHOTTISCHE

Formation:	Threesome, men facing LOD	Music: Bay Path Swing
Position:	Full-open, face-to-face, man holding outside hands	Record: Windsor 4675-B
		Rhythm: 4/4, 16 meas
Footwork:	Opposite (man L, ladies R)	

MEAS	CALL	INSTRUCTIONS
	forward and HOP	Forward (basic step): Run in LOD L,R,L, hop L. Repeat, starting R.
	READY FORWARD	
1-2	1 2 3 hop, ladies arch IN	Ladies arch in: In 4 step-hops, ladies arch under man's arms, ending with everyone facing fwd.
3-4	step-hop step-hop, GRAPEVINE LEFT	Grapevine: Step side L, cross R foot behind L, step side L, swing R foot over L. Repeat to R.
5-6	side behind step swing, ladies arch OUT	
		Ladies arch out: Ladies arch under man's arms in 4 step-hops to end facing partner. Drop hands.
7-8	step-hop step-hop, now change PARTNERS	
9-10	1 2 3 hop, now let's CLAP	Change partners: As ladies turn in place with basic step, man dances basic step fwd (L,R,L, hop L; R,L,R, hop R) to new partners. All clap hands above head twice (ct 1-2), hips twice (ct 3-4). Hold L hand on L hip, raise R forefinger high, and move hips L,R,L,R (ct 1-4).
11-12	hands hands hips hips, once again change partners	
13-14	1 2 3 hop, now let's CLAP	
15-16	hands hands hips hips, now start OVER	
		Repeat entire dance.

COMIN' 'ROUND THE MOUNTAIN

Formation:	Threesome	Music: Comin' 'Round the Mountain
Position:	Full-open	Record: Imperial 1012, Jubilee 806,
Footwork:	Opposite (man L, ladies R)	Windsor 7115, all sing
		Rhythm: 4/4, 8 meas

MEAS	CALL	INSTRUCTIONS
	READY SING	Take 8 walking steps fwd (meas 1-2).
1-2	She'll be comin' 'round the mountain when she comes.	Ladies join outside hands and all 3 circle 8 steps L to end in original place (meas 3-4).
3-4	She'll be comin' 'round the mountain when she comes.	In 8 steps, man steps fwd under raised

5	She'll be comin' 'round the mountain,	arms of ladies and pulls them under arch so that all end in circle back to back (meas 5-6).
6	She'll be comin' 'round the mountain,	Circle 8 steps L to end in original place. Ladies drop hands and walk back to new man, as man walks ahead to new partners (meas 7-8).
7-8	She'll be comin' 'round the mountain when she comes.	

Repeat entire dance, using following words.

<u>Verses 2, 3, and 4</u>

Oh, we'll all go out to meet her when she comes. . .

She'll be driving six white horses when she comes. . .

We will kill the old red rooster when she comes. . .

C O N G A

Formation:	Threesome	Music:	Conga
Position:	Full-open	Record:	Yates 731
Footwork:	All start L	Rhythm:	4/4, 16 meas

MEAS	CALL	INSTRUCTIONS
	WALK FORWARD	<u>Walk forward (basic step)</u>: Walk fwd 3 steps and kick R foot to R side. Walk fwd 3 steps and kick L foot to L side. Repeat.
	READY <u>WALK</u>	
1-2	1 2 3 kick, 1 2 3 kick	
3-4	1 2 3 kick, now to the <u>side</u>	<u>Side</u>: Step side L, cross R foot over L, step side L, kick R foot to R side. Repeat to R. Repeat meas 5-6.
5-6	side cross side kick, side cross side kick	
7-8	side cross side kick, forward and <u>CROSS</u>	<u>Cross</u>: Walk fwd 3 steps and kick R foot over L. Repeat, starting R. Repeat meas 9-10.
9-10	forward 2 3 cross, forward 2 3 cross	
11-12	forward 2 3 cross, center and <u>SNAP</u>	<u>Snap</u>: Move toward center of circle with basic step, turning ½ turn R on 3rd step and snapping fingers on kick. Repeat toward wall. Repeat meas 13-14.
13-14	in in turn snap, out out turn snap	Repeat entire dance.

15-16   in in turn snap, men forward
               start over

               C R O S S   O V E R   T H E   B R I D G E

Formation: Threesome   Music: Cross over the Bridge
Position: Full-open   Record: Windsor 4804-B
Footwork: All start L   Rhythm: 4/4, 8 meas

MEAS   CALL   INSTRUCTIONS

          grapevine to the left   Grapevine: Step side L, cross R foot
                                       behind L, step side L, swing R foot
          READY GRAPEVINE   over L. Repeat to R.

1   side behind side swing   Walk forward: Walk fwd 3 steps, brush
                                       R foot fwd.
2   now walk FORWARD
                                       Walk back: Walk back 3 steps and clap
3   forward 2 back now   own hands.

4   turn right-hand lady   Turn right-hand lady: Man takes R-
                                       hand lady with forearm grip and they
5   turn 2 3 brush   walk L,R,L, brush R; R,L,R brush L.
                                       Man takes L-hand lady with L forearm
6   left-hand LADY   grip, they walk L,R,L, brush R; R,L,R,
                                       brush L.
7   ladies back men forward
                                       Ladies back, men forward: In 4 steps,
8   NOW GRAPEVINE   man walks fwd and ladies walk back to
                                       new partners.

                                       Repeat entire dance.

               F E S T I V A L   S C H O T T I S C H E

Formation: Threesome   Music: Bay Path Swing
Position: Promenade, ladies'   Record: Windsor 4675-B
               inside hands on man's   Rhythm: 4/4, 32 meas
               shoulders
Footwork: Opposite (man L, ladies R)

MEAS   CALL   INSTRUCTIONS

          forward and HOP   Basic step: Fwd L,R,L, hop L; fwd
                                       R,L,R, hop R.
          READY BASIC
                                       Roll in: All step L, hop L, step R,
1   1 2 3 hop   hop R; repeat. On step-hops ladies
                                       roll toward man into skaters' position
2   ladies roll IN   with inside hands on man's shoulders.

                                       120

3	step-hop step-hop	Roll and arch: In 4 step-hops, ladies roll and arch out away from man 1½ turns to end facing man, inside hands joined. Man does 4 step-hops in LOD.
4	NOW BASIC	
5	1 2 3 hop	
6	roll and arch out	Chase: Man, holding ladies' inside hands, does 1 basic step fwd as ladies dance back.
7	step-hop step-hop	
8	now chase BACK	Roll in, roll out sequence: Ladies roll into skaters' position in 2 step-hops and out again in 2 more step-hops. Man does 4 step-hops in LOD.
9	1 2 3 hop	
10	1 2 roll in	Arch in: Ladies arch toward man into promenade position in 4 step-hops. Man does 4 step-hops in LOD.
11	step-hop roll out	
12	step-hop chase back	Slide: Take 3 slides L to center, swing R foot over L; take 3 slides R, swing L foot over R.
13	1 2 3 hop	
14	1 2 arch in	Circle slide: Ladies drop inside hands with man and join these hands with each other, and join outside hands with man to form circle. All repeat slide sequence in circle to L, then R. Ladies then drop hands to roll in.
15	step-hop step-hop	
16	now let's SLIDE	
17	slide slide slide reverse	
18	slide slide roll in	Half-circle slide: Repeat slide sequence in skaters' position, curving to L and R in half-circle.
19	step-hop step-hop	
20	now let's SLIDE	Roll out: Ladies roll away from man to promenade position in 4 step-hops. Man does 4 step-hops in LOD.
21	slide slide slide reverse	
22	now roll and arch	Repeat entire dance.
23	step-hop step-hop	
24	now circle SLIDE	
25	slide slide slide reverse	
26	slide slide roll in	
27	step-hop step-hop	
28	half-circle SLIDE	
29	slide slide slide reverse	

MEAS	CALL	
30	slide slide <u>roll out</u>	
31	step-hop step-hop	
32	step-hop <u>start over</u>	

G O O D - N I G H T ,   L A D I E S

Formation: Threesome
Position: Shine, face-to-face, man facing LOD, ladies facing agLOD
Footwork: Opposite (man L, lady R)

Music: Good-night, Ladies
Record: All sing
Rhythm: 4/4, 8 meas

MEAS	CALL	INSTRUCTIONS
	men sing first verse	**Verse**
	READY SING	Man bows to R lady (meas 1).
Verse		Man bows to L lady (meas 2).
1	Good-night, ladies,	Man turns R lady under arch with R-L cnt (meas 3).
2	Good-night, ladies,	
3	Good-night, ladies,	Man turns L lady under arch with L-R cnt and walks ahead to new set (meas 4).
4	We're going to leave you now.	**Chorus**
Chorus		Ladies hook man's elbows and all two-step fwd 8 two-steps. Repeat entire dance, using following words.
5	Merrily we roll along,	**Verses 2 and 3**
6	Roll along, roll along,	[Ladies sing] Farewell, gentlemen. . .
7	Merrily we roll along	[All sing] Sweet dreams, everyone. . .
8	O'er the deep blue sea.	**Suggestion**

If party is not too large continue until each man has said "Good-night" to every lady.

Variation

As get-acquainted dance, R-hand lady sings, "My name's _____," as man shakes her hand (meas 1).
L-hand lady sings, "My name's _____" as man shakes her hand (meas 2).
Man sings, "My name's _____" and

122

points to self with both thumbs (meas 3).

All sing, "Let's go to meet the rest," as man skips ahead to new partners and ladies turn in place (meas 4).

Repeat entire dance.

HOT PRETZELS

Formation: Threesome
Position: Varsouvienne
Footwork: All start L

Music: Hot Pretzels or medium foxtrot
Record: Capitol DAS 6016, Imperial 1146, or own choice
Rhythm: 4/4, 8 meas

MEAS   CALL

place L heel forward

READY HEEL

1-2   HEEL back step, STEP HEEL

3   back step STEP

4   HEEL walk forward

5-6   ONE TWO, THREE BRUSH

7   step brush heel brush

8   stomp stomp HEEL

INSTRUCTIONS

Heel (basic step): Put L heel fwd (ct 1-2), close L foot to R (ct 3), step in place, R,L (ct 4, 1-2). Repeat, starting R (ct 3-4, ct 1-4). Put L heel fwd (ct 1-2), step in place L,R (ct 3-4).

Walk: Walk fwd 4 slow steps.

Brush: Stomp L (ct 1), brush R foot fwd as L heel comes off floor (ct 2); drop L heel down (ct 3), brush R foot fwd while raising L heel again (ct 4); stomp R,L,R.

Repeat entire dance.

Suggestion

For mixer, ladies turn back as man goes ahead to new partner on walk step 2nd time through.

JESSIE POLKA

Formation: Threesome
Position: Skaters', man's arms around ladies' waists
Footwork: All start L

Music; Jessie Polka
Record; MacGregor 632
Rhythm: 4/4, 4 meas

MEAS   CALL

left heel FORWARD

READY HEEL

INSTRUCTIONS

Heel (basic step): Put L heel fwd, close L foot to R; point R toe back, touch R foot beside L. Kick R foot

1	heel stand back touch	fwd, close R foot to L; point L foot to side, cross L foot in front of R without changing weight.
2	kick stand two-step	
3	step' close' step step' close' step	Two-step: Starting L, take 4 two-steps fwd.
4	step' close' step now basic	Repeat entire dance.

Suggestion

For mixer, man goes ahead and ladies turn back to new partner on two-step 2nd time through.

J O L L Y   I S   T H E   M I L L E R

Formation:	Threesome	Music:	Jolly Is the Miller
Position:	Full-open	Record:	Old Timer 8089, Folkraft 1192, all sing
Footwork:	Opposite (man L, ladies R)	Rhythm:	4/4, 8 meas

MEAS	CALL	INSTRUCTIONS
	walk and SING	Take 8 walking steps fwd (meas 1-2).
	READY WALK	Ladies join outside hands; all circle L 8 steps (meas 3-4).
1-2	Jolly is the miller as he lives by the mill.	Man turns R-hand lady with R elbow hook in 4 steps (meas 5), then turns L-hand lady with L elbow hook in 4 steps (meas 6).
3-4	The wheel goes 'round with a right good will.	
5-6	One hand in the hopper and the other in the sack.	Ladies walk back and man fwd to new partners in 8 steps (meas 7-8).
7-8	The men step forward and the ladies step back.	Repeat entire dance.

Christmas Variation

Jolly is Saint Nicholas who lives up north.

He gives us a good time for all we're worth,

And we like to see him coming with his pack on his back.

The boys step forward and the girls step back.

LI'L LIZA JANE

Formation:	Threesome	Music: Li'l Liza Jane
Position:	Shine	Record: MacGregor 654, all sing
Footwork:	Opposite (man L, ladies R)	Rhythm: 4/4, 12 meas

MEAS	CALL	INSTRUCTIONS
	all stoop DOWN	**Chorus**
	READY STOOP	All quickly stoop down on word "O," then rise up high on toes, reach arms overhead, and turn L ½ turn individually while singing meas 1-2. Repeat for meas 3-4 to end facing LOD.
Chorus		
1-2	O Eliza, li'l Liza Jane,	
3-4	O Eliza, li'l Liza Jane.	**Verse**
Verse		Join hands and move fwd in LOD with 4 walking steps on words "Come, my love, and marry me." All stomp twice (ct 1), pause (ct 2), and repeat (ct 3-4) on words "Li'l Liza Jane."
5	Come, my love, an' marry me,	
6	Li'l Liza Jane.	
7	I will take good care of thee,	Repeat meas 5-6 twice more to words of meas 7-8 and 9-10.
8	Li'l Liza Jane.	
9	Come, my love, an' be my one,	On words "You got a gal an' I got none," ladies walk back 4 steps as man walks fwd 4 steps to new partners (meas 11). Repeat meas 6 to words of meas 12.
10	Li'l Liza Jane.	
11	You got a gal an' I got none,	Repeat entire dance.
12	Li'l Liza Jane.	

MORMON SCHOTTISCHE

Formation:	Threesome	Music: Frontier Schottische
Position:	Varsouvienne	Record: MacGregor 5005 B
Footwork:	Opposite (man L, ladies R)	Rhythm: 4/4, 8 meas

MEAS	CALL	INSTRUCTIONS
	basic step FORWARD	Basic step: Run fwd L,R,L, hop L. Run fwd R,L,R, hop R.
	READY FORWARD	
1	forward 2 3 hop	Step-hop: Step fwd L, hop L; step R, hop R. Repeat.
2	now let's step-hop	Heel-toe: Place L heel fwd, L toe back.

3	step-hop step-hop	Man steps in place L,R,L as ladies turn out to full-open position in 3 steps to end facing agLOD. Repeat heel-toe to R, then men run fwd, ladies back to new partners.
4	now heel-TOE	
5	HEEL-TOE	
6	out 2 THREE	Repeat entire dance.
7	CHANGE PARTNERS	
8	now basic STEP	

R A M B L I N'   R U B I N

Formation:	Threesome	Music:	Ramblin' Rubin
Position:	Full-open	Record:	Windsor 7624-A
Footwork:	All start L	Rhythm:	4/4, 8 meas

MEAS   CALL

INSTRUCTIONS

	face in and jump	Face in: Turn L to face center of circle and jump fwd, back, fwd, and back.
	READY JUMP	
1	jump jump face out	Face out: Turn R to face wall and jump fwd, back, fwd, and back.
2	jump jump now kick	
3	kick kick face out	Kick: Turn diag L of LOD and kick R foot fwd twice. Turn diag R of LOD and kick L foot fwd twice.
4	kick kick teeter-totter	
5-6	DOWN UP, STEP-HOP	Teeter-totter: Bending at knees, ladies go down (ct 1-2); as ladies come up, man goes down (ct 3-4). Repeat.
7	now change PARTNERS	
8	and start OVER	Step-hop: Step L, hop L, step R, hop R. Ladies turn 1 full individual turn out as man moves ahead to new set of ladies. All stomp 3 times.

Repeat entire dance.

S H O U L D   I?

Formation:	Threesome	Music:	Star Dust
Position:	Full-open	Record:	Windsor 4678-B
Footwork:	Opposite (man L, ladies R)	Rhythm:	4/4, 8 meas

MEAS   CALL

INSTRUCTIONS

WALK FORWARD

Walk: Take 8 steps fwd.

READY WALK

1-2	1 2 3 4, circle three hands 'round
3-4	1 2 3 4, turn right-hand lady
5	turn left-hand lady
6	turn right-hand lady
7	1 2 men forward
8	change partners start over

Circle three hands 'round: Ladies join outside hands and all circle 8 steps to L.

Turn right-hand lady: With R forearm grip, man turns R-hand lady 1 full turn in 4 steps.

Turn left-hand lady: With L forearm grip, man turns L-hand lady 1 full turn in 4 steps.

Men forward: Man moves ahead and ladies back to new partners in 4 walking steps.

Repeat entire dance.

T E N   P R E T T Y   G I R L S

Formation:	Threesome
Position:	Skaters', man's arms around ladies' waists
Footwork:	All start L

Music:	Ten Pretty Girls
Record:	MacGregor 604, Folk 1296, Old Timer 8004
Rhythm:	4/4, 16 meas

MEAS   CALL

INSTRUCTIONS

point left over right

READY CROSS

1-2	CROSS SIDE, back side FORWARD
3-4	CROSS SIDE, back side FORWARD
5-6	CROSS SIDE, back side FORWARD
7-8	CROSS SIDE, now let's WALK
9-10	SLOW SLOW, quick quick SLOW
11-12	SLOW SLOW, kick and STOMP
13-14	FORWARD BACK, now right FOOT
15-16	FORWARD BACK, NOW BASIC

Cross (basic step): Point L foot over R (ct 1-2), point L to side (ct 3-4), step L behind R (ct 1), step side with R foot (ct 2), step fwd L (ct 3-4). Repeat, starting R. Repeat meas 1-4.

Walk: Walk fwd, starting L (slow, slow, quick, quick, slow). Repeat, starting R.

Kick and stomp: Kick L foot fwd and back, raising as high as possible. Stomp L,R,L. Repeat, starting R.

Repeat entire dance.

Suggestions

For mixer, ladies turn back on walk as man moves ahead to new partners. Inside lady turns L, outside lady turns R.

TWO - FOR - ONE WALTZ

Formation: Threesome
Position: Full-open
Footwork: All start L

Music: Any waltz
Record: Own choice
Rhythm: 3/4, 16 meas

MEAS	CALL
	all <u>run forward</u>
	ready RUN
1-2	forward 2 3, now <u>right arch</u>
3-4	arch 2 3, reverse and <u>run</u>
5-6	run 2 3, now <u>left arch</u>
7-8	arch 2 3, now let's <u>balance</u>
9-10	FORWARD and, <u>left lady run</u>
11-12	forward 2 3, now let's <u>balance</u>
13-14	FORWARD and, <u>right lady run</u>
15-16	forward 2 3, now <u>run forward</u>

INSTRUCTIONS

<u>Run forward</u>: Run 6 steps in LOD.

<u>Right arch</u>: R lady turns ½ turn as man raises R arm and L lady goes under and pulls man under, all in 6 steps. Ladies have exchanged places and all end facing agLOD.

<u>Run</u>: Run 6 steps agLOD.

<u>Left arch</u>: L lady turns 1/2 turn as man raises L arm and R lady goes under and pulls man under, all in 6 steps. Ladies are back in original places and all end facing LOD.

<u>Balance</u>: Step fwd L, touch R, back on R, touch L.

<u>Left lady run</u>: Man balances fwd and back with R lady as L lady runs fwd in 6 steps to new couple.

<u>Right lady run</u>: Man and L lady balance fwd and back as R lady runs fwd in 6 steps to new couple.

Repeat entire dance.

<u>Suggestion</u>

While one lady runs forward, man may wheel 1 full turn back with other lady rather than balance.

SOCIAL DANCING

INTRODUCTION

Social dancing had its roots in European peasant dances but did not really begin to take its present form until the waltz united couples in a one-to-one embrace. The irresistible enthusiasm that sent these early waltzers spinning around the floor has since taken many forms and has varied in its expression but has never quite been lost.

In recent years dancing has not been taught in elementary schools, for the most part, and there is a resultant widespread ignorance among young people about even the most fundamental aspects of social dancing. Young people today participate in a form of dancing executed independently and requiring comparatively little skill and coordination. Watching, their parents and grandparents have often expressed pity. For social dancing, though not necessarily difficult, demands a higher degree of cooperation and coordination between partners, a sense of rhythm, and some knowledge of basic steps. It thus includes an excitement and an aesthetic sense of achievement that is generally lacking in modern popular dance and that many young people today never experience.

Without doubt, the best time to teach social dancing is in the elementary school before the self-consciousness and awkwardness of adolescence sets in. If a young person can master the skills of social dancing early, he can later perform with an adequacy that will encourage him at a time when achievement is especially important to him, and he may even become enthusiastic about dancing. Lacking these basic skills, the young person in his early teens, being easily embarrassed, is usually unwilling even to try to acquire them.

For any age group, the basic steps of social dancing should be taught in a circle without the complication of coping with a partner. If everyone holds hands, no one is without the guidance of his neighbors in moving in the right direction and in doing the steps correctly. Most dances in this chapter be-gin in a circle, either single or double. After the steps are learned, part-ners should try them in shine position first, then with both hands joined and finally in closed position. (If the dancers are children, when "fourth grade" is called, they should take partners holding both hands in a double circle, with the leader facing the center. At the call of "sixth grade," the dancers should do all the steps in closed position in a double circle, dancing to the center and out. In this way they gain an awareness of their own progress.) However, if the ladies outnumber the men or vice versa, it may be fun to learn in a threesome formation rather than in couples.

There are records and tunes suggested for each dance in this chapter. However, the choice is open. The dancers or teacher could bring their favor-ite records in the same rhythm as the dance to be learned (4/4 for foxtrot, 3/4 for waltz, and so forth). It is good for young people to realize that social dance steps can be danced to their contemporary music.

Social dances are not necessarily round or sequence dances, but sequences are often used to teach the basic steps. The dance descriptions in this chapter are for this purpose. Once the dancers have mastered these basic steps, there will be no need for them to follow a sequence and, except for mixers, no need for the leader to call the dances.

MUSIC FOR DANCING

The identification of dance rhythms in recorded music is often a real challenge. A few albums have the type of dance printed on the cover or on the label. A very few have the tempo indicated. Both the type of dance and the tempo are of much importance to the dance teacher or to the person conducting a dance party. Tempo is indicated by the number of measures per minute; thus, to find the tempo of a piece of music, count the measures for one minute.

The tempo range found most enjoyable for each of the social dance rhythms is given below.

Dance	Tempo	Dance	Tempo
Foxtrot 129	33-45	Bossa Nova	42-48
Society Foxtrot	38-50	Mambo	38-48
Waltz	30-36	Merengue	58-64
Viennese Waltz	54-64	Polka	50-60
Lindy or Swing	32-64	One-step	55-65
Western Swing	26-32	International Waltz	30-32
Cha-cha	26-34	International Slow Foxtrot	30-32
Rumba	32-36		
		International Tango	32-34
Tango	30-34		
		Quick-step	46-52
Samba 180	48-60		

FOXTROT RHYTHMS

Origin: The foxtrot is perhaps the most popular of all modern dance forms. It is of comparatively recent origin, being only a little over 60 years old. The basic step was introduced by a musical comedy star named Harry Fox in a Florenz Ziegfeld show during the 1913-14 season. The dance, a simple trotting step done to then-popular ragtime music, was a showstopper. Oscar Duryea was then asked to use Harry Fox's routine as ballroom material in a demonstration to a group in a New York hotel. In working with the dance he found that the combination of Harry Fox's running steps and the slow walking steps was most appealing to the group. The dance's popularity further expanded when it was readily adapted to blues rhythms. From this beginning it was fitted to numerous forms of popular music and came to include a great variety of steps. By the early twenties, the foxtrot had emerged as the basic dance form of our country, and it is now danced worldwide.

Of course, the old dance done by Harry Fox has been so streamlined and modernized through the years that most of the trotting has been eliminated. Today we glide across the floor; one does not see couples bobbing up and down as they did in Grandmother's day. The foxtrot has become a smooth and graceful dance. Actually, it is the only smooth ballroom dance of American origin.

Rhythm: The foxtrot has been danced in 4/4, 2/4, and 6/8 time. The most common is 4/4 time. This is a 4/4 measure with an accent beat on counts one and three, giving the music the feeling of 2/4 rhythm. Many of the step forms of the foxtrot do not conform to the music measure; therefore, it is best to think of the rhythm in quick and slow units.

Tempo: There is a wide range of foxtrot tempos varying from very fast to very slow; quick steps can be used frequently in slow tempos, while slow steps fit fast tempos also. For moderate tempos, quick and slow steps can be combined.

The best dancing tempo is from 33 to 45 measures per minute.

Style: Even though style in ballroom mixers is not as important as in competition dancing it is well to look good at all times when on the dance floor. When stepping forward, move the torso forward with the diaphragm leading and let the foot follow. When stepping backward, move the foot back at the same time the body moves back. When stepping sideward, lead with the rib cage and place the weight on the foot as it reaches the sideward position. Follow through closely with the free foot before moving the other foot sideward again.

When changing directions the body should counterbalance before the feet move. As feet come together, the body should rise; when progressing, the body falls or lowers. Good style can add a great deal of enjoyment to social dancing.

Teaching the foxtrot: Men and ladies should make a single circle, all holding hands. The man (or leader) should have his partner on his right.

Start with the two-step rhythm. Notice that in learning, the basic step is placed between all other steps. After the students have mastered the routine, the basic step can be left out. Use the part method, (breaking a step down, isolating each movement) only when necessary.

The first lesson should include learning to dance forward and backward, circle left and right, and dance a cross step. Dancers should be able to do this alone or with a partner, taking either the leader's or the follower's part. Calling ahead can save much time and the dancers will learn much faster.

After learning the rhythm, dancers should:
● watch the demonstration.
● hold hands for the walk-through.
● dance to music.

If the instructional record is used, all that is necessary is to get the dancers in the correct formation and stand just inside the circle where all can watch the teacher while dancing the steps to be learned.

After the dancers have learned the dance in a large circle, make circles of ten and have students take turns calling the steps as desired. The steps may next be danced with a partner, first in two-hand position and then in closed position. The lady dances opposite footwork and, as in all couple dances, the lady moves ahead for each change of partners.

F O X T R O T   T W O - S T E P   M I X E R

Formation: Single circle
Position: Hands joined
Footwork: All start L

Music: Dixie Land
Record: Windsor 4696-B
Rhythm: 4/4, 44 meas, qqS (two-step)

MEAS	CALL	INSTRUCTIONS
	basic to the side	Basic step: Step side L, close R foot to L, step side L, touch R foot to L; repeat to R. Repeat.
	READY BASIC	
1	side together side touch	
2	side together side touch	Progress forward: Step side L, close R foot to L, step fwd on L foot, touch R foot beside L; repeat, starting R. Repeat.
3	side together side touch	
4	progress forward NOW	
5	side together FORWARD	Progress backward: Step side L, close R foot to L, step back on L foot, touch R foot beside L; repeat, starting R. Repeat.
6	side together FORWARD	
7	side together FORWARD	Basic cross: Dance L unit of basic step; then step side R, close L foot to R, cross R foot over L, and hold 1 ct. Repeat 3 more times.
8	basic step NOW	
9	side together side touch	Circle left: All turn 1/4 turn L and step fwd L, close R foot to L, step fwd L, touch R foot beside L; repeat, starting R. Repeat. End facing center of circle.
10	side together side touch	
11	side together side touch	
12	progress backward NOW	Circle right: All turn 1/4 turn R and repeat meas 33-36.
13	side together BACK	
14	side together BACK	Repeat entire dance.
15	side together BACK	
16	basic step NOW	

17	side together side touch
18	side together side touch
19	side together side touch
20	basic cross NOW
21	side together side touch
22	side together CROSS
23	side together side touch
24	side together CROSS
25	side together side touch
26	side together CROSS
27	side together side touch
28	now the basic step
29	quick quick SLOW
30	quick quick SLOW
31	quick quick SLOW
32	circle left NOW
33	forward together FORWARD
34	forward together FORWARD
35	forward together FORWARD
36	now the basic step
37	side together side touch
38	side together side touch
39	side together side touch
40	circle right NOW
41	forward close FORWARD
42	forward close FORWARD
43	forward close FORWARD
44	now start OVER

MAGIC RHYTHM FOXTROT

Formation:	Double circle	Music:	To Each His Own; Jack Hansen
Position:	Semi-open	Record:	"Sweet and Gentle," Dance
Footwork:	Opposite (man L, lady R)		Along DAL-1320
		Rhythm:	4/4, 9 meas, SSqq (magic)

MEAS	CALL	INSTRUCTIONS
	BASIC FORWARD	Basic step: Step fwd L (slow). Step fwd R (slow), step side L (quick), close R foot to L (quick). Repeat.
	READY BASIC	
1-3	FORWARD FORWARD, side together FORWARD, FORWARD senior walk	Senior walk: Take R-side position and step fwd L, step fwd R, step side L to face partner, and close R foot to L.
4-6	FORWARD FORWARD, left-side BACK, BACK touch step	Left-side: Turn to L-side position and take 1 basic step with man going back and lady fwd.
7-9	side touch side touch, arch now CHANGE, PARTNERS semi-open	Touch step: In conversation position step side L, touch R foot to L; step side R, touch L foot to R; step side L, close R foot to L.
		Arch: Lady turns R under L-R arch and moves to new partner with 1 basic step while man repeats touch step.
		Repeat entire dance.

F O X T R O T   M I X E R
(Walk rhythm)

Formation:	Double circle	Music:	I Left My Heart in San Francis-
Position:	Semi-open		co; Jack Hansen
Footwork:	Opposite (man L, lady R)	Record:	"Nice 'n' Easy," Dance Along
			DAL-S1315
		Rhythm:	4/4, 8 meas, SSSS (walk)

MEAS	CALL	INSTRUCTIONS
	WALK FORWARD	Walk: Walk fwd 4 steps in semi-open position.
	READY WALK	
1-2	FORWARD FORWARD, right-side WHEEL	Right-side wheel: Assume R-side position and do 1 complete turn R in 4 walking steps fwd (lady same).
3-4	FORWARD FORWARD, ROCK NOW	Rock: Assume conversation position and step fwd on L foot, back on R, fwd on L, back on R (lady opposite).
5-6	ROCK ROCK, ARCH NOW	

| 7-8 | CHANGE PARTNERS, FORWARD WALK | Arch: Man dances side touch to L and R as lady makes 1 complete turn under L-R arch to man ahead in 4 slow walking steps. |

Repeat entire dance.

FOXTROT MIXED MIXER

Formation: Double circle
Position: Semi-open
Footwork: Opposite (man L, lady R)

Music: Easy to Love; Jack Hansen
Record: "Second Ball of the Year," Dance Along DAL S1316
Rhythm: 4/4, 8 meas, SSqq (magic) and qqqqqqS (chassé)

MEAS	CALL	INSTRUCTIONS
	MAGIC FORWARD	Magic: In semi-open position, man steps fwd L,R, turns 1/4 R toward partner and steps sideward L, and closes R foot to L. Lady steps fwd R,L, turns 1/4 turn L toward partner, steps sideward R, and closes L foot to R. Both repeat.
	READY MAGIC	
1-3	FORWARD FORWARD, side together FORWARD, CHASSÉ eight now	
4-5	1 2 3 4, semi-open MAGIC	Chassé: Assume conversation position. Step sideward L, close R foot to L; repeat 3 more times.
6-8	FORWARD FORWARD, ladies arch CHANGE, PARTNERS and magic	Ladies arch: Man dances 2 step-swings in place (starting L, then R), then steps L and closes R foot to L; lady dances 1 magic step while going under L-R arch and on to new partner ahead.

Repeat entire dance.

FOXTROT
(Threesome)

Formation: Threesome
Position: Full-open, face-to-face, outside hands joined
Footwork: Opposite (man L, lady R)

Music: Jealous; George Poole
Record: "Spotlight on Dancing," Windsor WLP 3-01
Rhythm: 4/4, 8 meas, SSqq (magic) and qqqqqqqq

MEAS	CALL	INSTRUCTIONS
	basic forward and roll	Basic forward: Walk fwd, L,R,L,R, 2 slow and 2 quick steps. Repeat.
	READY BASIC	
1-3	FORWARD FORWARD, forward forward	Roll in: Ladies roll 1/2 turn toward man into cuddle position in 1 basic step.

	FORWARD, FORWARD <u>roll in</u>	<u>Roll out</u>: Ladies roll out to starting position in 1 basic step.
4-6	FORWARD FORWARD, <u>roll out</u>	
	FORWARD, FORWARD <u>roll wheel</u>	<u>Roll wheel and spin out sequence</u>: Ladies roll in and all 3 wheel R 1 complete turn in 8 quick steps. On last 4 quick steps, ladies spin out 1-1/2 turns as man moves ahead between ladies to new partners.
7-8	1 2 <u>spin out</u>, 1 2 <u>start over</u>	

Repeat entire dance.

B A L B O A   R H Y T H M

Position: Full-open, R-L cnt
Position: Full-open
Footwork: Opposite (man L, lady R)

Music: Cabaret; Jack Hansen
Record: "Take It Easy," recorded by Dance Along
Rhythm: 4/4, 8 meas, SSqqS (balboa)

MEAS	CALL	INSTRUCTIONS
	WALK FORWARD	<u>Walk (balboa, basic step)</u>: In full-open position walk fwd 3 steps, L,R,L; change weight on balls of feet on 4th count, R,L. Walk back R,L,R, ball-change L,R. (Balboa step is danced all through routine.)
	READY <u>WALK</u>	
1	1 2 3 back	
2	back 2 3 <u>away</u>	<u>Away</u>: Turn to face partner, drop hands, and back away from each other with 1 balboa step.
3	away 2 3 <u>together</u>	<u>Together</u>: Come together with 1 balboa step.
4	a right-hand <u>wheel</u>	
5	1 2 3' ball'-change	<u>Wheel</u>: Join R hands, wheel around 3/4 turn in 2 balboa steps. Man joins L hands with lady behind.
6	<u>take a new partner</u>	
7	a left-hand wheel	<u>Take a new partner</u>: Do complete L-hand wheel in 2 balboa steps fwd, changing hands to full-open position.
8	now start <u>OVER</u>	

Repeat entire dance.

C H A S S É   R H Y T H M

Formation: Double circle
Position: Two-hand, arms extended
Footwork: Opposite (man L, lady R)

Music: Josephine; William Farmer
Record: "San Francisco Penthouse Party," Hoctor HLP-4092
Rhythm: 4/4, 8 meas, qqqqqqS (chassé)

MEAS	CALL	INSTRUCTIONS
	chassé sideward	Chassé (basic step): Step side L, close R foot to L. Repeat 2 more times (ct 1-6).
	READY CHASSÉ	
1	side close side close	Back-to-back: Step side R (slow), re-lease L hands, and turn 1/2 turn R to assume back-to-back position with part-ner (ct 7-8). Repeat chassé in back-to-back position, starting R (ct 1-6).
2	back-to-BACK	
3	side close side close	
4	face-to-FACE	Face-to-face: Step side L (slow) and turn 1/2 turn L to assume two-hand position, arms extended, facing part-ner (ct 7-8). Repeat chassé, starting L (ct 1-8).
5	side close side close	
6	now change PARTNERS	
7	loop the LADIES	Change partners: Man repeats chassé agLOD, moves R to new partner on R. Lady turns with 1 chassé under L-R arch to new partner.
8	now start OVER	

Repeat entire dance.

L I N D Y   R H Y T H M S

Origin: The most memorable event of 1927 was the solo airplane flight of Charles A. Lindbergh from New York to Paris. His feat captured the imagina-tion of all the world, and young Lindbergh became the great American hero of his time. It was not at all surprising for a new dance fad to be called the Lindbergh Hop. The name was later shortened to the lindy hop, and finally to the lindy. This is the lindy still danced today.

The origin of this foxtrot novelty is obscure. Some say it was first danced by sailors and their girl friends, others claim a Harlem origin for it, and still others suggest this or that professional teacher as its originator. Whatever its beginnings may have been, it spread like wildfire when it was named the Lindbergh Hop. It became so popular that contests were held and groups traveled from state to state to compete in them.

Before long, a related but much more acrobatic form of the hop came on the scene. This new fad combined the lindy, the Charleston, the black bot-tom, the big apple, and a tumbling act all in one. The wilder the antics of the dancers, the more proficient they were thought to be. The craze soon became known as "jitterbug."

Rhythm: The lindy is usually danced to 4/4 time music. However, there are several different rhythm combinations used in the lindy. The most common consists of two slow and two quick counts which require 1-1/2 measures of 4/4 music.

Tempo: The best tempo for the lindy is between 32 and 64 measures per min-ute. In single rhythm the music should be from 50 to 64 measures per minute, while double rhythm should be from 40 to 50 measures per minute. Triple rhythm is played from 32 to 40 measures per minute.

Style: For smooth dancing of the lindy, the posture is erect and steps are short. All that applies to smooth dancing in any rhythm applies to the lindy. Poor posture mars the style of the dance.

Teaching the lindy: Use the same basic techniques used in teaching the fox-trot. Teach the steps in single, double, and threesome circles. Beginners should dance the steps in a single circle, while intermediate dancers dance in a double circle in two-hand position. Advanced dancers dance in a closed position with the boys facing the center.

Use the basic step between all other steps during direct teaching and controlled practice. Remember that ladies start with the right foot and men start with the left. When students show signs of having mastered the steps, have a controlled practice period. Then give the dancers complete freedom with the music playing. During free practice walk around giving private help to individuals that need it.

At the conclusion of the first lesson the dancers should be able to dance forward, backward, and sideward; to turn both right and left with a partner; and to dance either the lady's or the man's part.

L I N D Y   S I N G L E   C I R C L E   D A N C E
(Single rhythm)

Formation: Single circle
Position: Hands joined
Footwork: All start L

Music: Green Door; George Poole
Record: "Spotlight on Dancing," Windsor WLP 3-01
Rhythm: 4/4, 36 meas, SSqq

MEAS	CALL	INSTRUCTIONS
	rock forward and back READY BASIC	Basic step: Step fwd L (slow), back R (slow), back L (quick), fwd R (quick). Repeat.
1-3	FORWARD BACK, back forward FORWARD, BACK basic again	
4-6	FORWARD BACK, back forward SLOW, CIRCLE left now	Circle left: Face front and dance 4 basic steps fwd and back, progressing sideward L in circle.
7-9	FORWARD BACK, side forward SLOW, SLOW quick quick	Circle right: Facing front, dance 4 basic steps, progressing sideward R in circle.
10-12	FORWARD BACK, side forward SLOW, CIRCLE right now	
13-15	FORWARD SIDE, back side FORWARD, SIDE back side	Left break turn: Drop hands and turn 1/2 turn L toward center of circle on slow steps of basic. Repeat to original position in circle.

○

| MEAS | CALL | INSTRUCTIONS |

MEAS	CALL

16-18   FORWARD SIDE, back side
        SLOW, SLOW <u>basic step</u>

19-21   FORWARD BACK, back forward
        SLOW, <u>LEFT break turn</u>

22-24   TURN TURN, back forward
        TURN, TURN <u>basic step</u>

25-27   FORWARD BACK, back forward
        SLOW, <u>RIGHT break turn</u>

28-30   TURN TURN, back forward
        TURN, TURN <u>basic step</u>

31-33   FORWARD BACK, back forward
        SLOW, <u>SPIN left now</u>

34-36   SPIN BACK, back forward
        SPIN, BACK <u>start over</u>

INSTRUCTIONS

<u>Right break turn</u>: Turn 1/2 turn R toward center of circle on slow steps of basic step. Repeat back to place.

<u>Spin</u>: Place L foot fwd and spin on L foot for 1 complete L turn (slow), step back on R (slow), step back L (quick), step fwd R (quick).

Repeat entire dance.

L I N D Y   D O U B L E   R H Y T H M

Formation: Single circle
Position: Hands joined
Footwork: All start L

Music: Ja-Da; George Poole
Record: "Spotlight on Dancing," Windsor
          WLP 3-01
Rhythm: 4/4, 33 meas, SSqq

MEAS	CALL

dig forward and back

READY <u>BASIC</u>

1-3   dig forward dig back, back
       forward
       dig forward, dig back <u>basic</u>
       again

4-6   dig forward dig back, back
       forward
       SLOW, SLOW <u>circle left</u>

7-9   dig forward dig back, side
       cross
       dig forward, dig back side
       cross

10-12 dig forward dig back, side
       cross

INSTRUCTIONS

<u>Basic step</u>: Dig L toe beside R foot, step fwd L; dig R toe beside L foot, step back R; step back L, step fwd R. Repeat.

<u>Circle left</u>: Facing fwd, dance basic, stepping back diag L on 1st quick step and crossing R foot over L on 2nd quick step. Repeat 3 more times.

<u>Circle right</u>: Facing fwd, dance basic, stepping back diag R and fwd diag R on quick steps. Repeat 3 more times.

<u>Left turn</u>: Turn 1/2 turn L toward center of circle on slow steps of basic; repeat to original place in circle.

<u>Right turn</u>: Turn 1/2 turn R toward center of circle on slow steps of basic; repeat to place.

MEAS	CALL	INSTRUCTIONS

	SLOW, SLOW <u>basic step</u>	Repeat entire dance.
13-15	SLOW SLOW, quick quick SLOW, SLOW <u>circle right</u>	
16-18	dig forward dig side, back forward dig forward, dig side back forward	
19-21	dig forward dig side, back forward SLOW, SLOW <u>basic step</u>	
22-24	SLOW SLOW, quick quick SLOW, SLOW <u>left turn</u>	
25-27	dig turn dig turn, back forward dig turn, dig turn <u>basic step</u>	
28-30	SLOW SLOW, quick quick dig forward, dig back <u>right</u> <u>turn</u>	
31-33	dig turn dig back, back forward dig turn, dig turn <u>start over</u>	

T R I P L E   R H Y T H M   L I N D Y   S T Y L I N G

Formation: Single circle
Position: Hands joined
Footwork: All start L

Music: Nice 'n' Easy; Jack Hansen
Record: "A Dance Is," Dance Along DAL-
         S1322
Rhythm: 4/4, 96 meas, qqS qqS SS

MEAS	CALL	INSTRUCTIONS
	SIDEWARD BASIC	Basic: Step side L, close R foot to L, and change weight momentarily; step side R, close L foot to R, and change weight momentarily; step back L, fwd R. Repeat.
	READY <u>BASIC</u>	
1-3	side close SIDE, side close SIDE, BACK FORWARD	Splits: Repeat basic step, jumping feet apart, then together, on slow counts.
4-6	side close SIDE, side close SIDE, <u>BASIC</u> AGAIN	Rock: Repeat basic step, placing heels

7-9	side close SIDE, side close SIDE, BACK FORWARD	together, rocking back, and turning toes out and in on slow counts.
10-12	side close SIDE, side close SIDE, BACK FORWARD	Dig: Repeat basic step, touching L toe behind R twice on slow counts.
13-15	side close SIDE, SPLITS NOW, OUT IN	Single kick: On slow counts of basic step, kick L foot fwd and close to R, changing weight momentarily. Repeat.
16-18	side close SIDE, side close SIDE, OUT IN	Circle: On slow counts of basic step, circle L foot from fwd around back and close to R, changing weight momentarily. Repeat.
19-21	side close SIDE, ROCK STEP, ROCK ROCK	
22-24	side close SIDE, side close SIDE, ROCK ROCK	Double kick: On slow counts of basic step, kick L foot fwd (ct 1) and close to R (ct 2), then kick R foot fwd (ct 3) and close to L (ct 4).
25-27	side close SIDE, DIG STEP, DIG DIG	
28-30	side close SIDE, side close SIDE, DIG DIG	Knee bend: On slow counts of basic step, bend both knees down, circling them from L to R.
31-33	side close SIDE, SINGLE KICK, kick ball-CHANGE	Heel-toe: On slow counts of basic step, put L heel fwd and L toe back, without changing weight.
34-36	1 2 THREE, 1 2 THREE, kick ball-CHANGE	Left turn: Drop hands and move 1/2 turn L to center of circle on slow counts of basic step. Repeat, moving back to place.
37-39	1 2 THREE, CIRCLE NOW, circle ball-CHANGE	
40-42	1 2 THREE, 1 2 THREE, circle ball-CHANGE	Right turn: Drop hands and move 1/2 turn R to center of circle on slow counts of basic. Repeat to place.
43-45	1 2 THREE, DOUBLE KICK, KICK KICK	Repeat entire dance.
46-48	1 2 THREE, 1 2 THREE, KICK KICK	
49-51	1 2 THREE, KNEE BEND, DOWN UP	
52-54	1 2 THREE, 1 2 THREE, DOWN UP	
55-57	1 2 THREE, BASIC STEP, BACK FORWARD	
58-60	1 2 THREE, 1 2 THREE, BACK FORWARD	
61-63	1 2 THREE, HEEL-TOE, TOE HEEL	

64-66	1 2 THREE, 1 2 THREE, TOE HEEL
67-69	1 2 THREE, <u>BASIC STEP</u>, BACK FORWARD
70-72	1 2 THREE, 1 2 THREE, BACK FORWARD
73-75	1 2 THREE, <u>LEFT TURN</u>, TURN TURN
76-78	1 2 THREE, 1 2 THREE, TURN TURN
79-81	1 2 THREE, <u>BASIC STEP</u>, BACK FORWARD
82-84	1 2 THREE, 1 2 THREE, BACK FORWARD
85-87	1 2 THREE, <u>RIGHT TURN</u>, TURN TURN
88-90	1 2 THREE, 1 2 THREE, TURN TURN
91-93	1 2 THREE, <u>BASIC STEP</u>, BACK FORWARD
94-96	1 2 THREE, 1 2 THREE, <u>START OVER</u>

L I N D Y   F O U R S O M E   D A N C E   R O U T I N E
(Single rhythm)

Formation: Double circle, team formation, couples facing

Position: Full-open, outside hands joined with other couple

Footwork: Opposite (man L, lady R)

Music: My Baby Just Cares for Me; Memo Bernabei

Record: "Dancing on Air," Windsor WLP 3-05

Rhythm: 4/4, 24 meas, SSqq

MEAS	CALL	INSTRUCTIONS
	rock forward and back	Basic step: Step fwd L (slow), in place R (slow), back L (quick), in place R (quick). Repeat.
	READY <u>BASIC</u>	
1-3	FORWARD BACK, step step <u>BACKWARD</u>, <u>ARCH ROLL</u>	Backward arch roll: In 1 basic step, man facing LOD arches both ladies back into cuddle position with 2nd man.
4-6	ARCH ARCH, <u>BASIC</u> FORWARD, BACK step step	Double roll: In 1 basic step, man facing agLOD rolls both ladies into cuddle position with 1st man; in next basic
7-9	NOW <u>DOUBLE</u>, ROLL ROLL, ROLL do' it' again	

142

10-12	ROLL ROLL, <u>BASIC</u> FORWARD, <u>BACK</u> step step
13-15	FORWARD BACK, <u>single roll</u> ROLL, ROLL do' it' again
16-18	ROLL ROLL, <u>arch home</u> ARCH, ARCH <u>BASIC</u>
19-21	FORWARD BACK, step step FORWARD, BACK <u>CUDDLE</u>
22-24	ARCH ARCH, DIP ARCH, ARCH <u>start over</u>

step, he rolls them back to 2nd man.

Single roll: In 1 basic step, 2nd man rolls L-hand lady to 1st man. In next basic step, each man rolls his partner to opposite man.

Arch home: In 1 basic step, both men raise R arms and arch ladies to original position.

Cuddle: Both men assume two-hand position with partner and, in 1 basic step, arch her back under R arm, without releasing either hand, to assume R cuddle position. On quick steps of this basic, ladies dip fwd and back across partner to L cuddle position. In next basic step, men loop ladies back to place under L arm.

Repeat entire dance.

L I N D Y   A R C H   M I X E R

Formation:	Double circle, men facing center	Music:	At Sundown; Memo Bernabei
Position:	Two-hand	Record:	"Dancing on Air," Windsor WLP 3-05
Footwork:	Opposite (man L, lady R)	Rhythm:	4/4, 9 meas, SSqq

MEAS	CALL
	rock forward and back
	READY <u>BASIC</u>
1-3	FORWARD BACK, back forward FORWARD, BACK back forward
4-6	SLOW <u>FORWARD</u>, arch now SLOW, <u>BACKWARD</u> arch now
7-9	CHANGE PARTNERS, and basic SLOW, SLOW <u>BASIC</u>

INSTRUCTIONS

Basic step: Step fwd L (slow), in place on R (slow), back on L (quick), in place on R (quick). Repeat 2 more times.

Forward arch: Step fwd L, back R, back L, in place R, so that man turns 1/2 turn L and changes places with partner and lady turns 1/2 turn R under L-R arch.

Backward arch: Step fwd L, back R, back L, in place R, so that man turns 1/2 turn R to original place and lady turns 1/2 turn L under L-R arch to original place.

Change partners: Man moves to lady on R in 1 basic step and takes her in two-hand position.

Repeat entire dance.

LINDY MIXER
(Single rhythm)

Formation:	Double circle, men facing center
Position:	Two-hand
Footwork:	Opposite (man L, lady R)

Music:	Telestar
Record:	"Popcorn," Musicar MS 3242-B
Rhythm:	4/4, 12 meas, SSqq

MEAS	CALL
	rock forward and back
	READY <u>BASIC</u>
1-3	FORWARD BACK, step step FORWARD, BACK <u>turn right</u>
4-6	TURN TURN, step step TURN, BACK now <u>basic</u>
7-9	FORWARD BACK, step step FORWARD, BACK <u>walk around</u>
10-12	TURN TURN, walk around CHANGE, PARTNERS <u>start over</u>

INSTRUCTIONS

<u>Basic step</u>: Step fwd on L, back on R, back on L, in place R. Repeat.

<u>Turn right</u>: Step fwd L, back R, back L, in place R, turning 1/2 turn R and changing places with partner. Repeat to end in original position.

<u>Walk around</u>: In 1 basic step, man turns 1/2 turn L, lady 1/2 turn R, so that man's back is to lady as he turns. Man changes lady's R hand to his L hand behind his back as they change places to complete the 1/2 turn. Repeat, taking lady on R in two-hand position.

Repeat entire dance.

LINDY TRIPLE MIXER

Formation:	Double circle, men facing in
Position:	Two-hand
Footwork:	Opposite (man L, lady R)

Music:	Hot Butter
Record:	"Popcorn," Musicar MS 3242-B
Rhythm:	4/4, 12 meas, SS qqS qqS

MEAS	CALL
	rock back and forward
	READY <u>BASIC</u>
1	BACK FORWARD
2	side close SIDE
3	side close SIDE
4	BACK FORWARD
5	side close SIDE

INSTRUCTIONS

<u>Basic</u>: Step back L (slow), in place R (slow); step side L (quick), close R foot to L (quick), step side L (slow); step side R (quick), close L foot to R (quick), step side R (slow). Repeat.

<u>Cuddle wheel</u>: While stepping back L (slow), in place R (slow), man crosses L hand high over lady's head bringing her into cuddle position. In 6 steps (quick, quick, slow, quick, quick, slow), man wheels fwd, lady back, for 1 complete wheel.

144

MEAS	CALL	INSTRUCTIONS

MEAS	CALL		INSTRUCTIONS
6	CUDDLE WHEEL		Top spin and change partners sequence: Starting in cuddle position and in 1 basic step, man raises L hand and pulls with R hand to spin lady under L-R arch to new partner on her R.
7	BACK FORWARD		
8	forward forward FORWARD		
9	forward forward FORWARD		Repeat entire dance.
10	TOP SPIN		
11	CHANGE PARTNERS		
12	START OVER		

L I N D Y   S I N G L E   R H Y T H M

Formation: Threesome
Position: Full-open
Footwork: Opposite (man L, ladies R)

Music: My Kind of Town; Jack Hansen
Record: "Hollywood," Dance Along DAL-1318
Rhythm: 4/4, 15 meas, SSqq

MEAS	CALL	INSTRUCTIONS
	rock forward and back	Basic step: Step fwd L (slow), back R (slow), back L (quick), fwd R (quick). Repeat.
	READY BASIC	
1-3	FORWARD BACK, back forward SLOW, SLOW backward arch	Backward arch: In 1 basic step L lady backs under L-R arch to face man and R lady backs under R-L arch to face man.
4-6	ARCH ARCH, BASIC FORWARD, BACK back forward	Sideward arch: Man dances basic step while both ladies turn R under arch toward center of hall in 1 basic step, then turn L under arch back to place in 1 basic step.
7-9	FORWARD BACK, sideward arch ARCH, ARCH arch back	
10-12	ARCH ARCH, BASIC FORWARD, BACK back forward	Forward arch: In 1 basic step, ladies arch fwd while man drops hands and progresses fwd to new partners.
13-15	SLOW FORWARD, arch now CHANGE, PARTNERS and basic	Repeat entire dance.

LINDY THREESOME MIXER

Formation:	Threesome	Music: I'm Happy Just to Dance with You; Jack Hansen
Position:	Full-open	Record: "Hollywood," Dance Along DAL-1318
Footwork:	Opposite (man L, ladies R)	Rhythm: 4/4, 24 meas, SSqq

MEAS	CALL	INSTRUCTIONS
	rock forward and back	**Basic step:** Step fwd L (slow), back R (slow), back L (quick), fwd R (quick). Repeat.
	READY <u>BASIC</u>	
1-3	FORWARD BACK, step step FORWARD, BACK <u>backward arch</u>	**Backward arch:** In 1 basic step man raises both hands high and both ladies back under arch to face man.
4-6	ARCH ARCH, <u>BASIC</u> FORWARD, BACK back forward	
7-9	FORWARD BACK, <u>roll in</u> ROLL, ROLL <u>BASIC</u>	**Roll in:** In 1 basic step man pulls both hands, rolling ladies into cuddle position so that all end facing fwd.
10-12	FORWARD BACK, back forward FORWARD, BACK <u>roll out</u>	**Roll out:** In 1 basic step ladies roll out to full-open position again.
13-15	ROLL ROLL, <u>BASIC</u> FORWARD, BACK back forward	**Spin:** In 1 basic step man pushes with both hands on second slow step and lets go, spinning both ladies 1 full turn around and catching their same hands.
16-18	FORWARD BACK, <u>spin now</u> SPIN, SPIN <u>BASIC</u>	
19-21	FORWARD BACK, back forward FORWARD, BACK back forward	**Forward arch:** In 1 basic step man lifts both hands high and out, pulling ladies fwd under arch, then drops hands and moves ahead to new partners.
22-24	FORWARD BACK, <u>forward arch</u> ARCH, ARCH <u>start over</u>	Repeat entire dance.

CHARLESTON

The Charleston, symbol of the "roaring '20s," was an ancestor of the lindy.

Formation:	Single circle	Music: I Love My Baby; Bonnie Lee
Position:	Hands joined	Record: "Spotlight on Dancing," Windsor WLP 3-04
Footwork:	All start L	Rhythm: 4/4, 30 meas, SS

MEAS	CALL	INSTRUCTIONS
	READY BASIC	<u>Styling</u>
1-2	forward point back point,	For all steps, styling is as follows.

MEAS	CALL	INSTRUCTIONS

	forward point <u>kick step</u>	Heels should be turned out while 1 foot is in air. Heels are turned in when toes are touching floor.
3-4	forward kick back kick, forward kick <u>basic step</u>	
5-6	forward point back point, forward point <u>paddle left</u>	Basic step: Step fwd L, bring R toe fwd, flicking foot out and in, step back R, bring L toe back, flicking foot out and in. Repeat.
7-8	1 2 3 4, 5 6 <u>paddle right</u>	
9-10	1 2 3 4, 5 6 <u>basic step</u>	Kick step: Repeat basic step, replacing point with kick.
11-12	forward point back point, forward point <u>side left</u>	Paddle left, right: Paddle in direction indicated for 8 ct each way.
13-14	1 2 3 4, 5 6 <u>side right</u>	Side left, right: Chassé in direction indicated for 8 ct each way.
15-16	1 2 3 4, 5 6 <u>basic step</u>	
17-18	forward point back point, forward point <u>travel forward</u>	Travel forward, back: Walk 8 quick steps each way in direction indicated, styling as described above.
19-20	1 2 3 4, 5 6 <u>travel back</u>	Knee cross: Start with toes pointed out and heels together, backs of hands resting on knees. With weight on toe of L foot and heel of R, turn toes in and heels out to move L, at same time turning hands over and crossing them to touch opposite knee. With weight on heel of L foot and toe of R, resume first position, still moving L. Repeat 3 more times, then reverse direction by reversing distribution of weight on feet and repeat above 4 times.
21-22	1 2 3 4, 5 6 <u>basic step</u>	
23-24	forward point back point, forward point <u>knee cross</u>	
25-26	1 2 3 4, 5 6 travel right	
27-28	1 2 3 4, 5 6 <u>basic step</u>	
29-30	forward point back point, forward point <u>start over</u>	
		Repeat entire dance.

BOP

This descendant of the lindy was popular in the 1950s.

Formation: Single circle
Position: Hands joined
Footwork: All start L

Music: Song of the Marobi Trio
Record: "Hot Butter," Musicar MS 3242B
Rhythm: 4/4, 52 meas

MEAS	CALL	INSTRUCTIONS
	TOE HEEL	Styling
	READY <u>BASIC</u>	Basic step is danced in place; all

MEAS	CALL	INSTRUCTIONS
1-2	toe-heel toe-heel, toe-heel toe'-heel' step	other steps progress 8 ct L, then change weight and progress 8 ct R. Supporting foot progresses with toe-heel weight distribution, as in Charleston, and free foot flicks out and in. All steps danced with bounce styling.
3-4	1 2 3 4, 5 6 7 reverse	
5-6	1 2 3 4, 5 6 basic step	
7-8	toe-heel toe-heel, toe-heel kick step	Basic step: Start with heels together, toes out. Turn toes in, heels out, at same time bringing L toe fwd; bring heels together and close L foot to R. Repeat with R foot.
9-10	1 2 3 4, 5 6 7 reverse	
11-12	1 2 3 4, 5 6 basic step	
13-14	toe-heel toe-heel, toe-heel circle foot	Toe-heel step: Touch toe (odd ct) and heel (even ct) of free foot to floor beside supporting foot while progressing 8 ct L, then 8 ct R.
15-16	1 2 3 4, 5 6 7 reverse	
17-18	1 2 3 4, 5 6 basic step	Kick step: Kick R foot fwd (odd ct) and back (even ct) on 1st 8 ct, and L foot on 2nd 8 ct, progressing L, then R.
19-20	toe-heel toe-heel, toe-heel turn body	
21-22	1 2 3 4, 5 6 7 reverse	Circle foot: Circle free foot in small circle beside supporting foot while progressing L, then R.
23-24	1 2 3 4, 5 6 basic step	
25-26	toe-heel toe-heel, toe-heel shuffle step	Turn body: Repeat toe-heel step, turning body with swivel action.
27-28	1 2 3 4, 5 6 7 reverse	Shuffle step: Progress L 8 ct, then R 8 ct, with toe-heel weight distribution, weight on both feet, keeping feet parallel at all times.
29-30	1 2 3 4, 5 6 basic step	
31-32	toe-heel toe-heel, toe-heel bop forward	Bop forward, backward: Progress 8 ct in direction indicated with basic step.
33-34	1 2 3 4, 5 6 basic step	Sideward left, right: Progress 8 ct in direction indicated with basic step.
35-36	toe-heel toe-heel, toe-heel bop backward	Turn left, right: In 8 ct, turn 1 full turn in small circle in direction indicated with basic step.
37-38	1 2 3 4, 5 6 basic step	
39-40	toe-heel toe-heel, toe-heel turn left	Repeat entire dance.
41-42	1 2 3 4, 5 6 turn right	
43-44	1 2 3 4, 5 6 basic step	

MEAS	CALL	INSTRUCTIONS
45-46	toe-heel toe-heel, toe-heel <u>sideward left</u>	
47-48	1 2 3 4, 5 6 <u>sideward right</u>	
49-50	1 2 3 4, 5 6 <u>basic step</u>	
51-52	toe-heel toe-heel, toe-heel <u>start over</u>	

W A L T Z   R H Y T H M S

<u>Origin</u>: Originating in Austria or Switzerland about the middle of the eighteenth century, the waltz is a dance with marked rhythm and a gliding motion. At first it was considered daring because of the close contact between partners, but later it became not only accepted but fashionable. The music of Johann Strauss added to the tremendous popularity of the waltz.

Today, although the steps are much the same, the execution and feeling of the various types of waltzes are entirely different. The Viennese waltz, fast and staccato, requires a great deal of agility. The American waltz is much smoother and slower in tempo, and is widely popular today. High styling with an intricate pattern of steps characterizes with international waltz, often used in dancing competition. Learning to waltz well helps one add grace and smoothness to all other dancing steps.

<u>Rhythm</u>: The waltz is in 3/4 time with the accent on the first of the three beats.

<u>Tempo</u>: Streamlined waltz (walk rhythm) is danced to the tempo of 23 to 33 measures per minute, a very slow tempo. In the box rhythm, the tempo is from 33 to 43 measures per minute, still a slow waltz. A medium tempo waltz is 43 to 53 measures per minute, as in the hesitation rhythm. The Viennese waltz, with a tempo of 53 to 73 measures to the minute, is the fastest waltz.

<u>Style</u>: The posture is erect, the movement smooth and continuous. The dancer who has mastered the waltz style is a true artist.

<u>Teaching the waltz</u>: The basic waltz steps can be learned most easily in a single circle with the learners holding hands first and then dancing individually as they learn. Waltzing with partners, first in two-hand position, then in closed position, is then easier. All should learn both how to lead and how to follow.

After the first lesson dancers should be able to dance forward and backward, circle left and right, and dance on the spot with a partner, taking either the man's or the lady's part.

Each dance in this section is designed to develop freedom and creativity in each dancer. For beginning dancers, the calls should be made well in advance, and then less far ahead as progress is made.
For example:

Beginners--[three beats ahead] <u>forward</u> waltz now

More advanced dancers--[two beats ahead] now _forward_ waltz
Experienced dancers--[one beat ahead] now waltz _forward_

W A L T Z   B O X   R H Y T H M

Formation: Single circle
Position: Hands joined
Footwork: All start L

Music: Somewhere, My Love; Jack Hansen
Record: "A Dance Is," Dance Along
            DAL-S1322
Rhythm: 3/4, 48 meas

MEAS	CALL	INSTRUCTIONS
	forward _box step_	Box step (basic step): Step fwd L, step side R, close L foot to R; step back R, step side L, close R foot to L. Repeat.
	ready BOX	
1	forward side together	Forward: Step fwd L, step side R, close L foot to R; step fwd R, step side L, close R foot to L. Repeat.
2	back side together	
3	forward side together	Backward: Step back L, step side R, close L foot to R; step back R, step side L, close R foot to L. Repeat.
4	waltz _forward_ now	
5	forward side together	Circle left, right: Turn 1/4 and repeat _forward_ step in direction indicated. End facing center of circle.
6	forward side together	
7	forward side together	Forward cross: Step fwd L, step side R, close L foot to R; cross R foot over L, step side L, close R foot to L. Repeat.
8	_box step_ now	
9	forward side together	Back cross: Step back L, step side R, close L foot to R; cross R foot behind L, step side L, close R foot to L. Repeat.
10	back side together	
11	forward side together	
12	_backward_ waltz now	Repeat entire dance.
13	back side together	
14	back side together	
15	back side together	
16	_box step_ now	
17	forward side together	
18	back side together	

150

MEAS	CALL	INSTRUCTIONS
19	forward side together	
20	circle left now	
21	forward 2 3	
22	forward 2 3	
23	forward 2 3	
24	box step now	
25	forward side together	
26	back side together	
27	forward side together	
28	circle right now	
29	forward 2 3	
30	forward 2 3	
31	forward 2 3	
32	box step now	
33	forward side together	
34	back side together	
35	forward side together	
36	forward cross now	
37	forward side together	
38	cross side together	
39	forward side together	
40	now box step	
41	forward side together	
42	back side together	
43	forward side together	
44	back cross now	

MEAS	CALL	INSTRUCTIONS

MEAS	CALL
45	back side together
46	cross side together
47	back side together
48	now start over

W A L T Z   B O X   A N D   H E S I T A T I O N   R H Y T H M S

Formation: Single circle
Position: Hands joined
Footwork: All start L

Music: Try to Remember; Jack Hansen
Record: "A Dance Is," Dance Along
DAL-S1322
Rhythm: 3/4, 56 meas

MEAS	CALL	INSTRUCTIONS
	FORWARD BASIC	Basic step: Step fwd L, step side R, close L foot to R; step back R (ct 1), touch L foot beside R (ct 2-3). Repeat.
	READY BASIC	
1-2	forward side together, BACK touch	Progress forward: Step fwd L, step side R, close L foot to R; step fwd R, touch L foot beside R. Repeat.
3-4	forward side together, BASIC again	Progress back: Step back L, step side R, close L foot to R; step back R, touch L foot beside R. Repeat.
5-6	forward side together, BACK touch	
7-8	forward side together, PROGRESS forward	Circle left, right: Turn 1/4 and repeat progress forward step in direction indicated. End facing center of circle.
9-10	forward side together, FORWARD touch	Forward cross: Step fwd L, step side R, close L foot to R; cross R foot over L, point L foot to side. Repeat.
11-12	forward side together, PROGRESS back	
13-14	back side together, BACK touch	Back cross: Step back L, step side R, close L foot to R; cross R foot behind L, point L foot to side. Repeat.
15-16	back side together, BASIC step	Repeat entire dance.
17-18	forward side together, BACK touch	
19-20	forward side together, PROGRESS back	

MEAS	CALL	INSTRUCTIONS
21-22	back side together, BACK touch	
23-24	back side together, <u>PROGRESS forward</u>	
25-26	forward side together, FORWARD balance	
27-28	forward side together, <u>CIRCLE left</u>	
29-30	forward 2 3, FORWARD balance	
31-32	forward 2 3, <u>BASIC step</u>	
33-34	forward side together, BACK balance	
35-36	forward side together, <u>CIRCLE right</u>	
37-38	forward side together, FORWARD balance	
39-40	forward side together, <u>BASIC step</u>	
41-42	forward side together, BACK balance	
43-44	forward side together, <u>FORWARD cross</u>	
45-46	forward side together, CROSS point	
47-48	forward side together, <u>BASIC step</u>	
49-50	forward side together, BACK balance	
51-52	forward side together, <u>BACK cross</u>	
53-54	back side together, CROSS point	
55-56	back side together, <u>START over</u>	

BOX RHYTHM WALTZ MIXER

Formation: Single circle
Position: Closed
Footwork: Opposite (man L, lady R)

Music: 'Til Tomorrow; Memo Bernabei
Record: "Dancing on Air," Windsor WLP 3-05
Rhythm: 3/4, 16 meas

MEAS	CALL
	forward box step
	ready BOX
1	forward side together
2	waltz forward now
3	forward side together
4	forward side together
5	forward side together
6	forward cross now
7	forward side together
8	cross side together
9	forward side together
10	box left turn
11	forward side together
12	back side together
13	forward side together
14	now change partners
15	forward side together
16	now box step

INSTRUCTIONS

Box: Step fwd L, step side R, close L foot to R. Step back R, step side L, close R foot to L.

Waltz forward: Step fwd L, step side R, close L foot to R; step fwd R, step side L, close R foot to L. Repeat.

Forward cross: Step fwd L, step side R, close L; man cross R foot over L (lady cross L foot behind her R), step side L, close R foot to L. Repeat.

Box left turn: Complete 1 full turn L while dancing 2 basic box steps.

Change partners: Lady turns R under L-R arch as man dances 1 progressive box step fwd to new partner ahead.

Repeat entire dance.

HESITATION WALTZ

Formation:	Single circle
Position:	Hands joined
Footwork:	All start L

Music: Viennese Waltz Medley; Jack Hansen

Record: "A Dance Is," Dance Along DAL-S1322

Rhythm: 3/4, 72 meas

MEAS	CALL	INSTRUCTIONS
	HESITATION FORWARD	Basic balance: Step fwd L, touch R foot to L; step back R, touch L foot to R. Repeat.
	READY basic balance	
1-2	FORWARD touch, BACK touch	Side balance: Step side L, touch R foot beside L; step side R, touch L foot beside R. Repeat.
3-4	FORWARD touch, SIDE balance	
5-6	SIDE touch, SIDE touch	Progress forward: Step fwd L, point R foot fwd; step fwd R, point L foot fwd. Repeat.
7-8	SIDE touch, PROGRESS forward	
9-10	FORWARD point, FORWARD point	Back lift: Step back L, lift R foot fwd; step back R, lift L foot fwd. Repeat.
11-12	FORWARD point, BACK lift	
13-14	BACK lift, BACK lift	Forward brush: Step fwd L, brush R foot fwd; step fwd R, brush L foot fwd. Repeat.
15-16	BACK lift, FORWARD brush	
17-18	FORWARD brush, FORWARD brush	Back touch: Step back L, touch R foot beside L; step back R, touch L foot beside R. Repeat.
19-20	FORWARD brush, BACK touch	
21-22	BACK touch, BACK touch	Sideward left: Step side L, touch R foot beside L, cross R foot over L, touch L foot beside R. Repeat 3 more times.
23-24	BACK touch, SIDEWARD left	
25-26	SIDE touch, CROSS touch	Sideward right: Cross R foot behind L, touch L foot beside R, step side R, touch L foot beside R. Repeat 3 more times.
27-28	SIDE touch, CROSS touch	
29-30	SIDE touch, CROSS touch	
31-32	SIDE touch, BASIC balance	Side draw: Repeat side balance sequence, replacing touch with draw.
33-34	FORWARD touch, BACK touch	
35-36	FORWARD touch, SIDEWARD right	Dot: Repeat side balance sequence, replacing touch with dot.
37-38	CROSS touch, SIDE touch	Sideward brush: Repeat side balance sequence, replacing touch with brush diag fwd.

MEAS	CALL	INSTRUCTIONS
39-40	CROSS touch, SIDE touch	Ball turn: Step side L, brush R foot diag fwd across L, step R in front of L and turn 1 full turn on balls of feet in 1 meas. Repeat, starting R.
41-42	CROSS touch, SIDE touch	
43-44	CROSS touch, BASIC balance	
45-46	FORWARD touch, BACK touch	Repeat entire dance.
47-48	FORWARD touch, SIDE draw	
49-50	SIDE draw, SIDE draw	
51-52	SIDE draw, DOT now	
53-54	SIDE dot, SIDE dot	
55-56	SIDE dot, BASIC balance	
57-58	FORWARD touch, BACK touch	
59-60	FORWARD touch, SIDEWARD brush	
61-62	SIDE brush, SIDE brush	
63-64	SIDE brush, BASIC balance	
65-66	FORWARD touch, BACK touch	
67-68	FORWARD touch, BALL turn	
69-70	SIDE brush, TURN turn	
71-72	SIDE brush, START over	

R U M B A   R H Y T H M S

Origin: The rumba is of Cuban origin and has probably the most pronounced rhythm of any modern ballroom dance. It is one of the most popular of all Latin-American dances and was the first dance from south of the border to interest Americans.

Rhythm: Rumba music is technically 2/4 in rhythm but for dance purposes is considered to be in 4/4 time.

Tempo: Slow rumba has 30 to 38 measures to the minute. The basic rumba is danced to this tempo. To the medium tempo of 38 to 50 measures per minute, combinations of break rhythms and the basic step are danced. Over 50 measures per minute is the tempo for fast break rhythms. The slow and medium tempos are best for ballroom dancing.

Style: The chief difference between the rumba and the two-step is in its style. The most important styles of rumba are Cuban-American, Cuban, and Puerto Rican; of these the Puerto Rican is the smoothest and therefore the most desirable for ballroom dancing.

Teaching the rumba: The techniques for teaching Latin dances are the same as those for teaching American dances, with perhaps the addition of a little extra styling. Elementary school dancers will learn the steps and little more. For them the similarity of dances should be stressed. Dancers of junior high age should be taught how to lead and follow. Dancers of high school age and above can be taught styling and the differences between dances.

At the conclusion of the first lesson each student should be able to dance forward, sideward, and backward; travel left and right; and dance a cross step with a partner. Dancers should be able to lead or follow.

A M E R I C A N   B A S I C   R U M B A   R H Y T H M

Formation: Single circle
Position: Hands joined
Footwork: All start L

Music: Yesterday Rumba; Jack Hansen
Record: "A Dance Is," Dance Along
DAL-S1322
Rhythm: 4/4, 30 meas, qqS

MEAS	CALL	INSTRUCTIONS
	SIDEWARD BASIC	**Basic:** Step side L (quick), close R foot to L (quick), step side L (slow), touch R foot to L. Repeat to R.
	READY BASIC	
1	side together side touch	**Cuban walk forward:** Step fwd L (quick), step fwd R (quick), step fwd L (slow). Repeat, starting R.
2	side together basic again	
3	side together side touch	**Backward:** Step back L,R,L (quick, quick, slow). Repeat, starting R.
4	Cuban walk FORWARD	
5	forward forward FORWARD	**Box step:** Step side L (quick), close R foot to L (quick), step fwd L (slow); step side R (quick), close L foot to R (quick), step back R (slow). Repeat.
6	now the basic step	
7	side together side touch	**Forward cross:** Step side L (quick), close R foot to L (quick), step fwd L (slow); step side R (quick), close L foot to R (quick), cross R foot over L (slow). Repeat.
8	Cuban walk BACKWARD	
9	back back BACK	
10	now the basic step	**Backward cross:** Step side L (quick), close R foot to L (quick), step back L (slow); step R (quick), close L foot to R (quick), cross R foot behind L (slow). Repeat.
11	side together side touch	
12	box step NOW	
13	side together FORWARD	Repeat entire dance.

157

MEAS	CALL	INSTRUCTIONS
14	side together BACK	<u>Suggestion</u>
15	side together FORWARD	After dancers have learned the steps, they may let go of hands; however, they learn much faster holding hands.
16	<u>basic step</u> NOW	
17	side together side touch	
18	<u>forward cross</u> NOW	
19	side together FORWARD	
20	side together CROSS	
21	side together FORWARD	
22	now the <u>basic step</u>	
23	side together side touch	
24	<u>backward cross</u> NOW	
25	side together BACK	
26	side together CROSS	
27	side together BACK	
28	<u>basic step</u> NOW	
29	side together side touch	
30	now <u>start OVER</u>	

R U M B A   B A S I C   A N D   B R E A K   S T E P S

Formation: Single circle
Position: Hands joined
Footwork: All start L

Music: Love Theme from "The Carpet-baggers"; Jack Hansen
Record: "Hollywood," Dance Along DAL-S1318
Rhythm: 4/4, 20 meas, qqS

MEAS	CALL	INSTRUCTIONS
	<u>sideward basic forward break</u>	<u>Sideward basic and forward break:</u> Step side L (quick), close R foot to L (quick), step side L (slow); step fwd R (quick), step back L (quick), close R foot to L (slow). Repeat.
	READY BASIC	
1	side together SIDE	

MEAS	CALL		INSTRUCTIONS
2	forward back TOGETHER		Backward break: Repeat sideward basic; then step back R, step fwd L, close R foot to L. Repeat.
3	side together SIDE		
4	backward break NOW		Back cross: Repeat sideward basic; then cross R foot behind L, step in place L, close R foot to L. Repeat.
5	side together SIDE		
6	back and TOGETHER		Forward cross: Repeat sideward basic; then cross R foot in front of L, step in place L, close R foot to L. Repeat.
7	side together SIDE		
8	back cross NOW		Side break: Repeat sideward basic, touching R foot to L on ct 4; step side R, step in place L, close R foot to L. Repeat.
9	side together SIDE		
10	back and TOGETHER		
11	side together SIDE		Note
12	forward cross NOW		Sideward basic or 1st unit starts L; 2nd unit starts R, and R foot does all break steps forward, backward, and sideward.
13	side together SIDE		
14	forward and TOGETHER		
15	side together SIDE		
16	now side BREAK		
17	side together SIDE		
18	side and TOGETHER		
19	side together SIDE		
20	now start OVER		

R U M B A
(Cuban box rhythm)

Formation: Single circle
Position: Hands joined
Footwork: All start L

Music: Magic Is the Moonlight; Memo Bernabei
Record: "Dancing On Air," Windsor WLP 3-05
Rhythm: 4/4, 42 meas, Sqq

MEAS	CALL	INSTRUCTIONS
	FORWARD BASIC	Basic step: Step fwd L (slow), close

MEAS	CALL	INSTRUCTIONS

MEAS	CALL
	READY basic step
1	FORWARD together break
2	BACK basic again
3	FORWARD together break
4	SIDEWARD break now
5	LEFT together break
6	RIGHT together break
7	LEFT together break
8	BACKWARD basic now
9	BACK together break
10	FORWARD together break
11	BACK together break
12	BASIC step now
13	FORWARD together break
14	PROGRESSIVE forward break
15	FORWARD together break
16	FORWARD together break
17	FORWARD together break
18	BASIC step now
19	FORWARD together break
20	PROGRESSIVE backward now
21	BACK together break
22	BACK together break
23	BACK together break
24	BASIC step now
25	FORWARD together break

INSTRUCTIONS

R foot to L (quick), shift weight back to L (quick). Repeat, stepping back on R.

Sideward break: Step side L (slow), close R foot to L (quick), shift weight back to L (quick); repeat, stepping to R. Repeat.

Backward basic: Step back L (slow), close R foot to L (quick), shift weight back to L (quick); repeat, stepping fwd on R. Repeat.

Progressive forward break: Step fwd L, close R foot to L, shift weight back to L; repeat, stepping fwd on R. Repeat.

Progressive backward: Step back L, close R foot to L, shift weight back to L; repeat, stepping back on R. Repeat.

Left turn in four: Dropping hands, dance 2 basic steps turning L 1 complete turn. Rejoin hands.

Stair step: Step side L, close R foot to L, shift weight back to L; step fwd R, close L foot to R, shift weight back to R. Repeat.

Backward stair step: Step side L, close R foot to L, shift weight back to L; step back R, close L foot to R, shift weight back to R. Repeat.

Repeat entire dance.

Note

All quick movements are danced with feet together; this is called "break." Slow movements are used to progress fwd, back, and sideward.

MEAS	CALL	INSTRUCTIONS
26	LEFT turn' in' four	
27	FORWARD together break	
28	BACK together break	
29	FORWARD together break	
30	BASIC step now	
31	FORWARD together break	
32	STAIR step now	
33	SIDE together break	
34	FORWARD together break	
35	SIDE together break	
36	BASIC step now	
37	FORWARD together break	
38	BACKWARD stair step	
39	SIDE together break	
40	BACK together break	
41	SIDE together break	
42	NOW start over	

R U M B A   M I X E R

Formation:	Double circle	Music:	Spanish Eyes; Joe Loss
Position:	Conversation	Record:	"Dancing Along the Hudson,"
Footwork:	Opposite (man L,		Telemark S 6400
	lady R)	Rhythm:	4/4, 8 meas, qqS

MEAS	CALL	INSTRUCTIONS
	SIDEWARD BASIC	Basic: Step side L, close R foot to L, step side L, touch R foot to L. Repeat to R.
	READY BASIC	
1	side together side touch	Arch out: Man does 1 basic step as lady, all in 1 basic step, turns R under L-R arch, then arches back,
2	now arch OUT	

161

MEAS	CALL	INSTRUCTIONS
3	now arch IN	turning L.
4	right-hand WHEEL	Wheel and spin sequence: Partners join R hands and wheel fwd 1 complete turn
5	quick quick SLOW	in 12 steps (quick quick slow). On last quick quick slow, man pushes with
6	quick quick SLOW	R hand, spinning lady 1 complete turn R to new partner.
7	now spin LADIES	
8	let's start OVER	Repeat entire dance.

R U M B A   T H R E E S O M E   M I X E R

Formation: Threesome
Position: Full-open, face-to-face, outside hands joined
Footwork: Opposite (man L, ladies R)

Music: Frenesi; Jack Hansen
Record: "Ball of the Year," Dance Along DAL-S1314
Rhythm: 4/4, 16 meas, qqS

MEAS	CALL	INSTRUCTIONS
	SIDEWARD BASIC	Basic: Step side L (quick), close R foot to L (quick), step side L (slow), touch R foot to L; repeat to R. Repeat.
	READY BASIC	
1	side close side touch	Cuban walk forward: Step fwd L (quick), fwd R (quick), fwd L (slow); repeat,
2	side close side touch	starting R; repeat, starting L.
3	side close side touch	Ladies roll in: L lady turns L and R lady R 1/2 turn toward man to cuddle
4	Cuban walk FORWARD	position while all take 1 Cuban walk unit fwd, starting R.
5	forward forward FORWARD	
6	forward forward FORWARD	Wheel right: L lady wheels fwd, R lady back for 1 complete turn in 4 meas of Cuban walk.
7	ladies roll IN	
8	now wheel RIGHT	Ladies roll out: Ladies roll out to original position in 1 basic step.
9	turn turn TURN	Change partners: All drop hands and Cuban walk (man fwd, ladies back) to
10	turn turn TURN	new partners in 3 meas.
11	quick quick SLOW	Repeat entire dance.
12	ladies roll OUT	

MEAS	CALL	INSTRUCTIONS
13	drop hands change partners	
14	forward forward FORWARD	
15	quick quick SLOW	
16	now start OVER	

M A M B O   R H Y T H M S

Origin: Although Haiti claims to be the birthplace of the mambo, it developed in this country, a product of the marriage of American swing music and the rumba rhythm. This occurred in Harlem when a group of jazz musicians decided it might be fun to have the rhythm section of a rumba band join them. Mambo music differs from all other in that the off-beat rather than the down-beat is accented.

Rhythm: The rhythm of the mambo is 4/4 time.

Tempo: The best mambo tempo is from 38 to 48 measures per minute.

Style: There is a pronounced rise and fall of the body on the basic step. As the feet break forward or back, the body is lowered. As the feet come together, the body rises. There is also a contra-body movement; as the left foot breaks forward, the left shoulder goes back. As the right foot moves back, the right shoulder moves forward.

Teaching the mambo: The mambo is best learned first in a single circle, and then in a double circle, dancing with partners in two-hand position. If the dancers add a little style to the mambo by going down on the quick movements and up on the slow movements, they will find that it is more fun. If all dancers try both the man's and lady's parts, they will find that each part has a different feeling, and they will be better dancers for having done so.

   At the conclusion of the first lesson dancers should be able to dance forward, backward, and sideward with a partner.

M A M B O   B A S I C   S T E P S

Formation:	Single circle	Music:	Mambo Pablón; Jack Hansen
Position:	Hands joined	Record:	"A Dance Is," Dance Along
Footwork:	All start L		DAL-S1322
		Rhythm:	4/4, 40 meas, qqS

MEAS	CALL	INSTRUCTIONS
	FORWARD BASIC	Basic step: Step fwd L (quick), step back R (quick), close L foot to R (slow); step back R (quick), step fwd L (quick), close R foot to L (slow). Repeat.
	READY BASIC	
1	forward back TOGETHER	

163

MEAS	CALL	INSTRUCTIONS
2	back forward TOGETHER	Side break: Step side L (quick), step in place R (quick), close L foot to R (slow); repeat to R. Repeat.
3	forward and TOGETHER	
4	side break now	Forward break: Step fwd L (quick), step back R (quick), close L foot to R (slow); step fwd R (quick), step back L (quick), close R foot to L (slow). Repeat.
5	side and TOGETHER	
6	side and TOGETHER	
7	side and TOGETHER	Back break: Step back L, step fwd R, close L foot to R; step back R, step fwd L, close R foot to L. Repeat.
8	basic step NOW	
9	forward and TOGETHER	Backward open break: Turn 1/4 L and step back L (quick), step fwd R (quick), close L foot to R (slow); turn 1/4 R and step back R (quick), step fwd L (quick), close R foot to L (slow). Repeat.
10	back and TOGETHER	
11	forward and TOGETHER	
12	forward break NOW	
13	forward and TOGETHER	Scallop: Cross L foot behind R, step in place R, close L foot to R; cross R foot behind L, step side L, close R foot to L. Repeat.
14	forward and TOGETHER	
15	forward and TOGETHER	Repeat entire dance.
16	basic step NOW	
17	forward and TOGETHER	
18	back and TOGETHER	
19	forward and TOGETHER	
20	back break NOW	
21	back and TOGETHER	
22	back and TOGETHER	
23	back and TOGETHER	
24	basic step NOW	
25	forward and TOGETHER	
26	back and TOGETHER	
27	forward and TOGETHER	

MEAS	CALL	INSTRUCTIONS
28	backward open BREAK	
29	back and TOGETHER	
30	back and TOGETHER	
31	back and TOGETHER	
32	basic step NOW	
33	forward and TOGETHER	
34	back and TOGETHER	
35	forward and TOGETHER	
36	scallop step NOW	
37	cross side TOGETHER	
38	open and TOGETHER	
39	cross side TOGETHER	
40	now basic STEP	

M A M B O

Formation: Single circle, facing in
Position: Shine
Footwork: All start L

Music: Mambo in the Moonlight; Jack Hansen
Record: "Ball of the Year," Dance Along DAL-S1314
Rhythm: 4/4, 16 meas, qqS

MEAS   CALL

INSTRUCTIONS

FORWARD BASIC

READY BASIC

Basic: Step fwd L (quick), step in place R (quick), close L foot to R (slow); step back R (quick), step in place L (quick), close R foot to L (slow). Repeat.

1 forward back TOGETHER

2 back forward TOGETHER

Right spin and back break sequence: Step fwd L, turning 1/2 turn R (quick), step fwd R, turning 1/2 to complete R turn (quick), close L foot to R (slow); step back R (quick), step in place L (quick), close R foot to L (slow). Repeat.

3 forward back TOGETHER

4 right spin' and' BREAK

5 forward spin TOGETHER

6 back and TOGETHER

Side step: Step side L (quick), step

165

MEAS	CALL	INSTRUCTIONS

MEAS	CALL
7	forward spin TOGETHER
8	now side STEP
9	side and TOGETHER
10	side and TOGETHER
11	side and TOGETHER
12	now side CROSS
13	side and CROSS
14	side and CROSS
15	side and CROSS
16	now start OVER

INSTRUCTIONS

in place R (quick), close L foot to R (slow); step side R (quick), step in place L (quick), close R foot to L (slow). Repeat.

Side cross: Step side L (quick), step in place R (quick), cross L foot over R (slow); step side R (quick), step in place L (quick), cross R foot over L (slow). Repeat.

Repeat entire dance.

M A M B O   M I X E R

Formation:	Double circle, men facing center
Position:	Closed
Footwork:	Opposite (man L, lady R)

Music:	Anything Can Happen Mambo; George Poole
Record:	"Spotlight on Dancing," Windsor WLP 3-03
Rhythm:	4/4, 8 meas, qqS

MEAS	CALL
	FORWARD BASIC
	READY BASIC
1	forward back TOGETHER
2	back forward TOGETHER
3	forward back TOGETHER
4	backward open BREAK
5	open and TOGETHER
6	open and TOGETHER
7	now loop the ladies
8	change partners and basic

INSTRUCTIONS

Basic: Step fwd L (quick), step back R (quick), close L foot to R (slow); step back R (quick), step fwd L (quick), close R foot to L (slow). Repeat.

Backward open break: Partners assume semi-open position and step back L agLOD (quick), step fwd R (quick), close L foot to R, coming into closed position (slow). Partners then open to reverse position and step back R (quick), step fwd L (quick), close R foot to L, coming into closed position (slow). Repeat meas 5.

Loop the ladies: Partners open to reverse position. As man dances 2nd unit of basic step, lady turns L under L-R arch to new partner on R.

Repeat entire dance.

MAMBO THREESOME MIXER

Formation: Threesome
Position: Full-open, face-to-face, outside hands joined
Footwork: Opposite (man L, ladies R)

Music: I Could Have Danced All Night; Jack Hansen
Record: "Hollywood," Dance Along DAL-1318
Rhythm: 4/4, 16 meas, qqS

MEAS	CALL	
	FORWARD BASIC	
	READY BASIC	
1	forward back TOGETHER	
2	back forward TOGETHER	
3	forward back TOGETHER	
4	now side BREAK	
5	side and TOGETHER	
6	side and TOGETHER	
7	side and TOGETHER	
8	now side ARCH	
9	side and ARCH	
10	let's do' it' AGAIN	
11	side and ARCH	
12	now basic STEP	
13	forward back TOGETHER	
14	back forward TOGETHER	
15	now spin LADIES	
16	change partners BASIC	

INSTRUCTIONS

Basic: Step fwd L (quick), step back R (quick), close L foot to R (slow); step back R (quick), step fwd L (quick), close R foot to L (slow). Repeat.

Side break: Step side L, step in place R, close L foot to R; step side R, step in place L, close L foot to R. Repeat.

Side arch: Repeat side break step, ladies turning L under arch on each 2nd unit.

Spin ladies: On last unit of basic, man pulls ladies' hands, spinning them once around to new partner as he progresses fwd between them to new partners.

Repeat entire dance.

CHA-CHA RHYTHMS

Origin: The provocative and colorful cha-cha comes from Cuba. This exciting rhythm is the latest development of the mambo, which in turn is an outgrowth of the rumba. The cha-cha has become one of the most popular Latin-American dances ever to invade the United States. Its international appeal may be attributed to its quick-moving pace that makes it fun and easy to perform.

Although the cha-cha resembles the rumba and mambo in that its movement is primarily in one spot, it does possess a character of its own. As with the mambo, many styles and variations of the cha-cha have been developed to suit individual preferences. For fun dancing, a "relaxed" styling that does not overemphasize body movements will make the cha-cha an entertaining dance for all.

Rhythm: Cha-cha music is written in 4/4 time.

Tempo: Slow cha-cha is from 23 to 28 measures to the minute; medium tempo is from 28 to 30, and fast cha-cha is 30 and up. The slow and medium tempos lend themselves best to ballroom dancing.

Style: As noted above, many style variations of the cha-cha are used to suit individual preferences. The same is also true of the timing.

Some dancers like to use the mambo or American approach to the cha-cha, which is to use the two slow counts first. Technically, it makes no difference whether the two slow counts come first or at the end of the measure, since the "cha-cha-cha" can begin on any beat. In this book the calls and dances are written for the American approach. In American styling, the forward rock should be made on the flat of the foot and the backward rock on the ball of the foot. On the first unit of the sideward step, the body leverage is to the left, and on the second unit to the right. (This is only on the sideward steps, not on the forward or backward movements.)

In the Cuban approach to the cha-cha, the break or "cha-cha-cha" portion comes on the second count. To do this, dancers step to the side with the left foot (slow count one), back with the right foot (slow count two), forward with the left foot (slow count three), and then cha-cha forward on counts four and one, continuing to any cha-cha step. (The rhythm is thus 1, 2, 3, 4 & 1, 2, 3, 4 & rather than 1, 2, 3 & 4, 1, 2, 3 & 4.)

Elements of Cuban styling include executing the "cha-cha-cha" portion (counts four and one) of the left and right basic cha-cha steps with the knees flexed and the steps flat-footed except for the step taken on the count "and," which is done on the ball of the foot. In doing the left cha-cha-cha, for example, the man's left shoulder and left hip are brought close together, and the weight is transferred from one foot to the other with a slight knee action.

Teaching the cha-cha: The cha-cha is learned in the same way any other dance is; however, the teacher should feel free to use whatever techniques seem appropriate. Using up-to-date music inspires added enthusiasm. Also, if the teacher allows a full measure to call a cha-cha step, the students will grasp the cha-cha faster and retain it longer. For example:

basic step do' it' now

1 2 3 4

2 2 3 4

3 2 3 4

sideward step do' it' now

168

After the first lesson, dancers should be able to dance forward, backward, and sideward with or without a partner.

Note

For ease of teaching and calling, the cha-chas in this book are altered rhythmically, each measure being treated as two measures, so that the rhythm is slow, slow, quick, quick, slow (SSqqS) rather than quick, quick, double-quick, quick (qqq'q'q).

C H A - C H A   S T Y L I N G

Formation: Single circle
Position: Hands joined
Footwork: All start L

Music: Third Man Theme; Jack Hansen
Record: "Ball of the Year," Dance Along DAL-S1314
Rhythm: 4/4, 72 meas, SSqqS

MEAS	CALL	INSTRUCTIONS
	in-place BASIC	In-place basic: Step fwd L, step back R, close L foot to R and change weight momentarily; step back R, step fwd L, close R foot to L and change weight momentarily. Repeat.
	READY BASIC	
1-2	FORWARD BACK, together ball-CHANGE	
3-4	BACK FORWARD, together ball-CHANGE	Progressive basic: Repeat in-place basic step, dancing 1 back two-step on 1st unit "cha-cha-cha" and 1 fwd two-step on 2nd unit "cha-cha-cha."
5-6	FORWARD BACK, together ball-CHANGE	Basic cross: Step fwd L, back R, back L, cross R foot in front of L, step back L; step back R, fwd L, fwd R, cross L foot behind R, step fwd R. Repeat.
7-8	BACK FORWARD, PROGRESSIVE BASIC	
9-10	FORWARD BACK, back close BACK	Dot: Repeat progressive basic step, touching toe of R foot behind L foot on 2nd slow step of 1st unit and touching toe of L foot in front of R foot on 2nd slow step of 2nd unit.
11-12	BACK FORWARD, forward close FORWARD	
13-14	FORWARD BACK, back close BACK	Tap: Tap L foot beside R (ct 4 of meas 32), step side L (ct 1), tap R foot beside L (ct 2), step side R (ct 3), tap L foot beside R (ct 4), step back L, close R foot to L, step back L; repeat, starting R and moving fwd. Repeat.
15-16	BASIC CROSS, cha-cha-CHA	
17-18	FORWARD BACK, back cross BACK	
19-20	BACK FORWARD, forward cross FORWARD	Hop cross: Hop on R foot (ct 4 of meas 40), cross L foot over R (ct 1), hop on L foot (ct 2), cross R foot over L

MEAS	CALL	INSTRUCTIONS

MEAS	CALL
21-22	FORWARD BACK, back cross BACK
23-24	BACK FORWARD, dot your TOE
25-26	FORWARD dot step, back close BACK
27-28	BACK dot step, forward close FORWARD
29-30	FORWARD dot step, back close BACK
31-32	BACK dot step, NOW tap tap
33-34	side tap side tap, cha-cha-cha tap
35-36	side tap side tap, cha-cha-cha tap
37-38	side tap side tap, cha-cha-cha tap
39-40	side tap side tap, hop cross now hop
41-42	forward hop back hop, back close back hop
43-44	back hop forward hop, forward close forward hop
45-46	forward hop back hop, back close back hop
47-48	back hop forward hop, SIDEWARD BASIC
49-50	FORWARD BACK, side together SIDE
51-52	BACK FORWARD, side together SIDE
53-54	FORWARD BACK, side together SIDE

INSTRUCTIONS

(ct 3), hop on R foot (ct 4), step back L, cross R foot over L, step back L; repeat, starting R, hopping behind supporting foot, and moving fwd. Repeat.

Sideward basic: Repeat in-place basic step, moving sideways (side, close, side) on "cha-cha-cha."

Sideward penguin: Repeat sideward basic step with arms close to sides, fingers out, and palms down, while swaying hips with steps.

Jump the rope: Hop on R foot (ct 4 of meas 64), step fwd L (ct 1), hop on L foot (ct 2), step back R (ct 3), hop on R foot (ct 4), step back L, close R foot to L, step back L, at same time swinging arms as if turning jump rope; repeat, reversing armswing, starting R, and moving fwd. Repeat.

Repeat entire dance.

MEAS	CALL	INSTRUCTIONS

MEAS	CALL
55-56	SIDEWARD PENGUIN, cha-cha-CHA
57-58	TOGETHER in place, side close SIDE
59-60	TOGETHER in place, side close SIDE
61-62	TOGETHER in place, side close SIDE
63-64	TOGETHER in place, jump the rope hop
65-66	forward hop back hop, back close back hop
67-68	back hop forward hop, forward close forward hop
69-70	forward hop back hop, back close back hop
71-72	back hop forward hop, START OVER

I N T E R M E D I A T E   C H A - C H A   S T E P S

Formation: Single circle
Position: Hands joined
Footwork: All start L

Music: My Man Cha-Cha; Memo Bernabei
Record: "Dancing On Air," Windsor WLP 3-05
Rhythm: 4/4, 64 meas, SSqqS

MEAS	CALL	INSTRUCTIONS
	basic step in place	**Basic step:** Step L in place (slow), step R beside L (slow), step side L (quick), close R foot to L (quick), step side L (slow); repeat, starting R. Repeat.
	READY BASIC	
1-2	in place in place, side close SIDE	
3-4	in place in place, side close SIDE	**Scoop:** Repeat basic step, bending knees and swinging arms down in place of 1st slow step, then straightening knees as arms come up in place of 2nd slow step.
5-6	in place in place, side close SIDE	
7-8	in place in place, SCOOP STEP	**Swivel:** Repeat basic step, turning L (ct 1-2) and R (ct 3-4) on balls of feet in place of 1st 2 slow steps, and

171

MEAS	CALL	INSTRUCTIONS

MEAS	CALL
9-10	in place in place, forward forward FORWARD
11-12	in place in place, back back BACK
13-14	in place in place, forward forward FORWARD
15-16	in place in place, SWIVEL NOW
17-18	SWIVEL SWIVEL, cha-cha-CHA
19-20	SWIVEL SWIVEL, cha-cha-CHA
21-22	SWIVEL SWIVEL, cha-cha-CHA
23-24	SWIVEL SWIVEL, CHICKEN SCRATCH
25-26	SCRATCH SCRATCH, cha-cha-CHA
27-28	SCRATCH SCRATCH, cha-cha-CHA
29-30	SCRATCH SCRATCH, cha-cha-CHA
31-32	SCRATCH SCRATCH, HEEL-TOE
33-34	HEEL-TOE, cha-cha-CHA
35-36	HEEL-TOE, cha-cha-CHA
37-38	HEEL-TOE, cha-cha-CHA
39-40	HEEL-TOE, BASIC STEP
41-42	FORWARD BACK, cha-cha-CHA
43-44	BACK FORWARD, cha-cha-CHA
45-46	FORWARD BACK, cha-cha-CHA
47-48	BACK FORWARD, MILITARY TURN
49-50	TURN AND, cha-cha-CHA

dancing "cha-cha-cha" in place.

Chicken scratch: Repeat basic step, brushing free foot back and stepping fwd on 1st 2 slow steps.

Heel-toe: Repeat basic step, placing L heel to side, then L toe by R instep in place of 1st 2 slow steps.

Military turn: Dropping hands, step fwd L (slow), turn 1/2 turn R on R foot (slow), and step fwd L,R,L toward wall (quick, quick, slow); repeat, starting R, to end facing center of circle. Repeat meas 49-52.

Military spin: Men step fwd L (slow), spin 1 full turn R on R foot (slow), and step back L,R,L (quick, quick, slow); then step back R (slow), fwd L (slow), and fwd R,L,R (quick, quick, slow). Repeat. Ladies do same step but start with 2nd unit.

Repeat entire dance.

MEAS	CALL	INSTRUCTIONS
51-52	TURN AND, cha-cha-CHA	
53-54	TURN AND, cha-cha-CHA	
55-56	NOW THE, MILITARY SPIN	
57-58	SPIN AND, cha-cha-CHA	
59-60	BACK AND, SPIN AGAIN	
61-62	SPIN AND, cha-cha-CHA	
63-64	BACK AND, START OVER	

C H A - C H A   M I X E R

Formation: Double circle
Position: Conversation
Footwork: Opposite (man L, lady R)

Music: The Cha-cha Song; Jack Hansen
Record: "A Dance Is," Dance Along
        DAL-S1322
Rhythm: 4/4, 16 meas, SSqqS

MEAS   CALL

INSTRUCTIONS

BASIC STEP

READY BASIC

Basic: Step fwd L (slow), back R (slow), close L foot to R (quick), step in place R (quick), in place L (slow); step back R (slow), fwd L (slow), close R foot to L (quick), step in place L (quick), in place R (slow). Repeat.

1-2   FORWARD BACK, cha-cha-CHA

3-4   BACK FORWARD, do it
        AGAIN

5-6   FORWARD BACK, cha-cha-CHA

7-8   OPEN BREAK, RIGHT NOW

9-10   OPEN AND, cha-cha-CHA

11-12   OPEN AND, cha-cha-CHA

13-14   GET READY, TURN NOW

15-16   CHANGE PARTNERS, START OVER

Open break: Cross L foot over R, turning 1/4 turn R (slow), step in place R, turning 1/4 turn L (slow). Close L foot to R (quick), step in place R (quick), in place L (slow). Cross R foot over L, turning 1/4 turn L (slow), step in place L, turning 1/4 turn R (slow), close R foot to L (quick), step in place R (quick), in place L (slow). Repeat, dancing 1 full individual turn, man L, lady R, on 2nd unit, so that both man and lady progress on cha-cha to new partner on R.

Repeat entire dance.

ROY'S CHA-CHA MIXER

Formation: Double circle, men facing center
Position: Conversation
Footwork: Opposite (man L, lady R)

Music: Puppet on a String; Joe Loss
Record: "Dancing Along the Hudson," Telemark S 6400
Rhythm: 4/4, 32 meas, SSqqS

MEAS	CALL
	FORWARD BASIC
	READY BASIC
1-2	FORWARD BACK, back close BACK
3-4	BACK FORWARD, forward close FORWARD
5-6	FORWARD BACK, back close BACK
7-8	SINGLE CIRCLE, ZIG-ZAG
9-10	FORWARD AND, cha-cha-CHA
11-12	BACK AND, cha-cha-CHA
13-14	FORWARD AND, cha-cha-CHA
15-16	BACK AND, clap your HANDS
17-18	PARTNER AND, now your CORNER
19-20	CLAP AND, now your PARTNER
21-22	CLAP AND, now your CORNER
23-24	RIGHT HANDS, around your PARTNER
25-26	LEFT HANDS, around your CORNER
27-28	AROUND AROUND, cha-cha-CHA
29-30	RIGHT HANDS, around your PARTNER
31-32	CONVERSATION POSITION, now start OVER

INSTRUCTIONS

Basic step and single circle sequence:
Step fwd L (slow), back R (slow), back L (quick), close R foot to L (quick), back L (slow); step back R (slow), fwd L (slow), fwd R (quick), close L foot to R (quick), fwd R (slow). Repeat, assuming L-side position on 2nd unit, then on ct 4 lady turns 1/2 turn to end L of partner. All dancers are facing in and join hands to form single circle; man's new partner is on his R.

Zig-zag: Repeat basic step, man stepping fwd as lady steps back; on next unit lady steps fwd as man steps back.

Clap: In 1 basic step, partners face and man claps lady's R hand with his L on ct 1, then turn to previous partners (ct 2-4). Man claps lady's L hand with his R (ct 1) and both turn back to new partner (ct 2-4). Repeat.

Right hands around: Man takes new partner in R forearm grip and they wheel 1 full turn R in 1st unit of basic step. Man then takes corner in L forearm grip and they wheel 1 full turn L in 2nd unit of basic step. Repeat R-hand wheel with partner, then partners take conversation position in 2nd unit of basic step.

Repeat entire dance.

THREESOME CHA-CHA

Formation:	Threesome	Music: Santa Isabel de las Lajas;
Position:	Full-open, face-to-face, outside hands joined	Jack Hansen
		Record: "Ball of the Year," Dance Along DAL-S1314
Footwork:	Opposite (man L, ladies R)	Rhythm: 4/4, 16 meas, SSqqS

MEAS   CALL

basic forward and back

READY BASIC

INSTRUCTIONS

Basic step: Step fwd L, step back R, step back L, close R foot to L, step back L; step back R, step fwd L, step fwd R, close L foot to R, step fwd R.

1-2   FORWARD BACK, back close BACK

3-4   BACK FORWARD, ROLL IN

Roll in: All dance 1 basic step, ladies rolling in to assume cuddle position on "cha-cha-cha" of 1st unit. All then dance 1st unit of basic step.

5-6   FORWARD BACK, back close BACK

7-8   BACK FORWARD, cha-cha-CHA

Roll out and arch sequence: Dancing 2nd unit of basic step, ladies roll out 1/2 turn on "cha-cha-cha" to face man. Then, in 1 basic step, ladies arch fwd under his raised arms to new partner as he dances in place.

9-10   FORWARD BACK, ROLL OUT

11-12 BACK FORWARD, forward close FORWARD

13-14 ARCH LADIES, and change PARTNERS

Repeat entire dance.

15-16 FORWARD FORWARD, START OVER

THREESOME CHA-CHA ROUTINE

Formation:	Threesome circle	Music: Mi Rival; George Poole
Position:	Shine	Record: "Spotlight on Dancing,"
Footwork:	All start L	Windsor WLP 3-02
		Rhythm: 4/4, 64 meas, SSqqS

MEAS   CALL

BASIC STEP

READY BASIC

INSTRUCTIONS

Basic step: Step fwd L, back R, back L, close R foot to L, step back L; step back R, fwd L, fwd R, close L foot to R, step fwd R.

1-2   FORWARD BACK, back close BACK

Basic cross: Step fwd L, back R, back

MEAS	CALL	INSTRUCTIONS

MEAS	CALL
3-4	BASIC CROSS, do it NOW
5-6	FORWARD BACK, back cross BACK
7-8	EAGLE STEP, do it NOW
9-10	POINT TOUCH, forward close FORWARD
11-12	FORWARD BACK, EAGLE AGAIN
13-14	POINT TOUCH, forward close FORWARD
15-16	FORWARD BACK, MILITARY cross turn
17-18	FORWARD TURN, forward cross FORWARD
19-20	FORWARD TURN, do it AGAIN
21-22	FORWARD TURN, forward cross FORWARD
23-24	CROSS OVER, PULL back hop
25-26	cross hop cross hop, dot hop STEP
27-28	BACK AND, do it again hop
29-30	cross hop cross hop, dot hop STEP
31-32	BACK AND, MILITARY SPIN
33-34	FORWARD SPIN, back close BACK
35-36	BACK FORWARD, SPIN AGAIN
37-38	FORWARD SPIN, back close BACK
39-40	BACK FORWARD, SUGAR SWITCH

INSTRUCTIONS

L, cross R foot in front of L, step back L; step back R, fwd L, fwd R, cross L foot in back of R, step fwd R.

Eagle step: Point L toe to side and extend arms, L arm down and R arm raised to make straight line through arms (ct 1); touch L toe to R and bring fingertips to chest, elbows extended (ct 2); step fwd L, close R foot to L, step fwd L. Repeat, starting R. Repeat meas 9-12.

Military cross turn: Step fwd L turning 1/2 turn R, step fwd R,L, cross R foot behind L, step fwd L; step fwd R turning 1/2 turn R, step fwd L,R, cross L foot behind R, step fwd R. Repeat.

Cross over pull back: Hop on R foot (ct 4 meas 24), cross L foot over R (ct 1), hop on L foot (ct 2), cross R foot over L (ct 3), hop on R (ct 4), dot L foot behind R (ct 1), hop on R foot (ct 2), step back on L (ct 3-4); step back R, fwd L,R, close L foot to R, step fwd R. Repeat.

Military spin: Step fwd L turning 1/2 turn R, fwd R turning 1/2 turn R, back L, close R foot to L, step back L; step back R, fwd L,R, close L foot to R, step fwd L. Repeat.

Sugar switch: Touch L toe to R instep, turn toe out and touch L heel to floor, cross L foot over R, step R foot behind L, cross L foot over R; repeat, starting R. Repeat.

Join hands: Partners join hands and take 1 basic step.

Roll in: In 1 basic step, man rolls ladies into cuddle position.

Wheel left: For 1 unit of basic cha-cha rhythm (SSqqS), man steps in place, R-hand lady fwd, and L-hand lady back to wheel 3/4 turn L. All then dance

MEAS	CALL	INSTRUCTIONS

MEAS	CALL
41-42	TOUCH HEEL, cross side CROSS
43-44	TOUCH HEEL, cross side CROSS
45-46	TOUCH HEEL, cross side CROSS
47-48	TOUCH HEEL, join hands BASIC
49-50	FORWARD BACK, back close BACK
51-52	BACK FORWARD, ROLL IN
53-54	FORWARD BACK, back close BACK
55-56	BACK FORWARD, WHEEL LEFT
57-58	STEP STEP, cha-cha-CHA
59-60	STEP STEP, WHEEL RIGHT
61-62	STEP STEP, cha-cha-CHA
63-64	spin the LADIES, and start OVER

INSTRUCTIONS

2nd unit of basic step.

Wheel right: For 1 unit of basic cha-cha rhythm, man steps in place, R-hand lady back, and L-hand lady fwd to wheel 1/2 turn R. For 2nd unit of basic cha-cha rhythm, man turns 1/4 turn R, spinning R-hand lady 1-1/4 turns and L-hand lady 3/4 turn to end beside him, facing LOD.

Repeat entire dance; on last beat stretch out arms as in eagle step for ending pose.

C O N G A   R H Y T H M S

Origin: The conga is a bit of Africa transplanted to the ballroom. The pulse-stirring rhythms of the conga drum, from which the dance derives its name, furnish an exciting interlude to the more melodious but slower-tempoed rumba music.

The history of the conga goes back many generations, probably to the west coast of Africa. However, one account states that the conga rhythm originated with African slaves brought to the West Indies. Their legs bound by heavy chains, they would walk three steps and rest. In Cuba the conga is an integral part of the annual street carnivals or comparasas. Celebrants in colorful costumes flock to Havana from all parts of the country to join in the semiritualistic parades and street dancing, which may continue for several days.

It remained for Americans to adapt the conga for the dance floor. Because of its simple basic pattern, the use of intriguing rhythm instruments, and its sociable nature, the conga soon caught the public fancy as a novelty dance. Since the conga was originally danced outdoors without partners, certain modifications have been necessary to adapt it to the ballroom. Without losing the characteristic style of Afro-Cuban dances, movements have been modified and steps confined to a smaller area.

Rhythm: Conga music is played somewhat like a fast rumba and can readily be recognized by the heavy drum beat on every fourth count. The rhythm is 4/4 time.

Tempo: The tempo of the conga is between 40 and 50 measures per minute.

Style: When the conga is danced to slower tempos dancers use a rock dance styling on each unit of the step; when it is danced to faster tempos the style becomes more like a schottische step. Instead of one, two, three, kick, it is one, two, three, hop. Thus, it is important that the tempo of the conga remain around 40 measures per minute so that the dancers may maintain the conga style.

Teaching the conga: As with other dances, conga steps are best learned in a single circle and done later with partners. By changing the record from conga music to current dance music, the teacher can change the dance from conga to rock although the dancers are doing the same steps. Doing this may lend added interest to the dance.

Dancers should kick to the side rather than backward or forward to avoid kicking those close by.

At the conclusion of the first lesson dancers should be able to dance forward, sideward, and backward in any formation, with or without a partner.

C O N G A

Formation: Single circle
Position: Hands joined
Footwork: All start L

Music: Hang on Sloopy; James Mitchell
Record: "Discotheque A Go-go,"
Hoctor HLP-4007
Rhythm: 4/4, 28 meas, qqS

MEAS	CALL	INSTRUCTIONS
	FORWARD BASIC	Basic step: Step sideward with 3 steps, L,R,L, and kick R foot fwd; repeat to R. Repeat.
	READY BASIC	
1	side together side kick	Progress forward: Step fwd L,R,L, kick R foot fwd; repeat, starting R. Repeat.
2	side together side kick	
3	side together side kick	Progress backward: Step back L,R,L, kick R foot fwd; repeat, starting R. Repeat.
4	progress forward NOW	
5	forward forward forward kick	Circle left, right: Turn 1/4 and repeat progress forward step in direction indicated. End facing center of circle.
6	forward forward forward kick	Side cross: Step side L (quick), cross R foot over L (quick), step side L (slow), kick R foot to side; repeat, starting R. Repeat.
7	forward forward forward kick	

MEAS	CALL	INSTRUCTIONS
8	progress backward NOW	Repeat entire dance.
9	back back back kick	
10	back back back kick	
11	back back back kick	
12	circle left NOW	
13	forward forward forward kick	
14	forward forward forward kick	
15	forward forward forward kick	
16	circle right NOW	
17	forward forward forward kick	
18	forward forward forward kick	
19	forward forward forward kick	
20	basic step NOW	
21	side together side kick	
22	side together side kick	
23	side together side kick	
24	side cross NOW	
25	side cross side kick	
26	side cross side kick	
27	side cross side kick	
28	now start OVER	

C O N G A   M I X E R

Formation:	Single circle	Music:	Tequila; James Mitchell
Position:	Two-hand, man facing LOD	Record:	"Discotheque A Go-go," Hoctor HLP-4007
Footwork:	Opposite (man L, lady R)	Rhythm:	4/4, 8 meas, qqS

MEAS	CALL	INSTRUCTIONS
	grand right-and-left	Basic step
	READY GRAND	Walk fwd 3 steps L,R,L; kick R diag back. Repeat, starting R. Repeat through entire dance.
1	1 2 3 kick	
2	1 2 3 kick	Grand right-and-left: Assuming full-open position, R-R cnt, walk fwd past partner in 3 steps, joining L hands with next person, kick; repeat, starting R. Repeat.
3	1 2 3 kick	
4	right-hand WHEEL	
5	1 2 3 kick	Wheel: Assume R-side position with 4th person. Wheel fwd twice around in 2 basic steps, backing up on 4th kick to join R hands with partner.
6	1 2 3 kick	
7	back right UP	
8	grand right-and-left	Repeat entire dance.

S A M B A   R H Y T H M S

Origin: The samba is a Brazilian dance with African roots. It first appeared in American ballrooms with a very bouncy style, but has since been modified to a smooth dance with an intriguing rhythm. In its original form and setting it was done much more slowly than we do it today. The unusual quality of the music is produced by the typical samba instruments (cabaca, reco-reco, chocalbo, and tambourine) above the syncopated beat of the drums.

Rhythm: Samba rhythm is unique in that the accent falls on the second beat of a 2/4 measure. Four measures are usually played to each phrase, and the dance step patterns should fall into this same phrasing. If drawn out musically the rhythm would be slow, quick, slow (according to the time elapsing after a step is made). It is the prolonging of the first beat and the sudden shift to a sixteenth note followed by a quarter note that gives the characteristic uneven samba rhythm, slow, quick, slow. For ease of calling, the rhythm count will be designated qqS.

Tempo: Less than 28 4/4 measures or 56 2/4 measures to the minute is considered slow samba; 28 to 33 4/4 measures is medium tempo, and over 33 4/4 measures is a fast samba.

Style: The exaggerated bounce of the early samba is now obsolete. The best style today has a smooth, lifting movement. The head is held still as the body moves forward, backward, sideward, like a swinging pendulum. To perform the rocking movement of the samba steps, bend the knees on count one and straighten them on count two.

A distinctive styling feature of the samba is its contra-body movement. For example, as the foot moves forward the shoulder and upper body sway slightly back, and vice versa. This is accomplished by a rapid backward shift of the shoulders immediately after the forward movement to designate the lead and, as the backward lead is accomplished, a forward shift of the shoulders. There is a natural springiness to the style resulting from the step itself, resulting in a controlled, easy undulation.

Teaching the samba: While the dancers are standing in place, have them bounce to the music. They should be able to tap, clap, and mark time with the music before trying the steps. A single circle is best for learning the steps; then progress to the two-hand and closed positions as the dancers' skill increases.

At the end of the first lesson the dancers should be able to dance forward, backward, and sideward with or without a partner.

Note

For ease of teaching and calling, the sambas in this book are considered to be in 4/4 time, each 2/4 measure becoming one 4/4 measure, so that their rhythm is quick, quick, slow (qqS) rather than double-quick, quick (q'q'q). Where a small a prefixes a numeral spelled out in capital letters, it indicates a rhythm of 1-3/4 beats, 1/4 beat, 2 beats in that measure.

S A M B A   B A S I C

Formation: Single circle
Position: Hands joined
Footwork: All start L

Music: Enjoy Yourself; Jack Hansen
Record: "A Dance Is," Dance Along
DAL-S1322
Rhythm: 4/4, 52 meas, qqS

MEAS	CALL	INSTRUCTIONS
	PENDULUM STEP	Pendulum (basic step): Step fwd L, close R foot to L, change weight momentarily; step back L, close R foot to L, change weight momentarily. Repeat.
	READY PENDULUM	
1-2	1 aTWO, 3 aFOUR	
3-4	FAVELA FORWARD, RIGHT NOW	Favela forward: Step fwd L, bring R foot behind L, draw L foot back slightly; step fwd R, bring L foot behind R, draw R foot back slightly. Repeat.
5-6	1 aTWO, 3 aFOUR	
7-8	PENDULUM STEP, RIGHT NOW	Favela backward: Step back L, bring R foot in front of L, change weight momentarily; step back R, bring L foot in front of R, change weight momentarily. Repeat.
9-10	1 aTWO, 3 aFOUR	
11-12	FAVELA BACKWARD, RIGHT NOW	

MEAS	CALL		INSTRUCTIONS
13-14	1 aTWO, 3 aFOUR		Side ball-change: Step side L, close R foot to L, changing weight momentarily; repeat to R. Repeat.
15-16	side ball-CHANGE, RIGHT NOW		
17-18	side ball-CHANGE, side ball-CHANGE		Spiral: Cross L foot in front of R (ct 1-2), step side R, changing weight momentarily (ct 3-4); cross R foot in front of L (ct 1-2), step side L, changing weight momentarily (ct 3-4). Repeat.
19-20	PENDULUM STEP, RIGHT NOW		
21-22	1 aTWO, 3 aFOUR		
23-24	1 aTWO, SPIRAL NOW		Chug: Chug 4 steps L; repeat to R.
25-26	cross aTWO, cross aTWO		Maxixe: Step L heel fwd and slide R foot to L (ct 1-2), step L toe back, slide R foot to L (ct 3-4); repeat. Repeat, starting R.
27-28	cross aTWO, PENDULUM NOW		
29-30	1 aTWO, 3 aFOUR		
31-32	1 aTWO, CHUG LEFT		Paddle left and right: In 4 steps, paddle 1 full turn to L. Repeat to R.
33-34	1 aTWO, CHUG RIGHT		
35-36	1 aTWO, PENDULUM NOW		Repeat entire dance.
37-38	1 aTWO, 3 aFOUR		
39-40	1 aTWO, 3 MAXIXE		
41-42	a1 a2, a3 a4		
43-44	a1 a2, a3 PENDULUM		
45-46	1 aTWO, 3 aFOUR		
47-48	PADDLE LEFT, AND RIGHT		
49-50	1 aTWO, NOW REVERSE		
51-52	1 aTWO, START OVER		

S A M B A   P A D D L E   M I X E R

Formation:	Single circle	Music:	Vem Vem; Jack Hansen
Position:	Hands joined	Record:	"Ball of the Year," Dance Along
Footwork:	Opposite (man L, lady R)		DAL-S1314
		Rhythm:	4/4, 16 meas, qqS

MEAS	CALL	INSTRUCTIONS

MEAS	CALL
	PENDULUM STEP
	READY PENDULUM
1-2	1 aTWO, do it AGAIN
3-4	1 aTWO, PADDLE LEFT
5-6	1 aTWO, PADDLE RIGHT
7-8	1 aTWO, PENDULUM NOW
9-10	1 aTWO, NOW ARCH
11-12	CHANGE PARTNERS, NOW CROSS
13-14	cross aTWO, cross aTWO
15-16	cross aTWO, START OVER

INSTRUCTIONS

Pendulum: Step fwd L, close R foot to L, change weight momentarily; step back on R, close L foot to R, change weight momentarily.

Paddle left: Man paddles L, lady R, for 1 complete individual turn.

Paddle right: Man paddles R, lady L for 1 complete individual turn. Partners end facing and join hands in L-R cnt.

Arch: Lady takes 1 favela step fwd under L-R arch as man dances 1 favela step fwd to lady ahead, all in 2 meas.

Cross: Assume two-hand position with new partner. Cross L foot over R, (ct 1-2), step side R and change weight momentarily (ct 3-4); cross R foot over L (ct 1-2), step side L and change weight momentarily (ct 3-4). Repeat; end facing center.

Repeat entire dance.

S A M B A   F A V E L A   M I X E R

Formation: Double circle
Position: Semi-open
Footwork: Opposite (man L, lady R)

Music: Cachita; Memo Bernabei
Record: "Dancing on Air," Windsor WLP 3-05
Rhythm: 4/4, 16 meas, qqS

MEAS	CALL
	FAVELA FORWARD
	READY FAVELA
1-2	1 aTWO, 3 aFOUR
3-4	1 aTWO, INDIVIDUAL TURN
5-6	1 aTWO, 3 aFOUR
7-8	1 aTWO, side ball-CHANGE
9-10	1 aTWO, 3 aFOUR

INSTRUCTIONS

Favela forward (basic step): Step fwd L, step R foot behind L, draw L foot back to R; repeat, starting R. Repeat.

Individual turn: Dancing favela step, man turns L, lady R, for 1 complete individual turn.

Side ball-change: Step side L (quick), step R foot beside L (quick), step in place L (slow); step side R (quick), step L foot beside R (quick), step in place R (slow). Repeat.

MEAS	CALL	INSTRUCTIONS

11-12	1 aTWO, <u>CHUG NOW</u>	Chug and change partners sequence: Partners turn to conversation position, drop hands, and chug 4 steps L. Man repeats chug to R to new partner, at same time looping original partner under L-R arch as she paddles in place.
13-14	1 aTWO, <u>CHANGE PARTNERS</u>	
15-16	1 aTWO, <u>FAVELA FORWARD</u>	

Repeat entire dance.

S A M B A   C R O S S   M I X E R

Formation: Double circle
Position: Conversation
Footwork: Opposite (man L, lady R)

Music: Celebration; Joe Loss
Record: "Dancing Along the Hudson," Telemark S 6400
Rhythm: 4/4, 8 meas, qqS

MEAS	CALL	INSTRUCTIONS
	<u>cross ball-CHANGE</u>	Cross ball-change: Step side L, cross R foot behind L, step in place L; step side R, cross L foot behind R, step in place R. Repeat.
	READY CROSS	
1	cross ball-CHANGE, cross ball-CHANGE	
2	cross ball-CHANGE, <u>chug left and right</u>	Chug left and right: Chug 4 steps L; repeat to R.
3	1 aTWO, NOW REVERSE	Favela step and arch sequence: Step fwd L, step R in front of L, pull L foot back; step fwd R, step L in back of R, pull R foot back. Repeat. Man does this in place while turning lady under L-R arch twice.
4	1 aTWO, <u>FAVELA ARCH</u>	
5	1 aTWO, 3 aFOUR	
6	1 aTWO, <u>INDIVIDUAL TURN</u>	Individual turn: In 4 favela steps, man turns L in place as lady turns R to new partner ahead.
7	1 aTWO, CHANGE PARTNERS	
8	1 aTWO, <u>cross ball-CHANGE</u>	Repeat entire dance.

S A M B A   R O L L   M I X E R
(Threesome)

Formation: Threesome
Position: Skaters'
Footwork: Opposite (man L, ladies R)

Music: Oye Negra; George Poole
Record: "Spotlight on Dancing," Windsor WLP 3-01
Rhythm: 4/4, 16 meas, qqS

184

MEAS	CALL	INSTRUCTIONS

MEAS	CALL	INSTRUCTIONS
	FAVELA FORWARD	**Favela (basic step):** Step fwd L, step R foot behind L, pull back a little with L foot; repeat, starting R. Repeat.
	READY FAVELA	
1-2	forward aTWO, 3 aFOUR	
3-4	LADIES ROLL, OUT NOW	**Ladies roll out:** Ladies roll out to face man with 2 favela steps.
5-6	1 aTWO, 3 aFOUR	
7-8	NOW CHUG, to the LEFT	**Chug left:** Chug 4 steps L; repeat to R.
9-10	1 aTWO, CHUG RIGHT	
11-12	DROP HANDS, CHANGE PARTNERS	**Change partners:** All drop hands and men dance fwd to new partners in 2 favela steps.
13-14	forward aTWO, 3 aFOUR	
15-16	NOW START, OVER AGAIN	Repeat entire dance.

T A N G O   R H Y T H M S

Origin: The tango had its beginning in Argentina, where its intensely emotional style made it known as a "love-dance." During the first part of the twentieth century, the tango became popular in the ballroom, where it was modified and refined. It was introduced to the United States as an exhibition dance about 1912, and from that time to the present has remained a favorite in both music and dance. The tango is considered one of the most perfect ballroom dances from the standpoint of stimulating music, simplicity of basic steps, ease of execution, adaptability to crowded floors, and attractiveness of style.

Rhythm: As it is currently played, the tango has four well-defined beats in each measure. The first beat is frequently preceded by a slur. For teaching purposes, each basic step is completed in two measures. The Argentine tango has a basic rhythm of slow, slow, quick, quick, draw.

Tempo: The tempo has an average of 32 measures per minute.

Style: The tango is the most highly styled of all the classic ballroom dances. It is frequently called the "dancer's dance," meaning that trained dancers find great enjoyment in dancing it and that only experienced dancers can do justice to its style. It is characterized by frequent dips and smooth, catlike movements. Dancers should take long steps and keep their knees slightly flexed in dancing the tango, as well as giving special attention to the line of balance.

Teaching the tango: Holding hands in a circle, the dancers should soon learn the special tango draw, which is always sideward. After they have learned all the steps, leave out the basic step and call at least one measure ahead. For example: SLOW SLOW, cross step NOW. Remember that there is no weight change on the fourth count; hold, touch, and draw indicate no transfer of weight.

Once dancers have progressed to the closed position, they should have plenty of free practice time, with the teacher giving individual help as needed to master the styling.

At the conclusion of the first lesson dancers should be able to keep the tango rhythm while dancing sideward, forward, and backward with a partner and taking either the leader's or follower's part.

T A N G O
(Basic Argentine rhythm)

Formation: Single circle
Position: Hands joined
Footwork: All start L

Music: Tango du Rita; Jack Hansen
Record: "A Dance Is," Dance Along
DAL-S1322
Rhythm: 4/4, 44 meas, SSqqS

MEAS	CALL	INSTRUCTIONS
	CONVERSATION DRAW	Conversation draw: Step side L (slow), cross R foot over L (slow), close L foot to R (quick), side R (quick), draw L foot to R (slow). Repeat.
	READY GO	
1-2	SIDE CROSS, together side DRAW	
3-4	SIDE CROSS, double cross NOW	Double cross: Step side L, cross R foot over L, cross L foot over R, step side R, draw L foot to R. Repeat.
5-6	SIDE CROSS, cross side DRAW	Forward box: Step side L, cross R foot over L, step fwd L, step side R, draw L foot to R. Repeat.
7-8	SIDE CROSS, CONVERSATION DRAW	
9-10	SIDE CROSS, together side DRAW	Backward box: Step side L, cross R foot over L, step back L, step side R, draw L foot to R. Repeat.
11-12	SIDE CROSS, forward box NOW	Cross point: Step side L, cross R foot over L, step side L, cross R foot behind L, point L foot to side. Repeat.
13-14	SIDE CROSS, forward side DRAW	
15-16	SIDE CROSS, backward box NOW	Forward basic: Step fwd L (slow), R (slow), L (quick), step side R (quick), draw L foot to R (slow). Repeat.
17-18	SIDE CROSS, back side DRAW	Backward basic: Step back L,R,L, step side R, draw L foot to R. Repeat.
19-20	SIDE CROSS, cross point NOW	Forward rock: Step fwd L, back R, fwd L, step side R, draw L foot to R. Repeat.
21-22	SIDE FORWARD, side back POINT	Backward rock: Step back L, fwd R, back L, step side R, draw L foot to R. Repeat.

MEAS	CALL	INSTRUCTIONS
23-24	SIDE CROSS, <u>forward basic</u> NOW	Corte: Step and dip back L, fwd R,L, side R, draw L foot to R. Repeat.
25-26	FORWARD FORWARD, forward side DRAW	Repeat entire dance.
27-28	FORWARD FORWARD, <u>backward basic</u> NOW	
29-30	BACK BACK, back side DRAW	
31-32	BACK BACK, <u>forward rock</u> NOW	
33-34	FORWARD BACK, forward side DRAW	
35-36	FORWARD BACK, <u>backward rock</u> NOW	
37-38	BACK FORWARD, back side DRAW	
39-40	BACK FORWARD, <u>CORTE</u> BACK	
41-42	BACK FORWARD, forward side DRAW	
43-44	BACK FORWARD, <u>START OVER</u>	

T A N G O   M I X E R

Formation:	Double circle	Music:	Jealousy; Memo Bernabei
Position:	Conversation	Record:	"Dancing On Air," Windsor
Footwork:	Opposite (man L, lady R)		WLP 3-05
		Rhythm:	4/4, 8 meas, SSqqS

MEAS	CALL	INSTRUCTIONS
	CORTE BACK	Corte: Step and dip back L, step fwd R,L, step side R, draw L foot to R. Repeat.
	READY <u>CORTE</u>	
1-2	BACK FORWARD, <u>CORTE AGAIN</u>	Semi-open basic: Both face center of circle and step fwd L,R,L; face partner and step side R; draw L foot to R while assuming L-side position.
3-4	BACK FORWARD, <u>semi-open BASIC</u>	
5-6	FORWARD FORWARD, now let's <u>ARCH</u>	Arch: Man does 1 basic step fwd, arching lady under L-R arch on 1st step. Lady turns 1 full turn R going back as

MEAS	CALL	INSTRUCTIONS

| 7-8 | CHANGE PARTNERS, NOW CORTE | man moves ahead on outside of circle to new partner. |

Repeat entire dance.

TANGO MIXER

Formation: Single circle
Position: Closed
Footwork: Opposite (man L, lady R)

Music: Inspiration; Jack Hansen
Record: "A Dance Is," Dance Along DAL-S1322
Rhythm: 4/4, 16 meas, SSqqS

MEAS	CALL	INSTRUCTIONS

FORWARD BASIC

READY FORWARD

Basic step: Step fwd L,R,L (slow, slow, quick), step side R (quick), draw L foot to R (slow).

| 1-2 | FORWARD FORWARD, basic left TURN | Basic left turn: Assume semi-open position and step toward center of circle L,R; turn 1/2 turn L while stepping back L (quick) and side R (quick), draw L foot to R (slow). Repeat, dancing toward wall. |

| 3-4 | FORWARD FORWARD, repeat left TURN | |

| 5-6 | FORWARD FORWARD, el sharon NOW | El sharon: Assume closed position and step fwd L (slow), cross R foot over L to R-side position (slow), step fwd L to closed position (quick), step side R (quick), draw L foot to R (slow). |

| 7-8 | FORWARD CROSS, do it AGAIN | |

| 9-10 | FORWARD CROSS, basic right TURN | Basic right turn: Assume semi-open position and step toward center of circle L,R; turn 1/2 turn R while stepping back L and side R, draw R foot to L. Repeat, dancing toward wall. |

| 11-12 | FORWARD FORWARD, repeat right TURN | |

| 13-14 | FORWARD FORWARD, change partners NOW | Change partners: As man dances 1 basic step fwd, lady turns R under L-R arch on inside of circle to new partner. |

| 15-16 | FORWARD FORWARD, now basic STEP | |

Repeat entire dance.

T A N G O   T H R E E S O M E   M I X E R

Formation:	Threesome
Position:	Full-open, face-to-face, outside hands joined
Footwork:	Opposite (man L, ladies R)

Music:	Noche de Amor; Jack Hansen
Record:	"Ball of the Year," Dance Along DAL-S1314
Rhythm:	4/4, 8 meas, SSqqS

MEAS	CALL	INSTRUCTIONS
	CORTE BACK	Corte: Step and dip back L (slow), step fwd R,L (slow, quick), step side R (quick), draw L foot to R (slow).
	READY CORTE	
1-2	BACK FORWARD, forward side DRAW	Walk to center: Step fwd L,R, step side L, side R, draw L foot to R.
3-4	BACK FORWARD, now walk to center	Change partners: Step fwd L,R,L, step side R, draw L foot to R as lady arches under man's arm to new partner.
5-6	FORWARD FORWARD, now change PARTNERS	Repeat entire dance.
7-8	FORWARD FORWARD, now start OVER	

B O S S A   N O V A   R H Y T H M S

Origin: The bossa nova was recently introduced to the United States by a group of American musicians who heard it played in Brazil. Bossa nova, translated into English, means "the new beat." In its faster tempo it closely resembles the samba, while the slower beat is more like that of the rumba. However, there is a subtle difference of rhythm that distinguishes the bossa nova from both samba and rumba. The characteristic features of the bossa nova are light melodic lines and an overall lightness and ease of expression.

The authentic bossa nova requires several specific percussion instruments. One of these is the beaded cabaso, somewhat like a gourd filled with seeds or beads to be shaken. Its sound is a little lighter than that of maracas. Another is the tubos shaker, which is a wooden tube, often of bamboo, filled with beads or pellets. A triangle, sounded by hitting from the inside and immediately deadening, is also used on certain accents. This definite accentuation is another characteristic distinguishing the bossa nova from the samba. The guitar is also important in the bossa nova.

Rhythm: The bossa nova is written in 4/4 time.

Tempo: The best tempo is 42 to 48 measures per minute.

Style: The bossa nova has a syncopated styling with a heavy bouncing of the body. The body goes up on count one and down on count two, up on count three and down on count four.

Teaching the bossa nova: When learning the bossa nova, the dancer should first listen to the music then bend and straighten his knees in time with the music. After the tempo and rhythm are mastered, the feet may then move into the steps as the body maintains the bounce. The bounce is the distinguishing factor, and sets the bossa nova apart from all other dances.

B O S S A   N O V A   H E S I T A T I O N   R H Y T H M   M I X E R

Formation: Double circle, men facing center
Position: Closed
Footwork: Opposite (man L, lady R)

Music: The Sweetest Sounds; Jack Hansen
Record: "Sweet and Gentle," Dance Along DAL-1320
Rhythm: 4/4, 8 meas, SS

MEAS	CALL	INSTRUCTIONS
	SIDEWARD BASIC	Sideward basic: Step side L, touch R foot beside L, step side R, touch L foot beside R. Repeat.
	READY SIDE	
1	side touch side touch	Open break: Step side L, touch R to L. Man then turns 1/4 turn R, lady 1/4 turn L to assume full-open position, L-R cnt, while stepping to side away from partner and touching free foot beside supporting foot. Both step-touch together, then away; repeat.
2	side touch open break	
3	side touch open touch	
4	together touch open touch	
5	together touch FLIRTATION	Flirtation: Maintaining L-R cnt and in 1 step-touch, man and lady come together, each drawing free foot in front of supporting foot to assume back-to-back position and look over shoulder at partner; then take 1 step-touch away from partner, drawing free heel in front of supporting foot to end facing partner. Repeat meas 6.
6	back'-to'-back face'-to'-face	
7	back'-to'-back ladies arch	
8	change partners now basic	

Ladies arch: Man dances 1 sideward basic step as lady turns R under L-R arch to new partner on R in 1 fwd basic step.

Repeat entire dance.

B O S S A   N O V A   M I X E R
(Two-step and hesitation rhythm)

Formation: Double circle, man facing center
Position: Two-hand

Music: More; Jack Hansen
Record: "Sweet and Gentle," Dance Along DAL-1320

Footwork: Opposite (man L,
            lady R)

Rhythm: 4/4, 16 meas, qqS, SS

MEAS	CALL		INSTRUCTIONS

SIDEWARD BASIC

READY <u>SIDE</u>

Basic: Step side L, close R foot to L, step side L, place R heel in front of L foot. Repeat to R.

1	side close side heel
2	side close side heel
3	side close side heel
4	now let's <u>CHARLESTON</u>

Charleston: Step fwd L into R-side position, kick R foot fwd, step back R, touch L foot to R. Repeat in L-side position, then step back to assume full-open position, L-R cnt. End facing LOD, arms extended.

5	FORWARD KICK
6	BACK TOUCH
7	FORWARD KICK
8	<u>OPEN BASIC</u>

Open basic: In 1 basic step, slide together and bump hips, looking at partner and snapping fingers. Men then move away from partner progressing diag fwd. Repeat, sliding in behind lady ahead of partner. Repeat 2 more times out and in to 4th lady.

9	side close side snap
10	men move AHEAD
11	side close side snap
12	men move AHEAD

Repeat entire dance.

<u>Suggestions</u>

13	side close side snap
14	men move AHEAD
15	keep this GIRL
16	and <u>start OVER</u>

Progressing 1 lady instead of 4 may be better for beginners. Men may also go back to new partner.

B O S S A   N O V A   T H R E E S O M E   M I X E R

Formation: Threesome
Position: Full-open
Footwork: All start L

Music: The Girl from Ipanema; Jack
         Hansen
Record: "Sweet and Gentle," Dance
         Along DAL-1320
Rhythm: 4/4, 8 meas, SS, qqqq, qqS

MEAS   CALL

INSTRUCTIONS

FORWARD TOUCH

Basic: Step fwd L, touch R foot to L, step back R, touch L foot to R. Repeat.

191

MEAS	CALL	INSTRUCTIONS

READY FORWARD

Cross: Step side L, cross R foot over L. Step side L, cross R foot behind L, step side L, cross R foot over L, step side L, touch R foot to L. Repeat to R, crossing back first.

1	forward touch back touch	
2	forward touch now cross	

Change partners: All drop hands and man two-steps fwd between ladies to new partners in 2 two-steps while ladies take 2 basic steps in place.

3	side forward side back	
4	side forward REVERSE	
5	side back side forward	

Repeat entire dance.

6	drop hands change partners
7	forward close FORWARD
8	now start OVER

MERENGUE RHYTHMS

Origin: The merengue is the national social dance of the Dominican Republic, and has acquired a high place among the perennial ballroom dances. It was created for one of the Republic's rulers, who had a wooden leg. There is also a Haitian merengue and a Puerto Rican merengue.

The merengue is an easy and colorful dance. After listening to the music a person immediately recognizes its Caribbean style. The music, as for most of the dances of the Caribbean, is of Latin origin and is lively and cheerful.

Rhythm: The music resembles a march, its time signature being 2/4 and the accent coming on every beat of the music. The step pattern is the simplest of all Latin American dances--step, close, step, close. The dance pattern follows the music's even beat, with a definite step on each beat of the measure in regular march time, and is danced quick, quick, quick, quick.

Tempo: Merengue music is played from 58 to 64 measures per minute.

Style: The merengue has a unique style. In the basic step, a slight forward bend or dip is taken on the side step. The body comes back to normal position after the side step is taken, and the feet return to closed position. Whether the step is taken forward, sideward, or backward, this slight bend or dip is used all the time.

This style resembles a man with a wooden right leg dragging it sideward as he moves to the left. No matter what the direction of movement, the following foot never passes the leading foot. When dancing the sideward steps the body leverage is to the left for the man and to the right for the lady, and the body is often pushed sideward with the heel of the right foot as the toe turns out. The body should move smoothly and the dancer should avoid combining slow and quick chassé steps.

Teaching the merengue: Following are suggestions to simplify learning

the merengue:
- Take small steps with the upper ribcage bent forward.
- Men keep the right leg stiff, or do not bend it much, while ladies keep the left leg stiff.
- There is motion in the left hip only for the lady and in the right hip only for the man.
- Head styling is from side to side.

At the end of the first lesson the dancers should be able to dance forward, backward, and sideward with or without a partner.

MERENGUE MIXER

Formation: Double circle
Position: Conversation
Footwork: Opposite (man L, lady R)

Music: Por un Pelito; Jack Hansen
Record: "A Dance Is," Dance Along DAL-S1322
Rhythm: 4/4, 8 meas, qqqqqqqq

MEAS	CALL	INSTRUCTIONS
	chassé and back away	Chassé: Step side L, close R foot to L. Repeat.
	READY CHASSÉ	
1	side close back away	Back away: Partners drop hands and step back L, close R foot to L; then step fwd L, close R foot to L, reassuming conversation position.
2	back together CHASSÉ	
3	side close heel check	Heel check: Raise R foot high and cross it over L (ct 1); touch heel to floor (ct 2). Bring R foot back to place in same way (ct 3-4).
4	up down stair step	
5	side close forward close	Stair step: Step side L, close R foot to L, step fwd L, close R foot to L; step back L, close R foot to L, step fwd L, close R foot to L.
6	back close CHASSÉ	
7	side close change partners	
8	side close start over	Chassé and change partners sequence: Partners chassé 4 ct L (side, close, side, touch), then man loops lady L 1 full turn in place under L-R arch in 3 steps (L,R,L, touch) as he continues to chassé in LOD to new partner.

Repeat entire dance.

ROCK RHYTHMS

Origin: Rock dances developed spontaneously from variations created by dancers performing other dances. Some were built around pantomime--the dance leader would call out the name of a bird or animal and the dancers would create new movements to imitate it. Rock dances have since become a means of individual expression for the dancer.

In the past dances were generally created to match music, but rock dances are frequently created and given a name first; then recording artists put out a record to go with the dance. Sometimes the orchestra even follows the dancer. The musician may be inspired to revise music to complement the dancer.

Rhythm: Most rock music is written in 4/4 time.

Tempo: Fast rock is 50 to 70 measures per minute. Slow is from 24 to 34 measures per minute.

Style: Dancers do not touch when doing a fast rock dance to avoid inhibiting each other's movements. This is why the individual position is called shine or challenge position because a person can shine or show off; it is a challenge to see who can create the best variations and movements. The form is entirely up to each dancer. However, the style for slow rock music is fairly standard-- dancers take a tightly closed position and keep the legs fairly stiff while rocking back and forth.

One recent fast rock dance fad shows a trend back to contact between partners. Dancers leave their feet in one spot and move their hips from side to side; partners bump hips once per measure or as desired. This dance's name, appropriately, is the bump.

Teaching rock dances: When teaching rock dances, choose music that is rhythmical, exciting, and appealing. Learn short routines first, phrasing the step pattern with the music and using a variety of steps and styles. Do not dance the same sequence to every tune. After learning set routines from the book, try creating original steps that phrase with the latest tunes.

Have fun!

C I N N A M O N   C I D E R

Formation:	Lines, 1 of men, 1 of ladies, facing	Music:	Playground in My Mind; Clint Holmes
Position:	Two-hand	Record:	Epic 5-10891
Footwork:	Opposite (man L, lady R)	Rhythm:	4/4, 4 meas

MEAS	CALL	INSTRUCTIONS
	READY SWAY	Sway: Sway the body L,R,L,R.
1	left right now kick	Kick: Step side L, kick R foot over L. Step side R, kick L foot over R.
2	step kick kick cross	Kick cross: Partners assume full-open position, R-L cnt, and step side L (ct 1), kick R foot over L (ct 2), cross R foot over L (ct 3), and step back L (ct 4), turning 1/2 turn to end back to back. Change hands to L-R cnt and repeat, starting R, to end face to face.
3	step kick cross back	
4	step kick sway now	

Repeat entire dance.

C O L D   S W E A T

Formation: Line
Position: Shine
Footwork: All start L

Music: Love Will Keep Us Together;
           The Captain and Tennille
Record: A & M Records 1672-S
Rhythm: 4/4, 3 meas

MEAS	CALL	INSTRUCTIONS
	kick ball-CHANGE	Kick ball-change: Kick L foot fwd, close feet and change weight momentarily, L,R. Repeat, crossing R foot over L on 4th ct.
	READY KICK	
1	kick ball'-change' point' and' cross	Point and cross: Point to L side (ct 1), point L foot over R (ct 2).
2	point' and' swivel back' and' stomp	Swivel back: Step back R, swiveling L; step back L, swiveling R.
3	step stomp start over	Stomp: Stomp R foot fwd, close R foot to L; stomp L foot fwd while turning 1/4 turn R, close L foot to R.

Repeat entire dance.

T H E   C O N T I N E N T A L

Formation: Double circle
Position: Shine
Footwork: All start L

Music: I Came, I Saw, I Conga'd;
           Sidney Thompson
Record: Yates Y-731
Rhythm: 4/4, 4 meas

MEAS	CALL	INSTRUCTIONS
	step swing and grapevine	Step swing: Step L, swing R foot across L, step R, swing L foot across R. Repeat.
	READY AND	
1	step swing step swing	Grapevine: Step side L (ct 1), cross R foot behind L (ct 2), step side L and pivot 1/2 turn L (ct 3), kick R foot fwd (ct 4).
2	step swing GRAPEVINE	
3	turn and go back	Back: Walk back, R,L,R, and swing L foot across R.
4	back back step swing	

Repeat entire dance.

Variations

Dancers may snap fingers on step-swing
and clap hands on turn kick. With
partners facing, dance routine through
twice. This brings dancers back to
place. For mixer, dancers clap neigh-
bor's hands on turn and move to new
partner on R after dancing routine
through twice.

C O N T I N E N T A L   H U S T L E

Formation: Double circle   Music: South of the Border; Herb
Position: Shine   Alpert's Tijuana Brass
Footwork: All start R   Record: A & M Records 755
                                     Rhythm: 4/4, 20 meas

MEAS   CALL   INSTRUCTIONS

        WALK BACKWARD, READY WALK   Walk (basic step): Take 2 slow steps
                                         back away from partner, then 2 quick
  1-2   BACK BACK, back together   steps, then 1 slow step; repeat, start-
        FORWARD   ing L and moving fwd. Repeat meas 1-4.

  3-4   FORWARD FORWARD, forward   Turn: Make 2 complete individual turns,
        together BACK   first to R and then to L, each in 1 unit
                                         of basic step.
  5-6   BACK BACK, back together
        FORWARD   Jump: Jump fwd on balls of both feet
                                         (ct 1-2) and then drop weight to heels
  7-8   FORWARD FORWARD, right turn   (ct 3-4). Jump back on balls of both
        NOW   feet (ct 1-2) and then drop weight to
                                         heels (ct 3-4).
  9-10 TURN TURN, left turn NOW
                                         Heel clicks: Click heels together twice,
 11-12 TURN TURN, jump forward   placing weight on L foot after 2nd click.
        and back
                                         Points and kick: For 2 ct each, point
 13-14 FORWARD DROP, HEEL CLICKS   R toe fwd twice, back twice, fwd once,
                                         back once, side once, and kick R foot
 15-16 points and KICK, FRONT FRONT   across L.

 17-18 BACK BACK, FRONT BACK   Change partners: Step side R to face
                                         new partner, closing L foot to R.
 19-20 CHANGE PARTNERS, START OVER
                                         Repeat entire dance.

ELEPHANT WALK

Formation:	Line, or single or double circle	
Position:	Shine	
Footwork:	All start R	

Music: Up Cherry Street; Herb Alpert's Tijuana Brass
Record: A & M Records 755
Rhythm: 4/4, 8 meas

MEAS	CALL
	READY POINT
1	out in left foot
2	out in right back
3	back and left back
4	back and lift knee
5	up down left knee
6	up down kick now
7	kick step jump now
8	jump' and' clap start over

INSTRUCTIONS

Point: Point R foot to side, touch R foot to L; point R foot to side, close R foot to L. Repeat to L.

Right back: Point R foot back, touch R foot to L; point R foot back, close R foot to L. Repeat with L.

Lift knee: Touch R knee to L elbow, point R foot to side; touch R knee to L elbow, close R foot to L. Repeat with L knee.

Kick: Kick R foot over L, close R foot to L; kick L foot over R, close L foot to R.

Jump: Jump side R. Clap hands on ct 3.

Repeat entire dance.

Variation

This dance can be done as mixer with partners in two-hand position. On jump, each jumps to new partner.

SNOOPY

Formation:	Line
Position:	Shine
Footwork:	All start L

Music: Rock the Boat; Hues Corporation
Record: RCA Victor APBO-0232
Rhythm: 4/4, 4 meas

MEAS	CALL
	SIDEWARD POINT
	READY POINT
1	point together point together

INSTRUCTIONS

Point: Point L to side, close L foot to R. Repeat to R, then again to L.

Kick ball-change: Kick R, step R, change weight momentarily.

Kick cross: Step fwd R (ct 1), kick

MEAS	CALL	INSTRUCTIONS
2	kick' ball'-change kick cross	and cross L foot over R (ct 2-3), step back R (ct 4). Step back L (ct 1), kick and point R foot over L (ct 2-3), step fwd R, turn 1/4 turn R (ct 4).
3	forward cross back' 2' 3	
4	kick ball'-change' turn point	Repeat entire dance.

FOLK DANCING

INTRODUCTION

The roots of folk dancing, a peculiar and tireless breed of dance, reach deep into the past. Its origin is elemental, springing from the everyday lives of nameless common people in every land. Folk dance has been preserved and perpetuated relatively unchanged, taking on the characteristics of each particular race and condition. An expression of joy and sorrow, folk dance has been influenced by Greek and barbarian, Jew and gentile, sinner and saint. It is a building, healing, ennobling force which can unite all mankind. Its language is universal. It is the timeless urge of nameless masses seeking expression.

Folk dancing provides an opportunity to learn foreign customs and beliefs, as well as the history and geography of different countries. It reveals enthusiasms that have evolved over the years as civilizations have developed. It brings additional understanding of the backgrounds of other peoples and increases our appreciation for our own heritage.

The language of folk dance is rhythm, which not only allows different peoples to forget their differences, but bridges most barriers and unites people on common ground. Watching dancers from any country can arouse an intense curiosity about them, their history, and their distinctive culture. To participate in their dancing can strengthen bonds of brotherhood with them.

Authenticity in a folk dance can be a rich and wonderful experience, or it can result in a rigid, lifeless formula. A dance is merely the framework for an expression of spirit. To dance as a people dance is to capture their spirit; to perform authentic folk dances thus produces an expression of this spirit. Therefore, when teaching, refrain from rearranging an authentic folk dance step. Instead, devote attention to the rhythm and styling of a dance. These are the most difficult aspects of folk dance.

Following is an explanation of the folk dance movement patterns; then the dances are presented, arranged alphabetically according to their country of origin.

FOLK DANCE MOVEMENT PATTERNS

Folk dances are composed of recurring patterns of positions and movements. Although originally most of these patterns were learned by example and demonstration rather than by the spoken or written word, it is convenient to refer to these patterns by name in order to clarify the description of the dances. The following description of step patterns should therefore be helpful.

The fundamental forms of movement are the walk, run, jump, hop, leap, gallop, slide, and skip. The first five are even rhythms while the last three are uneven rhythms.

EVEN RHYTHMS

Walk: An alternate transfer of weight from one foot to the other, during which one foot remains in contact with the floor.

Run: A rapid alternate transfer of weight from one foot to the other with a slight elevation.

Jump: A two-foot pattern which may be performed in one of three ways:
(1) Push off the floor with both feet and land on both feet.
(2) Push off the floor with both feet and land on one foot.
(3) Push off the floor with one foot and land on both feet.

Hop: A one-foot pattern performed by pushing off the floor with one foot and landing on the same foot.

Leap: An extended run with both feet off the floor momentarily, performed by pushing off with one foot and landing on the opposite foot.

UNEVEN RHYTHMS

Gallop: A combination of a step and a leap in a series of long-short rhythms.

Slide: A combination of a step and a leap in a series of long-short rhythms. It is smoother than a gallop and is always done in a sideward direction.

Skip: A combination of a step and a hop performed to a series of long-short rhythms.

STEP PATTERNS

The common folk dance steps are as follows.

Balance: To balance toward partner, step fwd on R, touch L to R. Step away from partner on L, touch R to L.

Buzz step: In square dance swing position, step R, push with L; repeat while turning.

Grapevine: Step side R, step L behind R, step side R, step L in front of R.

Polka: Hop L, step R, close L to R, step R. Repeat, starting on other foot. (Hop, step, close, step.)

Heel-toe polka: Hop on R, extend L heel to L side. Hop on R and place L toe by R heel, then polka to the L starting on R foot. Repeat, extending R foot to side. (Heel-toe, hop, step, close, step.)

Push-step or chug: Step to the R. Place weight on L toe momentarily, step sideward to R, bending R knee slightly. Bring L toe to side of R foot, and repeat.

Schottische: Step fwd with R foot; almost close L to R; step R fwd, hop R; swing L knee slightly fwd on hop. Repeat on L foot. (Step, step, step, hop.)

Step-hop: Step L and hop on L. Step R and hop on R. (Step, hop, step, hop.)

Two-step: Step fwd R, close L to R, step fwd R and hold (pause). (Step, close, step, hold.) Repeat, starting on other foot.

Waltz (progressive): Step fwd L, sideward R, close L to R. Step fwd R, sideward L, close R to L.

THE DANCES

DOUDLEBSKA POLKA
(Czechoslovakian)

Formation: Mass (couples anywhere)
Position: Closed or shoulder-waist
Footwork: Opposite (man L, lady R)

Music: Doudlebska Polka
Record: Folk Dancer MH-3016
Rhythm: 2/4, 48 meas

MEAS	CALL
	polka around the floor READY POLKA
1-4	1, 2, 3, 4
5-8	5, 6, 7, 8
9-12	9, 10, 11, 12
13-16	13, 14, 15, star' and' sing
17-20	1, 2, 3, 4
21-24	5, 6, 7, 8
25-28	9, 10, 11, 12
29-32	13, 14, men clap, ladies around
33-36	1, 2, 3, 4
37-40	5, 6, 7, 8
41-44	9, 10, 11, 12
45-48	13, 14, 15, start over

INSTRUCTIONS

Polka: Take 16 polkas anywhere on floor, turning cw, progressing ccw.

Star: Men star L in several circles, man's arm around lady's waist. Polka in circle and sing tra-la-la to tune.

Clap: Each man faces center, claps own hands twice on ct 1, and on ct 2 claps hand of men on each side once, as ladies circle cw around circle of men with 16 polka steps. Man turns around and polkas with lady behind him, getting new partner.

Repeat entire dance, moving anywhere on floor.

LITTLE MAN IN A FIX
(Danish)

Formation: 2 couples, mass (see
  INSTRUCTIONS below)
Position: Men hook L elbows
Footwork: All start R

Music: Little Man in a Fix
Record: Folk Dancer MH-1054
Rhythm: 3/4, 28 meas

MEAS	CALL	INSTRUCTIONS

MEAS	CALL
	all run forward
	ready, WHEEL
1-4	1 2 3, 4 5 6, 7 8 9,
	open NOW
5-8	1 2 3, 4 5 6, 7 8 9,
	ladies UNDER
9-12	1 2 3, 4 5 6, 7 8 9,
	paddle NOW
13-16	1 2 3, 4 5 6, 7 8 9,
	now WALTZ
17-28	1 2 3, 2 2 3,
	3 2 3, 4 2 3,
	5 2 3, 6 2 3,
	7 2 3, 8 2 3,
	9 2 3, 10 2 3,
	11 2 3, now WHEEL

INSTRUCTIONS

Formation

Sets of 2 couples standing side by side in single line and facing opposite directions. Men hook L elbows, put R arms around partners' backs; ladies place L hands on men's R shoulders.

Wheel: All run fwd 12 steps.

Open: Men and ladies join hands and stretch into line in 12 running steps.

Ladies under: In 12 steps, men run in place and raise joined L hands high to swing partners around in front of them and under arch formed by their joined hands. Each lady, retaining grasp of partner's hand, passes and turns toward partner to join R hands with other lady, making low 8-hand star.

Paddle: Dancers lean away from center with R foot fwd and paddle L 12 counts. Men drop hands and take closed dance position with partners.

Waltz: Couples waltz 12 measures; man then hooks elbows with nearest man.

Repeat entire dance.

S E V E N   J U M P S
(Danish)

Formation: Single circle
Position: Hands joined
Footwork: All start L

Music: Seven Jumps
Record: RCA Victor 41-6172
Rhythm: 4/4

MEAS	CALL
	step' on' L hop' on' L
	READY HOP

INSTRUCTIONS

Chorus

Hop: Hop 7 hops to L then jump once. Repeat to R.

Chorus

MEAS	CALL	INSTRUCTIONS

MEAS	CALL
1-2	1 hop 2 hop, 3 hop 4 hop
3-4	5 hop 6 hop, 7 hop 8 jump
5-6	right hop, 2 hop, 3 hop 4 hop
7-8	5 hop 6 hop, 7 hop right foot

Verse

right foot up now

right foot down' and' chorus

INSTRUCTIONS

Verse

Right foot up: Place hands on hips and raise R knee. Do not place foot on floor until 2nd note.

Left foot up: Repeat above, then add L foot.

Right knee down: Repeat all above, then kneel on R knee.

Left knee down: Repeat all above, then kneel on L knee.

Right elbow down: Repeat all above then place R elbow on floor.

Left elbow down: Repeat all above, then place L elbow on floor.

Head down: Repeat all above and place head on floor.
Finish dance with final chorus.

Breakdown of Actions

Calls for these actions are as the calls given above for R foot. Rhythm is uncountable. Repeat chorus between each part. Continue through until all parts of the body are used, then finish with chorus.

R foot up

R foot up, L foot up

R foot up, L foot up, R knee down

R foot up, L foot up, R knee down, L knee down

R foot up, L foot up, R knee down, L knee down, R elbow down

R foot up, L foot up, R knee down, L knee down, R elbow down, L elbow down

R foot up, L foot up, R knee down, L knee down, R elbow down, L elbow down, head down

203

GREENSLEEVES
(English)

Formation:	Double circle in groups of two couples, both facing ccw and designated as no. 1 and no. 2
Position:	Full-open, facing LOD
Footwork:	All start L

Music:	Greensleeves
Record:	RCA Victor EPA 414
Rhythm:	4/4, 12 meas

MEAS	CALL	INSTRUCTIONS
	WALK FORWARD READY WALK	Walk: All walk briskly fwd 16 steps.
1	1 2 3 4	Right-hand star: Couple no. 1 turns back to face no. 2, all taking R hand of opposite partner for R-hand star and walking 8 steps cw.
2	5 6 7 8	
3	9 10 11 12	Left-hand star: All turn 1/2 turn R and change to L-hand star for 8 steps ccw. On last step, couple no. 1 turns fwd taking original position.
4	13 14 right'-hand' star	
5	1 2 3 4	
6	5 6 left'-hand' star	Arch: Couple no. 2 forms arch with inside hands, walks fwd over no. 1, who moves back, all with 4 steps. Repeat with couple no. 1 forming arch for no. 2. Repeat meas 9-10. (This figure is often called turning the sleeves inside out.)
7	1 2 3 4	
8	5 6 arch now	
9	1 2 3 change	
10	1 2 3 change	
11	1 2 3 change	Repeat entire dance.
12	1 2 start over	

OSLO WALTZ
(English)

Also known as the "good-night" waltz, the Oslo waltz is often used as the final number of a program, giving the dancers a chance to bid their friends farewell.

Formation:	Single circle
Position:	Hands joined
Footwork:	Opposite (man L, lady R)

Music:	Oslo Waltz
Record:	Folk Dancer MH-3016
Rhythm:	3/4, 32 meas

MEAS	CALL	INSTRUCTIONS
	waltz NOW	Waltz balance, ladies turn sequence:

MEAS	CALL	INSTRUCTIONS

MEAS	CALL
1-2	forward 2 3, ladies TURN
3-4	1 2 3, forward AGAIN
5-6	forward 2 3, ladies TURN
7-8	1 2 3, forward AGAIN
9-10	forward 2 3, ladies TURN
11-12	1 2 3, forward AGAIN
13-14	forward 2 3, ladies TURN
15-16	1 2 3, side balance now
17-18	side ball-change, individual TURN
19-20	turn 2 3, hold HANDS
21-22	side ball-change, individual TURN
23-24	turn 2 3, balance and point
25-26	SIDE close, side POINT
27-28	SIDE close, waltz TURN
29-30	turn 2 3, turn 2 3
31-32	turn 2 3, start OVER

INSTRUCTIONS

All 2-step waltz balance fwd and back; lady begins with R foot, man with L. With 2 waltz steps in place, man takes lady on L side and brings her across in front of him to R side, changing hands. Lady takes 2 waltz steps as she turns R 1 full turn toward man while changing sides, and ends facing center of circle. Repeat waltz balance and crossover 3 times. On 4th time, lady faces man and takes closed dance position, man facing LOD.

Side balance: In ballroom position, balance toward center and away from center; man begins with L foot, lady with R. Turn away from partner, 1 full turn. Man turns L, lady turns R with 1 waltz step and 2 walks. Repeat meas 17-20, balancing away from center of circle, then toward center, with man turning R and lady L on turn.

Balance and point: Join hands with partner, elongated hold, shoulder height. Man beginning with L foot, lady with R, moving away from center, step sideways, close, step sideways, and point toe of free foot. Repeat toward center. In ballroom dance position, take 4 turning waltz steps moving ccw, turning R. Man starts turn on R foot, lady on L foot. On 4th waltz step open up to single circle.

Repeat entire dance.

R O A D   T O   T H E   I S L E S
(English)

Formation: Double circle
Position: Varsouvienne
Footwork: All start L

Music: Road to the Isles
Record: Folk Dancer MH-300 3-A
Rhythm: 4/4, 8 meas

MEAS	CALL	INSTRUCTIONS

MEAS   CALL

READY POINT

INSTRUCTIONS

Point and grapevine sequence: Place L toe fwd (ct 1-2) then step to R

MEAS	CALL	INSTRUCTIONS

MEAS	CALL
1	POINT behind side
2	STEP POINT
3	behind side STEP
4	heel-toe and schottische
5-6	1 2 3 hop, 1 2 3 turn
7-8	1 2 3 turn, stomp stomp STOMP

INSTRUCTIONS

side on L foot behind R (ct 3), step to R on R foot (ct 4), step on L foot in front of R foot (ct 1-2). Repeat step to L starting on R foot (this 2nd unit starts on ct 3, meas 2). Then in meas 4, place L heel fwd (ct 1-2), L toe back (ct 3-4).

Schottische: Run fwd L,R,L and hop on L. Repeat schottische step R,L, R and on R hop turn to face agLOD. Repeat 1 schottische step agLOD and turn back to ccw on last hop, and stomp 3 times.

Repeat entire dance.

Variation

To dance a mixer, man progresses to next lady on the last stomp.

R A K S I   J A A K
(Estonian)

Formation:	Threesome facing center of hall
Position:	Full-open, hands at shoulder height
Footwork:	All start L

Music:	Raksi Jaak
Record:	Folk Dancer MH-3007B
Rhythm:	4/4, 24 meas

MEAS   CALL

balance to the side
READY BALANCE

Chorus

1	step touch step touch
2	step touch forward now
3	1 2 3 kick
4	1 2 bow knot

Verse

5	hop' 1' 2' 3' hop' 2' 2' 3'

INSTRUCTIONS

Chorus

Balance: All step L to L, touch R beside L. All step R to R, touch L beside R. Repeat meas 1-2. Walk fwd 3 steps (L,R,L), kick R foot fwd. Walk back 4 steps (R,L,R,L).

Verses

Bow knot: Man polkas in place. Both ladies polka around man retaining handhold. As ladies cross in front, R lady arches over and L lady goes under arch. Ladies cross in back with L lady arching high as R lady goes

206

MEAS	CALL	INSTRUCTIONS

MEAS	CALL
6	hop' 3' 2' 3' hop' 4' 2' 3'
7	hop' 5' 2' 3' hop' 6' 2' 3'
8	hop' 7' 2' 3' now chorus

Chorus

9	step touch step touch
10	step touch forward now
11	1 2 3 kick
12	1 2 pull' to' center

Verse

13	hop' 1' 2' 3' hop' 2' 2' 3'
14	hop' 3' 2' 3' arch back
15	hop' 1' 2' 3' hop' 2' 2' 3'
16	hop' 3' 2' 3' now chorus

Chorus

17	step touch step touch
18	step touch forward now
19	1 2 3 kick
20	1 2 cuddle now

Verse

21	hop' 1' 2' 3' hop' 2' 2' 3'
22	hop' 3' 2' 3' back now
23	hop' 1' 2' 3' hop' 2' 2' 3'
24	roll out start over

INSTRUCTIONS

under. Keep hands high, as man faces front during arches.

Center: Ladies turn in to face man, forming triangle with ladies' backs to center of hall, man facing center. Polka 4 steps toward center of circle, ladies pulling man. All reverse direction and ladies release hands and arch under man's arms, turning toward him for 4 polka steps.

Cuddle: On last meas, ladies turn in toward man to cuddle position. (L lady makes R turn, R lady makes L turn. Man has arms around ladies' waists.) Dance 4 polka steps fwd. Dance 2 polka steps back. Ladies turn out to original positions with 2 polka steps.

Repeat entire dance.

COME LET US BE JOYFUL
(German)

Formation:	Triple circle, threesome team formation	Music:	Come Let Us Be Joyful
Position:	Hands joined	Record:	Folkraft 1195
Footwork:	All start L	Rhythm:	4/4, 12 meas

MEAS	CALL	INSTRUCTIONS
	walk forward and bow READY WALK	Walk and bow: Facing sets walk fwd 3 steps, bow to opposite on 4th step. Walk back to place in 4 steps.
1	1 2 3 back	Repeat.
2	1 2 3 forward	Elbow turn: Man (or center person) turns R-hand partner with R elbow
3	1 2 3 back	turn for 4 steps, then the L-hand partner with L elbow turn for 4 steps.
4	elbow turn right'-hand' lady	Repeat to R and L.
5	turn the left'-hand' lady	Walk and pass-through: Facing sets again walk fwd 3 steps, bow on 4th.
6	turn the right'-hand' lady	Back 4 steps. Each set passes R shoulders as they walk fwd with 8
7	turn the left'-hand' lady	steps to face a new set.
8	1 2 walk forward	Repeat entire dance.
9	1 2 3 back	
10	1 2 pass-through	
11	1 2 3 4	
12	now start OVER	

ZIGUENER POLKA
(German)

Formation:	Double circle	Music:	Ziguener Polka
Position:	Shine	Record:	Folkraft 1486 x 45 A
Footwork:	Opposite (man L, lady R)	Rhythm:	4/4, 12 meas

MEAS	CALL	INSTRUCTIONS
	now let's CURTSY	Curtsy: Curtsy to partner, then to dancer on L front, then to dancer on R front, and finally to partner again.
1	1 2 left lady	
2	1 2 right lady	Clap and walk sequence: Men move ccw, ladies cw around circle. On 1st

MEAS	CALL	INSTRUCTIONS

MEAS	CALL
3	1 2 PARTNER
4	1 2 clap' and' walk
5	clap hit' hit' 2 hit' hit'
6	3 hit' hit' 4 hit' hit'
7	5 hit' hit' 6 hit' hit'
8	7 hit' hit' 8 now' polka'
9-10	hop' 1' 2' 3' hop' 2' 2' 3', hop' 3' 2' 3' hop' 4' 2' 3'
11-12	hop' 5' 2' 3' hop' 6' 2' 3', hop' 7' 2' 3' now curtsy

INSTRUCTIONS

beat of each measure, clap own hands once; on 2nd beat, clap both hands twice with person passing, beginning with dancer at L; 1 change each bar.

Polka: Polka with 8th person in shoulder-waist position, turning cw and progressing ccw in circle; finish facing partners, men with backs to center, in shoulder-waist position.

Repeat entire dance with new partner.

M I S I R L O U
(Greek)

Created by Greek immigrants to America, Misirlou is widely popular and has many different versions.

Formation: Line
Position: Hands joined at shoulder height
Footwork: All start R

Music: Misirlou
Record: RCA Victor EPA 4129
Rhythm: 4/4, 4 meas

MEAS	CALL
	step side right foot
	READY SIDE
1	SIDE POINT
2	back side SWIVEL
3	forward forward BACK
4	now start OVER

INSTRUCTIONS

Side, point, swivel sequence: Step R (ct 1), pause (ct 2), tap L toe on floor in front of R (ct 3), swing L leg around to back of R foot in an arch (ct 4). Step L deep in back of R, bending knees slightly (ct 1), pivot 1/4 turn R while stepping R (ct 2), step fwd L still facing R (ct 3), pivot quickly 1/2 turn L on L foot to face cw, bringing R leg around to front with R knee bent and raised (ct 4). Starting R, take 3 very smooth, small steps fwd cw (ct 1-3), lift L foot in back (ct 4). Still facing cw, take 3 smooth steps back (ct 1-3), lift R foot and pivot 1/4 R to face front again (ct 4).

Repeat through entire dance.

H U K I - L A U
(Hawaiian)

The dance Huki-Lau represents a Hawaiian fishing party and banquet. The words to the song are given and explained below.

Formation: Single circle
Position: Shine
Footwork: All start L

Music: Huki-Lau
Record: Waikiki Records 45-538
Rhythm: 4/4

MEAS	CALL	INSTRUCTIONS

READY CHORUS, hitch and PULL

Basic Step

Side L, close R, side L, touch R, repeat to R. Continues throughout dance.

Chorus

1-2	HITCH HITCH, PULL PULL
3-4	PULL PULL, ARMS OUT
5-6	NOW LET'S, stir and EAT
7-8	STIR EAT, now throw nets out
9	make like' the' SEA
10	then like' a' FISH
11-12	SWIM AND, hitch and PULL
13-14	HITCH HITCH, PULL PULL
15-16	PULL AND, grand right-and-left

Chorus

Hitch and pull: Point L thumb over shoulder twice (meas 1). Place both hands to R side as though pulling rope and pull 2 times (meas 2); repeat pull to L, then again to R (meas 3-4).

Arms out: Extend both arms fwd to indicate everybody.

Stir and eat: Place R fingers in palm of L hand, stir and bring up to mouth as though eating.

Nets: Throw arms out.

Sea: Move hands up and down and from R to L, palms down.

Fish: Place R palm over back of L hand, wriggle thumbs.

Verse

17-18	quick quick SLOW, quick quick SLOW
19-20	quick quick SLOW, quick quick SLOW
21-22	quick quick SLOW, quick quick SLOW
23-24	quick quick quick quick, ready and CHORUS

Verse

Grand right-and-left (walking in quick, quick, SLOW rhythm) to the 5th person. With R hands joined, dance 1 complete turn around 5th person in 8 quick steps.

Repeat chorus, then entire dance. Sequence of dance from beginning to end is thus:

chorus	chorus
verse	verse
chorus	chorus

MEAS   CALL

INSTRUCTIONS

Words to Chorus

Oh, we're going to the huki-lau,
A huki, huki, huki, huki, huki-lau.
Everybody loves the huki-lau,
Where the lau-lau is the kau-kau
    at the huki-lau.
Oh, we'll throw our nets out into the
    sea
And all the uma-uma come swimming to
    me.
Oh, we're going to the huki-lau,
A huki, huki, huki, huki-lau.

INSTRUCTIONS (CONTINUED)

Word Meanings

Huki-lau--pulling in fish
Huki--pull
Lau-lau--baked fish
Kau-kau--food
Uma-uma--type of fish

Words to Verse

What a wonderful day for fishing
The old Hawaiian way.
And the huki-lau nets go swishing
Down in old Laie Bay.

Y A N K E E   H U L A
(Hawaiian)

The extremely simple Yankee Hula is intended for haoles (white visitors to
Hawaii) to dance.

Formation:	Single circle, partners facing, man facing LOD	Music:	Hula Mixer or Huki-Lau
Position:	Shine	Record:	Sets in Order S-1-0-3007, Waikiki Records 45-538
Footwork:	All start L	Rhythm:	4/4, 8 meas

MEAS   CALL   INSTRUCTIONS

        step sideward LEFT   Side (basic hula step): Extend both arms
                                        to R, step L side, close R to L, step
        READY SIDE   side L, touch R to L. Swing arms down
                                        and up on L side, repeat side movement
1   side together side touch   to R. Repeat meas 1-2.

2   let's do' it' AGAIN   Turn: Circling hands near R hip,
                                        palms down, turn L 1 complete turn in
3   side together side touch   4 slides.

4   now let's TURN   Change partners: Extend arms to sides.
                                        Take 2 slides to L and diag fwd, cross-
5-6   TURN TURN, CHANGE PARTNERS   ing arms so that backs of hands are
                                        together. In 2 slides R and diag fwd,
7-8   OUT IN, NOW SIDE   and while extending arms to sides,
                                        slide in behind partner to face new

MEAS	CALL	INSTRUCTIONS

partner. Say, "Aloha!"

Repeat entire dance.

H O R A

(Israeli)

Formation:	Single circle, facing center	Music: Hava Nagila or Hora
Position:	Hands on shoulders	Record: Folkraft 1110-B
Footwork:	All start L	Rhythm: 4/4, 3 meas

MEAS	CALL	INSTRUCTIONS

GRAPEVINE and swing

READY <u>VINE</u>

<u>Grapevine and swing</u>: Step sideward R on R foot, cross L back of R. Step sideward R, hop on R and swing L across in front of R. Step on L and swing R in front of L while hopping on L.

1 side behind side swing

2 side swing side behind

3 side swing side swing

Repeat through entire dance.

M A Y I M, M A Y I M
(Israeli)

The word <u>mayim</u> means "water." The dance depicts the significance of water in desert Israel.

Formation:	Single circle	Music: Mayim, Mayim
Position:	Hands joined	Record: Folkraft 110 8A
Footwork:	All start R	Rhythm: 4/4, 13 meas

MEAS	CALL	INSTRUCTIONS

GRAPEVINE and leap
READY <u>GRAPEVINE</u>

<u>Grapevine and leap</u>: Cross R over L, step L to L, cross R behind L, leap L with L. Repeat 3 times.

1 cross side back leap

2 cross side back leap

3 cross side back leap

4 cross side <u>walk' to' center</u>

<u>Walk</u>: Step R,L,R,L to center of circle, raising arms gradually above shoulder height. Reverse 4 steps back to place R,L,R,L, gradually lowering arms to starting position. Repeat meas 5-6.

5 forward forward back now

6 back back forward now

<u>Circle</u>: Facing cw, take 4 running steps starting R.

MEAS	CALL	INSTRUCTIONS

MEAS	CALL
7	forward forward back now
8	back back circle left
9	run run touch swing
10	touch swing touch swing
11	touch swing change' feet' and' clap'
12	swing clap swing clap
13	swing clap GRAPEVINE

Touch swing: Leap R, extend L toe directly fwd to touch floor, hop R and extend L toe to L side. Repeat 3 more times. Leap L, extend R toe directly fwd to touch floor, clapping hands at same time; hop L, touch R toe to R side, extending arms out to sides. Repeat 3 more times, clapping as R toe touches floor.

Repeat entire dance.

V A Y I V E N   U Z I Y A H U
(Israeli)

Originally composed for men, the dance Vayiven Uziyahu celebrates Israeli independence in 1956.

Formation:	Single circle	Music:	Vayiven Uziyahu
Position:	Facing ccw, hands joined low	Record:	Festival Records FS 201
		Rhythm:	4/4, 17 meas
Footwork:	All start R		

MEAS	CALL
	run to RIGHT
	READY RUN
1-2	run 2 3 4, bounce 2 3 4
3-4	run 2 bounce 2, run 2 bounce 2
5-6	run 2 3 4, bounce 2 3 4
7-8	run 2 bounce 2, run 2 walk now
9-10	walk walk STOMP, walk walk STOMP
11-12	walk walk run run, leap leap jump kick
13-14	jump kick walk walk, STOMP walk walk

INSTRUCTIONS

Run: Take 4 light running steps fwd ccw (ct 1-4). Bring feet together and face center of circle on 4th ct. Bounce in place 4 times (ct 1-4). Turn to face ccw, take 2 running steps fwd (ct 1-2); turn to face center of circle on ct 2, bounce in place 2 times (ct 3-4). Repeat meas 3. Repeat meas 1-4.

Walk, run, leap sequence: Face LOD, ccw. Take 2 strong, small walking steps fwd ccw, R,L (ct 1-2). Stomp R in front of L, R shoulder fwd (ct 3); bring R shoulder back sharply (ct 4). Repeat meas 9. Take 2 steps fwd, R, L (ct 1-2), clapping hands to R side at chest level on each step; rejoin hands. Take 2 light running steps fwd, R,L, (ct 3-4); leap fwd R,L (ct 1-2). Spring from L and land on both feet facing center so that feet are parallel and about 12 inches apart (ct 3). Leap on L, crossing L in front of R (ct 4).

MEAS	CALL	INSTRUCTIONS
15-16	STOMP walk walk, run run leap leap	Leap may be high and wide. R foot kicks behind L at same time. Again spring from L and land on both feet
17	jump kick start over	(ct 1). Leap L across in front of R (ct 2), kicking R foot behind L. Repeat entire sequence, beginning at meas 9. (Moves will be 2 ct off rhythm 2nd time through.)

Repeat entire dance.

V E' D A V I D

(Israeli)

The name Ve' David means "David of the beautiful eyes."

Formation: Double circle, facing LOD
Position: Full-open
Footwork: All start L

Music: Ve' David
Record: Festival Records FS 201
Rhythm: 4/4, 10 meas

MEAS	CALL	INSTRUCTIONS
	walk to single circle	Walk: Walk fwd ccw 4 steps.
	READY WALK	Circle: Man backs up 4 steps to end up L of lady, who takes 4 steps in place, both turning to face center.
1	1 2 single circle	
2	1 2 center now	Center and back: All join hands, walk 4 steps to center, raising hands shoulder-high, then 4 steps back, lowering hands.
3	1 2 back now	
4	1 2 ladies center	Ladies center: Lady walks 4 steps to center, raising arms shoulder-high, then takes 4 steps back, lowering arms. Man claps rhythm.
5	1 2 back now	
6	1 2 men center	
7	1 2 turn right	Men center and turn: Man walks 4 steps to center, clapping 4 times, turning 1/2 R on ct 4 to face new lady on R. Man walks 4 steps to new partner.
8	new partner buzz turn	
9	1 2 3 4	Buzz turn: In shoulder-waist position, both buzz step turn 8 counts.
10	5 6 start over	

Repeat entire dance.

MAORI STICK GAME

(Maori--New Zealand)

The words of this song tell of a boy singing to his father, "What I am doing may seem silly, but I am reminiscing about my departed sweetheart and counting the time until she returns to me." The father replies, "You are silly, because your sweetheart may not return at all." The game is played with pairs of painted sticks which the players pass to each other in patterns. The sticks are about one to two inches in diameter and about fifteen inches long and are painted in two colors (usually red and black), with the color changing at the middle of the stick. Each player has two sticks, one in each hand, and holds them upright, grasping them in the center. The man holds the sticks with the black ends up, and the lady holds them with the black ends down.

Formation: Lines or mass (in couples)

Position: Shine, sitting on floor, facing

Footwork: None (movements all with hands)

Music: Maori Stick Game

Record: See INSTRUCTIONS below

Rhythm: 3/4 (4/4 on last sequence, occasional 2/4 meas)

MEAS	CALL
	single PASS
	ready NOW
1-2	down clap right, down clap left
3-4	down clap right, down clap left
5-6	down clap right, down clap left
7-8	down clap right, now double pass
9-10	down clap right, right down clap
11-12	left left down, clap right right
13-14	down clap left, left down clap
15-16	right right down, clap and hold
17-18	down 2 3, man out down

INSTRUCTIONS

Basic Movements

Down: Hit bottom ends of sticks on floor.

Clap: Hit own upright sticks together.

Pass: Toss stick or sticks to partner gently in vertical position. Toss straight across or in slightly upward arc so that they can be caught without hitting floor.

Drum: Hit top ends of sticks on floor by sliding shafts of sticks through hands to grasp nearer bottom ends.

Flip: Toss sticks into air so that they revolve end for end (one-half revolution) and catch them.

Hold: Pause for number of ct indicated, resting bottoms of sticks on floor. Words "e aue" and "ra" following instruction "hold" are words of song at this point, and provide means of distinguishing two types of holds.

Sequences

215

MEAS	CALL	INSTRUCTIONS

19-20	clap pass, down clap pass	Single pass: Down (ct 1), clap (ct 2), pass R sticks (ct 3); down (ct 1), clap (ct 2), pass L sticks (ct 3). Repeat for total of 8 passes, 4 per stick (meas 1-8).
21-22	down clap pass, down and hold	
23-24	down 2 3, 4 in' and' out	Double pass: Down (ct 1), clap (ct 2), pass R sticks (ct 3), pass R sticks (ct 1); down (ct 2), clap (ct 3), pass L sticks (ct 1), pass L sticks (ct 2). Repeat for total of 6 double passes, 3 per stick (meas 9-16).
25-26	down clap pass, down clap pass	
27-28	down clap pass, down clap pass	
29-30	down clap pass, down clap pass	Hold (e aue): Down (ct 1), hold (ct 2-3), down (ct 1), hold (ct 2).
31-32	down clap pass, down and hold	Man out: Down (ct 3 of meas 18), clap (ct 1), pass L stick to partner's R hand and R stick to partner's L hand simultaneously (ct 2 of meas 19 [2/4 meter]), man passing his sticks outside lady's. Down (ct 1), clap (ct 2), pass simultaneously as for meas 19, man passing his sticks outside lady's (ct 3). Repeat for total of 4 simultaneous passes (through meas 22).
33-34	down 2 3, in' and' out down	
35-36	clap pass, down clap pass	
37-38	down clap pass, down and hold	
39-40	down 2 3, now single flip	Hold (ra): Down (ct 1), hold (ct 2-3, 1-3 next meas).
41-42	drum flip down, right drum flip	In and out: Down, clap, pass simultaneously as for man out sequence, except that sticks with black ends up are always passed outside. Sequence begins on ct 1 of meas 25 and continues for 8 passes to hold (e aue), then begins after hold on ct 3 of meas 34 and continues for 4 more passes to hold (ra).
43-44	down left drum, flip down right	
45-46	drum flip down, left drum flip	
47-48	down right drum, flip down left	Single flip: Drum to R (ct 1), flip (ct 2), down (ct 3), pass R sticks (ct 1); drum to L (ct 2), flip (ct 3), down (ct 1), pass L sticks (ct 2). Repeat for total of 12 drum-flips and passes, 6 per side (meas 41-56).
49-50	drum flip down, right drum flip	
51-52	down left drum, flip down right	
53-54	drum flip down, left drum flip	Double flip: Drum to R, flip twice (in 2 ct), down, pass R. Sequence begins on ct 3 of meas 58 and continues for 2 passes, 1 per stick, to hold (ra),

MEAS	CALL	INSTRUCTIONS

MEAS	CALL
55-56	down right drum, flip down hold
57-58	down 2 3, double flip drum
59-60	flip flip, down right drum
61-62	flip flip down, left drum' and' hold
63-64	down 2 3, 4 double flip
65-66	drum flip flip, down right drum
67-68	flip flip down, left drum flip
69-70	flip down right, drum flip flip
71-72	down left drum, flip down' and' hold
73-74	down 2 3, double flip drum
75-76	flip flip, down right down
77-78	flip flip down, left drum' and' hold
79-80	down 2 3, now single exchange
81-82	down change down, right down change
83-84	down left down, change down right
85-86	down change down, left down change
87-88	down right down, now double exchange
89-90	down change change, down right down
91-92	change change down, left down change

INSTRUCTIONS

ending with drum in middle, flip, down in middle. Sequence begins after hold on ct 1 of meas 65 and continues for 4 passes, 2 per stick, to hold (e aue), ending with drum in middle, 2 flips, down. Sequence then repeats actions from ct 3 of meas 58 to meas 64, ending with hold (ra).

Single exchange: Down (ct 1), pass R stick to own L hand and L stick to own R hand simultaneously, with L stick passing closest to body (ct 2); down (ct 3), pass R stick to partner (ct 1); down (ct 2), pass R stick to L hand and L stick to R hand (exchange) as above (ct 3); down (ct 1), pass L stick to partner (ct 4). Repeat for total of 6 exchanges (meas 81-88).

Double exchange: Down (ct 1), exchange (ct 2), exchange (ct 3), down (ct 1), pass R sticks (ct 2); down (ct 3), exchange (ct 1), exchange (ct 2), down (ct 3), pass L sticks (ct 1). Repeat for total of 4 double exchanges and passes, 2 per stick, ending with down, 2 exchanges, down at hold (e aue).

Box: Down (ct 3 of meas 98), clap (ct 1), pass R stick to partner's L hand, L stick to own R hand simultaneously (ct 2 of meas 99 [2/4 meter]). Repeat for total of 4 passes to hold (ra).

Bounce-back: Down (ct 1), clap (ct 2), pass simultaneously as for in and out sequence (ct 3); pass simultaneously again, keeping sticks with black ends up on outside (ct 1). Repeat for total of 6 double simultaneous passes (meas 105-12).

Mix: Down (ct 1), clap (ct 2), pass R stick (ct 3), pass L stick (ct 1), pass R stick (ct 2).

Reverse box: Down (ct 3 of meas 114), clap (ct 1), pass sticks as for box sequence (ct 2 of meas 115 [2/4 meter]),

| MEAS | CALL | INSTRUCTIONS |

MEAS	CALL

93-94 change down right, down
       change change

95-96 down left down, change
       and hold

97-98 down 2 3, now box down

99-100 clap pass, down clap pass

101-102 down clap pass, down and
         hold

103-104 down 2 3, now bounce-back

105-106 down clap pass, back
         down clap

107-108 pass back down, clap
         pass back

109-110 down clap pass, back
         down clap

111-112 pass back down, clap
         and mix

113-114 down clap pass, reverse
         box down

115-116 clap pass, back down clap

117-118 pass back down, clap and
         hold

119-120 down 2 3, 4 and flourish

[spoken] down clap

121-130 1 2 3 4, 2 2 3 4
         3 2 3 4, 4 2 3 4
         5 2 3 4, 6 2 3 4
         7 2 3 4, 8 2 3 4
         9 2 3 4, 10 that's ALL

INSTRUCTIONS

reverse stick motion by passing R
stick to own L hand and L stick to
partner's R hand simultaneously (ct 1).
Repeat for total of 3 reverses to
hold (ra).

Flourish: Down, clap on spoken word
"toru-fa," then pass R sticks (ct 1),
L sticks (ct 2), R sticks (ct 3),
L sticks (ct 4) continuously for total
of 39 passes, holding sticks in air
for final ct of meas 130.

Words of Song

E papa wai rangi taku nei mahi,
Taku nei mahi he tuku roimata,
E papa wai rangi taku nei mahi,
Taku nei mahi he tuku roimata.

E aue ka mate ahau,
E hine hoki iho ra.
Maku e kau teo hi-koi tanga,
Maku e kau teo hi-koi tanga.
E aue ka mate ahau,
E hine hoki iho ra.

[Spoken] Toru-fa

Huri, huri, huri, huri, o mahara e,
Ki te tau, ki te tau, i o ra rawa e,
Ko ra rawa, ko ra rawa, o mahara e,
Kia koe ra e hine,
Kia koe ra e hine.

Record

To obtain record, write to:

   Dr. Leona Holbrook
   Richards Building
   Brigham Young University
   Provo, Utah 84602

Price is $1.75 postpaid.

MAORI STICK GAME

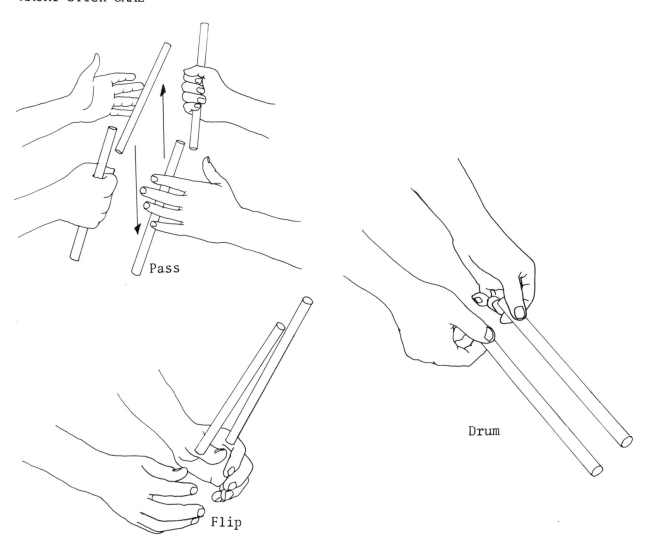

Pass

Flip

Drum

TINIKLING

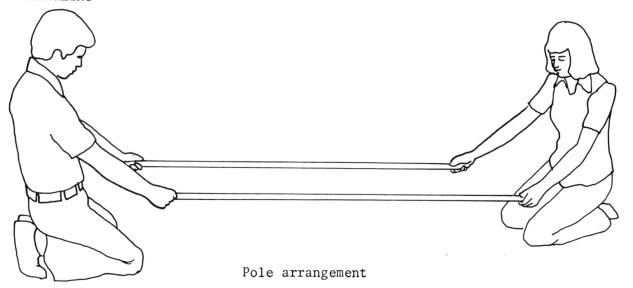

Pole arrangement

LA CUCARACHA

(Mexican)

Formation: Single circle
Position: Shine, partners facing
Footwork: All start L

Music: La Cucaracha
Record: RCA Victor EPA 4134
Rhythm: 3/4, 32 meas

MEAS	CALL
	stomp and clap
	ready STOMP
1	left stomp stomp
2	right stomp stomp
3	stomp stomp stomp
4	HOLD and
5	left stomp stomp
6	right turn around
7	1 2 3
8	REPEAT and
9	left stomp stomp
10	right stomp stomp
11	stomp stomp stomp
12	HOLD and
13	left stomp stomp
14	right turn around
15	1 2 3
16	grand right'-and'-left
17-18	step close step, step close step
19-20	step close step, stomp STOMP
21-22	step close step, step close step

INSTRUCTIONS

Stomp and clap: Partners stand facing each other about 2 feet apart. Stomp L, as partners turn to R and clap L hands; stomp 2 more times. Turn 1/4 L, stomp R, clapping R hands. Stomp twice more. Stomp 4 more times in place (ct 1-4) and hold (ct 5-6). Repeat meas 1-3, except turn around in place on last 4 stomps. Repeat all above.

Grand right-and-left: Proceed with 3 two-steps and 2 stomps. Repeat 3 more times to 9th person.

Repeat entire dance.

Variations

With hands on hips, touch elbows rather than clap hands. Weave rather than grand right-and-left by keeping hands on hips while moving as for grand right-and-left.

MEAS	CALL	INSTRUCTIONS

23-24	step close step, stomp STOMP	
25-26	step close step, step close step	
27-28	step close step, stomp STOMP	
29-30	step close step, step close step	
31-32	step close step, start OVER	

LA RASPA

(Mexican)

Formation: Double circle
Position: Two-hand, right-side
Footwork: All start R

Music: La Raspa
Record: MIA Dance Record #50 R
Rhythm: 4/4, 16 meas

MEAS	CALL	INSTRUCTIONS

READY KICK

Kick: Starting in R-side position, kick R foot fwd (ct 1). Bring R back to place and kick L fwd (ct 2). Kick R fwd, bring L back to place, at same time turning 1/4 turn to L-side position (ct 3); hold (ct 4). Repeat in L-side position. Repeat, changing sides, 6 more times, to end in L-side position.

1 kick kick left side
2 kick kick right side
3 kick kick left side
4 kick kick right side
5 kick kick left side
6 kick kick right side
7 kick kick left side

8 right arm TURN

Right arm turn: Hook R elbows with partner. Turn once around in 7 running steps, and clap on ct 8. Man hook L elbows with next lady ahead; turn once around in 7 running steps and clap on ct 8. Alternate R and L turn to 4th lady.

9-10 1 2 3 4, left hands AROUND

Repeat entire dance.

11-12 1 2 3 4, right hands AROUND

13-14 1 2 3 4, left hands AROUND

15-16 1 2 3 4, 5 6 start over

MEXICAN CLAP DANCE

(Mexican)

Formation: Double circle   Music: Chiapanecas
Position: Full-open   Record: MacGregor 608, Old Timer/8100
Footwork: Opposite (man L, lady R)   Rhythm: 3/4, 32 meas

MEAS	CALL	INSTRUCTIONS
	WALK and, CLAP	Note
	READY, WALK	In "Call" column capital letters represent either two beats or three, as needed to complete measure. (End of measure is indicated by comma or by end of line.)
1-4	ONE, TWO, THREE, REVERSE	
5-8	ONE, TWO, THREE, BALANCE	
9-12	AWAY, TOGETHER, AWAY, clap CLAP	
13-16	TOGETHER, AWAY, AROUND, ROCK	Walk and clap: Beginning with outside foot, walk fwd 3 steps. On 4th meas, turn to face partner, clap own hands twice. Repeat agLOD.
17-20	FORWARD, BACK, FORWARD, BACK	
21-24	FORWARD, BACK, FORWARD, BACK	Balance: Facing each other with both hands joined, put R foot back, balance away, together, away (meas 9-11). Clap hands twice (meas 12). Both hands joined, balance together, away, together (meas 13-15). Man then places arms around and behind partner's waist and claps hands twice; lady places arms around man's neck and claps twice (meas 16).
25-28	FORWARD, BACK, FORWARD, BACK	
29-30	under the arm, new PARTNER	
31-32	NOW, WALK	

Rock turn: Partners take closed dance position and in 12 meas rock fwd and back, as to make 2 complete revolutions turning L in place. Man raises L hand and arches lady under arm to go to next man.

Repeat entire dance.

TINIKLING

(Philippine)

Tinikling birds have long necks and long legs. This dance imitates these birds as they walk or run in the tall grass or over fallen branches. Two bamboo poles about nine feet long are placed horizontally on the ground. The large end of one pole and the small end of the other pole are placed together, pointing slightly diagonally toward the music. Two pieces of board about 30 inches long and two inches thick are placed under the poles, about one foot from the ends. Two bamboo players sit on the ground opposite each other holding the ends of the poles, one with the back of the left shoulder toward the music. The dance is performed along the length of the poles as the players move the poles together and apart, sliding them on the boards.

Formation: Partners' R sides to poles
Position: Shine, man's hands on his waist, lady's hands to sides
Footwork: All start R

Music: Tinikling
Record: Villar MLP 5000, Mico TM-006
Rhythm: 3/4

MEAS	CALL
1	ready WALTZ
2-4	1 2 3, 2 2 3, 3 2 3
5-7	1 tap tap, 2 tap tap, 3 tap tap
8	TINIKLING
9-10	hop in in, right in in
11-12	left in in, right in in
13-14	left in in, right in in
15-16	left in in, double hop turn
17-18	right in in, left in in
19-20	right in in, left in in
21-22	right in in, left in in
23-24	men TURN, ready and chase
25-26	left right left, turn in in
27-28	left right left, turn in in
29-30	left right left, turn in in
31-32	left right left, double hop reverse
33-34	right left right, turn in in

INSTRUCTIONS

Note

In "Call" column capital letters represent either two beats or three, as needed to complete measure. (End of measure is indicated by comma or by end of line.)

Bamboo Rhythm

On ct 1, strike poles together; on ct 2-3 separate them about 2 feet and hit them twice against the floor. Continuous rhythm with the poles is 1 2 3, 1 2 3, in each measure of the dance except meas 1-4 of introduction.

Basic Step

Tinikling step R: Hop L foot at L side of bamboos (ct 1), small leap onto R between the poles (ct 2), small leap onto L in same spot (ct 3). (Footwork call would be out, in, in.) R arm up high, hand circling ccw in motion like screwing in a light bulb; man's L hand on his waist, lady's L arm at right angles to R arm, hand circling cw as described for R hand.

Tinikling step L: Reverse hands. Hop (or leap) on R foot on R side of bamboo poles (ct 1), small leap onto L between poles (ct 2), small leap onto R in same spot (ct 3).

Sequences

MEAS	CALL	INSTRUCTIONS

MEAS	CALL
35-36	right left right, turn in in
37-38	right left right, turn in in
39-40	right left right, now <u>feet apart</u>
41-42	1 in in, 2 in in
43-44	3 in in, 4 and turn
45-46	1 in in, 2 in in
47-48	3 in in, 4 turn back
49-50	1 in in, 2 in in
51-52	3 in in, 4 and turn
53-54	1 in in, 2 in in
55-56	3 in in, turn <u>back' to' back</u>
57-58	right in in, left in in
59-60	right in in, left in in
61-62	right in in, left in in
63-64	right in in, double hop reverse
65-66	left in in, right in in
67-68	left in in, right in in
69-70	left in in, right in in
71-72	left in in, now <u>DIAGONAL</u>
73-74	left in in, right in in
75-76	left in in, right in in
77-78	left in in, right in in
79-80	left in in, change place' and' turn

Introduction: Beginning R, dance 3 waltz steps fwd to places on L side, partners facing same direction of pole, man's hands on his waist, lady's hands at her sides. (Bamboo: Meas 1-4 silent; meas 5 to end of dance strike together on ct 1 of each meas.) Stand with weight on L (ct 1), tap R twice between poles (ct 2-3). Repeat 3 more times.

Tinikling: Dance 7 tinikling steps, R and L alternately. Small leap R outside R pole (ct 1), small leap onto L inside (ct 2), hop L in same place, making 1/2 turn L ccw (ct 3). Dance 7 tinikling steps, L and R alternately. Man leaps onto L outside pole to his L (ct 1), turns ccw by taking small leap R inside, and hops R in same place (ct 2-3), to finish facing partner. Lady leaps onto L outside pole to her L (ct 1), takes small leap onto R inside (ct 2), hops R inside, moving back near bamboo player (ct 3). Partners will now be working in opposition.

Chase: Both beginning L, partners take 4 running steps (L,R,L,R) fwd and diag to own L outside poles (ct 1, 2, 3, 1), turning 1/2 R cw on 4th step; leap onto L, R between poles (ct 2-3). Moving cw around poles, repeat action of meas 25-26 3 more times. On last count (meas 32, ct 3), hop L to reverse. Repeat in reverse action of meas 25-31, beginning R, moving ccw. Both partners finish with double hop on R foot.

Feet apart: Jump with both feet apart, outside poles (ct 1); jump twice with feet together between poles (ct 2-3). Both hands joined straight across, swing joined hands outward, shoulder-high (ct 1); swing joined hands down in front, between partners (ct 2-3). Repeat action of meas 41 2 more times. Jump with both feet apart outside poles (ct 1); release hands and jump twice between poles making 1/2 turn R to finish with partners back to back

MEAS	CALL	INSTRUCTIONS

MEAS   CALL

INSTRUCTIONS

81-82	left in in, right in in
83-84	left in in, right in in
85-86	left in in, right in in
87-88	left change place, now feet apart
89-90	1 in in, 2 in in
91-92	3 in in, 4 and turn
93-94	1 in in, 2 in in
95-96	3 in in, 4 turn back
97-98	1 in in, 2 in in
99-100	3 in in, 4 and turn
101-102	1 in in, 2 in in
103-104	3 in in, turn and chase
105-106	left right left, turn in in
107-108	left right left, turn in in
109-110	left right left, turn in in
111-112	left right left, double hop reverse
113-114	right left right, turn in in
115-116	right left right, turn in in
117-118	right left right, turn in in
119-120	right ladies turn, now TINIKLING
121-122	left in in, right in in

(ct 2-3). Partners repeat action of meas 41-44. Hands are at sides and are raised slightly on each ct 1. Finish facing partner. Repeat action of meas 41-48 to finish with partners to own L of poles, facing and dancing diag across poles.

Back-to-back: With 2 tinikling steps, partners pass L shoulders, pass back to back and move back to place (L do-si-do). Repeat action of meas 57-58 3 more times. On last count, hop R to reverse. Repeat action of meas 57-64 in reverse, passing R shoulders (R do-si-do). Finish inside poles.

Diagonal: Leap onto L outside poles (ct 1); leap R diag fwd toward center between poles (ct 2); leap L in same spot (ct 3). Join R hands on ct 2-3. Both turn 1/4 L and leap R diag back across other pole, releasing R hands (ct 1); leap L diag fwd toward center between poles (ct 2); leap R in same spot (ct 3). Join L hands on ct 2-3. Repeat action of meas 73-74 2 more times. Repeat action of meas 73. With 1 tinikling step, double-hop down poles on L foot to exchange places with partner. Finish with partners facing. Repeat action of meas 73-80.

Chase and ladies turn sequence: Repeat action of meas 25-40, with ladies turning 1/2 R cw on last double-hop (meas 120, ct 2-3).

Tinikling and bow sequence: Repeat action of meas 9-15. On meas 128, double hop L in poles to reverse. Repeat action of meas 17-22. On meas 135-36 step out of poles, walk forward, and bow.

MEAS	CALL	INSTRUCTIONS
123-124	left in in, right in in	
125-126	left in in, right in in	
127-128	left in in, right hop reverse	
129-130	right in in, left in in	
131-132	right in in, left in in	
133-134	right in in, forward and bow	
135-136	1 2 3, HOLD	

A L U N E L U L

(Romanian)

The name Alunelul means "little hazelnut."

Formation: Single circle
Position: Hands on shoulders
Footwork: All start R

Music: Alunelul
Record: Folk Dancer MH-1120
Rhythm: 4/4, 16 meas

MEAS	CALL	INSTRUCTIONS
	side cross' and' stomp twice	Side cross: Step R side, cross L foot behind R, step R side, cross L foot behind R. Step R, stomp L heel beside R foot twice. Repeat meas 1-2 to L. Repeat from beginning.
	READY SIDE	
1-2	side cross side cross, now to' the' LEFT	
3-4	side cross side cross, now to' the' RIGHT	One cross: Step R, cross L foot behind, and step R. Stomp L heel beside R foot. Repeat to L. Repeat meas 9-10.
5-6	side cross side cross, now to' the' LEFT	Stomp: In place, step R, stomp L; step L, stomp R; step R, stomp L twice. Then step L, stomp R; step R, stomp L; step L, stomp R twice.
7-8	side cross side cross, one cross STEP	
9	side cross left now	Repeat entire dance.
10	side cross right now	
11	side cross left now	
12	side cross stomp' in' place	

| MEAS | CALL | INSTRUCTIONS |

| 13-14 | side stomp side stomp, now left FOOT |
| 15-16 | side stomp side stomp, now side CROSS |

K O R O B U S H K A

(Russian)

The name Korobushka means "little basket," and the dance depicts a peddler showing the various articles in his basket.

Formation: Double circle
Position: Two-hand
Footwork: Opposite (man L, lady R)

Music: Korobushka
Record: Kismet A-106, Victor 26-5017, Folk Dancer 1059
Rhythm: 4/4, 12 meas

MEAS	CALL	INSTRUCTIONS

schottische forward and back

READY FORWARD

1	1 2 3 back
2	1 2 3 forward
3	1 2 BOKAZO
4	now turn RIGHT
5	now turn LEFT
6	turn and WINDOWS
7	BALANCE ARCH
8	arch and TURN
9	turn and CLAP
10	turn and WINDOWS
11	BALANCE ARCH
12	now let's SCHOTTISCHE

Schottische step: Walk fwd (lady back) L,R, step-hop L, extending R foot on step-hop. Repeat, moving back toward center, starting R (R,L, step-hop R). Repeat, moving away from center, starting L (L,R, step-hop L).

Bokazo (Hungarian break step): Hop L, tapping R toe fwd (ct 1), hop L, tap R toe sideward in pigeon-toe motion (ct 2), hop L, closing R to L with heel click (ct 3), pause (ct 4).

Turning step: Drop hands and move away, each making 1 turn R with steps R,L,R (ct 1-3); pause and clap hands on ct 4. Repeat by turning L back to place.

Windows: Partners, facing with R-L contact, balance toward each other on R, back on L. Man and lady then change places with 4 walking steps, R,L,R,L, lady arching L under man's arm. Repeat meas 5-8, but turn L in place to balance and arch turn with new partner.

Repeat entire dance.

MAKAZICE

(Serbian)

Formation: Line
Position: Hands joined
Footwork: All start R

Music: Makazice
Record: Folk Dancer MH-3023
Rhythm: 4/4, 8 meas

MEAS	CALL	
	CHASSÉ RIGHT	
	READY CHASSÉ	
1-2	1 2 3 4, 5 6 REVERSE	
3-4	1 2 3 4, 5 6 CHARLESTON	
5	FORWARD CROSS	
6	BACK TOGETHER	
7	FORWARD CROSS	
8	NOW CHASSÉ	

INSTRUCTIONS

Chassé: Step side R, behind L (7 ct), hop (ct 8), repeat L.

Charleston: Step fwd R, cross and point L in front of R (Charleston step), bring L foot back across R foot and chug back once, then chug back again with feet side by side and drop to heels. Repeat above step.

Repeat entire dance.

MILANOVO KOLO

(Serbian)

Formation: Single circle
Position: Hands joined
Footwork: All start R

Music: Stanctiello
Record: RCA SP 45-144
Rhythm: 2/4, 12 meas

MEAS	CALL
	step-hop to right
	READY CIRCLE
1	step-hop GRAPEVINE
2	circle to the left
3	step-hop GRAPEVINE
4	two-step to center
5	step close STEP
6	step close STEP

INSTRUCTIONS

Circle and grapevine: Move 2 step-hops R,L, ccw. Step side R, step L behind R, take 3 quick light steps in place, R,L,R. Repeat to L.

Two-step: Bring joined hands straight fwd to shoulder level, elbow straight. Two-step very quickly to center starting R (step-together-step, pause), then L, for a total of 4 two-steps. Repeat two-steps moving backward R, still very quickly.

Repeat entire dance.

MEAS	CALL	INSTRUCTIONS
7	step close STEP	
8	two-step BACK	
9	step close STEP	
10	step close STEP	
11	step close STEP	
12	now step-HOP	

H I E R   E K   W E E R

(South African)

The words hier ek weer mean "here I am again."

Formation:	Double circle, partners facing opposite directions (men cw, ladies ccw)	Music:	Little Shoemaker
		Record:	Windsor 4141
		Rhythm:	4/4, 16 meas
Position:	Shine		
Footwork:	All start L		

MEAS   CALL

WALK OPPOSITE

READY WALK

Walk: Man turns R and walks 16 steps cw as lady turns R and walks 16 steps ccw. Each stomps 3 times while turning to face opposite direction. Walk back 13 steps, going past partner to new partner, facing ccw.

MEAS	CALL
1	1 2 3 4
2	5 6 7 8
3	9 10 11 12
4	now walk OPPOSITE
5	1 2 3 4
6	5 6 7 8
7	9 10 11 12
8	now clap' and' WALK
9-10	clap hit clap hit, 1'2'3'4' SWING

Clap and walk: March fwd in LOD while doing the following.
Clap own hands once (ct 1).
Clap partner's hands once (ct 2).
Clap own hands once (ct 3).
Clap partner's hands once (ct 4).
Clap own hands five times (ct 1-3).

Swing: Take shoulder-waist swing position on last ct. Swing partner with buzz step turn, 8 ct. Repeat meas 9-12.

Repeat entire dance, changing partners each time through.

MEAS	CALL	INSTRUCTIONS
11	1 2 3 4	
12	now clap' and' WALK	
13-14	clap hit clap hit, 1'2'3'4' SWING	
15	1 2 3 4	
16	5 6 walk opposite	

T A N T' H E S S I E

(South African)

The name Tant' Hessie means "Aunt Esther's white horse."

Formation: Double circle
Position: Shine, partners facing
Footwork: All start L

Music: Tant' Hessie
Record: Folkraft 337-006
Rhythm: 2/4, 24 meas

MEAS	CALL	INSTRUCTIONS
1-2	1' and' 2' and', now back	Step-bend (basic step): Step on L on ct 1; bend knee on the "and," then repeat on R foot, moving fwd for 4 ct to partner's R shoulder then backward for 4 ct. Then repeat, moving fwd to L shoulder and back.
3-4	1' and' 2' and', left side	
5-6	1' and' 2' and', 3' and' back	
7-8	1' and' 2' and', do'-si'-do	Do-si-do: With 8 step-bends pass R shoulders. Then repeat, passing L shoulders. On ct 8 stomp foot.
9-10	1' and' 2' and', 3' and' 4' and'	
11-12	5' and' 6' and', 7' and' now' reverse'	Swing: Swing partner 16 steps--accent down on ct 1 and up on ct "and." Repeat entire dance moving to new partner on L.
13-14	1' and' 2' and', 3' and' 4' and'	
15-16	5' and' 6' and', now' stomp' and' swing'	Repeat entire dance.
17-18	1' and' 2' and', 3' and' 4' and'	
19-20	5' and' 6' and', 7' and' 8' and'	

MEAS	CALL	INSTRUCTIONS

21-22   9' and' 10' and', 11' and'
12' and'

23-24   13' and' 14' and', step'-
bend' change' partners'

S O U R C E S   O F   F O L K   D A N C E   B O O K S   A N D   R E C O R D S

B O O K S

Teachers' Dance Handbook, No. 1
Olga Kulbitsky and Frank Kaltman
Folkraft Records
1159 Broad Street
Newark, New Jersey 07114

Fun Dances and Games
Alma Heaton
BYU Bookstore
Provo, Utah 84602

Folk Dancing
Mary Bee Jensen and Clayne R. Jensen
BYU Bookstore
Provo, Utah 84602

Handy Play Party Book
Cooperative Recreation Service, Inc.
Radnor Road, Route 1
Delaware, Ohio 43015

Folk Dance Manual
Cooperative Recreation Service, Inc.
Radnor Road, Route 1
Delaware, Ohio 43015

R E C O R D S

Folkraft Records
1159 Broad Street
Newark, New Jersey 07114

MacGregor Records
729 S. Western Avenue
Los Angeles, California 90005

Bomar Records
10515 Burbank Blvd.
North Hollywood, California 91601

Phil Maron's Folk Shop
1531 Clay Street
Oakland, California 94612

RCA Victor Records
155 East 24th Street
New York, New York 10010

Folk Dancer
Yates Record Shop
436 East 400 South
Salt Lake City, Utah 84111

Festival Folkshop
161 Turk Street
San Francisco, California 94102

Square formation

Basket formation

SQUARE DANCING

INTRODUCTION

Four couples, a square of open floor space, music, and a caller--the makings of an evening of long-to-be-remembered fun, American style. No other form of dance in this country, from the grass roots to the city sidewalks, is more deeply implanted in our history or more enthusiastically executed by its adherents of every generation.

The reason for the perennial durability of square dancing is, quite simply, that it's fun. It is fun for grandparents, their kindergarten grandchildren, and everyone in between. It can be simple or intricate, graceful or rambunctious, but it is fun. It is great exercise, calculated to improve the circulation and to warm the heart. A rewarding sense of achievement comes from stepping through the paces of square dance; and once a person has done it well, he looks forward with anticipation to the time when he can do it again.

Social barriers break down as dancers follow the instruction "You swing my girl and I'll swing yours." It makes no difference that "my girl" is the president's wife and "yours" is the custodian's daughter. The grand right-and-left mixes farmers and pharmacists, bankers and bakers, teachers and typists. Wherever and by whomever it is performed, square dancing has the capacity to close generation gaps and open up channels of communication through vigorous, rhythmic group activity.

Although square dancing is usually considered American, it stems from the folk dances of Europe that preceded it by hundreds of years. The formation known as the "square" and most of the movements used in square dancing originated with the old European formation dances. Elements of the square dance have been traced back to English morris dances, the elegant ballroom dancing of the French aristocracy, Scottish reels, Irish jigs, mazurka quadrilles, the polka, and the waltz. Along with Europe's contribution, Spanish-American and Mexican dances of the Southwest have also contributed to the American square dance. Through the years, square dancing has undergone almost constant change. Even today movements and terminology are not static. Because of this dynamic quality, square dancing continues to be challenging, interesting, and exciting for even the more experienced dancers.

This chapter contains the most widely used square dance calls and their various movements, which can be endlessly combined. Technically, square dancing is done in a hollow square by four couples; however, the steps can be adapted to single circle, double circle, team, and threesome dancing.

Following in this chapter are some general hints for square dancing, a discussion of square dance calling, a glossary of terms, and the dances. Dance formations discussed consist of the single circle, the double circle, teams, threesomes, and the traditional square.

Note

Because the repetition of figures and the patter used in calling them makes further detailed instruction redundant, and because the names of the figures are often long and cumbersome to reuse, as well as quite variable, the format for writing the dances in this chapter departs from that used elsewhere.

Instead, the names of the figures have been underlined where no instructions at all are given with the call, or instructions without the name of the figure have been placed opposite the corresponding line in the call. However, two dances written in the conventional format of this book--"Oh, Johnny!" and "Fun with Swing"--have been purposely left to enable the reader to contrast the methods of writing.

A FEW GENERAL HINTS

●Directions in the calls are for the men. Ladies must usually reverse the directions. For example, with the call allemande left the man turns to his left-hand lady, but the lady turns right and gives her left hand to the man on her right.

●Smoothness in square dancing is a must; skipping or bouncing up and down is bad form and wears a dancer out quickly. Develop a smooth, easy gliding step and swing.

●Listen to the caller. Never try to anticipate what he might say; wait for the call.

●Eliminate clapping, stomping, and any other unnecessary noise. In good western square dancing clapping is permitted only when the caller calls for it.

●Any mistake made in square dancing is caused by at least two people, never just one. Remember this when you want to blame someone else for mistakes made in your square.

●When doing a grand right-and-left, look the dancers you meet straight in the eye and give them a smile. Some dancers never do look at each other; they just grab one hand after another until they meet their partners, and thus miss a lot of the social enjoyment of square dancing.

●Maintain good posture. Keep your weight forward on the balls of your feet, not back on your heels.

●Men! Bone-crusher grips and bull-by-the-tail swings have no place in square dancing. When swinging, lean back to get enough centrifugal force for a smooth, rhythmic swing but avoid roughness or a sudden release of your partner which may throw her off balance.

●Be courteous and polite at all times. Thank the members of your set for the dance. After a mixer, don't leave a partner stranded in the middle of the floor; escort her back to her partner before dashing off to find yours.

●Don't worry about making errors. Half the fun of square dancing is making occasional mistakes.

SQUARE DANCE CALLS

A good caller is vital to an evening of square dancing; without him there can be no dance. It is the caller who keeps the dancers together by instructing their movements, and who maintains the pace and enthusiasm of the evening by his efficient leadership. Becoming a good caller takes practice, however, and development of the qualities discussed hereafter.

The caller's voice must be clear. If any call is not clearly understandable, the dancers will be lost. Also, the pitch of his voice should be pleasant to the ear. If he fails to pitch his voice to harmonize with the music, the sound of it will be distressing to the dancers and will hamper much of the pleasure of the evening.

There is a quality of any voice perhaps best defined by calling it excitement. It attracts attention and makes people want to listen. It creates the impression that what is being said is important. Although to an extent some have it and some don't, this quality can be developed and is essential in a good caller's voice.

A deadpan caller is no addition to any party. He needs to empathize with the dancers, making them feel that he is part of what they are doing and that he is glad to be there. In this way the caller participates in the dancing. If he withdraws from that participation, everyone feels the difference.

Personality is a quality hard to define, but good callers have it in their voices. In striving to achieve an individual style, the beginner may overdo and become artificial and unnatural. But if he works to master the other basic elements of good calling, the personality will probably come naturally.

In addition to these qualities of his voice, the caller must have a good sense of timing. The pattern of his rhythms must be precise and clear. The rests must be properly distributed without interfering with the dance routine. In western square dancing, where timing is flexible and not based on a regular eight-measure phrase, it is particularly important for the caller to sense the right timing. The following call makes a good illustration of this necessity.

> Two gents swing with the elbow swing,
> Opposite partners elbow swing.
> Now two gents with the same old thing,
> Now your partners, elbow swing.

Each line of the above call is exactly four counts long and the meter continues from line to line without pause. However, a set of dancers cannot keep up with that mechanical perfection. They have too far to go around each other, too much floor to cover. It is necessary to introduce waits. Perhaps the call should be counted something like this:

> Two gents swing with the elbow swing (wait wait),
> Opposite partners elbow swing.
> Now two gents with the same old thing (wait wait),
> Now your partners, elbow swing.

The overall rate of speed of calling depends on how well the group dances. Generally speaking, however, 132 to 140 beats to the minute is about right. If the dance is too slow the group will lose interest. The better the dancers, of course, the faster the tempo.

The good caller has, in addition to a properly trained voice and a fine sense of timing, the personal qualifications that make it possible for him to relate well to the group. Among these are the ability to command, a sense of pattern, and a warmth that maintains contact with the dancers. Of course, the caller cannot be a tyrant, and part of the quality that makes for good command comes from the excitement in his voice. There is, however, a personal characteristic that penetrates the laughter, the scuffle of feet, the music, and even the patter of the call, that reaches out to the dancers and makes them pay attention and try their best.

Dance patterns can become boggled if the caller does not know exactly what he is doing. Good calling depends on a detailed knowledge of the skills and the limitations of square dancing. The composition of the dance depends on the caller, and he can frustrate the dancers if he tries to put too many changes into one dance.

Some singing calls have been written out for the caller and are properly timed to allow the dancers to move at a comfortable speed. A number of singing-call records have been recorded with the calls already on them. These may be used with success if the program is properly outlined and the selected records have only simple calls on them.

If the leader wishes to call his own dance but is not experienced in calling, he can obtain records which have the music and calls on one side of the record and the instrumental version only on the other side. He may then practice with a professional caller's recording as an aid in both pitch and timing.

The leader should first become completely familiar with the calls to be used and with the actions expected of the dancers. The calls below will provide an introduction to the art of square dance calling. When using them, remember to--

- Demonstrate the figure as you explain it
- "Talk" the dancers through the figure, using the call given
- Call the dancers through the figure without music, calling one or two beats ahead of the dancers' movements
- Play the appropriate band on the record or call the dance with the music

TYPES OF CALLS

In the chapter of this book on techniques of teaching, the calls were listed as directional, rhythm, counting, chanting, and prompting. Square dance calls are generally prompting calls that cue the dancers to the next dance figure and are called ahead, except in some singing calls where the call is spoken on the same beat on which the dancers execute the command. In such cases, the dancers must have the dance memorized or they will always be behind the caller and the music.

A square dance call is usually divided into four parts:
a. introduction,
b. breaks,
c. body or figures, and
d. ending.

The introduction, breaks, and ending often contain the same dance pattern, and their calls are correspondingly similar.

Introductory calls are those used to get the dancers started and accustomed to the caller and the tempo of the music before the main figure of the dance commences.

Trimmings are the break calls called between the main figures of the dance.

Patter or hash calls comprise the main figures of the dance. They are chanting calls made up by the caller and serve mainly as a rhythmic background for the dancers; they do not follow the melody of the music. These calls may be quite entertaining if the caller is imaginative and creative. The calling of hash or patter calls requires a thorough knowledge of square dancing, hours of practice, and good use of the vocal apparatus, including clear diction, clear vocal tones, proper pitch, emphasis of the important commands, and an excited quality in the voice. It requires proper timing so that the dancers move at a comfortable speed and are not too hurried, and yet do not have to stop and wait for the next call. Acquiring these skills requires so much practice that unless one is a professional caller or is learning to be one it is best not to attempt to call "hash" for an entire evening, but to use square dancing as only part of an evening's entertainment.

Ending calls are similar to introductory and trimming calls, but generally contain words that indicate the end of the dance.

For a number of the dances in this chapter, only the figure has been described. Introductions, breaks, and endings may therefore be added as desired; examples of these follow.

EXAMPLES OF CALLS

<u>Introductory calls</u>: Listed below are a few introductory calls used mainly in the West.

All jump up and never come down,
Swing your honey,
Go 'round and 'round.
You promenade, boys,
Promenade.

All join hands and go the middle;
Make your feet keep time to the fiddle.
When you do that remember my call:
Swing on the corners and promenade all.
    [repeat three more times]

First you whistle and then you sing,
Now all join hands and make a ring.

Allemande left and ladies star,
The gents walk around but not too far.
Allemande left and gents star,
The gals walk around but not too far.
Allemande left with the ol' left hand,
A right to your honey in a right-and-left grand.

<u>Trimmings</u>: An important part of any square dance call, trimmings are patter calls filling in between the hash calls of the figures and providing a rhythmical background for the dancers. Not every trimming is satisfactory for any given call, and the caller must make his selection wisely. Following are examples of trimmings used in connection with various square dance movements.

    For an allemande left and grand right-and-left:
Allemande left when you come down;
Now the grand ol' right-and-left.
And a hand over hand and a heel over heel--
The faster you go the better you feel.

Allemande left with the ol' left hand,
A right to your honey in a right-and-left grand.
Right and left on a heel and toe,
Around the ring and away you go.

Right and left on a heel and toe;
Hi, Mary, hello, Joe.

Swing your corner with your left hand,
Your partner right in a right-and-left grand.

237

Go right and left around the ring
While the roosters crow and the birdies sing.

Allemande left as pretty as you can
And you dance right into a right-and-left grand.
Hand over hand and around you go
And you dance right off on your heel and toe.

Meet your Sally, meet your Sue,
Meet that gal with a rundown shoe.

    For a promenade:
Greet your honey and promenade eight;
Promenade eight 'til you get straight.

Meet your taw and promenade 'round
Like a jaybird walking on frozen ground.

Meet your honey, don't be afraid
To take that gal and promenade.

Meet your taw, pretty little squaw,
And promenade to Arkansas.

    For a square-through:
With a left hand back and you pull her through,
And the right hand out with a howdy do, how are you?
Shufflin' along with the ol' shu shu.

Step on it, boys, you're right in the pink.
Enjoy yourself; it's later than you think.

Snap it up, you're doing fine;
A step in time will save you nine.

Late to bed and early to rise
Will pack the bags under your eyes.

Rush 'em, gals, and give 'em a push;
A bird in the hand is worth two in the bush.

Squeeze 'em, girls, and hold 'em right;
A barking dog will never bite.

Put your eggs all in a basket.
If he won't dance, he's headed for the casket.

Squeeze your honey and watch him squirm;
Getting a man is like catching a worm.

    For a swing:
Swing 'em high and whirl 'em low,
Keep on swingin' your calico.

Swing 'em all day, swing 'em all night.
Go allemande left, go left and right.

Swing that gal around and 'round.
Kiss her, boys, and go to town.

Swing that gal, that pretty little miss.
Squeeze her tight and steal a kiss.

  For any movement:
Hurry up, boys, and meet your boss;
He who hesitates is surely lost.

Rush 'em, boys, and give 'em a push;
A bird in the hand is worth two in the bush.

The early bird catches the worm,
So grab your honey and give her a turn.

Here comes one that hasn't been caught,
So strike now while the iron is hot.

It's hotter than heck but don't mind the weather
When good friends get together.

I went out to milk but I didn't know how;
I milked the goat instead of the cow.

Step on it, girls, you're right in the pink.
You can coax a man to dance but you can't make him think.

If you're behind and missed a call,
Don't stop to scratch, just get on the ball.

Ending calls:

That's all, boys, that's all.

Keeno, boys, that's all.

Promenade around the square,
Now take her out for a little fresh air.

Promenade around the hall,
That's it, boys, that's all.

Promenade your lady fair,
Take her over to an easy chair.

Promenade all, it's the end of the call;
Promenade out through the hole in the wall.

Swing your honey around and around;
When you get tired just set her down.

Men to the center and form a star.
Run along, girls, leave them right thar.

Swing 'em hard and let 'em go,
Take those gals to the old maid's row.

Ladies to their places with the gents on a halter.
Thank the band and kiss the caller.

That's all there is, the dance is ended.
Go sit down; the caller is winded.

Your gal's pretty, but she's so frank.
Take them heifers to the water tank.

Meet your honey, whoop and holler,
Take her to chow for a whole silver dollar.

Wink to your honey, kiss her on the sly,
Take her in your arms and home you fly.

S Q U A R E   D A N C E   T E R M S

The following is a list of terms unique to square dancing. Terms not
defined here may be found in the main list of terms in the section entitled,
"How to Use the Book."

Active couple: The couple performing a particular movement at a given time.
If the caller directs the head couples to perform a right-and-left through,
the head couples would become active; the side couples would be inactive.

All around your left-hand lady: A movement in which the man faces his
corner, passes right shoulders around her, and returns to place, passing
left shoulders.

All eight chain: A movement in which each dancer joins right hands with the
person designated, and moves past that person to join left hands with the
next dancer. Each couple then performs a courtesy turn to face the center of
the set.

Allemande left: A movement in which each dancer takes his corner in a left
forearm grip and walks completely around her to face his own partner and
there waits for the next call.

Allemande right: A movement similar to an allemande left, except that it is
done with the partner or with the right-hand person and with a right forearm
grip.

Allemande thar: A movement in which the dancers face their corners, join
left hands and walk around each other, then turn counterclockwise back to
their partners to join right hands and pull by to the next person and join
left hands. Holding on to this person but shifting to a forearm grip, the
men move in and form a right-hand star, walking backward. Ladies are on the

outside walking forward. The men break the star but retain their forearm grip with the ladies, and couples make a half-turn right so that the men are facing counterclockwise and the ladies clockwise. The dancers then move on to the person each is facing, join right hands, and pull by to the next person and join left hands. Holding on to this person but again shifting to a forearm grip, the men move in and form a right-hand star walking backward, with the ladies on the outside walking forward. The men break the star but retain their forearm grip with the ladies, and couples make a half-turn right so that the men are facing counterclockwise and the ladies clockwise. Each person should now be facing his original partner, if there are four couples in a square.

    Call:
Allemande left and allemande thar,
With a right and a left, and form a star.
Let that star through the heavens whirl,
And a right and left to the second girl.
And star again.
Shoot that star and find your own;
There she is, boys; promenade home.

Along the line: A command given when dancers are in line formation (for example, in two lines of four facing each other), instructing them to perform the movement in the direction of the line, rather than across the set to the opposite line.

Appropriate command: Any command to perform a movement which the dancers are in position to perform.

Arky style: A term referring to figures done by two dancers of the same sex working together as a couple.

Arm turn: A movement in which two dancers facing each other assume a forearm hold, with the hand of each person placed just below and inside the elbow of the other person. The two walk around each other in a clockwise direction. The center of the turn (point of pivot) should be halfway between the hands of the two dancers. See also Allemande left.

Around one to a line: A movement in which the active dancers split the inactive couple and separate. Each one moves in his or her direction around an inactive dancer and steps up beside that dancer to form a line of four with the inactive couple in the center.

Back by the left: A movement in which the dancers change from a right-hand star to a left-hand star by releasing the right handhold, making a half turn in to the right to form a left-hand star, and then moving forward counter-clockwise.

Balance: A movement which may be performed in either of the following ways.
(a) Partners face each other with right hands joined, take one step forward, close or touch with the other foot, and then step back and close or touch. This is the movement that dancers would do unless directed otherwise.
(b) Partners face each other with right hands joined, step with the right foot and swing the left foot in front, then step with the left foot and swing the right foot in front.

Balance four in line, or balance your line: A movement in which two couples join hands and stand in a straight line so that partners have their right hands joined and are facing in opposite directions. All balance in place.

Balance swing: A movement in which the couple balances and then takes swing position; the man holds the lady's right hand in his extended left hand, and puts his right hand on her waist, while she places her left hand on his right shoulder. Each should stand slightly left of the other so that right hips almost touch. They then swing clockwise with rapid walking steps.

Barge-through: A movement in which two facing lines of four approach each other, and all dancers do a half-square-through (two hands). Then those facing inward do a pass-through while those facing outward do a partner trade. The movement ends in eight-chain-through formation.

Basic: A generally accepted, time-tested movement.

Bend the line: A movement in which a line with an even number of dancers breaks in the middle; the end dancers move forward while the center dancers move back until the halves are facing.

Boomps-a-daisy: A movement executed by swinging the hips so as to bump the person designated in the call.

Box the gnat: A movement in which partners join right hands and the lady makes a half-turn left under the joined hands as the man walks forward, making a half-turn right, so that they exchange places and end facing each other. See also Swat the flea.

Break: The call telling the dancers to let go of or drop hands.

Break and trail, or single file Indian style: A movement in which the dancers circle left, then, on command, drop hands and reverse direction, walking in single file back to their original positions. This is sometimes done with the right hand on the left shoulder of the person ahead. In Indian style, the ladies give an Indian call while each man holds his free hand at the back of his head with the fingers vertical to represent feathers.

Buzz swing: A movement executed in closed dance position. Partners lean apart at the waist with inside feet close together and swing clockwise, shifting inside feet just enough to keep their balance and pushing with the outside feet as if on a scooter. Couples should not bounce. The swing should be done with as little up-and-down movement as possible.

Cast off: A movement executed from a line of four dancers in which the middle dancers drop hands and separate, walking forward three-quarters turn around the end dancers, turning them also. The end person helps by backing up slightly as the other moves around him to act as a pivot. Dancers end as two couples facing at right angles to the original line.

Catch all eight: A movement in which partners face each other, assume a right forearm grip, and swing clockwise for two steps. They then do a quick half-turn and change to a left forearm grip, and swing counterclockwise for four or more steps as directed by the caller.

Centers in: A movement executed with two couples facing the same direction, one couple directly behind the other. The lead couple steps apart, and the couple behind moves between the separated lead couple, resulting in a line of four people facing in the same direction.

Chain, ladies chain, or ladies change: A movement, executed by two couples facing each other, in which the ladies clasp right hands and cross toward each other's place. Each lady extends her left hand to take the opposite man's left hand and places her right hand at the back of her waist to receive his right hand. He takes her right hand and they turn counterclockwise to end facing the other couple.

Chanting call: A call done in harmony and rhythm with the music.

Circle four: A movement in which two couples face each other, join hands, and circle left (clockwise).

Circle left: A movement in which the group joins hands and circles clock-wise.

Circle right: A movement in which the group joins hands and circles counter-clockwise.

Circle to a line: A movement executed with two couples forming a ring and circling to the left. The man indicated by the caller breaks his left hand-clasp while retaining the hold with his right hand. All others in the circle retain their handholds, and the four dancers spread out to form a line of four, facing toward the center of the set.

Circle to a two-faced line: A movement in which two couples join hands and circle four (to the left or clockwise). Just before reaching the halfway mark, each couple releases the hands of the other couple and continues a few steps further left, then steps forward into a two-faced line.

Circulate: A movement starting with the dancers in two lines of four where those indicated move forward one position.

Closer, or ending: The final sequence of square dance movements which follows the figure, or main portion, of the dance.

Cloverleaf: A movement executed from a completed double-pass-through forma-tion. The dancers in the two outside couples step forward slightly and separate, and each moves one-quarter of the way around the outside of the square until he meets another dancer coming toward him. They then turn to face the square and step toward its center. The couples second in line in the formation have followed the couples in front of them by first moving forward, then dividing and moving one-quarter of the way around the square until each dancer meets another person. They then face the center of the original square directly behind the other couple to end in double-pass-through formation at right angles to the original formation.

Coordinate: A smooth action figure which starts from single-file columns and ends in two-faced lines. (To get to the columns, heads may lead to the right and circle with the sides to a line, then all do a curlique.) On

243

command, all circulate single file one and one-half positions to set up three pairs of dancers in column formation with right hands adjacent and two men as lonesome ends, each facing his right. The three pairs then assume right forearm grips and turn one-half turn. The center pair of these, consisting of two men, will then separate and each man will step forward to end beside the lady in front of him, as the lonesome men on the ends of the set step ahead and beside the lady in front of them to form two two-faced lines at right angles to the columns.

Corner: For a man, the lady on his left in a single circle or square; for a lady, the man on her right.

Couples backtrack: A movement executed from promenade position in which the man and lady each do an individual about-face turn toward each other while retaining handholds to end with the man on the right and the lady on the left, facing opposite the original direction.

Couples separate: A movement in which partners turn their backs on each other and follow the directions of the next call separately. Usually they are told to promenade around the outside of the square. When they pass on the other side, the man should pass on the outside while the lady stays close to the square. All those not active should "close ranks" so that the active dancers will not have so far to go.

Courtesy turn: A movement where partners face and join left hands, with the lady placing her right hand on her right hip, palm out, and the man placing his right hand on the lady's right hand. Both then turn counterclockwise to face the center of the square, with the man backing up and the lady moving forward.

Cross-trail, or trail-through: A movement executed like a pass-through except that after each person has passed right shoulders with the dancer facing him, each man turns diagonally to his right and crosses behind his partner, who advances diagonally to the left. The movement ends with the couples facing away from the center, the lady on her partner's left.

Curlique: A movement where a man and lady face, joining and raising right hands. The man then does the equivalent of a star-through while the lady does a three-fourths twirl left under the man's arm, so that they end facing opposite directions, their right shoulders close together, at right angles to their original position.

Daisy chain: A movement similar to a grand right-and-left. The dancers, however, progress forward, pulling by with the right hand and the left hand, and then turn back to make a right-hand turn with the person behind them. The dancers repeat this action, moving forward two hands and back one, to progress around the set until original partners meet or the caller terminates the movement.

Dive-through: A movement executed by two couples facing each other. The couple whose back is to the center of the square makes an arch with joined inside hands; the other couple joins hands and moves forward, ducking under the arch. The couple who made the arch moves forward and does a frontier whirl to face the square.

Dixie chain: A movement executed by two couples facing each other in a single line formation, ladies standing in front of their partners. The couples advance toward each other and perform a movement similar to the grand right-and-left: the two ladies join right hands and pass right shoulders, then join left hands with the men facing them and pass left shoulders; the two men join right hands and pass right shoulders. The couples end facing out, ladies in front of their partners, all still in single file.

Do paso: A movement in which partners join left hands and circle each other, then join right hands with their corner and circle, then join left hands (with partner) and turn to position. It is usually executed in a circle or square.

Dos-a-partner, dos-a-corner: Terms indicating a do-si-do around the partner or the corner as indicated.

Do-si-do Alamo style: A movement performed by two couples in a circle, generally following a circle four movement, the ladies brushing left shoulders and giving their left hand to their partner and their right hand to the other man. This forms a circle with the men facing in and the ladies facing out. Each dancer rocks forward one step and back one step, then repeats these rocking steps. The dancers then release right hands and each couple wheels one-half turn counterclockwise to join right hands with other dancers, re-forming the circle with the ladies facing in and the men facing out. The rocking forward and back is repeated. Then the dancers release left hands and wheel one-half turn clockwise with the right-hand person, then step forward, each man to his own partner with his left hand and turn with her to finish with a courtesy turn.

Double elbow: A movement in which partners lock right elbows and turn two steps clockwise, then turn one-half turn in two steps to shift from the right to the left elbows and turn in the opposite direction for four steps. Dancers then lock right elbows with the next person and repeat the movement until otherwise directed by the caller.

Double-pass-through: A movement executed from a completed wheel-and-deal formation in which all four couples advance forward, passing right shoulders with the dancers facing them so that each couple passes through two other couples.

Eight-chain-through: A movement performed by head couples facing side couples (this may be set up by head couples executing a star-through and a frontier whirl). Each dancer joins right hands with the person designated, moves past that person, and joins left hands with the next dancer. The end couples then perform a courtesy turn to face the center of the set, as the center couples join left hands with their opposite and pull by to face the ends.

Elbow swing: A movement in which the persons indicated by the caller join designated arms in an elbow lock and wheel one full turn.

Elbow swing one and one-half, or once and one-half: A movement generally done similar to a grand right-and-left with hooked elbows. Each dancer hooks right elbows with his partner and walks around her one full turn, then hooks left elbows with the next person and turns around her one full turn.

All repeat this action, continuing as in a grand right-and-left, until partners meet or other directions are called.

Ends turn in: A movement performed by lines of four dancers facing out from the center of the set. The two dancers in the middle of the line join inside hands and hold them high; the two on the ends step forward, perform a half-turn, and dive under the arch. The two who formed the arch then perform a frontier whirl to end facing the center of the set.

Fan the top: A movement executed from an ocean wave formation (right or left hand) where the center dancers turn three-quarters while the end dancers release handholds and move up one position to form an ocean wave at right angles to the original wave.

Figure: A sequence of square dance movements which ends with the men at their home positions. The ladies are also usually at their original positions at the end of a figure. The figure or figures compose the main portion of the dance. Several figures placed together in a set sequence constitute a routine or round dance.

Fill-in calls, or patter calls: Calls given between command calls. They do not direct the dancers to perform movements, but give continuity to the calls.

Flutter wheel: A movement performed by two facing couples in which the ladies (or right-hand persons) go into the center and turn by the right forearm, taking the opposite man's right hand with their free left hand as they pass and taking him along and back to their original position. The ladies then release right forearms and couples end facing each other.

Foot couples: Couples number two and four, more commonly known as side couples.

Forearm grip: See One-hand turn.

Forward and back: A movement in which the individuals or couples designated by the caller move forward three steps, then back three steps. (Count: forward, two, three, touch, back, two, three, touch.)

Four hands 'round, or four hands up: A movement in which two couples join hands and circle clockwise one full turn.

Four ladies chain, or grand chain: A movement in which the four ladies form a right-hand star and rotate clockwise one-half turn. Each lady then joins left hands with the man opposite her, and he courtesy turns her.

Frontier whirl, or California twirl: A movement executed by two dancers standing side by side, the lady on the right. They join inside hands and make one-half turn toward each other as they exchange places, the lady walking under the raised right arm of the man, to end facing opposite their original direction.

Grand right-and-left Alamo style: A movement performed by couples holding hands in a circle. In four counts, each man does an allemande left with his corner and, keeping hold of her left hand, takes hold of his partner's right hand. This forms a circle with the men facing in and the ladies facing out. Men then balance into the circle on the next four counts as ladies balance out; then all balance back four counts. (Step forward on left foot, swing right foot forward, step back on right foot, lift left foot forward.) Men then drop left hands and, keeping hold of their partner's right hand, walk clockwise four counts to take the next lady in the line by the left hand. Men are now facing out of the circle and ladies are facing in. All balance forward and back again. Men drop right hands and walk counterclockwise around the ladies for four counts, join right hands with the next lady, repeat the balance, and so continue around the ring until they meet their own partners. They then turn them into place and promenade.

Grand square: A metered figure in which the side couples in a square perform one movement and the head couples another simultaneously. The dancers take four steps to complete each movement. First the side couples face their partners and back away from each other four steps, then turn to face their opposites and come together in four steps, then turn to face each other and walk toward each other four steps, then face their opposites and back away four steps. At the same time the head couples move into the center of the square in four steps, turn to face their partners and back away four steps, turn to face their opposites and back away four steps, and turn to face their partners and come together in four steps. At this point all dancers are now in home position. The head couples now perform the movements of the side couples as the side couples perform those of the head couples to reverse the figure and end in home position as at the beginning.

Half-promenade, or promenade half: A movement executed by two couples facing each other in which they exchange places by promenading counterclockwise past each other to occupy each other's former position. If opposite couples in the square half-promenade, they will promenade halfway around the inside of the square. Sometimes couples are directed by the caller to half-promenade on the outside of the square, but they would do this only when specifically directed.

Half-sashay: Another term for Rollaway.

Hand-over-hand: Another term for Grand right-and-left.

Hands: A term meaning dancers, used as a short form in calling movements. For example, circle four (six, eight) hands around commands a designated group of people to join hands and circle left or right as the caller indicates.

Hash: A collection of calls for various movements arranged in an appropriate sequence and called as a chant. These calls form the main figure or figures of the dance.

Head couples, heads: (a) Couples one and three. (b) In team formation, the couple facing in the line of dance (visiting couple).

Hoedown music: Lively hillbilly music with a strong beat, used to accompany folk or square dancing.

Home, home position, or home station: The position in which couples started the dance. Actually, the ladies do not have home positions since they change partners throughout the dance.

Honors all: A command for men to bow and ladies to curtsy to their partners.

Hub: The star formed by the inside dancers in a star promenade or allemande thar position.

Hub back out--rim turn in: A movement executed from a star promenade position where the couples keep hold of each other while the centers (those forming the star) drop hands and back out; those on the outside then move forward into the center and form a star. This results in a star promenade position with the ladies on the inside forming a right-hand star rotating clockwise.

Inappropriate command: A command to perform a movement that the dancers are not in position to execute.

Indian style: A command for dancers to circle single file.

Inside out--outside in: A movement executed in 8 steps by couples facing each other. The couple designated ducks forward under the arch made by the joined inside hands of the other couple. At the same time the arching couple moves forward until both couples are back to back. Then the couple who had gone under the arch joins and raises inside hands and moves backward and over the other couple, who backs under the arch, so that the couples end facing each other.

Ladies chain: A movement in which two ladies in opposite couples advance, join right hands to pull past each other, then give their left hands to the opposite men, who courtesy turn them.

Ladies to the center, back to the bar: A movement, often preceding star movements, in which the ladies move three steps forward toward the center of the square, then three steps back to their home positions.

Make a basket: A movement in which the ladies move to the center of the set and stand in a circle with hands joined, while the men walk once around the circle to the right, then raise their joined hands up and over the ladies' heads and down in front of them. Usually a buzz step follows.

Mark time: The command to change weight from one foot to the other in one spot in time with the music. Marking time prepares dancers to move forward and keeps them in rhythm while waiting for the next call.

Men run: From a swing-through, men run around the lady on their right to come back to a position facing the same direction as the lady.

Ocean wave: A line of dancers facing in alternating directions with hands joined, in which the dancers rock forward two counts and back two counts.

On to the next: A command given to a person or couple after executing a movement with another couple (or single dancer), indicating to him to leave that position, move to the next couple or person in his direction of movement, and repeat the movement with them.

One-hand turn, forearm grip, or forearm turn: A grip in which the forearms are held horizontally and each person clasps the forearm of the other person near the elbow (right arm with right arm or left with left). This gives a short grasp for fast turns.

Opener: A preliminary sequence of square dance movements which precede the figure, or main portion, of the dance.

Opposite: The dancer facing a person whose partner is beside him. For example, when two couples face each other the man's opposite is the lady facing him and the lady's opposite is the man facing her. The two couples are also termed opposite.

Partner: The dancer on the man's right or lady's left (a) at the beginning of a dance, or (b) at the beginning of any figure of the dance. Other terms for partner are mother, ma, pa, and so on.

Pass-through: A movement in which two facing couples (or threesomes) walk forward and past each other, each person passing right shoulders with his opposite and moving to the position occupied by the other couple.

Patter calls: Calls, done to music with little melody, that serve mainly as rhythmic background and entertainment. In patter calls the caller does not follow the melody.

Promenade: The act of walking with a shuffle step in the line of dance in couples with the lady on the man's right. Their arms are crossed with hands clasped in front of them; the lady's right hand is in the man's right and her left hand is in his left hand. His right arm should be above her left arm. Occasionally a two-step is used instead of the shuffle.

Promenade all with a left-hand star: A movement in which each man puts his left hand in the center, clasping the other men's hands to form a star, and puts his right arm around his partner. All then walk counterclockwise around the set.

Pull her by, or pull by: A movement in which two dancers each clasp the other's hand, pass each other, and move on as directed by the next call.

Red hot: A movement usually started from a promenade position in which each lady makes one-half turn left, moving in front of her partner, as each man moves to his right-hand lady and they wheel one-half turn around with a right forearm swing. Then each man returns to his partner and they perform a complete turn with a left forearm swing. The man then moves to his corner lady and they do a right forearm swing for one-half turn; then all return to their partners for another complete left forearm swing.

Reel: A movement performed by two facing lines, one of men and one of ladies. The couple at the head of the set hooks right elbows, turning 1-1/2 times clockwise so that the lady faces the man's line and the man faces the lady's line. They then separate, and the head lady swings the next man in line one full turn with a left elbow swing as the head man turns the next lady in line one full turn, also using a left-elbow swing. The head couple now swings together 1-1/2 times using a right elbow swing, then move on to the next lady and man in the lines, swinging them with a left elbow swing. The action is repeated until everyone in the lines has been turned.

Reverse: The command to repeat any given action in the opposite direction. Examples include the call to change a right-hand star to a left-hand star, or to change a clockwise-moving circle to a counterclockwise-moving circle.

Right-and-left back: A movement executed after a right-and-left through where the same two couples pass back in the same way, returning to their original positions.

Right-and-left through: A movement executed while two couples are facing each other. Each person advances and takes the right hand of the person opposite, pulling the person by. Immediately upon passing through the other couple, the man gives his left hand to his partner and courtesy turns her, so that the couples end facing one another, but have exchanged places.

Rim: The outside persons in a star promenade or allemande thar formation.

Rip 'n' snort: A movement executed from a circle with all hands joined in which the couple indicated by the caller moves across to the couple opposite, who makes an arch. Leading the other dancers with them, the lead dancers go under the arch, then separate, moving away from each other and leading the other dancers around the outside of the original circle until they once again meet and join hands in a circle facing in. After all have gone under the arch, the arching dancers turn under their own arms, without releasing handholds, to face the center of the circle. Occasionally, the call will indicate that facing lines are to be formed rather than a circle; in this case, the arching dancers drop hands and follow the other dancers to end in facing lines.

Rollaway, rollaway with a half-sashay, whirl away with a half-sashay, or half-sashay: A movement executed when the lady is on the man's right in which she rolls across in front of him in a full turn from his right side to his left side.

Run: A movement done from an ocean wave formation by either the center two or the end two dancers in the line. If the centers are directed to run, they walk forward one-half turn around the two people on the ends of the line, as the ends move in to occupy the vacancies left by the centers; thus the center two become the new ends of a two-faced line. If the ends are directed to run, they walk halfway around the centers while the centers move out to allow space for them, and they end in a two-faced line.

Sashay: Originally, a series of short sliding steps to the side. In many of today's figures, sashay refers merely to partners exchanging places with the lady passing in front of the man. See also Rollaway (Half-sashay).

Scootback: A movement executed from parallel ocean waves in which the dancers facing in step forward to meet in the center and do a turn-through, as the dancers facing out make one-half turn to fold into the spot vacated by the dancers who were previously beside them facing in. These dancers, on completing the turn-through, take the places of those who were originally facing out to re-form the waves. (When done from a right-hand wave with partners touching right shoulders, the turn-through is done with a right forearm turn and the fold is also to the right. When done from a left-hand wave, the turn-through is with a left forearm grip and the fold is to the left.) This movement can also be done by two couples parallel to each other with partners facing opposite directions.

Seesaw, seesaw your pretty little taw: A movement, usually made when the man returns to place after a do-si-do with his corner, in which partners circle each other by passing left shoulders and returning to place passing right shoulders. If so directed, a man may seesaw his corner in the same manner.

Set: In square dance, four couples in a square formation.

Shoot the star: A movement used to shift out of the allemande thar formation. The four men break their right-hand star but maintain their left forearm grips with their partners. Each couple then does one-half turn counterclockwise to end facing in the line of dance.

Shuffle walk: Short walking steps, the feet always close to the floor, taken in a loose-jointed glide with no up-and-down motion of the shoulders.

Side couples, sides: Couples two and four in the square.

Singing calls: Calls done to music with a melody which the caller follows. These calls are written specifically for the melody and cannot be called ahead.

Slide-through: A movement in which two facing couples pass-through, the men then making one-quarter turn right and the ladies one-quarter turn left to end with partners facing.

Slip the clutch: See Throw in the cluth.

Spin chain-through: A variation of a swing-through using three-quarter turns instead of one-quarter turns. From two parallel ocean wave formations the end dancers turn one-half into the center, then turn three-quarters to form a wave across the set; the center dancers in this new wave then turn one-half to exchange places, then turn three-quarters with the other center dancers of the original waves to re-form the parallel ocean waves.

Spin the top: A movement executed from an ocean wave formation in which all turn one-half by the right hand, then the new centers swing three-quarters by the left hand while the ends move up one position (one-quarter of a full-circle sweep) to join hands with them in a new ocean wave at right angles to the original wave.

Split the ring: A movement in which the designated couple advances forward and between the dancers in the opposite couple. Unless otherwise directed, the lady would then turn to her right and the man to his left and they would continue around the outside of the set back to their original place.

Square: A set of four couples facing each other, each couple forming one side in a square formation.

Square-through: A movement executed by two couples facing each other in which each dancer takes his opposite's right hand and pulls by, then makes one-quarter turn to face his partner. He then takes his partner's left hand and pulls by, then turns one-quarter to face his opposite, and takes his opposite's right hand and pulls by without turning.

Star: A movement in which each person holds the designated arm out at a little lower than shoulder height, men grasping the wrist of the man ahead and ladies using a handhold, and all circle in the direction indicated by the caller.

Star promenade: A movement in which the four men in a square form a left-hand star, placing their right arms around the waists of their partners, and each lady places her left arm around the waist of her partner or on his right shoulder. All promenade forward.

Star-through: A movement executed by two facing dancers in which the man's right hand joins the lady's left, palm to palm and fingers up, and the hands are raised as the two walk toward each other; the lady turns one-quarter turn left under the man's arm as he does one-quarter turn right. They finish side by side with the lady on the man's right.

Swap: Exchange partners with the person indicated.

Swat the flea: A movement in which partners join left hands and the lady makes a half-turn right under the joined hands as the man walks forward and does a half-turn left, so that the dancers exchange places and end facing each other. See also Box the gnat.

Sweep a quarter: A movement in which facing couples in full-open position continue in their previous direction of movement for a 90-degree circling turn (a movement of one position).

Swing: A movement in which the designated man and lady take ballroom dance position, except that they stand to the left of each other so that the outsides of their right feet are touching, and both turn forward.

Swing your opposite: A movement in which the ladies stand still while each man moves left around the inside of the ring to swing his opposite lady. (If the man then comes back to swing his own partner, he should continue around the inside of the set to his left.)

Swing-through: A movement usually done from an ocean wave formation in which the line breaks in the middle and the couples wheel one-half turn clockwise. The new center two persons then join hands and wheel counterclockwise one-half turn to make a new ocean wave line with the dancers originally on the ends of the line now in the center.

Those who can: Those so situated at the time of the call that they can execute the movement. This assumes that some of the dancers are not in position to perform it.

Three-quarter chain: A movement similar to a two-ladies chain or four-ladies chain except that the ladies rotate three-quarters instead of one-half. The ladies form a right-hand star in the center of the square and walk forward three-quarters turn so that each lady meets her corner man; she then joins left hands with him and they perform a courtesy turn.

Throw in the clutch, or slip the clutch: A movement executed from an allemande thar star or a wrong-way thar star in which those in the center retain the star but release handholds with those on the outside. The dancers forming the star then change direction and move forward, while those on the outside continue to walk forward around the outside.

Tip: Two or three successive dances followed by a rest period.

Trade: A movement executed from any line formation where the dancers are not facing within the line. The two dancers designated by the caller in each line trade places in the same line by walking forward and around in a half-circle, passing right shoulders, and each taking the place of the other person. Each active dancer ends facing the opposite direction from which he started.

Trade-by: A movement executed from an eight-chain-through position where the dancers have passed through so that the center four are facing inward and the end four are facing outward. On command, those facing inward pass-through while those facing outward trade.

Trimming: A break call given between the main figures of the dance.

Turn alone, U-turn back, or you turn back: A movement in which each dancer makes an individual one-half turn to reverse direction.

Turn and left through: A movement in which two facing couples, each having done a half-sashay, do a normal turn-through. As they pull by, the men take the ladies' left hands in their left hands and courtesy turn them to end facing the other couple.

Turn right back, or around your own the other way home: A movement executed in a grand right-and-left movement. When the man meets his own partner on the opposite side of the square, he takes her by the right hand and they wheel one-half turn to face the opposite direction, then continue the grand right-and-left in this opposite direction to home position.

Turn the basket inside out: A movement executed from basket formation in which, keeping hands joined, the men raise their hands up over the ladies' heads and down in back; the ladies then do the same, forming a new basket with the hands outside. Usually a buzz-step circle right follows.

Turn-through: A movement in which two facing dancers turn each other one-half by a right-forearm turn, release the arm grip, and move a step forward to end back to back with each other.

Twirl: A movement in which a man and a lady join right (or left) hands and the man either turns the lady under his raised right (or left) arm.

Two-couple basket: A basket formation executed by two couples. As the two ladies bow, the men raise their joined hands over the ladies' heads and lower them behind the ladies' waists. Then the men bow as the ladies raise their joined hands over the men's heads and down behind their waists. Each dancer then leans outward from the waist and moves slowly clockwise with a buzz step.

Two-faced line: A line of four consisting of two couples standing side by side and facing opposite directions.

U-turn back: See Turn alone.

Veer left (right): A movement in which two facing couples move diagonally left (or right if called) and forward to end in a two-faced line.

Wagon wheel: A movement in which all couples allemande left, then men take a right forearm grip with their partners. As each man comes into line with his partner as if to pass her, he flips her or quickly turns her one-half turn clockwise, hooking his right elbow with her left and simultaneously forming a star by putting his left hand in the center and walking forward, or counterclockwise. On command each man breaks the star with his left hand, turns one full turn counterclockwise with his partner, turns her into position facing him, and takes her right hand. After a balance, he continues the grand right-and-left past his partner with his right hand and flips the next lady, hooks elbows, and forms the star as above. When the wagon wheel is again broken, the grand right-and-left is continued until partners meet and promenade.
    Call:
Now allemande left and right to your girl,
Form a wagon wheel and make it whirl;
The hub flies out and the rim flies in,
Now right-hand whirl and another wheel.
The faster you go the better you feel.
It's a right-and-left and a-going again,
Find your partner, find your maid--
There she is, boys, promenade.

Walk and dodge: A movement executed from parallel ocean waves or by two parallel couples with partners facing in opposite directions. Dancers facing in walk across the set (circulate) to take the place of the person who was directly in front of them, while those facing out sidestep (dodge) to fill the spot vacated by the dancer who was formerly facing in beside them, so that all end facing out.

Weathervane: A movement performed by two couples facing each other in which the men move diagonally forward to hook left elbows, reaching behind each other to take the opposite lady's left hand with their left hand, and putting his right arm around his partner's waist. All walk forward. (If desired, all may run forward until the ladies' feet leave the ground and they "fly.")

Weave the ring: The same movement as a grand right-and-left, except that the dancers do not join hands.

Wheel-and-deal: A movement performed by a line of four dancers in which the right-hand couple wheels one-half turn left, with the inside person holding the pivot, as the couple on the left moves forward and wheels one-half turn right to fall in behind the other couple to end in double-pass-through formation.

Wheel-around: A movement executed from star promenade or allemande thar position in which the hub dancers back out and the rim dancers move forward, turning one-half to reverse direction.

Whirl away with a half-sashay: See Rollaway.

Wrong-way thar: A movement following a hand or forearm couple turn in which the dancers designated hold onto the partners they have just turned and move into a left-hand star. The dancers are in the same formation as in an allemande thar except that they are facing in the opposite direction.

You turn back: See Turn alone.

Zoom: A movement executed by two couples, one standing directly in front of the other, facing the same direction. The back couple moves forward while the leading couple separates and these dancers circle back 360 degrees to end directly behind the former back couple.

S Q U A R E   D A N C I N G   I N   A   S I N G L E   C I R C L E

A single circle is a good formation in which to learn square dance figures and steps. It lends itself well to a group of people of assorted ages and sizes or of the same sex. It is also excellent for dance parties and one-night engagements.

For the following figures, a record is available called "Square Dancing in a Single Circle." The price is $6.95. It may be purchased from: Recreation Department, Alma Heaton, 273-H Richards Building, Brigham Young University, Provo, Utah 84602. Checks should be made payable to Alma Heaton. If this record is used, no caller is necessary; and if you listen long enough to the calls, you will have them learned.

This discussion of square dancing in a single circle consists of seven lessons which correspond to bands on the instructional record. Each lesson except the first and last includes a walk-through to familiarize the dancers with the figures to be learned and a call during which dancers may execute and practice the figures.

For each of the lessons, the leader may play the appropriate band of the record "Square Dancing in a Single Circle" or call the written call to any good hoedown record. On the calls the timing is not too important, but the caller's words should match the rhythm of the music.

L E S S O N   O N E

FIGURE   CALL

Circle left   Join your hands and circle left,
                     Circle left, around you go.
                     Well, circle left on a heel and toe.

255

FIGURE	CALL
	Come on, cowboy, don't be slow.
Circle right	Now reverse round the other way back; Make your feet go wickity-wack. Come on, boys, take up the slack, Circle to the right and don't look back.
Swing	Now take your own and give her a swing-- Go 'round and 'round with the dear little thing. Swing her high and swing her low, Swing your gal in calico.
Run to the middle	Now join your hands and stretch way out, Then run to the middle and give a shout. One, two, three, four.
Circle left	Well back right out to the outside ring; Circle to the left like everything. Around you go, around that hall, Now stop where you are and listen to my call.
Men center	Just the fellows, just the gents Run to the middle and give a shout. One, two, three, four.
Swing partner	Then back right out to the outside ring And find your own and give her a swing. Well, swing that gal, go 'round and 'round; Go any old way but upside down.
Girls center	Then just the pretty ones, just the ladies Run to the middle and yell. One, two, three, four.
Circle left	Then back right out to the outside ring; Join your hands and circle. (Repeat as desired.)

L E S S O N   T W O

FIGURES	WALK-THROUGH
Corner and partner	Be sure your partner is on your right, men. Face your partner. Now face the lady on your left; she's your corner. Face your partner; now face your corner.
Do-si-do corner	Now let's do a do-si-do. Face your corner. With the men moving on the outside, pass right shoulders and move sideward to the right, passing back to back, and back into your original position.

FIGURES	WALK-THROUGH
Do-si-do partner	Now let's try a do-si-do with our partners. Again we will pass right shoulders, so this time the men will go to the inside of the ring. Here we go; do-si-do your partners. Move forward passing right shoulders, then back to back, and finally back into your original position.
Buzz swing	To do a buzz swing, let's first take our partners in normal ballroom closed position. Now put your partner to your right side. Put your right foot by your partner's right foot and put your weight on it. With a pushing motion of your left foot, push yourself around your partner and you're swinging. You will find it will help if you lean slightly away from your partner at the waist.
Promenade	Men, step just inside the circle and face your partner. Join right hands with your partner. Reach under your right hand with your left hand and join it with your partner's so that your joined hands are now crossed. Now, both turn and face counterclockwise around the hall. Walk forward with a gliding step and you're promenading.
Ladies turn back	Keep walking, keep promenading around. Now release hands and ladies turn around and go the other way around, while you men keep going the way you are. This is called a turn back. Find a new partner, men, and give her a swing, unless the caller says find your own--or pass your own and swing the next.

CALL

All jump up and never come down,
Then swing your honey, go 'round and 'round,
Any old way but upside down.
Well, join your hands and circle the town.

Circle left around that hall,
Circle left and don't you fall,
Around you go, let's have a ball.
Stop where you are and listen to the call.

Face your corner, the gal on your left,
Do-si-do that corner girl.
Back to back, around you go,
Then face your own and don't be slow.

Well, do-si-do the one you know,
Around you go on a heel and toe.
Then take that gal and give her a swing
And promenade, go 'round the ring.

Now, girls turn back on the outside track,
Around you go and don't come back.

CALL

Keep on walkin' 'round the town,
The big foot up and the little one down.

Well now, gents, just take a gal,
Just any old gal and give her a swing.
Swing that gal 'round and 'round,
Kick her in the shins and don't fall down.

L E S S O N   T H R E E

FIGURES   WALK-THROUGH

Allemande left   Take your corner in a left forearm grip. Walk around her
                    until you are facing your partner and let go of hands.
                    Let's try it again. Allemande left with your corner; take
                    a forearm grip and walk around each other until you are
                    facing your partner.

Allemande right   Take a right forearm grip with your partner. Walk around
                    her until you are facing your corner. This is an
                    allemande right with your partner. Let's try it again.
                    Allemande right with your partner; forearm grip with your
                    partner and walk around her until you are facing your
                    corner.

Balance   Join two hands with your corner lady and both step on
                    your left feet. Swing the right foot across the left,
                    then step on your right foot and swing the left foot
                    across. This is a balance. Let's try it again. Starting
                    on the left foot, step swing, step swing.

                    CALL

                    Allemande left your corners all;
                    It's corner lady with a left hand 'round.
                    Allemande right your partners all,
                    Turn your honey with a right hand 'round.

                    Then find your corner and balance now,
                    Balance left and balance right.
                    Then swing your corner in the middle of the night,
                    Swing her 'round and hold on tight.

                    Then promenade this new little Sue;
                    Promenade, go two by two.
                    She's that gal from Salt Lake City.
                    Golly gee, but ain't she pretty?

                    Well, join your hands in a great big ring,
                    Circle left like everything.
                    Circle left and don't be slow--
                    Like a barefoot boy on frozen snow.
                    (Repeat as desired.)

258

LESSON FOUR

FIGURES	WALK-THROUGH
Grand right-and-left	Allemande left your corner, then stop, facing your partner. Now we are going to go grand right-and-left. Join right hands with your partner, pull her by, and keep going in the same direction. Take the next lady by the left and pull her by, take the next by the right, the next by the left, and swing the next lady. Let's try it again. Allemande left your new corner. Now, starting with your partner, count five hands around the ring. Take your own by the right hand for one, the next by the left for two, a right to the next for three, a left to the next for four, and swing that lady number five.

CALL

Allemande left with the old left hand,
A right to your own; go right-left grand.
Count five hands around the ring;
When you get to five, that fifth little gal--
Well, give her a swing.
Swing that gal with eyes so blue,
She's the gal with the rundown shoe.
Now promenade, go two by two.

LESSON FIVE

FIGURES	WALK-THROUGH
Alamo style	Face your corner for an Alamo style. Allemande left but don't let go of hands. Join hands with your partner. The men should be facing in and the ladies should be facing out. Now all take a step forward, then back. Release left hands and turn your partner halfway around so that the men are facing out and the ladies are facing in, and join left hands with the next lady. Step forward and back again. Release right hands with your partner and turn with a left-hand turn halfway around and join right hands with the next. Rock forward and back again. Release left hands and turn a right-hand turn halfway around to the next and join left hands. Rock forward and back. Release right hands and turn a left-hand turn halfway around, take the next, and promenade.
Whirl away with a half-sashay	Join your hands in a big ring, ladies on their partner's right. Men, pulling with your right hand, roll your partner across to your other side. Ladies, go across turning one full turn to the left. That's a whirl away with a half-sashay. You now have a new partner on your right. Remember, men, the lady on your right is always

259

FIGURES   WALK-THROUGH

your partner, no matter who she is.

CALL

Allemande left in the Alamo style.
A right to your own, gonna balance awhile--
Balance in, balance out.
Turn by the right, it's half about.

Balance out, balance in,
Turn by the left, you're goin' again.
Balance in, balance out.
Turn by the right, it's half about.

Balance out, balance in.
Turn by the left and take that maid,
Take that maid and promenade.
Take that Sue along with you.

Join your hands and circle to the left.
Circle left around I say,
Circle left and hear my say:
All the ladies half-sashay.

Circle left in the same old way,
Circle left; now hear me say:
All the ladies half-sashay.
Swing that gal that's comin' your way.
(Repeat as desired.)

L E S S O N   S I X

FIGURES   WALK-THROUGH

Swat the flea   Face your corner. Join left hands with her and instead
                 of just walking around, men, raise your left hand to form
                 an arch. Ladies, turn under the arch; turn right as you
                 back under the arch. End facing each other and exchanging
                 places. That's what you do when you swat the flea.

Box the gnat   Now, to box the gnat, face your partner. Join right hands
                 with her and, men, raise your right hand to form an arch.
                 Ladies, turn under the arch, turning left as you back
                 under the arch. End facing each other and exchanging
                 places.

Elbow swing   For an elbow swing, start with an allemande left with
                 your corner. Then hook right elbows with your partner
                 and go all the way around her until you meet the next
                 lady--not your corner, but the one past your partner.
                 Hook left elbows with her and go all the way around until

260

you meet the next, hook right elbows with her and go all
the way around until you meet the next and hook left elbows with her and go all the way around, then promenade
the next little maid.

CALL

Face your corner, swat the flea.
Then pull her by and find your own.
Box the gnat with your own little maid,
Pull her by and find old corner.

Well, allemande left. Meet them all with an elbow swing.
Meet your own with a right elbow.
Go all the way 'round, go on to the next
With the left elbow.
Go all the way 'round, then on to the next
With a right elbow.
Go all the way 'round, then on to the next
With a left elbow, a left elbow.
Go all the way 'round, go on to the next
And promenade that sweet little maid.
If she won't drink root beer give her lemonade.

Then join your hands, around you go.
Hurry up, Nellie; come along, Joe.
Circle left, around I say,
Circle left in the usual way.
(Repeat as desired.)

O H, J O H N N Y!

Formation:	Single circle	
Position:	Hands joined	
Footwork:	Opposite (man L, lady R)	

Music: Oh, Johnny!
Record: Old Timer 8209
Rhythm: 4/4, 16 meas

MEAS	CALL	INSTRUCTIONS
1-2	All join hands and circle the ring.	Circle: All circle R.
3-4	Stop where you are and give her a swing.	Swing: Swing partner, then corner, then partner with hip or buzz swing.
5-6	Swing that girl behind you; now your own	
7-8	If you have found she's not flown.	Allemande left: Take corner in L forearm grip and walk 1 full turn around to partner.
9-10	Allemande left with the sweet corner maid,	
11-12	Do-si-do your own.	Do-si-do: Pass R shoulders, moving around and behind partner to pass L shoulders and back into place.

MEAS	CALL	INSTRUCTIONS

13-14 All <u>promenade</u> with your sweet <u>corner</u> maid,

<u>Promenade corner</u>: Assuming promenade position with corner, walk around circle to end in man's home position.

15-16 Singing oh, Johnny! Oh, Johnny, oh!

Repeat entire dance.

L E S S O N   S E V E N

CALL

All join hands and <u>circle right</u>; <u>circle left</u> the other way back.
<u>Walk all around your corner</u>, <u>see-saw your partner</u>.
<u>Allemande left</u> your corner girl.
Meet your honey with a <u>double elbow</u>.
First by the right, then by the left,
On to the next; you're not through yet.
First by the right, then by the left,
On to the next; you're not through yet.
First by the right, then by the left,
On to the next; you're not through yet.
First by the right, then by the left,
On to the next, and promenade.
Promenade with a great big smile;
Promenade, go 'bout a mile.

All join hands and <u>circle left</u>
Around, around, don't be slow.
Break it all up with a <u>do-pas-o</u>.
Partner by the left, go all the way 'round;
Corner by the right, go all the way 'round.
Back to your honey if she ain't too tall,
Back to your corners and promenade all.
Promenade two by two,
Promenade like you used to do.

F U N   W I T H   S W I N G

Formation: Single circle
Position: Hands joined
Footwork: Opposite (man L, lady R)

Music: Any with a good medium tempo
Record: Own choice
Rhythm: 4/4, 56 meas

MEAS	CALL	INSTRUCTIONS

all walk to <u>center</u>

READY FORWARD

<u>Center</u>: All walk to center 4 steps, then back 4 steps.

<u>Ladies in</u>: Ladies walk to

MEAS	CALL	INSTRUCTIONS

MEAS	CALL
1-2	1 2 back now, 1 2 <u>ladies in</u>
3-4	1 2 3 back, 1 2 <u>men in</u>
5	1 2 turn left
6	<u>waist swing</u> corner lady
7-8	1 2 3 4, 5 6 <u>center</u> now
9-10	1 2 3 back, 1 2 <u>ladies in</u>
11-12	1 2 3 back, 1 2 <u>men in</u>
13	1 2 turn left
14	<u>shoulder swing</u> corner lady
15-16	1 2 3 4, 5 6 <u>center</u> now
17-18	1 2 3 back, 1 2 <u>ladies in</u>
19-20	1 2 3 back, 1 2 <u>men in</u>
21	1 2 turn left
22	<u>Irish swing</u> corner lady
23-24	1 2 3 4, 5 6 <u>center</u> now
25-26	1 2 3 back, 1 2 <u>ladies in</u>
27-28	1 2 3 back, 1 2 <u>men in</u>
29	1 2 turn left
30	<u>elbow swing</u> corner lady
31-32	1 2 3 4, 5 6 <u>center</u> now
33-34	1 2 3 back, 1 2 <u>ladies in</u>
35-36	1 2 3 back, 1 2 <u>men in</u>
37	1 2 turn left
38	<u>buzz swing</u> corner lady
39-40	1 2 3 4, 5 6 <u>center</u> now
41-42	1 2 3 back, 1 2 <u>ladies in</u>

INSTRUCTIONS

center 4 steps, then walk back 4 steps.

<u>Men in</u>: Men walk 4 steps to center, turn to face corner, and walk to this new partner in 4 steps.

<u>Waist swing</u>: Putting R arm around partner's waist and holding L hand high, swing 8 ct.

<u>Shoulder swing</u>: Both man and lady place R hand on partner's R shoulder, join L hands, and swing 8 ct.

<u>Irish swing</u>: Partners join R hands, holding them high, and hold partner's R elbow with L hand, and swing 8 ct.

<u>Elbow swing</u>: Partners link R elbows and swing 8 ct.

<u>Buzz swing</u>: Partners assume R-side position and swing 8 ct. This is regular square dance swing.

<u>Backhand swing</u>: Partners put L hands behind own backs, interlock R elbows, join hands in L-R, R-L cnt, and swing 8 ct.

<u>Give her the lead</u>: Lady leads man in 8 ct of any swing.

Repeat entire dance.

MEAS	CALL	INSTRUCTIONS

MEAS	CALL
43-44	1 2 3 back, 1 2 <u>men in</u>
45	1 2 turn left
46	<u>backhand swing</u> corner lady
47-48	1 2 3 4, 5 6 <u>center</u> now
49-50	1 2 3 back, 1 2 <u>ladies in</u>
51-52	1 2 3 back, 1 2 <u>men in</u>
53-54	<u>give her the lead</u>, you're on your own
55-56	1 2 3 4, 5 6 <u>start over</u>

S Q U A R E   D A N C I N G   I N   A   D O U B L E   C I R C L E

Square dancing in a double circle means that couples are facing in team formation with the lady on the man's right. If the dancers were in a square it would be as if one couple were visiting another couple in the set. However, each couple has a chance to visit all the couples instead of just those that would comprise a square. As in other types of team dances, visiting couples face the line of dance and hosts face against the line of dance. This formation is especially good for one-night engagements.

Following are four lessons which correspond to bands on the instructional record "Square Dancing in a Double Circle," which may be obtained, if desired, in the same way as the record "Square Dancing in a Single Circle." The lessons contain figures to be learned first, then walk-throughs of the figures, then calls putting the figures together. Following these lessons are descriptions of dances, all designed for team formation.

L E S S O N   O N E

FIGURES	WALK-THROUGH
Right-and-left through	Now, for a <u>right-and-left through</u>, join right hands with the person <u>opposite</u> you and pull by, looking towards your partner. Join left hands with your partner; men, put your right arm around your partner's waist and turn to face the other couple with men moving back and ladies forward. Let's try it again. [Repeat.]
Pass-through	With the men going on the outside and the ladies going between the dancers in the other couple, all move forward now and do a <u>pass-through</u>. Don't turn around. [At this point, the dancers should meet another couple coming the other way around the circle and the right-and-left through may be reviewed.]

CALL

It's <u>forward up and back</u> with you;
Forward again with your right hand,
Go <u>right-left through</u> across the land.
A right to the opposite, then left to your own.

The gents back up with an arm around.
Now face those two, now here we go.
It's a <u>right-left through</u> across from you;
Go right, then left and turn around.

Well, forward up and back with you,
It's up again and <u>pass-through</u>.
Go on to the next with your right hand,
Go <u>right-left through</u> across the land.

It's a right, then left and turn around.
Face those two, that's what you do;
With the one you're facin' <u>do-si-do</u>,
It's back to back around with you.

Now <u>pass-through</u>, go on to the next.
Join your hands with the next old two.
<u>Circle left</u> just once around,
Go exactly once around.
(Repeat as desired.)

L E S S O N   T W O

FIGURES

Ladies chain

Right- and
left-hand
star

WALK-THROUGH

The two <u>ladies chain</u> by joining right hands and pulling
each other by. Join left hands with the opposite man.
Men, turn this lady as at the end of a right-and-left
through. Let's try it again. [When this figure is repeated the dancers will have their original partners.]

Everybody, put your right hand in so that your hands are
touching. Now walk forward until you are back where you
started. This is a <u>right-hand star</u>. Now make it a <u>left-
hand star</u>; put your <u>left</u> hands in and walk just once
around.

CALL

Two <u>ladies chain</u> and don't be slow;
A right, then left to the gent.
Turn around and face those two;
Two <u>ladies chain</u> back home.

A right, then left and turn around,
Go up and back and don't you frown.
<u>Pass-through</u> to go on to the next,

CALL

It's on to the next with your right hand.

Make a right-hand star.
Go once around them where you are.
Go back by the left and don't be slow,
Around you go on a heel and toe.

And when you're straight
Go forward up and back with you,
Forward again and pass-through.
Go on to the next and meet those two.
(Repeat as desired.)

L E S S O N   T H R E E

FIGURES   WALK-THROUGH

Star-through   Men, reach forward with your right hand and take the
                     opposite lady's left hand. Now raise this hand to form
                     an arch. Ladies, go forward under the arch; men, stay on
                     the outside and turn to face your original partner. You
                     now have a new partner by your side. Go right-and-left
                     through across from you. Face those two and star through
                     again. You should now be back to your original position
                     with your original partner.

Square-through,   Now, square-through, three-quarters around. Join right
three-quarters   hands with your opposite, pull each other by, and face
around   your partner; join left hands with her, pull her by, and
                     face the other lady. Join right hands with her and pull
                     her by but don't turn. You should now be back to back
                     with the couple you were facing, with your original part-
                     ner by your side, lady on the right. Go on to the next
                     couple and let's try it again. [Repeat.]

                     CALL

                     Go forward up and back with you,
                     Forward again and star-through.
                     Go right-left through across from you;
                     Turn around and face those two.

                     Square-through three-quarters 'round
                     Go right, then left,
                     Then right, go on to the next
                     And do-si-do, go all the way around.
                     (Repeat as desired.)

LESSON   FOUR

FIGURES	WALK-THROUGH

Ocean wave

Do-si-do your opposite lady and go all the way around her. Now all step forward with the men on the outside so that you are in one line, facing alternate directions. All join hands. Now if you will step forward and back you will make an ocean wave.

Swing-through

Do-si-do to an ocean wave, rock up and back. Now, ladies, keep holding the man's hand, but let go of each other and everyone walk forward one-half turn. Now, men, release the ladies' hands, join left hands with each other, and turn one-half while the ladies just stand. All join hands, and you've got another ocean wave with the men in the center. Now let's swing-through from this position. Men, release hands and turn halfway around with the ladies. Ladies, let go of the men's hands, join left hands with each other, and turn halfway around while the men just stand. All join hands in another ocean wave. Now, ladies, let go of hands. Go right-and-left through. You should be back in your original positions now.

CALL

Do-si-do, around with you,
Make an ocean wave when you come down.
Rock up and back to town
Swing through.
Turn a girl by the right; now men turn left.
Rock once more, swing-through.
Turn a girl by the right; now the girls turn left.
Rock again.

Go right-left through across from you
Turn around and face those two.
Go up and back then pass-through
On to the next and meet those two.
(Repeat as desired.)

Following are square dance figures in set routines. These sequence dances may also be danced in a square formation if the visiting couple travels to each other couple and performs the figure before going to their home position.

Since the visiting couple does most of the actions, it is good to turn each team halfway around frequently so that couple two becomes couple one. This change could well come after each dance.

BIRDY IN THE CAGE

Formation: Double circle, team formation
Position: Hands joined
Footwork: Opposite (man L, lady R)

Music: Own choice
Record: Own choice
Rhythm: 4/4

CALLS

INSTRUCTIONS

Four hands up and around you go,

Circle 4 to L.

Birdy in the cage.

"Birdy" or head girl goes to center of circle.

Circle three hands 'round,

"Birdy" turns L as other 3 dancers circle around her.

Around and around and around you go.

Birdy hop out and the crow hop in,

Head girl joins circle; "crow," or head man, goes to center.

Keep on going around again.

Circle 3 hands around "crow."

The crow hop out and circle four,

Head man joins circle, and all circle L.

Arch and on to the next.

Hosts arch and visiting couple goes under arch to new couple.

Repeat entire dance.

BROWN-EYED MARY

Formation: Double circle
Position: Promenade
Footwork: Opposite (man L, lady R)

Music: Brown-eyed Mary
Record: Old Timer 8209
Rhythm: 4/4

CALL

INSTRUCTIONS

Turn your partner halfway 'round,

Partners join R hands and walk around for 1/2 turn.

Turn the corner lady.

Each man joins L hands with lady behind him and turns her completely around.

Turn your partner all the way 'round,

Man then joins R hand with original partner and turns her 1 full turn around.

CALL	INSTRUCTIONS
And take the forward lady.	Man continues toward lady in front of him.
I'll call the pattern just once more	Take fwd lady in promenade position for a new partner and two-step as you promenade.
And tell you what to do;	Repeat entire dance.
You can do this circle dance	

INSTRUCTIONS column continued:

And take the forward lady.

Man continues toward lady in front of him.

I'll call the pattern just once more

Take fwd lady in promenade position for a new partner and two-step as you promenade.

And tell you what to do;

Repeat entire dance.

You can do this circle dance

Note

Without my telling you.

For more fun, caller can make up his own rhymes about his dance, community, or people attending dance. Following are examples of 4-line rhymes which can be used during promenade.

. . .

As you promenade your new little maid,

Here's what you should do:

_____ sells groceries
And only grade A meat.
We wish he'd tell us how to live
On what it costs to eat.

Make up a rhyme, just in time

While the music plays for you.

. . .

Insurance is _____'s game
And does he love to sell it.
He'll sell a million dollars' worth
In the time it takes to tell it.

And now my little song is through;

You've danced away the night.

So tell that pretty girl adieu

With all you dancers on the floor
It's such a pleasant sight.
We're glad you came to

And come bid me good-night!

To dance with us tonight.

B U Z Z'S   M I X E R

Formation: Double circle
Position: Two-hand
Footwork: All start L

Music: Buzz's Mixer
Record: Windsor 7637B or own choice
Rhythm: 4/4

CALL

INSTRUCTIONS

Shuffle in and shuffle back,
Shuffle across the track.

Starting L, all take 1 shuffling two-step fwd

CALL	INSTRUCTIONS

toward partner; starting R, take 1 shuffling two-step back from partner. Starting L, take 2 shuffling two-steps to exchange places with partner, man making 1/2 turn R in crossing over to finish facing center of circle and lady making 1/2 turn L under joined hands to finish facing wall.

Shuffle in and shuffle back,
Shuffle across the track.

Repeat above action to end in original position.

Turn away and take up the slack,
Slide three times, then both hands clap.

Partners release hands and man turns 1 full turn L with 4 steps, L,R,L,R, as lady turns 1 full turn R with 4 steps, R,L,R,L, to end facing; then, resuming two-hand position, partners take 3 sliding steps L and clap hands sharply.

Swing your lady and she'll swing you,
Promenade that girl in blue.

Taking square dance swing position, partners swing once around, then promenade.

Now flip 'em in--the pretty side in--
Promenade, you're gone again.

By pulling on R hands, partners change sides, lady crossing over in front of man with 1 full turn L as man walks diag fwd and to R to end with lady on man's L with hands still crossed; all continue to promenade in LOD.

Gents turn back on the outside track,
Meet any ol' girl that's comin' back.

As lady continues to walk fwd in LOD on inside, man releases hands, turns 1/2 turn R, and walks fwd agLOD on outside until call comes to swing; then each man swings nearest lady.

Swing, swing that pretty little maid,
Take this one and promenade.
Promenade and don't be slow;
Face your partners--here we go!

New partners swing and promenade in LOD. Partners face with men facing wall and release L hands, but keep R hands joined.

CALL	INSTRUCTIONS
	Repeat entire dance.

Note

When men turn back and swing nearest lady, anyone missing a partner should go to inside of circle to find one, then swing and promenade with other dancers.

D E E R   H U N T E R ' S   H O E D O W N

Formation: Double circle, team formation
Position: Hands joined
Footwork: Opposite (man L, lady R)

Music: Own choice
Record: Any good patter calling record
Rhythm: 4/4

CALL	INSTRUCTIONS
Circle left and show no fear,	All circle L.
Look around for that darn deer.	Drop hands and continue circling, or shade eyes with R hand while circling, or raise arms as if aiming rifle while circling.
Circle right, that buck is near;	Join hands and circle R.
Hear that bellow loud and clear.	Drop hands and continue circling, or shade eyes with L hand while circling.
I'll comb the forest with my gun, If I don't get him, I'll make him run.	Men do-si-do opposite lady.
That ain't no deer, but we're not done. I've got that	Swing partner.
Buck fever.	Dance sugar foot (swiveling walk) fwd 4 steps, or raise arms to square representing deer's antlers while moving fwd 4 steps with sugar foot.
Fever in my blood,	Back up 4 steps.
Buck fever all the time.	Irish swing with partner.
I've got buck fever,	Sugar foot fwd 4 steps.

CALL	INSTRUCTIONS
Fever in my blood.	Walk back 4 steps.
I've got that buck fever, All the time.	Irish swing with partner.
Pass-through.	Drop hands, pass R shoulders with opposite to meet new couple.
	Repeat entire dance.

Suggestion

On "fever" steps, give some freedom to dancers and let them create their own steps.

D I V E   F O R   T H E   O Y S T E R

Formation:	Double circle, team formation	Music:	Own choice
Position:	Hands joined	Record:	Own choice
Footwork:	Opposite (man L, lady R)	Rhythm:	4/4

CALL	INSTRUCTIONS
Circle four, circle four. One, two, three, four.	All 4 circle once around.
Dive for the oyster, One, two, three, four.	Visiting couple steps forward 2 steps under arch formed by host couple, and comes back to place in 2 steps back.
Dig for the clam, One, two, three, four.	Host couple takes 2 steps under arch formed by visiting couple and backs to place in 2 steps.
Dive for the sardine and Take a full can.	Visiting couple goes under host couple's arch, pulling host couple into dishrag, then releases handclasp with hosts.
On to the next. One, two, three, four.	Visiting couple goes in direction facing to next couple as hosts turn to face new visiting couple.
	Repeat entire dance.

HONEY BEE SQUARE DANCE

Formation:	Double circle, team formation	Music:	Own choice
Position:	Hands joined	Record:	Own choice
Footwork:	Opposite (man L, lady R)	Rhythm:	4/4

CALL	INSTRUCTIONS
All join hands and circle left, Buzz, buzz, buzz, buzz.	Circle left 1 complete turn.
Now turn right back and circle right. Buzz, buzz, buzz, buzz.	Circle R.
Right-hand star around the hive, Zoom, zoom, zoom, zoom.	All form R-hand star and walk fwd.
Step right up and boomps-a-daisy.	All go up to opposite dancer and on 4th count turn back while clapping opposite person's hand. If desired, dancers may bump hips at same time hands are clapped.
Come back, drones, you're too darn lazy. Swing your opposite honey, Go round and round. Buzz, buzz, buzz, buzz.	Walk back to place. Men swing opposite lady.
Swing your own queen bee Right off the ground. Zoom, zoom, zoom, zoom.	All swing own partner.
Forward and bow and back with you,	Couple bows to opposite couple.
Forward again and pass-through.	Dancers drop hands, walk 8 steps fwd passing R shoulder with opposite dancer; end facing new couple.
Meet a new two, they will dance with you. Bow to them, they'll bow to you.	Bow to new couple.
	Repeat entire dance.

I'LL SWING YOUR GIRL

Formation:	Double circle, team formation	Music:	Own choice
Position:	Shine	Record:	Own choice
Footwork:	Opposite (man L, lady R)	Rhythm:	4/4

CALL	INSTRUCTIONS
Do-si-do the opposite, Do-si-do your own.	Dancers do-si-do around opposite person, then around own partner.
I'll swing your girl, You swing mine; An even swap, a fair trade-- Your pretty girl for my old maid.	Swing opposite with regular buzz swing.
Now we'll trade and swing once more; Swing 'em harder than you did before.	Swing own partner.
Circle four, circle four,	All join hands and circle once around to L.
Arch and on to the next.	Visiting couple goes under arch made by host couple to move on to new couple.
	Repeat entire dance.

LADY 'ROUND TWO, GENT FALL THROUGH

Formation:	Double circle, team formation	Music:	Own choice
Position:	Full-open, R-L cnt	Record:	Own choice
Footwork:	Opposite (man L, lady R)	Rhythm:	4/4

CALL	INSTRUCTIONS
Everybody bow, everybody swing,	Bow to opposite, then swing partner.
Lady 'round two, gent fall through.	Visiting couple, lady in lead and man following, goes around cw behind host couple, lady going around both dancers while man goes between dancers of host couple and around man.
Swing in the inside, outside too.	Partners meet and swing; man follows his partner back to place. Both couples swing.
Four hands up and make it go, Break into a circle four,	Circle 4 once around.
Arch and on to the next.	Host couple forms arch, visiting couple goes under and on to new couple.

Repeat entire dance.

P O L K A   H O E D O W N

Formation: Double circle, team formation	Music: Own choice
Position: Full-open, R-L cnt	Record: Own choice
Footwork: Opposite (man L, lady R)	Rhythm: 4/4

CALL

INSTRUCTIONS

Everybody balance and swing around
And around with the pretty little thing.

All balance, then swing partner.

Sashay four to the center of the set,

Partners face and couples take 3 sliding steps toward each other, so that ladies end facing.

Re-sashay; you're not through yet.

All take 3 sliding steps back to place.

Sashay back and form a row,
The gals reach back, and there's your beau.

Still facing each other, partners slide 3 steps toward other couple to form single row, then ladies reach back over their shoulders and men behind them take them in varsouvienne position.

A heel and toe and a one, two, three,
A heel and a toe with your honey bee.
A heel and toe and a one, two, three,

Execute heel-and-toe polka starting with L foot and moving sideward to L by pointing L toe fwd, then back, then taking 1 polka step L; repeat, starting R. Repeat L and R. (Couples are facing and moving opposite directions on heel-toe and polka.)

A heel and a toe, on to the next.
One, two, three, four.

Drop hands and slide through to face new couple, retaining original partner.

Repeat entire dance.

ROLL THE BARREL

Formation: Double circle, team formation
Position: Hands joined
Footwork: Opposite (man L, lady R)

Music: Own choice
Record: Own choice
Rhythm: 4/4

CALL

INSTRUCTIONS

Roll the barrel, tap the keg.

Visiting couple steps forward under arch formed by host couple and backs to place without releasing hands.

Save the oyster, break the egg.

Visiting couple again goes under arch formed by host couple.

Open the book, write the check.

Visiting couple separates and partners go around hosts, retaining handholds with them, to turn them 1 full turn and end in original position.

Turn them inside out,
Arch and on to the next.

Visiting couple goes under arch formed by host couple and walks to next couple.

Repeat entire dance.

SHOOT THAT PRETTY GIRL

Formation: Double circle, team formation
Position: Hands joined
Footwork: Opposite (man L, lady R)

Music: Own choice
Record: Own choice
Rhythm: 4/4

CALL

INSTRUCTIONS

First couple up, the couple you're facing,
And circle four, oh, circle four.
Drop that gent and circle three, circle three,
Go halfway around and

All 4 circle 1 complete turn L. Visiting man leaves circle and stands alone in home position; others continue circling 1/2 turn more.

Shoot that pretty girl through to me.

Host couple raises hands and pulls visiting lady under arch toward her partner.

And swing, boys, swing.

All swing partners.

And promenade.

Partners walk to next couple,

CALL	INSTRUCTIONS
	ladies passing R shoulders, men keeping arm around partner's waist.
	Repeat entire dance.

S W I N G   O L '   A D A M

Formation:	Double circle, team formation	Music:	Own choice
Position:	Full-open, R-L cnt	Record:	Own choice
Footwork:	Opposite (man L, lady R)	Rhythm:	4/4

CALL	INSTRUCTIONS
The first lady out with a balance and swing,	All balance and swing partners.
Then swing ol' Adam.	Visiting lady turns once around with opposite man in R elbow swing.
Then swing miss Eve,	Visiting lady swings once around with opposite lady in L elbow swing.
And swing ol' Adam before you leave,	Visiting lady swings opposite man with R elbow swing once around.
And don't forget your own.	All swing own partners.
Arch on to the next.	Visiting couple goes under arch made by hosts and on to new couple.
	Repeat entire dance.

T A K E   A   P E E K

Formation:	Double circle, team formation	Music:	Own choice
Position:	Shine	Record:	Own choice
Footwork:	Opposite (man L, lady R)	Rhythm:	4/4

CALL	INSTRUCTIONS
Around the couple and take a peek,	Visiting couple separates and walks around host couple to peek at eack other.
Back to your honey and swing your sweet.	Visiting couple returns to

CALL	INSTRUCTIONS
	place and swings.
Around that couple and peek once more,	Visiting couple repeats peek.
Back to the center and circle four.	All 4 circle 1 complete turn to L.
Second couple arch and on to the next.	Host couple raises hands to form arch, and visiting couple walks under to new couple.
	Repeat entire dance.

T E X A S   S T A R

Formation: Double circle, team formation
Position: Full-open, R-L cnt
Footwork: Opposite (man L, lady R)

Music: Own choice
Record: Own choice
Rhythm: 4/4

CALL	INSTRUCTIONS
First couple balance and swing;	Partners in visiting couple bow to each other and swing.
Head and foot, form a ring, Circle right like everything.	Both couples circle 4.
Now form a star with your right hand.	All place R hands in to form R-hand star and walk fwd.
Back with your left and don't get lost.	Reverse to L-hand star and walk fwd.
Swing your opposite with your right hand, Now your own with your left hand.	All swing opposite with R forearm grip, then partner with L forearm grip.
Four hands up and here we go,	Circle 4.
'Round and 'round with a do-si-do. Do-si-do with the gent you know; The lady go si and the gent go do. Do-si-do and a do-si-ding,	Do-si-do partner, then do-si-do opposite.
Balance home and everybody swing.	All swing partner.
Keep your arm around And on to the next.	Men keep arm around partner and ladies pass R shoulders as all walk to a new couple.

Repeat entire dance.

T H R E E S O M E   S Q U A R I N G   A N D   T H R E E S O M E   C I R C L E S

Threesome square dance figures are used only when there are twice as many ladies as men. Often ladies prefer to dance in threesomes rather than take the man's part in a couple and dance with another lady.

When threesomes are square dancing, two threesomes always face each other to make a team. The threesome facing the line of dance is the head, or visiting, threesome. To change, dancers drop hands and pass right shoulders with those they are facing, moving around the circle to a new threesome.

B O O M P S - A - D A I S Y

Formation: Threesome team   Music: Own choice
Position: Hands joined   Record: Own choice
Footwork: Opposite (man L, ladies R)   Rhythm: 4/4

CALL

INSTRUCTIONS

All join hands and go to the middle,
Make your foot keep time with the fiddle.
While you are there, keep time with the beat;
Tip tap with your big feet.
One, two, three, four.

All 6 dancers walk fwd to center of circle and tap feet.

Clap your hands, slap your knees,

All clap own hands and knees.

Boomps-a-daisy if you please.

Bump hips with dancers on either side.

Turn your right-hand lady
With the right hand around,

Men turn R-hand lady 1 complete turn with R forearm grip.

Left-hand lady when she comes down.

Men turn L-hand lady 1 complete turn with L forearm grip.

Forward and bow and back you go

Walk fwd and bow to facing threesome, then walk back to place.

Forward again and pass-through.
On to the next.

Drop hands and pass R shoulders with opposite, walking to new threesome.

Repeat entire dance.

BUILD-UM TEEPEE

Formation: Threesome team
Position: Full-open
Footwork: Opposite (man L, ladies R)

Music: Own choice
Record: Own choice
Rhythm: 4/4

CALL

INSTRUCTIONS

Squaws in center, hands up high;
Build-um teepee, don't be shy.

All 4 ladies move to center
of set and hold both hands
high and together to form
teepee shape.

Chief duck under on a heel and toe
And hurry up, Indian; don't be slow.
In and out, out and under,
Meet-um squaw, swing like thunder,
Swing like thunder.

Each man weaves in and out
under arch to R, around
opposite lady, and under L
arch, then swings either one
of his partners.

Swing the right-hand lady once around.

Each man swings other partner to alternate swinging
R- and L-hand ladies.

Forward and bow and forward again
And on to the next.

All walk fwd, bow, return
to place, and pass-through
to new threesome.

Repeat entire dance.

CHASE THE RABBIT

Formation: Threesome team
Position: Shine
Footwork: Opposite (man L, ladies R)

Music: Own choice
Record: Own choice
Rhythm: 4/4

CALL

INSTRUCTIONS

Head gent swing and whirl the right-hand girl.

Man in visiting threesome
swings R-hand partner.

Chase that rabbit, chase that squirrel,
Chase that pretty girl 'round the world.

Visiting man **chases** R-hand
lady around set.

Girl, chase that baboon, chase that 'coon,
Chase that man, go 'round the moon.
Forward and bow, forward again,

R-hand lady turns and chases
visiting man back home.

Pass-through
And on to the next.

Threesomes pass-through.

Head gent swing and whirl the left-hand girl

Visiting man swings L-hand
partner.

CALL	INSTRUCTIONS
And chase that rabbit, chase that squirrel, Chase that girl, go 'round the world.	Visiting man chases L-hand lady around set.
Girl, chase that baboon, chase that 'coon, Chase that man, go 'round the moon.	L-hand lady turns and chases visiting man back home.
Forward and bow, forward again, Pass-through, and on to the next.	Threesomes walk fwd, bow, walk back, then pass-through to new set.
	Repeat entire dance.

H A P P Y   M A N

Formation:	Threesome teams	Music:	Own choice
Position:	Hands joined	Record:	Own choice
Footwork:	Opposite (man L, ladies R)	Rhythm:	4/4

CALL	INSTRUCTIONS
All join hands and circle left six hands round.	All circle L once around.
You're going wrong; the other way back, Make your feet go wickity-wack.	Circle R back to home position.
A right-hand star; say, "How do you do?"	All place R hands together and walk once around; drop hands and turn.
Back by the left; say, "How are you?"	Join L hands and star to home position.
Forward and bow, drop your hands, Pass-through, and on to the next.	All walk fwd, bow, walk back, then drop hands and pass-through on to next set.
	Repeat entire dance.

I N D I A N   S T Y L E

Formation:	Threesome team	Music:	Own choice
Position:	Hands joined	Record:	Own choice
Footwork:	Opposite (man L, ladies R)	Rhythm:	4/4

CALL	INSTRUCTIONS
All join hands and circle left, circle left.	Circle 6 hands around.
Break and trail, single file, Indian style.	All walk R around circle single file.

CALL	INSTRUCTIONS
Swing that girl behind you; She's that girl with a great big smile. Break and trail, single file, Indian style, Lady in the lead.	Man shoulder swings lady behind him, ending with lady in front of man; all walk R around circle single file.
Swing that girl behind you. Hurry up, boys, you're right in the pink; Enjoy yourself; it's later than you think. Break and trail, single file, Indian style, Lady in the lead.	Man swings lady behind him with neck swing, ending with lady in front, then walks behind her single file R around circle.
Swing that girl behind you. Hurry up, boys, and pound the leather; It's hotter than heck but don't mind the weather.	Man swings lady behind him with Irish swing, ending with lady in front of man, then man walks behind her in single file.
Swing that girl behind you.	Man backhand swings lady behind him.
Forward and bow.	Threesomes walk fwd 3 steps and bow, then back 3 steps.
Forward again and pass-through On to the next.	All drop hands and pass-through to next threesome.
	Repeat entire dance.

R E D   H O T   R E E L

Formation: Threesome team
Position: Full-open
Footwork: Opposite (man L, ladies R)

Music: Own choice
Record: Own choice
Rhythm: 4/4

CALL	INSTRUCTIONS
Allemande left the left-hand lady, Go all the way, all the way around.	Turn L-hand lady 1 complete turn with L forearm grip.
Right to the opposite, Go all the way, all the way around.	Turn opposite man's R-hand lady 1 full turn with R forearm grip.
Next by the left, Go all the way, all the way around.	Turn opposite man's L-hand lady 1 full turn with L forearm grip.
Own by the right, Go all the way, all the way around.	Turn own R-hand lady 1 full turn with R forearm grip.

CALL	INSTRUCTIONS
Forward and bow,	All walk fwd 3 steps and bow to opposite threesome, then walk back 3 steps.
Forward again, pass-through, On to the next.	Pass-through to new threesome.
	Repeat entire dance.

S W I N G ' S   T H E   T H I N G

Formation: Threesome team   Music: Own choice
Position: Hands joined   Record: Own choice
Footwork: Opposite (man L, ladies R)   Rhythm: 4/4

CALL	INSTRUCTIONS
All join hands and circle left six hands 'round.	Circle 6 to L.
Circle right, go the other way back; Make your feet go wickity-wack.	Circle R.
A right-hand star; say, "How do you do?"	All 6 place R hands in center to form R-hand star and walk fwd.
Back by the left; say, "How are you?"	Place L hands in star and walk fwd.
Swing that girl behind you.	Man swings own L-hand lady once around.
Swing the next little girl down the line; Keep on swinging, you're doing fine.	Man swings opposite man's R-hand lady.
Swing the next little girl; you're right on time.	Man swings opposite man's L-hand lady.
One more girl; you're on your way-- Give her a swing and don't you stay.	Man swings own R-hand lady.
Forward and bow, forward again and	All step fwd and bow to opposite threesome, then step back.
Pass-through and on to the next.	Drop hands, pass R shoulders, and walk to new threesome.
	Repeat entire dance.

T E X A S   S T A R

Formation:	Threesome team	Music:	Own choice
Position:	Full-open	Record:	Own choice
Footwork:	Opposite (man L, ladies R)	Rhythm:	4/4

CALL	INSTRUCTIONS
Ladies to the center and back to the bar;	All 4 ladies walk fwd, touch R hands high, and walk back to place.
Gents to the center and form a star.	Both men form R-hand star and walk fwd.
Back by the left but not too far.	Both men form L-hand star and walk fwd.
Pick up your right-hand girl. Go all the way round.	Without breaking star, each man picks up his R-hand partner.
Ladies in and the men back out, And you've turned that Texas star about.	Men break star and step back, keeping L arm around R-hand lady, as ladies move to center and form R-hand star.
Pick up the left-hand lady, go all the way.	Men pick up L-hand partner and walk fwd in star with both ladies.
Break in the middle, wheel once around.	Inside ladies drop hands when they arrive at home position, and both threesomes wheel once around to R.
Forward and back and on to the next.	All walk forward, bow, and walk back, then drop hands and pass-through to next threesome.
	Repeat entire dance.

T E X A N   W H I R L

Formation:	Threesome team	Music:	Own choice
Position:	Shine	Record:	Own choice
Footwork:	Opposite (man L, ladies R)	Rhythm:	4/4

CALL	INSTRUCTIONS
Gents to the center and back to your boss;	Men walk to center of set, touch L hands high, and walk back.
Ladies to the center and form a cross. Turn, turn and don't get lost.	Ladies join R hands to form R-hand star and walk fwd once around.
Gents step in with a right-hand cross.	Men step in between own partners, put R hand in center, and star R.
The gents turn with a Texan whirl, Now join your hands and go 'round the world.	Men release handhold, pivot individually left, and come back into star position behind lady immediately following, as star keeps moving.
The gents turn to the left once more. Join your hands and around the floor.	Men release hold again, turn L lady behind them into another six-handed star.
Now gents turn with a fancy little spin, Join your hands and you're goin' again. Now listen, gents, 'cause you should know	Men again release hold and turn L around lady behind them into six-handed star.
'Tis time to break with a do paso. Now back with your left with the left hand 'round, Left-hand girl with the right-hand 'round.	Men reach over R shoulder and join L hands with partner behind them, then all do paso, ending in original formation.
Forward and bow, pass-through, And on to the next.	All step fwd, bow, step back, and pass-through to new threesome.
	Repeat entire dance.

SQUARE DANCING IN A SQUARE FORMATION

After dancers have learned the fundamental figures in a single, double, or threesome circle, it is a challenge and a lot of fun to try following a good hash caller with four couples in a square formation.

Many more square dance figures and patterns can be danced in a square than in a large circle. However, one couple can foul up a square and cause more problems than in a circle. Thus, a dancer's first obligation when dancing in a square is to listen to the caller for instructions.

Dancers in clubs usually dance in a square, because it is the most challenging formation.

In a square, the couples are numbered for easy identification. Couple number one is closest to but facing away from the source of music; couple number two stands to the right of couple number one; couple number three is opposite to and facing couple number one; and couple number four stands to the left of couple number one. Couples one and three are referred to as the head couples, while couples two and four are the side couples.

BRINGIN' HOME THE BACON

Formation: Square
Position: Full-open, R-L cnt
Footwork: Opposite (man L, lady R)

Music: Own choice
Record: Own choice
Rhythm: 4/4

CALL

INSTRUCTIONS

Docey 'round the corner girl,
Come back home and swing and whirl.

Do-si-do with corner, then walk back to partner and swing.

Ladies promenade inside the ring,

All 4 ladies circle single file to R inside ring of men.

Meet your partner, turn 'em by the right.

Turn partner with R forearm grip.

Allemande left,

Turn corner with L forearm grip.

A grand ol' right-and-left
Until you meet your beau.
Do-si-do around her,
Swing her high and low; then

Grand right-and-left halfway around circle to meet partner, do-si-do, and swing.

Promenade to Macon,
We're bringin' home the bacon,
Rakin', bakin', makin' happiness.

Turn partner, take promenade position, and walk home.

Repeat entire dance.

DIP AND DIVE

Formation: Square
Position: Full-open, R-L cnt
Footwork: Opposite (man L, lady R)

Music: Own choice
Record: Own choice
Rhythm: 4/4

CALL

INSTRUCTIONS

First and third balance and swing,
First and third to the right of the ring,
Four hands full around,

Head couples balance, swing, and move to side couples and circle 4 with them for 1 full turn.

Second and third arch so big.

Couples 2 and 3 raise arms;

CALL	INSTRUCTIONS

CALL

Now dip and dive, oh, duck and dive--
Go, my boys, and go like thunder.
Keep on going 'til you reach the wall,
Then turn right back and through 'em all.
Dip and dive, oh, duck and dive,
Act alive, man, alive.
Dip and dive, duck and dive,
Some'll batch and some'll wive.
Dip and dive, oh, duck and dive--
Cost one spot, but worth a five.
Dip and dive, duck and dive,
Regular old-time cattle drive.

Now you're home and all eight swing,
A left allemande and a right-hand grand;
Promenade eight when you come straight.

Second and fourth balance and swing.
Second and fourth to the right of the ring.
Four hands full around,
Third and fourth arch so big.

[Repeat the patter of B and C of the
Lengthwise Dip and Dive.]

INSTRUCTIONS

couple no. 1 ducks under
arch of couple no. 2, and
couple no. 4 goes under arch
made by couple no. 3, and
all dip and dive. Ladies in
couples facing out go under
arch made by their partners,
changing places with them,
then raise arms to start
traveling across set. Dip
and dive is repeated across
set and back until all 4
couples are in positions
they started in.

Couples 1 and 3 go home, and
all swing and promenade once
around set.

Repeat entire dance with
side couples leading and
couples 3 and 4 arching.

D I V I D E   T H E   R I N G   A N D   D O S - A - C O R N E R S

Formation: Square
Position: Full-open, R-L cnt
Footwork: Opposite (man L, lady R)

Music: Own choice
Record: Own choice
Rhythm: 4/4

CALL

[Figure]

First couple balance, first couple swing,
Down the center and split the ring.
The lady goes right and the gent goes left,
Dos-a-partners, one and all.

Down the center as you did before,
Down the center and cut away four.
Dos-a-corners, don't you fall,
Dos-a-partners, one and all.

Down the center as you used to do,
Down the center and cut away two.

INSTRUCTIONS

Couple no. 1 balances and
swings, then walks between
dancers of couple no. 3; man
turns L, lady R, and they
walk home. All do-si-do.

Couple no. 1 swings, then
man walks between couples 3
and 4 as lady walks between
couples 2 and 3; they return
home, and all do-si-do.

Couple no. 1 walks down
center of set, and man goes

CALL	INSTRUCTIONS
Dos-a-corners, don't you fall, Dos-a-partners, one and all.	between dancers of couple no. 4 as lady goes between dancers of couple no. 2; then they return home, and all do-si-do. Repeat entire dance.

<u>Note</u>

The figure should be re-peated 4 times, with each couple taking active part in turn. Figure repetitions are separated by trimmings.

F O R W A R D   S I X   A N D   F A L L   B A C K   S I X
(Line figures)

Formation:	Square	Music:	Own choice
Position:	Full-open, R-L cnt	Record:	Own choice
Footwork:	Opposite (man L, lady R)	Rhythm:	4/4

CALL	INSTRUCTIONS
First couple out to the couple on the right And circle four.	Couple no. 1 goes to couple no. 2 and they circle L.
Leave that girl, go on to the next, And circle three.	Man no. 1 goes alone to couple no. 3 and they circle L.
Take that girl, go on to the next, And circle four.	Man no. 1 takes lady no. 3 to couple no. 4 and they circle L.
Leave that girl and go home alone.	Man no. 1 goes alone to home position; at this point, men no. 2 and no. 4 have a lady at each side and men no. 1 and no. 3 stand alone in their home posi-tions.
Forward six and fall back six,	Threesomes walk fwd and bow to each other, then walk back.
Forward two and fall back two,	Lone men walk fwd and bow, then walk back.

CALL	INSTRUCTIONS
Forward six and arch right through.	Threesomes move fwd and man arches R-hand lady under L arm and on to lone man on L while moving L-hand lady to own R side.
Swing on the corner like swinging on a gate; And now your own if you're not too late.	All swing corner, then partner.
	Repeat entire dance with each couple leading out.

F O R W A R D   S I X   A N D   R I G H T   H A N D   O V E R
(Line figures)

Formation: Square
Position: Full-open, R-L cnt
Footwork: Opposite (man L, lady R)

Music: Own choice
Record: Own choice
Rhythm: 4/4

CALL	INSTRUCTIONS
First couple out to the couple on the right, Circle four with all your might. Leave that lady where she be, On to the next and circle three.	Couple no. 1 goes to couple no. 2 and they circle L; man no. 1 then leaves his partner in line with couple no. 2 and goes to couple no. 3 and circles L once.
Steal that girl from her back door, Go to the next and circle four.	Man no. 1 takes lady no. 3 on to couple no. 4 and they circle L.
Leave that girl with that new man, Go back home as fast as you can.	Man no. 1 goes home, leaving lady no. 3 with couple no. 4, so that sides are 2 threesomes and heads are 2 lone men.
Forward six and back you go.	Threesomes walk to center and back.
Two gents loop with a do-si-do; Right hand over, left hand under, Spin those girls--they go like thunder.	Men no. 2 and no. 4 raise R hands high and lead L-hand lady under arch, spinning her to new partner; at same time R-hand lady trades sides with L-hand lady and spins on to new partner, to end with men no. 2 and no. 4 standing alone.

CALL	INSTRUCTIONS
[Repeat from "Forward six . . . " 3 more times.]	Repeat walk to center and arch and spin 3 more times.
Allemande left with your left hand; Right to your partner With a right-and-left grand. Meet your honey and promenade.	Allemande left with corner, then execute grand right-and-left to meet original partner, then promenade to home position. Repeat entire dance.

F O U R   G E N T S   S T A R
(Star figure)

Formation:	Square	Music:	Own choice
Position:	Full-open, R-L cnt	Record:	Own choice
Footwork:	Opposite (man L, lady R)	Rhythm:	4/4

CALL	INSTRUCTIONS
Four gents star in the center of the square;	Men form R-hand star and wheel 1/2 turn cw.
Turn the opposite lady and leave her there.	Each man turns opposite lady 1 full turn with L forearm grip.
Star right back in the center of the set.	Men form R-hand star and wheel 1/2 turn cw.
Turn your own; you're not through yet.	Each man turns partner 1 full turn with L forearm grip.
Star right back in the center of the town;	Men form L-hand star and wheel 3/4 turn cw.
Turn the right-hand lady with the left hand 'round.	Each man turns R-hand lady 1 full turn with L forearm grip.
Star right back in the center of the floor;	Men form R-hand star and wheel 1/2 turn cw.
Turn the left-hand lady or she might get sore.	Each man turns L-hand lady 1 full turn with L forearm grip.
Star right back and you should know--	Men form R-hand star and wheel 3/4 turn cw.

CALL	INSTRUCTIONS
Meet your own with a do paso. It's partner left and corner right, Partner left with a left all around, And promenade your corner when she comes down.	All execute do paso, then promenade with corner.
	Repeat entire dance. (To get to original partner, repeat 3 times.)

I'LL SWING YOURS
(Visiting figure)

Formation:	Square	Music:	Own choice
Position:	Full-open, R-L cnt	Record:	Own choice
Footwork:	Opposite (man L, lady R)	Rhythm:	4/4

CALL	INSTRUCTIONS
The head two men with your own pretty girl-- Swing, boys, swing, you swing and whirl.	Head men swing partners.
Lead to the right when you hit the floor; Join up hands and circle four.	Head couples walk to side couples and circle 4.
I'll swing your girl, you swing mine,	Change partners and swing.
Then I'll swing my girl half the time.	All swing own partners.
The same four circle; around you go And break right into a do-si-do. One foot up and the other foot down, Hit it up, boys, you're goin' to town. Now take your honey and travel on.	Circle 4 again, then do-si-do with opposite.
	Repeat entire dance with other couple on other side.

MOUNTAIN MUSIC
(Promenade outside the square figure)

Formation:	Square	Music:	I Like Mountain Music
Position:	Full-open, R-L cnt	Record:	MacGregor 658-A, Top Record 25031
Footwork:	Opposite (man L, lady R)	Rhythm:	4/4

CALL	INSTRUCTIONS
[Introduction, break, and ending]	

CALL	INSTRUCTIONS
Allemande left your corner;	Take corner with L forearm grip and turn once.
Right-hand turn your partner.	Take partner with R forearm grip and turn once.
Men star left in the middle, go once around.	Men place L hands to center of set and walk fwd ccw.
Turn partner right a wrong-way thar;	Partners assume R forearm grip and turn once around.
Men back up in a left-hand star. Back that star and move it right along.	Men join hands in L-hand star and back up, still holding partners with R forearm grip, as ladies walk fwd.
Shoot that star.	Men release L hands and turn partners 1 full turn with R forearm grip.
Allemande left with corners;	All turn corners once with L forearm grip.
Grand right-and-left.	All grand right-and-left, continuing until meeting original partner.
When you meet your girl, Promenade and sing with me. I like mountain music, good ol' mountain music, Played by a real hillbilly band.	Turn partner under R arm, assume promenade position, and walk to home position.

[Figure or body]

Walk all around your corner.	Do-si-do corner and return to place.
Turn partner by the left.	Allemande L with partner.
Head couples promenade halfway around	Couple no. 1 promenades around couple no. 2; couple no. 3 promenades around couple no. 4.
Down the middle. Pass on through,	Couples 1 and 3 walk to center and pass-through.
U-turn back, star-through.	Partners in couples 1 and 3 turn individually 1/2 turn and star-through with opposite to end facing side

CALL	INSTRUCTIONS
	couples.
Circle up four about halfway around.	Head couples join hands with side couples and circle 4, moving 1/2 turn L.
Dive-through.	Head couples dive under arch made by side couples, and head men arch ladies to original place.
Circle up four in the middle of the ring One full turn, Then rear back.	Head couples join hands in middle of set and circle L 1 full turn; then, still holding hands, all 4 lean back, raising free foot.
Pass-through. Swing, swing that corner girl,	Head couples pass-through to meet original corner, and all swing.
Promenade. I like mountain music, good ol' mountain music, Played by a real hillbilly band.	All promenade while singing, "I like mountain music, good ol' mountain music, / Played by a real hillbilly band." Head men with new partner repeat the figure. Repeat the break. Couples 2 and 4 repeat figure twice. Repeat break, ending with original partner.

Repeat dance.

Note

To end with original partner, order of dance is as follows.

    introduction
    body--head couples
    body--head couples
    break
    body--side couples
    body--side couples
    ending

STAR-THROUGH

Formation:	Square	Music:	Own choice
Position:	Full-open, R-L cnt	Record:	Own choice
Footwork:	Opposite (man L, lady R)	Rhythm:	4/4

CALL

INSTRUCTIONS

[Figure]

One and three go up and back,

Head couples walk to center of the set and walk back to place.

Star-through across the track.

Dancers in head couples star-through with opposite to end facing in toward center of set.

Right-and-left through a full turn and Face the outside two.

Head couples execute right-and-left through with each other to end facing side couples (no courtesy turn).

Pass-through then face your own.

Dancers in head couples pass-through with side couples and turn to face own partners, while side couples courtesy turn.

Star-through,

Head couples star-through to end facing side couples.

Dive-through,

Head couples go under arch made by side couples.

Pass-through,

Head couples meet in center of set and pass-through.

And swing the corner one.

All swing original corner.

Allemande left the corner girl,

Assume L forearm grip with corner and walk around 1 full turn.

Grand right-and-left. When you meet That gal of yours,

All grand right-and-left to meet partner.

Do-si-do around your pet.
Then promenade to Macon;
We're bringin' home the bacon,
Rakin', bakin', makin' happiness.

Partners do-si-do, then promenade to home position.

Repeat entire dance. There
is a break before side
couples dance through the
figure twice. Finally, an
ending is called.

Note

Order of dance from beginning to end is as follows:
Figure is repeated twice
by head couples, then break
is called, then figure is
repeated twice by side
couples, then ending is
called.

Hints

Star-through always requires
the man's R hand and the
lady's L hand joined. Both
turn just 1/4 turn, lady L
under arch and man R. When
teaching star-through, have
men put L hands in pockets
and ladies place R hands
behind own backs. After
star-through partners are
never facing each other
since they only complete
1/4 turn.

T E X A S   S T A R
(Star figure)

Formation: Square
Position: Full-open, R-L cnt
Footwork: Opposite (man L, lady R)

Music: Own choice
Record: Own choice
Rhythm: 4/4

CALL

INSTRUCTIONS

Girls to the center and back to the bar.

Ladies take two steps to
the center and two steps
back to place.

Men to the center and form a star
With a right-hand cross.

Men form R-hand star and
move cw.

Back with the left and don't get lost;

Men change to L contact and
wheel star ccw.

CALL	INSTRUCTIONS
Meet your partner, pass her by, Catch the next girl on the fly.	Men pass partner and link R elbow with next lady's L elbow, bringing her along. Star keeps moving.
The men back out and the girls swing in And you form that Texas star again.	Men keep partner on R but break L-hand star and back out as ladies walk fwd and in to form R-hand star, wheeling cw.
Men go in and the ladies back out And you turn that Texas star about.	Ladies back out and men move in to form L-hand star, wheeling ccw.
Now the men back out with a full turn around Like a jaybird walking on frozen ground.	Men back out and partners wheel 1-1/2 turns to end with ladies in R-hand star.
Now the ladies back out with a full turn around Like a scared old rabbit chased by a hound.	Ladies back out and partners wheel 1-1/2 turns to end with men in L-hand star.
Break in the center and everyone swing And promenade. Go 'round that ring.	All swing partner and promenade to end in home position.

Repeat entire dance.

Variation

Men run to new set at call of "skat," made when men are on outside of star, while ladies keep star intact. When ladies are on outside, caller may call "skit," and ladies find new set. Caller may end dance by calling, "Skit, skat, and skedaddle."

T I P P E R A R Y

Formation:	Square	Music:	It's a Long Way to Tipperary
Position:	Full-open, R-L cnt	Record:	Balance Xii0
Footwork:	Opposite (man L, lady R)	Rhythm:	4/4

CALL

[Figure]

INSTRUCTIONS

CALL	INSTRUCTIONS

CALL

Head two couples promenade,
Halfway around the square;

Chain those girls across the set
And turn the lady there.

Go to the right, you circle four,
And make a line for me;
Go forward eight and back
One and three diagonally.

Right-and-left through, you turn
And pass-through,
Hook the sides and turn that line all the way.

Bend the line and chain the ladies;
Same two, go forward up and back with you.

Now you star-through, your
Corner swing now.
Swing and promenade the ring.
It's a long, long way to Tipperary
But my heart's right there.

[Ending] . . .

Bow to your partners all;
Thanks, lady, that'll be all.

INSTRUCTIONS

Couples 1 and 3 promenade
halfway around outside of
set.

Head ladies chain across set
and men courtesy turn them.

Head couples lead to couple
on R and circle 4 once around
to lines of 4 facing each
other and diag to original
set; lines move fwd and back.

Head couples do right-and-
left through on diag, then
turn back with courtesy turn
and pass-through on same
diag. Each head man hooks
L elbows with man (in side
couple) he meets to make
2-faced line of 4, and all
turn line 1 full turn.

All bend line; facing ladies
then chain and couples walk
fwd and back.

All star-through and swing
corner, then promenade to
home position.

Repeat entire dance.

Note

Order of dance from beginning
to end is as follows: Figure
is repeated twice by head
couples, then twice by side
couples, then ending is
called.

VENUS AND MARS
(Star figure)

Formation: Square
Position: Full-open, R-L cnt
Footwork: Opposite (man L, lady R)

Music: Own choice
Record: Own choice
Rhythm: 4/4

CALL

INSTRUCTIONS

Eight to the center for a right-hand star;

All form R-hand star and walk fwd cw.

Back with the left but not too far.

All change to L-hand star and walk fwd ccw.

Now the first lady out and form two stars,
One like Venus and one like Mars.

With lady no. 1 leading, all 4 ladies leave L-hand star and go out to R to form R-hand star, as men keep L-hand star moving.

Now the ladies go in and the men go out
And you turn these two stars 'round about.

With lady no. 1 leading, ladies step in front of their partners to rejoin L-hand star; at same time men leave L-hand star and form R-hand star.

Now the ladies go out and the men go in
And turn those two stars back again.

Again, with lady no. 1 leading, ladies step in front of their partners to join R-hand star of men; at same time men move out to L to form L-hand star.

Now turn it around till you meet your own;
Pick her off and promenade home.

As men meet partners, they leave stars and promenade to home position.

Repeat entire dance, with ladies 2, 3, and 4 leading in turn.

YOU'RE THE REASON
(Cross-trail figure)

Formation: Square
Position: Full-open, R-L cnt
Footwork: Opposite (man L, lady R)

Music: You're the Reason
Record: Sets in Order 128,
Flip instrumental
called by Johnny
LeClair
Rhythm: 4/4

CALL

[Figure]

Well, here we go--

The four ladies chain;
Turn 'em around.
Chain 'em right back;
Turn the sweetest in town.

And then the heads star-through,
Square-through three-fourths 'round,
  split the sides,
'Round one to the middle.

A right-and-left through,
Turn back and cross-trail.
Allemande left the corner;
Do-si-do 'round your own
One time around.
Same girl, you swing and whirl.

Sides face, everybody grand square.
I'm bettin' you're not losin'
Sleep over me;
And if I am wrong,
Don't fail to call.

Go all the way home; do left allemande.
Do-si-do 'round your partner,
That corner you swing;
Swing the corner lady, promenade that ring.
Baby, you're the reason
I don't sleep at night.

INSTRUCTIONS

All 4 ladies chain across
set and are courtesy turned,
then chain back across to
original partner and are
courtesy turned.

Head couples move to center
and star-through with person
opposite, then square-through
3/4 to end facing original
corners; each head couple
then walks between dancers
of side couple facing them,
separate, and go around side
dancers to come back to
center of set.

Head couples execute right-
and-left through, courtesy
turn, cross-trail to corner,
and allemande left; then
do-si-do and swing partners.

Side couples face partners
and all execute grand square.

All allemande left with
corner, then do-si-do partner. Swing corner and
promenade to home position.

CALL	INSTRUCTIONS
	Repeat entire dance.
[Ending]	
Swing the girl;	All swing partner.
You're the reason I don't sleep at night.	

<u>Note</u>

Order of dance from beginning to end is as follows: Figure is repeated twice by head couples, then twice by side couples, then ending is called.

Sequence: Call twice through; then change third and fourth lines to make the sides active and call twice more.

S Q U A R E   D A N C E   R E C O R D   C O M P A N I E S

Blue Star Records
P.O. Box 7308
Houston, Texas 77008

Educational Record Sales
157 Chambers Street
New York, New York 10007

Hi Hat
P.O. Box 69833
Los Angeles, California 90069

Imperial Records
137 N. Western Avenue
Los Angeles, California 90004

Jubilee Records
8811 N. 38 Drive
Phoenix, Arizona 85021

MacGregor Records
729 S. Western Avenue
Los Angeles, California 90005

Wagon Wheel Records
9500 53rd Avenue
Arvada, Colorado 80002

Folkraft Records
1159 Broad Street
Newark, New Jersey 07114

Green, Inc.
P.O. Box 216
Bath, Ohio 44210

Honor Your Partner Records
Educational Activities, Inc.
P.O. Box 392
Freeport, New York 11520

J-Bar-L Records
Sets in Order
462 N. Robertson Boulevard
Los Angeles, California 90048

Kalox Records
316 Starr Street
Dallas, Texas 75203

Old Timer Records
P.O. Box 64343
Los Angeles, California 90064

TAP DANCING

INTRODUCTION

Everyone occasionally feels an urge to tap a toe, shuffle a foot, or stomp to lively music. For this reason tap dancing has been popular for over a hundred years. Tap dancing is unique in that its appeal is not only to sight, like other dances, but to hearing as well. Some classify tap dancing as the playing of a percussion instrument, but most see it as a form of dancing.

Tap dancing is an excellent way to teach dance rhythms, for if the dancer is off, his ear will tell him. Since sound is involved in a musical way, the dancer becomes aware of phrasing, measures, and subdivided beats more rapidly than with other kinds of dancing.

Tap dancing is versatile and useful because it can be danced alone, in couples, in small groups, or in large groups; in groups of all ladies or all men, or in mixed groups with an unequal distribution of males and females. Both sexes enjoy tap dancing, whereas men often shy away from other forms of dancing, feeling that such forms are too effeminate.

TEACHING TECHNIQUES

In teaching a tap sequence, each measure should be broken down with a precise counting call. It is easiest for the student to learn if the tap step is done very slowly, but with the proper rhythm maintained. As the student learns the step, the tempo can be speeded up to normal.

Another important teaching technique is to simplify the tap step to its easiest form. For example, instead of teaching a shuffle-hop-shuffle step, the instructor could teach a tap-hop-tap step, and when the students have mastered the simplified form the shuffle can be added in place of the tap.

It is also a good idea in teaching tap to repeat one measure several times until it is learned, then to repeat the next measure several times. After both are mastered, the two can be combined.

BASIC TAP STEPS

Tap: The production of a single sound by touching the ball of the foot on the floor and raising it.

Brush: A tap produced while moving the foot forward.

Slap: A tap produced while moving the foot backward.

Shuffle: A brush and slap grouped together without a weight change.

Step: A change of weight accomplished by stepping on the ball of the foot.

Flap: A brush and step grouped together either forward or to the side.

Flap-back: A slap and step backward grouped together.

Heel: A single sound produced by tapping the heel of the foot on the floor.

Heel-drop: A single sound produced by dropping the heel to the floor when the weight is on the ball of the foot.

Jump: A movement executed by pushing off the floor from both feet and landing on both feet.

Hop: A movement executed by pushing off the floor from one foot and landing on the same foot.

Leap: A movement executed by pushing off the floor from one foot and landing on the other foot.

Stomp: A sound produced by placing the entire foot solidly on the floor.

Dot: A sound produced by tapping the toe behind or in front of the supporting leg.

R H Y T H M

In the following exercises and routines the ampersand (&) will be used for the count and (one-half beat), and a will indicate one-fourth beat, in duple rhythm (e.g., 2/4, 4/4). In triple rhythm (e.g., 3/4, 6/8, or notes grouped and labeled above with a 3) both & and a indicate one-third beat.
Most tap steps fit into single, double, and triple rhythm counts.

The interval in which no sound is made is called a rest. It is not called in a counting call. The following notes and rests are equal:

$$\text{♩} = \text{𝄽} \qquad\qquad \text{♪} = \text{𝄾}$$

The following rhythms would be called as indicated:

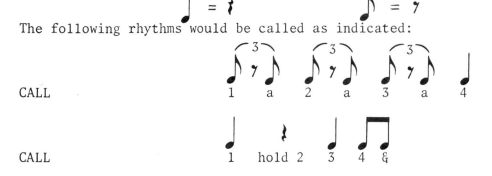

302

CALL   1 a 2 hold 3 & 4

Rhythm holds are usually placed in parentheses. The last line above would be written: 1 a 2   (3) &   4.

Often when a count from one measure is grouped with the following measure, it is written with that group. For example, several measures of shuffles would be written:

        a1   a2   a3   a4
        a1   a2   a3   a4

rather than

                                a
  1   a2   a3   a4   a
  1   a2   a3   a4.

T A P   E X E R C I S E S

T A P

MEAS	CT	INSTRUCTIONS
1	1&2&	4 taps fwd
	3&4&	4 taps diag fwd R
2	1&2&	4 taps side R
	3&4	3 taps diag back R
	&	close R to L
3	1&2&	4 taps fwd L
	3&4&	4 taps diag fwd L
4	1&2&	4 taps side L
	3&4	3 taps diag back L
	&	close L to R

Repeat.

B R U S H

MEAS	CT	INSTRUCTIONS
1	1 2	2 brushes fwd R
	3 4	2 brushes diag fwd R
2	1 2	2 brushes side R
	3	1 brush diag back R
	4	close R to L

MEAS	CT	INSTRUCTIONS
3	1 2	2 brushes fwd L
	3 4	2 brushes diag fwd L
4	1 2	2 brushes side L
	3	1 brush diag back L
	4	close L to R

Repeat.

B R U S H   A N D   S L A P

MEAS	CT	INSTRUCTIONS
1	1&2&	brush and slap fwd R 2 times
	3&4&	brush and slap diag fwd R 2 times
2	1&2&	brush and slap side R 2 times
	3&	brush and slap diag back R
	4	close R to L
3	1&2&	brush and slap fwd L 2 times
	3&4&	brush and slap diag fwd L 2 times
4	1&2&	brush and slap side L 2 times
	3&	brush and slap diag back L
	4	close L to R

Repeat.

S H U F F L E

MEAS	CT	INSTRUCTIONS
1	a1 a2 a3 a4	shuffle fwd R 4 times
2	a1 a2 a3 a4	shuffle diag fwd R 4 times
3	a1 a2 a3 a4	shuffle side R 4 times
4	a1 a2 a3	shuffle diag back R 3 times
	4	close L to R
5	a1 a2 a3 a4	shuffle fwd L 4 times
6	a1 a2 a3 a4	shuffle diag fwd L 4 times
7	a1 a2 a3 a4	shuffle side L 4 times

MEAS	CT	INSTRUCTIONS
8	a1 a2 a3	shuffle diag back L 3 times
	4	close R to L

Repeat.

<u>Variation</u>

The shuffle may also be done in 4 meas with 2 shuffles in each direction instead of 4.

F L A P

MEAS	CT	INSTRUCTIONS
1	a1	flap (brush step) fwd L
	a2	flap fwd R
	a3	flap fwd L
	a4	flap fwd R

Repeat.

F L A P - B A C K

MEAS	CT	INSTRUCTIONS
1	a1	flap-back (slap step) R
	a2	flap-back L
	a3	flap-back R
	a4	flap-back L

Repeat.

F L A P   A N D   H E E L   D R O P

MEAS	CT	INSTRUCTIONS
1	a1	flap fwd R
	2	heel-drop R
	a3	flap fwd L
	4	heel-drop L

Repeat.

F L A P   A N D   H O P

MEAS	CT	INSTRUCTIONS
1	a1	flap fwd R
	2	hop R
	a3	flap fwd L
	4	hop L

Repeat.

F L A P - B A C K   A N D   H E E L - D R O P

MEAS	CT	INSTRUCTIONS
1	a1	flap-back R
	2	heel-drop R
	a3	flap-back L
	4	heel-drop L

Repeat.

F L A P   A N D   B A L L - C H A N G E

MEAS	CT	INSTRUCTIONS
1	a1	flap fwd R
	a2	flap fwd L
	a3	flap fwd R
	&4	ball-change L R
2	a1	flap fwd L
	a2	flap fwd R
	a3	flap fwd L
	&4	ball-change R L

Repeat.

Variation

This exercise can also be done
moving back by flapping back
instead of fwd.

F L A P   A N D   H E E L - D R O P ,   F L A P   A N D   B A L L - C H A N G E

MEAS	CT	INSTRUCTIONS
1	a1	flap fwd R
	2	heel-drop R
	a3	flap fwd L
	4	heel-drop L

MEAS	CT	INSTRUCTIONS
2	a1	flap fwd R
	a2	flap fwd L
	a3	flap fwd R
	&4	ball-change L R
3	a1	flap fwd L
	2	heel-drop L
	a3	flap fwd R
	4	heel-drop R
4	a1	flap fwd L
	a2	flap fwd R
	a3	flap fwd L
	&4	ball-change R L

Repeat.

Variation

This exercise can also be done moving back by flapping back instead of fwd.

Action round

DANCING FOR CHILDREN

This chapter is divided into two sections. The first concerns traditional rhythmic experiences for children and includes musical mixers, grand march figures, action rounds, musical games, sequence dances, elementary dances, and rope jumping.

Creative dance for children, introducing them to the elements and concepts of dance and including six mini-lessons designed to stimulate creativity in movement, comprises the second section.

TRADITIONAL DANCE

INTRODUCTION

Rhythmic experiences are valuable to a young child in that they satisfy his need for movement. They also give him a means of expressing ideas and feelings.

TYPES OF RHYTHMIC ACTIVITIES

Experiences in rhythmic movement for young children include activities of four different types. A balanced program provides experiences in each of the following.

FUNDAMENTAL RHYTHMS

Basic movements necessary for successful performance in all types of rhythmic activities. They are also a complete experience in themselves, and as such are satisfying to children.

RHYTHMIC PANTOMIME

Rhythms which give children the opportunity to show the movements of people, animals, mechanical devices, or forces of nature. The vivid imaginations of young children help them to identify themselves completely with the objects they represent.

INTERPRETIVE RHYTHMS

Rhythms concerned with the expression of feelings rather than with ideas as in rhythmic pantomime. Children respond spontaneously with free rhythmic movement to music or other motivating stimuli.

SINGING GAMES

Traditional rhythmic experiences that have given pleasure to generations of young children. Large or small groups can participate, singing and moving about together.

GENERAL SUGGESTIONS

One of the teacher's first problems is to arrange for adequate space so that children may have freedom of movement. Auditoriums and playgrounds provide ample space, but classrooms and living rooms often present a problem. However, in a small space a workable solution is to divide the children into two or three groups so that each can be completely active in turn. Provide accompaniment by singing, clapping, or using rhythm instruments. Kindergarten teachers sometimes have rhythms with half their pupils while the others are engaged with storybooks or puzzles.

Children need to learn to use all the space available to them as well as to make allowance for the movement of others. Individuals should be commended for using space well.

Finally, the teacher can make exercises fun by effective use of imagery. Further discussion and examples of this concept are found in the creative section of this chapter.

MUSICAL MIXERS

CHAIN LINE FIGURES

HOLDING HANDS

Any march in 2/4 or 4/4 time makes good accompaniment for chain line figures. To begin, all join hands, and the leader starts the music. At the same time, he starts pulling the dancers into a circle. The person at the end of the chain pulls up and into the line any who are left seated.

After all are in a chain line, the leader may pull them into any of the following formations. No instructions are necessary for a chain line, making it a good opener for dance parties.

Inside out: The leader pulls the line into one big circle, then cuts across the center of the circle and through the other side without dropping hands on either side. As the dancers follow, the circle is turned inside out with all the dancers facing out. The leader then drops his right hand and turns left while his right-hand partner turns right. Both walk around, pulling the other dancers with them, to form the circle again, facing in.

Tie the knot: In a variation of the inside out pattern, the leader, once he has cut the circle and pulled all the dancers through, keeps hands joined and leads the dancers in a full loop around the person cut. This person does not turn with the others but stands still and lets his arms be crossed in front of him by the movements of the other dancers. The leader continues this pattern, looping around one person at a time until all are in a knot. To untie themselves the dancers, retaining handclasps, raise their arms above their heads, and turn halfway around.

Spiral: The leader pulls the dancers into a tight spiral by circling around and around, making the circles smaller as he travels.

Spiral

Snail

Spiral

Unwinding spiral

Unwinding spiral

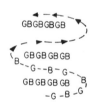

Serpentine

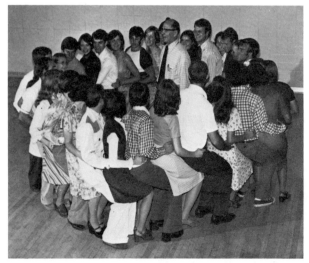

Dominoes

Weave

Unwinding spiral: When the leader has led the group into a rather tight spiral, he turns to face the opposite direction and walks through the spiral aisles formed by the dancers, bringing them out of spiral formation. Hands are still joined.

Thread the needle: When the dancers are in one big circle or line, the leader reverses direction and weaves in and out under the arms of the dancers, thus reversing the direction of the entire chain.

Snail: From a tight spiral, the leader in the center ducks under the joined arms forming each circle and pulls the dancers through to the outside into one line.

Serpentine: The leader weaves the line between relay lines.

Weave or Snake: The leader moves the line down the floor in S-curves like a snake.

NOT HOLDING HANDS

Basic Step

Everyone stands in a single circle, facing in the line of dance, and music (again any march in 2/4 or 4/4 time) is played. The footwork is three steps forward (L,R,L on ct 1,2,3), then a pause to clap hands twice (ct and 4). The sequence is then repeated, starting with the opposite foot (R,L,R, clap, clap). The above two measures are repeated to make four measures in all. This basic step should be repeated until the group is familiar enough with it to do it easily. Then it may be alternated with four measures of each of the following variations. These variations should be taught one by one and added to the series already learned as the dancers master them. In the series they should be called ahead, during the fourth measure of the basic step, so that the rhythm will continue without interruption.

Variations

Step and clap: Step sideward L (ct 1), clap hands at L (ct 2), step sideward R back to place (ct 3), clap hands at R (ct 4); repeat for 4 meas.

Turn in place: Turn L in place, L,R,L, touch (meas 1). Repeat to R (meas 2). Repeat L and R for 4 meas in all.

Drum major: Step fwd L (ct 1), lift R knee high, leaning backward and swinging arms in the style of a drum major (ct 2). Repeat, stepping fwd R (ct 3), lifting L knee high (ct 4). Repeat for total of 4 meas.

Indian: Step fwd on L toe (ct 1), lower L heel (ct 2), repeat R (ct 3-4). Repeat for total of 4 meas. Bend body forward from waist and drop head low on first 2 meas; raise body high and bend head back on last 2 meas. Arms swing alternately fwd and back with elbows slightly bent.

Indian--on the double: Repeat Indian variation twice as fast, moving 4 steps fwd L,R,L,R, and turning in place next 4 steps, L,R,L,R.

Military turn: Step fwd L (ct 1), fwd R (ct 2), fwd L toe pivoting 1/2 turn R (ct 3), step R in place (ct 4); repeat, returning to original position. Repeat entire sequence for a total of 4 meas.

Dominoes: End the conga line in a tight round circle. When dancers have bodies touching, the leader calls for all to sit down, each person on the knees of the person behind him. Then if one dancer is pushed over, the circle will fall down like a line of dominoes.

Knee sit in a line: Place a chair under the last person in the line so that he may sit in it and instruct the line to back up until they are all sitting on the knees of the person behind them as for the dominoes variation. For either of these variations, the leader may have a contest to see which circle or line can stand up and sit down the most times in one minute without falling.

Follow me (chain line or marching): With a group that has once experienced fun with mixers and had good leadership, all the leader needs to do is drop hands and say, "Follow me." Then, without further verbal instructions, the leader can dance different steps (swing, slide, swagger, and so on) and the group will try to imitate them. This is an effective way of getting the children's attention.

   These variations will probably foster ideas for many more. Creativity is the key. Participants could take turns being leader and calling the variations in the order they want, or calling original ones. Each child could think of a new one and teach it to the others.

G R A N D   M A R C H   F I G U R E S

GENERAL INFORMATION

   The leader should provide steady march music and have two file leaders who understand the movements. Dancers march in single file.
   If the group has the same number of boys and girls, have the boys form a file on one side of the room and the girls on the other, both facing the front of the room where the director stands.

MOVEMENTS

   The following movements may be done in any order, but the file leaders must know the order so as to avoid confusion. Also, the group must be in the correct formation to execute each movement; the leader should keep this in mind when planning the order of movements in a grand march.

Grand right-and-left: Two single files march toward each other along the perimeter of the room. When they meet, dancers grand right-and-left through the other file to its end.

By twos: Two single files march toward each other, meet at one end of the room, and come up the center of the room two by two (in couples).

By fours: From a double file, partners stay together and turn in alternate directions, the first couple going right, the second left, the third right, and so on, to march back around the perimeter of the room. When the two files of couples meet at the other end of the room, a couple from each file joins the

313

GRAND MARCH FIGURES

Split the ring

By twos

Reverse bridges

Grand right-and-left, singles

Grand right-and-left in couples

Eight abreast

By fours

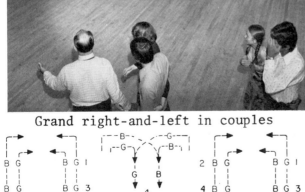

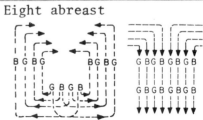

Reverse bridges   Eight abreast

other to come up the center by fours. When the file of four reaches the other end of the room, it may continue the doubling pattern as described to form eights, or it may divide into double files again, one couple turning to the right, the other to the left.

Circle bridges: Two files of partners march toward each other to meet at an end of the room. As both files of couples continue to march forward, the couples in the file at the director's right form a bridge by joining inside hands and holding them up high, and the other file marches under this bridge. When the two files meet again at the other end of the room, the other file forms a bridge under which the first file marches. This movement may be repeated as often as desired.

Dip and dive: Two files of couples march toward each other. When they meet, the first couple from the file on the leader's right goes under a single arch formed by the first couple in the other file, then forms an arch to go over the second couple, thus alternating with each couple coming the other way. The second couple in the right-hand file does the same, but starts by going over a couple. This pattern continues all down the files.

Skin the snake: Head couples in a double file lift their joined inside hands to form a bridge, then reverse direction and go back over their own lines. Each couple follows the head couple over the entire file until all have been over. Girls end on the other side of their partners. (It is usually necessary to couple this movement with either the reverse bridges or partners change arch movement to get the girls back on the right side of their partners.)

Reverse bridges: The head couple of a double file reverses direction and goes under the raised arms (bridges) of the rest of the couples. Each couple turns and follows the first couple until all have gone under the file. Girls end on the other side of their partners.

Split the ring: As two files of couples approach each other, everyone drops hands and the girls in each line march between the opposite couples. Boys march opposite their partners, either on the inside of the circle (if the boy is walking counterclockwise), or on the outside of the circle (if the girl is marching counterclockwise).

Grand right-and-left singles: As files of couples approach, each dancer extends his hand, boy to girl, and does a grand right-and-left all the way through the opposite file. Partners should come out even to continue the march in double files.

Grand right-and-left in couples: As files of couples approach each other, the boy puts his right arm around the girl's waist and the girl puts her left arm around the boy's waist. Girls join right hands as the first couples meet and pass; boys join left hands as they meet and pass the second couple, and all continue on in a grand right-and-left pattern through the entire file.

Partners change arch: In a file of four (two couples abreast), the center boy and girl join their nearest hands, form an arch, and stop. The outside boys and girls continue marching forward and turn one-half turn to face the arch, then join inside hands and go under the arch. The center couples, led by the last of the inside couples, go under the arch as for the reverse bridges movement. At the end of this movement, half the girls will be on the boys' left side. To get the girls back on the right side, this movement should be coupled with either the <u>reverse arches</u> or <u>skin the snake</u> movement.

<u>Cross</u>: Two files of couples march down the center of the floor from opposite directions to meet in the center of the hall. When couples from the two files meet, they trade partners by dropping hands, taking the hand of the person facing them, and turning their back on their original partner. Each dancer marches with his new partner to the side of the hall, then down the side and halfway across the end of the hall, then up the center to meet the other file and cross again to get back his original partner.

<u>Figure eight</u>: Either in single file or in a file of couples, dancers march around the room in the pattern of an "8," crossing in the center by cutting between dancers or couples in the file to be crossed.

<u>Sixteen abreast</u>: Starting with either single or double files, and using the same pattern as for the <u>by twos</u> and <u>by fours</u> movements, create files of four, eight, and sixteen. The group may divide back down to narrower files as described in the <u>by fours</u> movement, or they may be halted in this formation to go through relays or action rounds. From this formation the leader may create a chain line or a single circle by taking the hand of the person on the end of an outside line and leading that line around in a large circle. The first person on the end of the second line grasps the hand of the last person in the line, and so on until all are in one line being led by the leader. The line may then go into chain line figures or close to form a circle for action rounds, musical games, or sequence dances.

A C T I O N   R O U N D S

Elementary dances are necessarily sequence dances. They are actions composed to match the phrases of poems and songs. Start with simple action rounds that need little instruction, so that the dancers can walk and still have their minds free to listen for changes in formation. Later, the teacher should let the children make up their own movements to the words. Their imaginations should be their only limitation.

Different formations, such as single, double, or triple circles and lines, may be used.

Begin by using locomotor movements only. After the students are familiar with the songs, gradually add movements of the arms, hands, head, and body.

FAMILIAR ACTION ROUNDS

Following are samples of creative action rounds.

FRIENDS, FRIENDS, FRIENDS

Formation: Four parallel lines, facing fwd in single file
Tune: "Row, Row, Row Your Boat" sung as round with each line taking one part

Words	Actions
Friends, friends, friends, you say,	Walk fwd 4 steps and shake hands with person opposite.

All along the way.	Walk back 4 steps.
Smile, smile, smile, smile	Slide R 4 steps with hands over head, moving hands and fingers.
Every single day.	Slide L 4 steps, with hands as described above.

EENSIE-WEENSIE SPIDER

Formation: Single circle, facing in, hands free
Tune: Familiar

Words	Actions
Eensie-weensie spider went up the water spout.	All tiptoe 8 steps fwd to center of circle.
Down came the rain and washed the spider out.	Bring arms down, fluttering fingers (4 ct). Push arms away from center of body in opposite directions (4 ct).
Out came the sun and dried up all the rain.	All join hands high over heads and step-swing (step L, swing R foot, then reverse).
So eensie-weensie spider went up the spout again.	All tiptoe 8 steps fwd to center of circle.

This may also be done as a round with several small circles or one large circle.

SCOTLAND'S BURNING

Formation: Lines forming a square, facing center
Tune: Familiar, as four-voice round

Words	Actions
Scotland's burning. Scotland's burning.	Paddle L with hands raised, then paddle R with hands raised.
Look out, look out!	Arms folded on head, jump back twice for each "Look out!"
Fire, fire, fire, fire!	Wave arms in circles while walking back 4 steps.
Pour on water, pour on water.	Walk fwd 4 steps, moving arms as if water buckets are being passed.

PERFECT POSTURE

Formation: Four, 8, or 16 drill lines facing head of hall and divided into 4 sections of 1, 2, or more lines each
Tune: "Are You Sleeping?" as four-voice round

Words	Actions
Perfect posture! Perfect posture!	Stand perfectly straight at attention.

Do not slump! Do not slump!	Bend over with arms hanging and step fwd shaking head "no."
You must grow up handsome. You must grow up handsome.	Walk fwd with strutting motions (cock head high, fold arms behind back, and so on). Then walk back.
Hide that hump! Hide that hump!	Stand straight at attention.

LITTLE TOM TINKER

Formation: Four, 8, or 16 drill lines facing head of hall (usually as they march up center in grand march) and divided into 4 sections of 1 or more lines each

Tune: Familiar, as four-voice round

Words	Actions
Little Tom Tinker got burnt with a clinker	Walk 4 steps fwd.
	Walk 4 steps back.
And he began to cry	Raise hands twice over head.
Ma! Ma!	Turn in place once.
What a poor boy am I!	

Create your own foot, body, hand, and head movements to the following rounds.

DOWN AT THE STATION

Down at the station early in the morning
See the little puffer billies standing in a row.
See the engine driver turn the little handle.
Choo! Choo! Toot! Toot! Off they go!

ROW, ROW, ROW YOUR BOAT

Row, row, row your boat
Gently down the stream.
Merrily, merrily, merrily, merrily,
Life is but a dream.

THE GOOSE

Why doesn't my goose
Sing as well as thy goose,
When I paid for my goose
Twice as much as thou?

ARE YOU SLEEPING?

Are you sleeping, are you sleeping,
Brother John, Brother John?
Morning bells are ringing,
Morning bells are ringing,
Ding, ding, dong. Ding, ding, dong.

SWEETLY SINGS THE DONKEY

Sweetly sings the donkey at the break of day;
If you do not feed him, this is what he'll say:
"Hee-haw! Hee-haw! Hee-haw, hee-haw, hee-hay!"

MY DAME HAD A LAME TAME CRANE

My dame had a lame tame crane.
My dame had a crane that was lame.
Oh, pray gently, Jane, let my dame's lame tame crane
Drink and come home again.

BELLS ARE RINGING

Tune: "Are You Sleeping?"

Bells are ringing,
Bells are ringing;
Hear them sing,
Hear them sing:
Merry, Merry Christmas,
Merry, Merry Christmas,
Santa Claus, Santa Claus.

SANTA CLAUS

Tune: "Three Blind Mice"

Santa Claus, Santa Claus,
Reindeer paws, reindeer paws.
He comes in the night when the children sleep;
He slips with his pack down the chimney steep;
He piles all his toys 'neath the Christmas tree--
Dear Santa Claus.

HERE COMES SANTA CLAUS

Tune: "Row, Row, Row Your Boat"

Here comes Santa Claus
Riding in his sleigh.
He leaves all his toys for the girls and boys
All along the way.

M U S I C A L   G A M E S

AS YOU WERE

     Players form a double circle with the boys inside and march forward coun-
terclockwise. The leader calls various commands, such as "Boys in front of
girls," "Girls inside," "Boys behind girls," "Stop; girls about-face and all

319

grand right-and-left," "Circle four," "Walk with the other boy's girl," and terminating with "As you were." At this last command, everyone runs to find his original partner and continues marching. In the scramble, the leader takes a partner and the one player left out is "it." "It" calls various activities until he gets a partner.

COME ALONG

Players stand or sit shoulder-to-shoulder in a circle, holding their right hands out. One person stands in the middle and, when the music starts, runs around the circle clockwise and grabs someone by the hand, taking this person along. He, in turn, grabs someone else, and so on. When the music stops, all run to their places and the person left out is "it." For a ball-room mixer, boys take girls and girls take boys--from this formation the leader can shift readily to other activities by calling, "Everybody dance with the girl on the left," "March in a double circle," or "Dance in a line."
Variation
The circle faces out. When the music stops, each dancer runs to the closest vacancy.

INTRODUCTION

Partners face each other in a double circle--boys inside and girls outside. Both circles move to their right in time to the music. When the music stops, those facing each other shake hands and introduce themselves. Anyone without a partner moves to center of circle where he will find a partner. If someone without a partner can find a person not talking, he can take his partner. The game continues until each player has met ten or twelve people.

CONVERSATION CIRCLE

Partners face in a double circle, boys inside. The leader gives the group a subject to talk about. In time to the music, both circles move to their right. When the music stops, boys and girls face each other and start talking at the same time. Anyone without a partner walks around and listens to the conversation. If he finds someone not talking, he can take his place.

CRAZY HANDSHAKES

The group forms a double circle, the boys walking clockwise and the girls counterclockwise in time to the music. When the music stops, the boys talk to the girls while performing one of the following handshakes. The leader may call the handshakes or give the dancers free choice. (These actions may also be done in mass formation.)

Model T: Turn hand as though cranking a car.

Pump handle: Move hands up and down as though pumping for water.

Missionary: Squeeze hand tightly while shaking.

Milkmaid: Boy interlocks his fingers and turns thumbs down while girl holds his thumbs.

Barnyard: Scrape feet while shaking hands.

Royalty: Hold hands high and clasp fingertips.

Cocoa Drinkers: Clasp hands with thumbs up and pour into cupped free hands.

Tailor: Pinch material of partner's clothing with one hand while shaking hands with other.

Barber: Dust hair off partner's shoulders with free hand while shaking hands.

Dentist: Show teeth while shaking hands.

Doctor: Open mouth and say "aaahhh" while shaking hands.

Garbage man: Hold partner's arm above elbow, then slide hand down arm and off fingertips and shake in the air.

Fish: Let arm go limp and move hand from side to side.

Optometrist: Hold partner's eyebrow up with free hand and look into his eye while shaking hands.

Hitchhike: Start to shake hands and instead point thumb over own right shoulder.

Champion: Shake own hands above head.

Parachutist: Clasp hands, then throw hands in the air, breaking clasp, and let hands float down like parachutes.

Variations

Crazy handshakes may be used for other purposes.

Starter: Teach several of the handshakes to the first dancers that arrive and instruct them to teach the handshakes to all dancers as they arrive. Dancers should introduce themselves and get acquainted while shaking.

Conversational Handshakes: If all the dancers are acquainted, give them a subject to talk about while they are shaking hands. For example, the girl could take the affirmative on a subject such as "There is a Santa Claus," or "Cheese is better than marriage." This device can also be used in a mixer to find a new partner.

MUSICAL ELBOWS

The group forms a double circle with boys on the inside, right hands on hips. As the music is played, the boys march counterclockwise and the girls march clockwise. When the music stops each girl must hook a boy's elbow. Girls without partners go to the center and sing as the rest march. Extra girls must stay in the center until the music is stopped, when they may run to the outside and try to hook a boy's elbow.

Variation

If there are twice as many girls as boys, the boys should hold both elbows out.

MUSICAL MADHOUSE

The players form a single circle without holding hands. When the music begins, all march single file around the hall. The leader suddenly blows, for example, four blasts on his whistle. The march is stopped, and the players form small circles of four with hands joined. Those left out of a small circle of four must stand in the center of the hall. One blast starts the march again in a single circle. The next signal may be six blasts, at which circles of six are formed. While the circles are being formed, those in the center try to join one.

Variations

For a mixer, have the dancers keep in couples and exchange within the circle after the whistle is blown. To form squares for square dancing from couples, blow the whistle four times. For a threesome, one boy must find two girls. Those not finding a partner can provide the music by singing to replace played music; everyone tries harder for a partner when he has to pay this forfeit. For signaling, a cap pistol may be used instead of a whistle.

POPULARITY

With girls on the inside and boys on the outside of a double circle, all march in opposite directions. When the whistle blows, girls about-face, hook onto a boy's arm, and march with him. Extra girls go to the center. When the whistle blows again, boys and girls resume marching in opposite directions. Girls in the center may try to hook a boy's arm on subsequent signals.

Variations

If there are two girls to one boy, two girls may get one on each side of a boy. If there are still too many girls, let them fall in behind a boy-- seven girls on each boy's shirttail, for example. However, always have a few girls left over to go to the center.

STOOP

The group forms a double circle with boys on the inside and girls on the outside. When the music starts, the girls stand still while the boys march counterclockwise. When the music stops, every boy runs to his partner and takes her hands in his, and both stoop. The last person to stoop is a slow-poke. To end the game, the group may also be told to find seats for quiet games or to line up for refreshments instead of stooping.

KNEES

From a single circle, boy-girl formation, the girls march clockwise to the music, weaving in and out between the boys; boys go down on one knee to make a chair for their partners. When the music stops, girls run to their partners and sit on their knees.

Variation

To make this game a mixer, each girl could sit on the knee of the nearest boy.

REFRESHMENTS

Boys and girls march in opposite directions in double circle formation. When the music stops, all find partners wherever they can and line up for refreshments.

S E Q U E N C E   D A N C E S

Sequence dances are the same as round dances in that a few steps or movements are repeated in sequence, over and over again. Unlike social dancing, which has no set pattern or sequence and where each dancer is on his own, in sequence dances all dance the same step at the same time.

In this section of dances, the words of a familiar nursery rhyme or song have been used in preference to instructional calls and without the usual call format; only where there is no rhyme or where the dance is rather complicated has an instructional call been provided. The leader must teach the dance to the children first, then play or sing the nursery rhyme or song to cue them as they dance.

The dances are placed in alphabetical order, but they vary in degree of difficulty and appropriateness for various age levels. The leader will need to keep these factors in mind when selecting dances for a group.

Records are suggested for most of the dances, but the leader and children could provide the music by singing if they prefer.

A - H U N T I N G   W E   W I L L   G O

Formation:	Two lines, 1 of boys, 1 of girls, facing	Music:	A-Hunting We Will Go
Position:	Shine	Record:	Folkraft 1191
Footwork:	Opposite (boy L, girl R)	Rhythm:	4/4, 8 meas

MEAS	CALL	INSTRUCTIONS
	skip and all sing	Head couple joins inside hands and skips down between lines in 8 skips (meas 1-2). Other couples clap hands in rhythm.
	READY SKIP	
1	Oh, a-hunting we will go,	Head couple faces about by turning inward and changing hands and skips 8 skips back to head of set (meas 3-4).
2	A-hunting we will go,	For meas 5-8, all partners join inside
3	We'll catch a fox and put-him-in-a-box,	hands and follow head couple as they lead in a circle to L. When the head

4	And then we'll let him go.	couple reaches spot previously occupied by last couple, form arch by raising joined hands. All other couples skip under. The 2nd couple is now head couple.
5	1 2 3 4	
6	1 2 3 4	Repeat entire dance.
7	1 2 3 4	
8	now start OVER	

B E A N   P O R R I D G E   H O T

Formation: Double circle, partners facing
Position: Shine
Footwork: Opposite (boy L, girl R)

Music: Pease Porridge Hot
Record: Folkraft 1190
Rhythm: 4/4, 12 meas

MEAS   CALL

clap own hands' and' sing

READY CLAP

INSTRUCTIONS

Verses

Clap own hands to thighs, clap own hands together, clap partner's hands (meas 1).
Repeat (meas 2).
Clap own hands to thighs, clap own hands together, clap partner's R hand with own R hand, clap own hands (meas 3).
Clap partner's L hand with own L hand, clap own hands, clap partner's 2 hands (meas 4).

Verse 1

1	Bean porridge hot,
2	Bean porridge cold,
3	Bean porridge in the pot
4	Nine days old.

Chorus

5	1 2 3 4
6	5 6 7 8
7	9 10 11 12
8	13 14 15 reverse
9	1 2 3 4
10	5 6 7 8
11	9 10 11 12
12	13 14 second verse

Chorus

With both hands joined, partners take 16 slides ccw, then reverse for 16 slides cw.

Repeat entire dance, using the following words.

Verse 2

Some like it hot,

Some like it cold,

Some like it in the pot

Nine days old.

DID YOU EVER SEE A LASSIE?

Formation: Single circle
Position: Hands joined
Footwork: All start L

Music: Did You Ever See a Lassie?
Record: Folkraft 1183
Rhythm: 3/4, 16 meas

MEAS	CALL
	circle LEFT
	ready CIRCLE
1-2	Did you ever see a lassie (or laddie),
3-4	A lassie, a lassie,
5-6	Did you ever see a lassie
7-8	Do this way and that?
9-10	Do this way and that way,
11-12	Do this way and that way,
13-14	Did you ever see a lassie
15-16	Do this way and that?

INSTRUCTIONS

Circle moves L by skipping or walking in rhythm to words of meas 1-8.
For meas 9-16, circle stops moving, drops hands, faces in, and imitates leader's movements to words.

Repeat entire dance.

Note

New leader is chosen during the musical interlude. Leaders should be encouraged to use large, vigorous movements that can be imitated in definite rhythmical patterns.

THE FARMER IN THE DELL

Formation: Single circle, 1 in center
Position: Hands joined
Footwork: All start L

Music: The Farmer in the Dell
Record: Folkraft 1182
Rhythm: 4/4, 36 meas

MEAS	CALL
	circle left and sing
	READY WALK
1	The farmer in the dell,
2	The farmer in the dell,
3	Heigh ho, the derry-O!
4	The farmer in the dell.
5	The farmer takes a wife,

INSTRUCTIONS

All in circle sing while marching L to rhythm of song (meas 1-4).
Singing and moving continues as person in center (farmer) chooses another person (wife) to join him in the center (meas 5-8).
On following verses, newest person in center chooses next person, until last verse. Then all but last person rejoin circle, leaving him (the cheese) alone in center.
Repeat entire dance, with cheese as new farmer.

MEAS	CALL	INSTRUCTIONS

6	The farmer takes a wife,
7	Heigh ho, the derry-O!
8	The farmer takes a wife.

Breakdown of Verses

The farmer in the dell. . .
The farmer takes a wife. . .
The wife takes a child. . .
The child takes a nurse. . .
The nurse takes a dog. . .
The dog takes a cat. . .
The cat takes a rat. . .
The rat takes the cheese. . .
The cheese stands alone. . .

H O K E Y - P O K E Y

This is a story about a child ready to take a bath and finding that the water is too hot.

Formation: Single circle
Position: Shine
Footwork: All start R

Music: Hokey-Pokey
Record: MacGregor 6995, Capitol 2427
Rhythm: 4/4

MEAS   CALL

right foot IN

READY GO

1	You put your right foot in,
2	You put your right foot out,
3	You put your right foot in,
4	And you shake it all about;
5	You do the hokey-pokey
6	And you turn yourself around;
7-8	That's what it's all about.

. . .

89-90	You do the ho--key-pokey,
91-92	You do the ho--key-pokey,
93-94	You do the ho--key-pokey;
95-96	And that's what it's all about.

INSTRUCTIONS

Dancers act out words of song. On words "You do the hokey pokey and you turn yourself around," dancers may either raise hands above head and shake them or put left hand on stomach and raise right finger while turning around. On words "That's what it's all about," dancers jump 2 short jumps back, clapping hands, then make 1 long jump fwd to center.
For last verse, on words "You do the ho--key-pokey," dancers kneel and clap floor with hands, rising in time for regular sequence of actions on words "That's what it's all about."

Breakdown of Verses

Verse order may vary in different recordings, but is easily adapted from the following:

right foot	head
left foot	right hip
right arm	left hip
left arm	whole self
right elbow	back side
left elbow	ho--key-pokey

I SEE YOU

Formation:	Four lines (see diagram under INSTRUCTIONS), A and B facing C and D
Position:	Hands on shoulders of person ahead
Footwork:	Opposite (boy L, girl R)

Music:	I See You
Record:	Folkraft 1197
Rhythm:	4/4, 8 meas

MEAS	CALL
	peek and all sing
	READY PEEK
1	I see you, I see you,
2	Tra la la la la la la la la.
3	I see you, I see you,
4	Tra la la la la la la la la.
5	You see me and I see you,
6	You take me and I take you,
7	Tra la la la la la la la la,
8	Tra la la la la la la la la.

INSTRUCTIONS

Dancers in lines A and D play peek-a-boo with each other by bending head to L and looking over L shoulder of partner in line in front of them to the words "I see you." Bend head and look over partner's R shoulder to words "I see you." Look over L shoulder, R, L in double time to words "Tra la la la la la la la la" (meas 1-2).

Repeat all above, starting R (meas 3-4).

Boys in line A and girls in line D skip forward, passing partners' L shoulder on words "You see me and I see you." On words "You take me and I take you," each active dancer takes hands of person with whom he has been playing peek-a-boo and they turn 1 full turn (meas 5-6).

Active dancers drop hands with these partners and return to own partners, join hands in two-hand position, and skip around in couple turn to "Tra la la la. . ." of meas 7-8. At the end, dancers have reversed positions such that those in lines A and D form lines B and C.

Repeat entire dance with new active dancers.

Formation

A--XXXXX (boys)
B--OOOOO (girls)

C--XXXXX (boys)
D--OOOOO (girls)

JUMP JIM CROW

Formation: Double circle
Position: Two-hand
Footwork: Jump on both feet

Music: Jump Jim Jo
Record: Folkraft 1180
Rhythm: 4/4, 8 meas

MEAS	CALL	INSTRUCTIONS

jump in PLACE

READY JUMP

Jump 2 slow, 3 quick jumps in place.
Turn partner in 8 small running steps.
Drop hands and move to own R in 2 slides; stomp 3 times in front of new partner.
with 4 runs ending with 3 jumps in place.

1-2   Jump, jump, and jump Jim Crow.

3-4   Take a little twirl and then away we go,

5-6   Slide, slide, and stamp just so.

Repeat entire dance.

7-8   Then you take another partner and you jump Jim Crow.

LONDON BRIDGE

Formation: Single lines with 1 couple at head of each line
Position: Couples in two-hand arch, other dancers in shine
Footwork: All start L

Music: London Bridge
Record: All sing
Rhythm: 4/4, 16 meas

MEAS	CALL	INSTRUCTIONS

all march and sing

READY MARCH

1   London Bridge is falling down,

2   Falling down, falling down.

3-4   London Bridge is falling down, my fair lady.

5   What did the robber do to you?

6   Do to you? Do to you?

7-8   What did the robber do to you, my fair lady?

Dancers sing while marching under arch and around to end of line; all continue going under arch until words "off to prison" are sung. On these words arch is lowered to catch dancer then passing under. This dancer is taken to side and asked: "Will you have----or---?" The 2 dancers forming arch, or guardians of bridge, have previously chosen object for each to represent. When "caught" dancer chooses 1 of these objects, he is placed behind guardian representing this object.

Repeat entire dance until all are caught and in lines behind guardians.

MEAS	CALL	INSTRUCTIONS
9	He broke my watch and stole my keys,	Ends with "tug-of-war" between lines.
10	Stole my keys, stole my keys,	
11-12	He broke my watch and stole my keys, my fair lady.	
13	Then off to prison he must go,	
14	He must go, he must go.	
15-16	Then off to prison he must go, my fair lady.	

L O O B Y - L O O

Formation: Single circle
Position: Hands joined
Footwork: All start L

Music: Here We Go Looby-Loo
Record: Folkraft 1184
Rhythm: 4/4

MEAS   CALL

all skip and sing

READY SKIP

INSTRUCTIONS

Chorus

Skip to L until words "Saturday night" are sung.

Chorus

1	Here we dance looby-loo,
2	Here we dance looby-light.
3	Here we dance looby-loo,
4	All on a Saturday night.

Verse

5	Put you right hand in,
6	Put your right hand out,
7	Shake your right hand a little, a little,
8	And turn yourself about. Oh!

Verse

All stop, put R hand in toward center of circle, then stretch R hand away from center of circle. All shake R hand and turn in place.
Repeat for following verses, with chorus after each verse, suiting actions to words.

Breakdown of Verses

right hand
left hand
right foot
left foot
whole self

MAYPOLE DANCE

The object of the maypole dance is to braid a tall pole with ribbons while dancing around it. Four different colors of ribbons, attached to the top of the pole, leave it in a beautiful array of colors when the dance is finished. A pole six to eight inches in diameter looks better when braided than a smaller pole. The ribbons should be about ten feet longer than the pole.

Formation: Single circle around pole, partners facing
Position: Shine, each person holding one ribbon in both hands
Footwork: Opposite (boy L, girl R)

Music: Own choice
Record: Own choice
Rhythm: Duple or triple

MEAS   CALL

Because of the freedom of choice given in this dance, calls and measures are not given. However, the leader will be expected to call the steps to the dancers to avoid confusion.

INSTRUCTIONS

Girls move clockwise, and boys counterclockwise. Still holding ribbon in both hands, each dancer dips and dives over one and under another of dancers coming from opposite direction. As each dancer meets new partner, both execute dance step called by leader. Steps that may be used in progressing to each new partner include walk, two-step, conga, schottische, varsouvienne, polka, or any social dance step. Suggestions for steps to be danced by newly-met partners are as follows.

Balance--forward, backward, or sideward.
Arch--under own arm to center or outside and back.
Slide--to own right and left, in and out of circle (partner moving opposite).
Grapevine--to own right and left, in and out of circle.
Chug--to own right and left, in and out of circle.

Variations

If desired, dancers may perform progressive version of any of following dances while braiding the maypole; foxtrot, waltz, lindy, rumba, samba, tango, Charleston, mambo, meringue, bossa nova, rock, and many of the round dances.

MULBERRY BUSH

Formation: Single circle
Position: Hands joined
Footwork: All start L

Music: Here We Go 'Round the Mulberry Bush
Record: Folkraft 1183
Rhythm: 2/4

MEAS   CALL

INSTRUCTIONS

slide left, and sing

Chorus

READY, SLIDE

All take 16 slides to L while singing.

Chorus

Verse

1-2   Here we go 'round the mulberry bush,

All stop, drop hands, and dramatize the action.

3-4   The mulberry bush, the mulberry bush,

Repeat following verses, with chorus after each verse, suiting actions to words.

5-6   Here we go 'round the mulberry bush,

7-8   So early in the morning.

Breakdown of Verses

Verse

This is the way we iron our clothes. . .
So early Tuesday morning.

9-10   This is the way we wash our clothes,

This is the way we scrub the floor. . .
So early Wednesday morning.

11-12   Wash our clothes, wash our clothes,

13-14   This is the way we wash our clothes

This is the way we mend our clothes. . .
So early Thursday morning.

15-16   So early Monday morning.

This is the way we sweep the floor. . .
So early Friday morning.

Thus we play when our work is done. . .
So early Saturday morning.

MUSICANA

Formation: Single circle
Position: Hands joined
Footwork: All start L

Music: Own choice
Record: Own choice
Rhythm: 4/4, 52 meas

MEAS   CALL

INSTRUCTIONS

slide left and clap

Slide: Slide slowly to L (L,R,L,R,L,

MEAS	CALL	INSTRUCTIONS

READY <u>SLIDE</u>

MEAS	CALL
1-2	1 2 3 4, 5 6 REVERSE
3-4	1 2 3 4, 5 6 <u>CLAP</u>
5-6	slap slap slap slap, clap clap clap clap
7-8	turn 2 3 4, play a <u>VIOLIN</u>
9-10	1 2 3 4, 5 6 REVERSE
11-12	1 2 3 4, 5 6 <u>CLAP</u>
13-14	slap slap slap slap, clap clap clap clap
15-16	turn 2 3 4, play a <u>TROMBONE</u>
17-18	1 2 3 4, 5 6 REVERSE
19-20	1 2 3 4, 5 6 <u>CLAP</u>
21-22	slap slap slap slap, clap clap clap clap
23-24	turn 2 3 4, play a <u>PIANO</u>
25-26	1 2 3 4, 5 6 REVERSE
27-28	1 2 3 4, 5 6 <u>CLAP</u>
29-30	slap slap slap slap, clap clap clap clap
31-32	turn 2 3 4, play a <u>DRUM</u>
33-34	1 2 3 4, 5 6 REVERSE
35-36	1 2 3 4, 5 6 <u>CLAP</u>
37-38	slap slap slap slap, clap clap clap clap
39-40	turn 2 3 4, play a <u>TRUMPET</u>
41-42	1 2 3 4, 5 6 REVERSE
43-44	1 2 3 4, 5 6 <u>CLAP</u>
45-46	slap slap slap slap, clap clap clap clap

R). Let go of hands momentarily and clap own hands together once. Slide slowly to R (R,L,R,L,R,L). Clap own hands.

Clap sequence: Slap knees with both hands 4 times, clap own hands together 4 times. Turn to L 1 individual turn (L,R,L,R,L,R,L,R). Alternative is to turn (L,R,L,R) in 4 ct and clap knees, hips, and hands on remaining 4 ct.

Violin: Slide as above, imitating holding violin with L hand and bowing with R hand, and making noise like a violin. Clap and reverse direction, using same hand movements.

Trombone: Slide with L hand to mouth while pushing and pulling with R hand and making noise like a trombone. Clap and reverse.

Piano: Slide while moving fingers along keyboard. Clap and reverse.

Drum: Slide while using both hands to beat drum. Clap and reverse.

Trumpet: Slide while holding hands up as if holding trumpet to mouth and moving fingers of R hand up and down as if operating valves.

French horn: Puff cheeks as if blowing French horn.

<u>Variation</u>

Each person may take turn deciding what instrument to play. Dancer indicated by leader takes 2 steps fwd to center of circle and leads others in "playing" instrument of his choosing. Dancer rejoins circle for slide and clap sequences. Each dancer around circle takes his turn.

MEAS	CALL	INSTRUCTIONS
47-48	turn 2 3 4, play a <u>French</u> <u>horn</u>	
49-50	1 2 3 4, 5 6 REVERSE	
51-52	1 2 3 4, 5 6 that's all	

O A T S ,   P E A S ,   B E A N S

Formation: Single circle, 1 in center
Position: Hands joined
Footwork: All start R

Music: Oats, Peas, Beans, and Barley
Record: Folkraft 1182
Rhythm: 4/4, 16 meas

MEAS	CALL
	skip right and sing
	READY SKIP
1	Oats, peas, beans, and barley grow,
2	Oats, peas, beans, and barley grow,
3	Can you or I or anyone know
4	How oats, peas, beans, and barley grow?
5	Thus the farmer sows his seed,
6	Then stands back and takes his ease;
7	He stamps his foot and claps his hands,
8	And turns around to view the land.
9	Waiting for a partner,
10	Waiting for a partner,
11	Open the ring and choose one in,

INSTRUCTIONS

All skip 4 ct (meas 1) then slide 4 ct (meas 2) then walk 8 ct (meas 3-4) to R while singing.
Circle stops, all follow actions of farmer as they sing (meas 5-8).
All stand still and sing while farmer chooses partner (meas 9-12).
Circle skips R as farmer and his wife skip L inside circle (meas 13-14).
On meas 15-16, center couple chooses new farmer and rejoins outside circle in his place.

Repeat entire dance.

MEAS	CALL	INSTRUCTIONS

12   While we all gaily dance
        and sing.

13   Now you're married, you
        must obey,

14   You must be true to all
        you say,

15   You must be kind, you must
        be good,

16   And keep your wife in
        kindling wood.

OLD BRASS WAGON

Formation:	Two lines, 1 of boys, 1 of girls, facing	Music:	Ten Little Indians
Position:	Shine	Record:	Folkraft 1197, all sing
Footwork:	Opposite (boy L, girl R)	Rhythm:	4/4, 16 meas

MEAS	CALL

INSTRUCTIONS

sing head couple skip

READY GO

1   Skip up and down, little
     brass wagon,

2   Skip up and down, little
     brass wagon,

3   Skip up and down, little
     brass wagon.

4   You're the one, my darling.

5   One wheel off and the other
     one a-draggin',

6   One wheel off and the other
     one a-draggin',

7   One wheel off and the other
     one a-draggin',

8   You're the one, my darling.

9   Now run away in the old
     brass wagon,

Head couple skips 8 ct to foot of line and 8 ct back while all sing (meas 1-4).
Head couple hook R elbows and turn 1 full turn, then hook L elbow with 2nd dancer in other line and turn 1/2 turn to meet partner in middle. Hook R elbows and turn 1/2 turn, then hook L elbow with 3rd dancer in other line for 1/2 turn. Repeat pattern all down line (meas 5-8). If this movement takes longer than 4 meas, dancers may sing this verse over until head couple reaches foot of line, or head couple may continue on to next sequence from wherever they are in line without reeling all the way to foot.
Head boy and girl skip around outside of set in opposite directions, finishing in place at head of set (meas 9-12).
Head boy turns L and head girl R, and lead lines to where foot of set was.
Head couple joins hands to form arch and other couples meet, join inside hands and go under arch to reform set with 2nd couple as new head

MEAS	CALL	INSTRUCTIONS

MEAS	CALL
10	Now run away in the old brass wagon,
11	Now run away in the old brass wagon,
12	You're the one, my darling.
13	Wheel and turn with the old brass wagon,
14	Wheel and turn with the old brass wagon,
15	Wheel and turn with the old brass wagon,
16	You're the one, my darling.

INSTRUCTIONS

couple (meas 13-16).

Repeat entire dance.

<u>Variations</u>

Dancers may create new verses and movements to go with them; for example, a skipping or step-hop movement to words such as "Bouncing up and down in the old brass wagon. . . ." For mixer, dancers may adapt or create verses to fit a double circle formation. To words "Swing, oh, swing the old brass wagon, . . ." boy could elbow-swing partner (meas 1), girl on L (meas 2), and partner again (meas 3-4) to end in promenade position. Group could then promenade in circle to words "Promenade home, old brass wagon. . . ."

OLD MACDONALD'S FARM

Formation: Mass
Position: Shine
Footwork: All start L

Music: Old MacDonald's Farm
Record: All sing
Rhythm: 4/4, 6 meas

MEAS   CALL

sing and wiggle ears

READY SING

<u>Chorus</u>

1	Old MacDonald had a farm,
2	E - I - E - I - O.

<u>Verse 1</u>

3	And on this farm he had some ducks,
4	E - I - E - I - O.
5	With a quack-quack here and a quack-quack there,
6	Here a quack, there a quack, everywhere a quack-quack.

INSTRUCTIONS

<u>Chorus</u>

Bob up and down, bending and straightening knees (meas 1). Place thumbs to ears and move hands up and down imitating donkey's ears (meas 2).

<u>Verse 1</u>

Repeat actions of meas 1-2 (meas 3-4). Put palms of hands together and hold them up to mouth to form bill, moving them open and closed while keeping wrists touching. Everyone meander and zigzag around room, singing and moving hands as described (meas 5-8).

<u>Verse 2</u>

Repeat action of meas 1-2 (meas 7-8), then use fingers to poke each other with, in imitation of pecking.

MEAS	CALL	INSTRUCTIONS

| | | |

Chorus

Verse 3

7 Old MacDonald had a farm,

Repeat action of meas 1-2 (meas 15-16).
Wind tail in cranking motion.

8 E - I - E - I - O.

Verse 2

9 And on this farm he had some chicks,

10 E - I - E - I - O.

11 With a peck-peck here and a peck-peck there,

12 Here a peck, there a peck, everywhere a peck-peck.

Chorus

13 Old MacDonald had a farm,

14 E - I - E - I - O.

Verse 3

15 And on this farm he had a pig,

16 E - I - E - I - O.

17 With an oink-oink here and an oink-oink there,

18 Here an oink, there an oink, everywhere an oink-oink.

INSTRUCTIONS (CONTINUED)

Breakdown of Other Verses

Any number of these verses or others may be used in any order, with group creating actions to match. Repeat chorus between verses and end with chorus.

Cow	moo-moo	Bell	tinkle-tinkle
Owl	who-who	Indian	(war whoop like Indian, hand over mouth)
Wife	gimme-gimme		
Gun	bang-bang	Pain	(moan or groan)
Baby	cry-cry	Itch	scratch-scratch
Ford	chug-chug	Worm	wiggle-wiggle
Hen	cackle-cackle	Phone	ring-ring
Turkey	gobble-gobble	Train	toot-toot

INSTRUCTIONS (CONTINUED)

Lamb	baa-baa	Dog	bow-wow
Cat	meow-meow	Bed	snore-snore
Bees	buzz-buzz	Tree	sway-sway
Rabbit	hop-hop	Airplane	zoom-zoom

P I C K I N ' U P P A W P A W S

Formation: Two lines, 1 of boys,
1 of girls, facing,
4 to 6 couples per set
Position: Shine
Footwork: Opposite (boy L, girl R)

Music: Pawpaw Patch
Record: Folkraft 1181
Rhythm: 2/4, 24 meas

MEAS   CALL

head girl, CIRCLE

READY, GO

1-2   Where, oh, where is dear
little Nellie (use name of
active dancer)?

3-4   Where, oh, where is dear
little Nellie?

5-6   Where, oh, where is dear
little Nellie?

7-8   'Way down yonder in the
pawpaw patch.

9-10   Come on, boys, and let's
go find her,

11-12   Come on, boys, and let's
go find her,

13-14   Come on, boys, and let's
go find her,

15-16   'Way down yonder in the
pawpaw patch.

17-18   Pickin' up pawpaws, put 'em
in your pocket,

19-20   Pickin' up pawpaws, put 'em
in your pocket,

21-22   Pickin' up pawpaws, put 'em
in your pocket,

INSTRUCTIONS

While group sings, girl of head
couple turns to her R and circles
around outside of set cw and returns
to place (meas 1-8).
Girl circles set again as above, this
time followed by line of boys (meas
9-16). They may motion to each other
to follow, and so on. Remaining
girls use motions and expressions to
indicate indignation, sulkiness,
petulance, and so on.
Couples face head of set and join
inside hands, and head couple leads
others in small circle to L. When
head couple reaches place where foot
of set was, stop and make arch
(meas 17-22). Remaining couples run
under arch and reform set with second
couple as new head couple (meas 23-
24).

Repeat entire dance.

23-24   'Way down yonder in the
         pawpaw patch.

'R O U N D   A N D   'R O U N D   T H E   V I L L A G E

Formation: Single circle, 1 in   Music: 'Round and 'Round the
            center   Village
Position: Hands joined   Record: Folkraft 1191
Footwork: L   Rhythm: 2/4, 16 meas

MEAS   CALL   INSTRUCTIONS

        all sing, one skips   Those in circle hold hands up high
                                          while dancer in center weaves in and
        READY, SING   out under joined hands around circle.
                                          On last line of 2nd verse, dancer in
 1-2   Go 'round and 'round the   center stands in front of another
        village,   person in circle, and takes his
                                          place as he goes into center.
 3-4   Go 'round and 'round the
        village,   Repeat entire dance.

 5-6   Go 'round and 'round the
        village,   Variation

 7-8   As we have done before.   Leader and all dancers chosen stay
                                          in center instead of rejoining circle
 9-10   Go in and out the windows,   and follow leader in line through
                                          motions of dance.
11-12   Go in and out the windows,

13-14   Go in and out the windows,

15-16   As we have done before.

S K I P   T O   M Y   L O U

Formation: Double circle, several   Music: Skip to My Lou
            boys extra in center   Record: Folkraft 1192
Position: Shine   Rhythm: 4/4, 4 meas
Footwork: Opposite (boy L, girl R)

MEAS   CALL   INSTRUCTIONS

        skip and SING   Dancers in double circle skip or
                                          walk. Each boy in center chooses 1
        READY SKIP   couple from double circle and brings
                                          it into center. There they join
 1   I've lost my gal, now what'll   hands in small circle of 3 and skip
        I do?   or walk (meas 1-3).
                                          Boy from center and girl raise their

MEAS	CALL	INSTRUCTIONS

MEAS	CALL
2	I've lost my gal, now what'll I do?
3	I've lost my gal, now what'll I do?
4	Skip to my lou, my darling.

arms to form an arch; girl's original partner goes under arch toward center of circle to become extra boy in center, leaving other boy and girl to become new partners and join double circle (meas 4).

Repeat entire dance.

Other Verses

Actions are same for all verses.

Little red wagon painted blue. . .

Get me another purty as you. . .

Purty as a red bird, purtier too. . .

T H E   S W I N G

Formation: Triple circle
Position: Couple in two-hand, third person facing LOD between their joined hands
Footwork: Opposite (boy L, girl R)

Music: Any Viennese waltz
Record: Own choice
Rhythm: 3/4, 16 meas

MEAS	CALL
	swing 2 3
	forward NOW
1-2	forward 2 3, back 2 3
3-4	forward 2 3, back 2 3
5-6	forward 2 3, back 2 3
7-8	forward 2 3, back 2 3
9-10	forward 2 3, back 2 3
11-12	forward 2 3, back 2 3
13-14	forward 2 3, back push through
15-16	forward 2 3, 4 start over

INSTRUCTIONS

Forward swing sequence: All 3 dancers shift weight to the front foot for 3 ct and then to the back foot for 3 ct, swinging arms in same direction at same time, as if pushing swing. Continue for 14 meas.

Push through: On meas 15, which is fwd, swinger goes under arched arms of couple and progresses to next swing.

Repeat entire dance.

TEDDY BEAR'S PICNIC

Formation:	Double circle	Music: Teddy Bear's Picnic
Position:	Full-open, R-L cnt	Record: Recorded by Windsor
Footwork:	Opposite (boy L, girl R)	Rhythm: 4/4, 8 meas

MEAS	CALL	INSTRUCTIONS
	walk and BRUSH	Walk and brush sequence: Walk fwd 3 steps, brush R foot, repeat walk and brush starting R.
	READY WALK	
1	forward 2 3 brush	Pas de basque: Step to side L, cross R over L, change weight momentarily, R, L. Repeat to R.
2	now let's pas' de' basque	
3	pas' de' basque out' now' cross	Cross, cross back: Girl cross in front of boy without turning (4 ct).
4	cross and pas' de' basque	Individual turn: In 4 two-steps boy turn L in circle, girl turn R and ahead to new partner.
5	pas' de' basque in' cross' back	
6	now individual TURN	Repeat entire dance.
7	step' close' step step' close' step	
8	change partners now walk	

TEN LITTLE INDIANS

Formation:	Single circle with 1 dancer outside circle	Music: Ten Little Indians
Position:	Shine	Record: Folkraft 1197
Footwork:	L	Rhythm: 4/4, 16 meas

MEAS	CALL	INSTRUCTIONS
	all sing one skips	Verse 1
	READY SKIP	Dancers in circle stand still and sing. Dancer outside circle runs around outside and tags 10 dancers. Tagged dancers step inside circle and join hands to form small circle.
1	One little, two little, three little Indians,	
2	Four little, five little, six little Indians,	Chorus
3	Seven little, eight little, nine little Indians,	Outside circle join hands and slide L. Inside circle with hands joined

MEAS	CALL	INSTRUCTIONS

4   Ten little Indian boys.   slide R.

5   Tra la la, la la la,   <u>Verse 2</u>
        la la la la,
                                                Inside circle players return to outer
6   Tra la la, la la la,   circle in reverse order, as verse 2
        la la la la,   of song, with numbers in reverse
                                                order, is repeated.
7   Tra la la, la la la,
        la la la la,   All join hands after all 10 players
                                                have returned to outer circle and
8   Tra la la la la.   circle L on repeat of chorus. Leader
                                                remains in center until last line,
9   Ten little, nine little,   then chooses new leader and takes
        eight little Indians,   his place in circle.

10   Seven little, six little,   Repeat entire dance.
        five little Indians,

11   Four little, three little,
        two little Indians,

12   One little Indian boy.

13   Tra la la, la la la,
        la la la la,

14   Tra la la, la la la,
        la la la la,

15   Tra la la, la la la,
        la la la la,

16   Tra la la la la.

T E N N E S S E E   S A T U R D A Y   N I G H T

Formation: Double circle   Music: Tennessee Saturday Night
Position: Two-hand   Record: Decca 4613
Footwork: Opposite (boy L, girl R)   Rhythm: 4/4, 8 meas

MEAS   CALL   INSTRUCTIONS

        READY <u>STOMP</u>   <u>Stomp</u>: Stomp L foot twice. Stomp
                                  L,R,L. Repeat, starting R.
1   stomp stomp left' right'
        left   <u>Do-si-do</u>: Pass R shoulders and move
                                  back to place in 8 steps.
2   stomp stomp <u>do'-si'-do</u>
                                  <u>Jump</u>: Jump with both feet together
3   1 2 3 4   to L,R,L,R,L. Repeat, starting to R.

MEAS	CALL	INSTRUCTIONS

MEAS	CALL
4	1 2 jump now
5	left right left' right' left
6	right left now' let's' wheel
7	step' close' step change partners
8	swing swing start over

Wheel: Hook R elbows and do 2 two-steps once around and on to girl behind (meas 7).

Waist swing: Both boy and girl hold each other around waist with R arms, holding L arm up, and swing once around (meas 8).

Repeat entire dance.

Y A N K E E   D O O D L E

Formation: Single circle facing R
Position: Shine
Footwork: All start R

Music: Yankee Doodle
Record: All sing
Rhythm: 2/4, 16 meas

INSTRUCTIONS

MEAS	CALL
	all circle, RIGHT
	READY, GALLOP
1-2	Yankee Doodle went to town
3-4	Riding on a pony.
5-6	He stuck a feather in his cap
7-8	And called it macaroni.
9-10	Yankee Doodle, ha ha ha,
11-12	Yankee Doodle Dandy.
13-14	Yankee Doodle, ha ha ha,
15-16	Now give the girls some candy.

All gallop 8 times to R (meas 1-4). All stop and face center. All point to head on word "cap," all bow on word "macaroni" (meas 5-8). All join hands and take 6 slides to R, stamp feet 2 times on word "dandy" (meas 9-12).
Slide 6 times to L, clap hands 2 times on word "candy" (meas 13-16).

Repeat entire dance.

R O P E   J U M P I N G

Rope jumping can be a means of introducing an individual, a group, or a family to a wholesome, interesting, and challenging activity for a lifetime of enjoyment.

The rope should be 3/8"cotton sash cord. To measure the length, have the participant stand across the center of the rope and measure the ends up to his armpits on each side. Knot the two ends. A commercial rope with wooden or plastic handles can be purchased at sporting goods departments. Be sure the rope is made of 3/8" sash cord so that it has body and weight for ease of handling.

For effective use of the rope, keep the arms down rather close, but loose, at the sides of the body. Use flexible wrist movement. Keep the body erect, with the head held high and the eyes focused out in front.

S K I L L S

First, teach the skills without the rope. As soon as an individual has learned a skill, he can then practice it while turning the rope. Start with the basic skills to get the participant used to the rope and to help him develop the coordination for the more advanced skills.

Locomotor skills are necessary for developing demonstrations--try the ones listed and encourage the participants to create their own. The dance steps performed with jump ropes can be an interesting and challenging rhythmical experience.

KEEPING RHYTHM

While holding the rope handles together in front of the body with both hands, swing the rope first on one side of the body and then the other. Participants can do this while stationary or when moving. It is effective in a routine as background movement during individual demonstrations and can also be a means of moving participants onstage or offstage as they maintain a rhythm with the rope.

D E M O N S T R A T I O N S

As soon as a group have developed the basic and locomotor skills and one or more dance skills, they are ready to put the skills to music and to choreograph a routine for demonstration.

Select a popular tune with a good beat and experiment with skills as they are learned. Start the demonstration with locomotor skills that the participants can perform well. These skills need not be the same for each person, but can be their own choices as long as they can be performed to the same rhythms. The second phase of the demonstration could be skills performed by everyone in unison. The third phase could be individual skills performed by one or more of the participants at a time while the others keep rhythm.

ROPE JUMPING

KEY
F--Forward
B--Backward
R--Right Foot
L--Left Foot
_____ One Full Count
_____ One Half of a Count
____ One Third of a Count

Margaret Greenwood Blake
Brigham Young University Press
Provo, Utah

BASIC SKILLS

1. HIGH KNEE

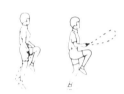

Spring L to R   Spring R to L
Rope   Rope
Spring L to R   Spring R to L
Rope   Rope

2. SINGLE TOE TAP

Spring R to L, Tap R-B
Rope
Spring L to R, Tap L-B
Rope

3. DOUBLE TOE TAP

Spring L to R,
Rope
Tap L-B   Tap L-B
Spring R to L,
Rope
Tap R-B   Tap R-B

4. STEP KICK

Spring R to L, Kick R-F
Rope
Spring L to R, Kick L-F
Rope

5. STEP KICK-PULL

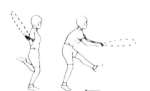

Spring L to R, Kick L-F, Pull R-B
Rope
Spring R to L, Kick R-F, Pull L-B
Rope

6. CROSS LEGS

Jump Crossing L over R
Rope
Jump Crossing R over L
Rope

7. COMBINATION

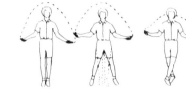

Stride   Together
Rope   Rope

Cross L over R   Together
Rope   Rope

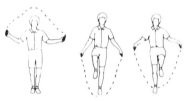

8. INDIAN HOP

Jump from R and L   Hop on L
Jump from L to R and L
Rope
Jump from R and L   Hop on R
Jump from R to R and L
Rope

9. CROSS ARMS FORWARD

Jump from R and L
Rope
Jump, Cross R arm over L
Rope

LOCOMOTOR SKILLS

10. RUN

Spring F-R to L
Rope
Spring F-L to R
Rope

11. SKIP

Step F-L to R, Hop on R
Rope
Step F-R to L, Hop on L
Rope

12. SLIDE

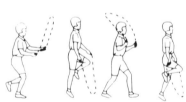

Step left to L, Spring L to R
Rope
Step left to L, Spring L to R
Rope

13. GALLOP

Step F-R to L, Lifting R knee
Rope
Spring L to R, Lifting L knee

DANCE SKILLS

14. SAMBA

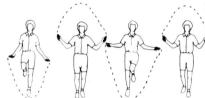

Spring F- L to R, Step L, Step R
Rope

Spring B- R to L, Step R, Step L
Rope

15. POLKA

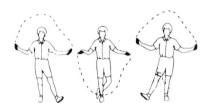

Hop on L, Step R, Step L, Step R
Rope

Hop on R, Step L, Step R, Step L
Rope

16. CHA-CHA

Spring F- L to R   Spring B- R to L
Rope

Step R, Step L, Step R
Rope

Spring F- R to L   Spring B- L to R
Rope

Step L, Step R, Step L
Rope

17. FINNISH REEL

Hop on R, L heel F
Rope

Hop on R, L toe B
Rope

Hop on L, R heel F
Rope

Hop on L, R toe B

18. GRAPEVINE

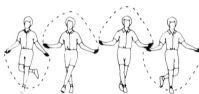

Spring left R to L
Rope

Spring B- L to R
Rope

Spring left R to L
Rope

Spring F- L to R
Rope

19. CHARLESTON

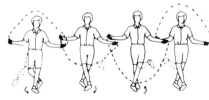

Jump F- R over L   Hop on R
Rope

Jump F- L over R   Hop on R
Rope

Jump B- L behind R   Hop on L
Rope

Jump B- R behind L   Hop on L
Rope

20. EAST SIDE

Spring L to R, Brush L- F and B
Rope

Step L, Step R

Spring R to L, Brush R- F and B
Rope

Step R, Step L

ADVANCED SKILLS

21. CRADLE

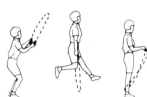

Spring F- R to L
Rope

Spring B- L to R
Rope

22. SCISSOR JUMP

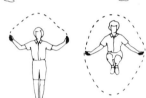

Jump, Scissor L- F and R- B
Rope

Jump, Scissor L- F and R- B
Rope

23. DOUBLE-TURN

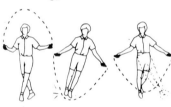

Jump from R and L

Rope, Rope

24. BELLS

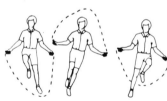

Step Crossing L over R
Rope

Hop from L, Click heels together

Step Crossing R over L
Rope

Hop from R, Click heels tog

25. FLEA HOP

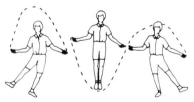

Step R to L
Rope

Hop on L - Slide R

Step L to R
Rope

Hop on R - Slide L

26. CUT STEP

Spring R to L, Extend R leg
Rope

Spring L to R, Extend L leg
Rope

CREATIVE DANCE

Creative dance for children is the expression of the child's inner being through movement. Movement is the language of dance and the body is the instrument. Through the use of his body the child interprets and expresses thoughts and feelings in his own way. The discovery and exploration of body parts--how they move, what can be done with them, and their general use to express that which is within the realm of the child's experiences--form the basis of creative dance.

The opinion that there is a place for creative dance in education is probably more widely held today than ever before, except in the ancient Greek civilization.

> The general end of education in America at the present time is the fullest possible development of the individual within the framework of our present industrialized democratic society.[1]

William James observed that the strength of any society is best judged by the creativity it induces in its citizens.[2] Because movement is basic in a child's learning and can thus meet some of the educational goals for developing an individual's potential, all children, not just the talented, should be given the opportunity to learn through creative dance. Creativity is a means of learning, of problem solving, of self-discovery and expression. "Creative dance is the only activity in which physical movement is used nonfunctionally and as a personal experience."[3] The child does not have to concentrate on an object or game and can therefore discover a great deal about his mind, his body, his thoughts, his language, his imagination, and his own ideas. He becomes aware of rhythm, space, energy, and the control of movement. His perception of the other arts is sharpened, and thus he may see that the elements of dance are also present in music, literature, and painting. Because creative dance requires the use of the whole personality, it helps develop high self-esteem; since no one is a failure, each child can achieve success in his own expressions and discoveries. Creative dance also provides physical development, positive emotional release, and aesthetic appreciation due to heightened sensitivity to the environment. Many classroom situations leave little opportunity for creativity: children are taught to color inside the lines, follow strict instructions in arithmetic, and so forth. Creative dance is therefore an essential part of the physical education program for the elementary child, for it enables him to express himself freely and to discover more about himself and others.

ELEMENTS AND CONCEPTS OF DANCE

Although we cannot "talk" dance, we can communicate concepts or fundamental ideas. It is through this "dance language" that teacher and student achieve some understanding of what each is trying to accomplish. Stated briefly, "the <u>body</u> moves in and through <u>space</u>, which requires <u>time</u>; and since movement functions in relation to gravity, use of body weight or <u>force</u> is introduced. Put together in unique combinations, they become the means

346

through which movement is explored through the full scope and potential of the body."[4] It is important for the teacher to know the elements and to be able to call upon them. Here they are listed in a more detailed form.

ELEMENT 1--THE BODY'S MOVEMENT FUNDAMENTALS

Body movements: Movements which emanate around the axis of the body from a fixed base, such as a sitting, standing, kneeling, or lying position. They include bending, stretching, swinging, swaying, pushing, pulling, turning, and twisting.

Locomotor movements: Movements which propel the body from one place to another through space, and include walking, running, leaping, jumping, hopping, galloping, skipping, and sliding. (Definitions are given below.)

Combinations of movements: Sequences involving a series of two or more locomotor movements (such as running and skipping), a series of two or more body movements (such as pushing and pulling), or a combination of locomotor and body movements (such as running and swinging, or walking and stretching).[5]

Definitions of Locomotor Movements

Walk: A transfer of weight from one foot to the other, in a smooth and even rhythm, during which one foot remains in contact with the ground.

Run: A transfer of weight from one foot to the other with increased tempo and a moment when both feet are off the ground at the same time.

Leap: An extended run.

Jump: An elevation movement executed by taking off and landing on both feet.

Hop: An elevation movement executed by taking off and landing on the same foot.

Skip: A combination step-hop with a long-short rhythm.

Gallop: A combination of a step-leap with a long-short rhythm.

Slide: A combination of a step-hop in a long-short rhythm. The body moves in a lateral position through space, with a moment of elevation.

The locomotor movements are very familiar and comfortable to children, for they use them every day in play or in covering space. In a dance lesson a teacher may encourage the child to "run more lightly" or "lift your knees as high as the ceiling when you go skipping," offering a challenge to the child to perform better what he may already know.

ELEMENT 2--SPACE

Direction: The line of motion made by the body moving through space; for example, forward, backward, sideward, diagonal, or up and down.

347

Levels: The altitude of the body moving in space: high, middle, or low.

Range: The amount of space the body occupies as it moves; for example, large, small, narrow, or wide.

Focus: The direction of gaze or intent of the individual as he moves through space.

Shape: A visual-kinetic image or a body design in space; for example, angular, circular, or linear.

Floor pattern: Designs made by the feet as they travel in various paths through space; for example, straight, curvilinear, zigzag, triangular, circular.

Density: Different tensions established between an individual and the space through which he moves; for example, moving through thick honey, pushing through a large body of water, moving through lightly falling snow.

Design: The arrangement of the shape, including off-centered shapes (asymmetrical designs) or centered ones (symmetrical designs).

ELEMENT 3--TIME

Time is expressed in the body as rhythm, and rhythm is in everything as a measuring of time, space, and energy. It may be countable (metric) or uncountable, such as breath or rhapsodic rhythms. Children should be exposed to both, but especially they love the breath rhythms, such as the feeling and timing of waves in the ocean or a lake; the bouncing of a ball as it moves from slow to fast and finally stops; and the rhythms of the wind, rain, and other natural phenomena. The teacher has all his surroundings from which to gather wonderful and imaginative ideas for rhythm experiences.

Rhythmic pattern: An organized ordering of beats or measured energy.

Metric rhythm: An organized beat pattern in a countable cycle.

Beat: The underlying pulse or basic unit of a pattern.

Accent: Emphasis.

Meter: The grouping of beats by their accents.

Tempo: The rate of speed of a movement or pattern.

Measure: A group of beats, one of which has a primary (heavier) accent.

Phrasing: The formation of measures into larger rhythmic structures.

ELEMENT 4--FORCE (OR ENERGY)

Force is experienced as the amount of tension or stress of a movement. It is the flow and control of energy.

Sustained movement: A smooth, constant flow of energy.

Swinging movement (swaying movement): A release into gravity, causing an increase in momentum, which carries the movement again to a point of suspension against gravity, which in turn causes a reversal of direction, increase of momentum, and a repetition of the cycle.

Collapse: Total lack of energy.

Vibratory movement: A continual pattern of rapid expanding and checking of energy.

Percussive movement: A sudden release of energy.

     Explosive: A large expenditure of energy.
     Staccato: Quick, sharp releases of energy.
     Pulsating: Quick, even releases of energy (less sharp than staccato).

Suspension: A sensation of buoyancy, such as at the end of a breath.

ELEMENT 5--SENSORY AND IDEATIONAL STIMULI (MOTIVATORS)

Other factors that affect movement are motivators, or stimuli. Children are deeply influenced by their surroundings--those things they see, hear, touch, or feel. They may translate these into movement, or their perceptions may provide impetus for movement or modify it. Here is a list of stimuli a teacher could use.[6]

Visual stimuli (sense of sight): Visual stimuli may be pictorial (such as the picture of a butterfly) or abstract (such as a zigzag line drawn on a piece of paper and suggesting many things, one being lightning). This category includes everything one can see which inspires movement. Color would be an important stimulating factor for children.

Tactile stimuli (sense of touch): Textures of cloths, objects, and liquids could be used as stimuli. The feeling of a soft cotton ball, for example, suggests soft and light movement. One could explore the contour and shape of objects such as a small, round rock or a twisted limb of a tree. Temperatures can also motivate movement ideas. For example, the teacher could ask the class, "How does it make you feel to be cold?" or "What kinds of play take place in the cold snow? How can you show me the same idea of movement but in a larger, stretching manner?"

Olfactory stimuli (sense of smell): Different odors, such as the burning leaves of autumn time, can provide ideas for movement.

Gustatory stimuli (sense of taste): A teacher could let a child taste something, watching the expression on the child's face. They could discuss what happened. Then the child could try to feel with his whole body how the item tasted. A pickle, for example, could evoke twisted, puckering movements.

Auditory stimuli (sense of hearing): Auditory stimuli could include percussive instruments, melodic instruments, the human voice, or verbal sounds.

<u>Moods and emotions</u>: Children can dance about anger, fear, loneliness, and so forth.

<u>Stories, poems, records</u>: Children love this area. They like the happenings of yesterday (primitive dance movement) as well as those of the present (astronauts and rockets).

TIPS FOR TEACHERS

A teacher should be sensitive to the students, willing to learn through trial and error, and unafraid to change ideas if necessary. Learn the students' names and create an atmosphere of informality within the structure of the class. Children should learn self-control but should also be allowed the freedom of individuality and the opportunity to exchange ideas verbally. Watch the students and comment in a positive manner about what you see them doing, letting them know that you like the different shapes they make, and so on. Ask questions to help the children be creative. Here are some leading questions referring to the elements of dance that we have already read about.

SPACE

1. Can you find a space in the room where you can turn or stand and not touch anyone else?
2. How small can you make yourself? How tall?
3. Can you move quickly forward? Backward? Sideways?

FORCE

1. How quietly can you walk? How heavily?
2. How would you use your entire body to push a giant doorbell? How would you walk against a strong wind? How would you lift a light feather with your back?
3. How could your body show me a happy feeling? A feeling of anger?

TIME

1. Can you move your arm slowly but your head quickly?
2. How fast can you move in this room? How slowly?

BODY MOVEMENTS AND LOCOMOTOR STEPS

1. Can you stretch while standing on one leg? On the other?
2. How far forward can you bend without falling over?
3. How many parts of your body can you twist separately? Together?
4. Who can slide forward? Backward?
5. Can you think of other ways to jump? Run? Walk?
6. Can you gallop in a circle? A square? A triangle?

As a teacher you are very important, for you open new windows for the child. You need not be a dancer, but you do need to give the children security, understanding, encouragement, and friendship. Help the students know that they will not be laughed at and that each can and will succeed. Cooperation and accomplishment, rather than competition, are the goals of the class.

It is usually a good idea to let the class dance barefoot in order to cut down on accidents. Also, the children will be freer in the use of their ankles, feet, and legs. Make sure the floor is clean or at least free from harmful bits of rock, glass, or other debris. For the girls, wearing long pants or shorts rather than dresses usually helps to release movement. Grouping children sometimes helps when many children are involved, and circles are good for the expression of intimate ideas. There must be time enough for the children to be able to explore an idea fully, and you should have in mind what you want your students to learn each day. The room and whatever might be in it could serve as stimuli for ideas. Percussion instruments or music can be put to good use. The voice is important too. Do not let it become monotonous, but use it to help the children.

Know the age characteristics of the children with whom you work. Know what to expect from them in terms of general capabilities and interests, and appeal to this knowledge in teaching them. Create stimulating concepts and provide variety in your teaching, trying new ideas yourself so as to release new discoveries in your students. Be aware of and alive to your environment.

MINI-LESSONS

The following ideas are to be regarded as mini-lessons. They are suggestions only and are written as if the teacher were really talking to the children. When you become inspired you can take off from these ideas and do what you want to do, remembering that you are working with one or two elements of dance per lesson and that the use of imagery or stimuli will help to make the experience more interesting. You are not trying to entertain the class but to help release creative movement and ideas from within the class members. These 6 mini-lessons do **not** even begin to cover all the areas that could be taught but they do provide some ideas and illustrate the structure of one main element per lesson, as mentioned earlier. Eventually you can and should make up your own lessons.

MINI-LESSON ONE

Elements concerned: Primarily locomotor steps and shapes, some tempo and imagery.

"Children, show me how you came walking into the school building today. Go anywhere in the room, but be careful not to bump into each other. Some of you walked into the building very quickly. I bet you were happy to come to school. We'll all walk quickly too just like those happy children did. Here we go.

"Could we go faster and faster until we must run? Good, I can see you running now. Let's try to run quietly as if our floor were made of foam rubber and we couldn't make a sound. Now stop quickly with your body in an interesting shape. Could your shape be one that is bent over? Could your shape be a stretched one? What if some of you found a shape on the floor, and maybe some an upside-down one? I see some very interesting stopping shapes, all kinds. Let's look at all of these different shapes you have found.

"I wonder if we could make a running pattern that would take you somewhere else in our room and then stop quickly in another different shape, one that you have never done before. Here we go. [Guide them rhythmically with the voice or a drum helping them to know when to run and when to stop quickly. Let them create a couple of stopping shapes.]

"Good, and yet my eyes are getting tired of just seeing you run. What other ways can you find to move all over the room? [Listen to their answers and try to use them, especially if they name some of the other locomotor steps.]

"Yes, see if you can go skipping, and stop in your favorite unusual shape. Now, try galloping, and stop in another shape. This time try one of my favorite steps. It is called a leap. Imagine that there is a stream of water running across our room and we don't want to fall in. Leap over it. Stretch your legs wide apart--here we go.

"You have worked very hard and have done some wonderful shapes and steps. Try to do some of these on your way home today. Thank you, children, and good-bye."

MINI-LESSON TWO

Elements concerned: Exploring time or rhythm: concentrating on tempo with contrast of fast and slow, using ideational stimuli of hide and seek.

"Imagine that each one of you is hiding behind a large colorful box right here in our room. I'll pretend to close my eyes so that I can't see you. You are all curled up so small that I don't even know you are there. Suppose you wanted to play hide and seek with me from behind your box. Here you come peeking, very slowly, up from behind your box. Slowly, slowly, ever so slowly, come peeking with your head. Now add your arms; now add your body and legs. See how you can stretch and peek from behind your pretend box. Peek at me in your own reaching-out pattern. What if I opened my eyes like this [open eyes wide]? What will you do? Yes, some of you may want to hide again. Will you hide slowly? No, quickly this time. Could you pull yourself in as quickly as this sound I'm going to make on the drum? Bang! Let's try it again. Out you come slowly, slowly, and stretch in your own way. Now quickly hide again: bang!

"See if this time you could reach out from behind the box quickly, as if you are saying 'Boo,' and then go back in slowly. Here we go. [At this point you can try all kinds of rhythmic changes. You can have the children quickly or slowly change positions, going to others' pretend boxes, or take off on any other new idea that may occur to you.]"

MINI-LESSON THREE

Elements concerned: Exploring body movements using silly putty as ideational stimuli. (Work with the qualities of the putty and show how it can be stretched, pressed flat, curled and twisted, and bounced. Use these qualities to stimulate movement in the body, showing that the body can also stretch, lie low and flat to the ground, curl, twist, and bounce. There are other qualities to be discovered too.

"Today I have a surprise for you right here in my hand. [Hold your hand in fist form hiding the silly putty.] What do you think it is? [Let them guess.] Those are all good guesses, and maybe another day we could dance about some of the things you've mentioned, but none of those answers are correct because here is what I have [open hand]. Yes, it is silly putty, and see what it can do. It can be stretched. [Show its qualities first and then begin to explore them in movement.]

"Find you own special place on the floor in the room. Imagine that I am pulling two parts of you and stretching them apart from each other. I am pulling two parts just as if you were the silly putty. See, you stretch and stretch. Stretch in your own way. [Explore some more.] The putty could be pressed flat. What if I were pressing you flat against the floor from your last stretching shape? Here I go, pressing slowly until you are close to the floor. Some of you are so flat and low you look just like melted silly putty. Those are very good patterns. I'm going to gather you up into a little ball. Curl up into your own little ball. Can you be as small as a period or a dot? Good! You know how the round silly putty ball went bouncing from big bounces to little ones? See if you can do just the opposite and go from little bounces to big ones. Begin to bounce higher and higher and higher until you must stop standing high. I'm going to make the putty go twisting around. Show me how you can go twisting around too. Good!

"You have done stretches, melting, twisting, bouncing, and curling into a little ball. Decide what were your favorite three movements and put them together in your own pattern just the way you would like to do them. [Some child might do a slow twist, then move directly into curling into a ball and finish with a low stretch. There will be all kinds of movement possibilities. Encourage them to be imaginative. Let the children view the finished studies they have composed.]"

MINI-LESSON FOUR

Elements concerned: Exploring space, involving range, with contrast of big and little; levels with contrast of low and high; and moving in space. Ideational stimuli are a balloon and its properties.

"How can you make yourselves as big as possible? Show me. Good, I can see you really reaching and trying to touch the walls in this room. You make me think of a large balloon when it is all blown up big and round. I just happen to have one behind my desk. Look at it. See if you can make yourselves still larger. If I let the air out of the balloon it will slowly go down until it is very small and low to the floor, see? Try this: let the air out of your large shape slowly until you become very small and low to the ground. Let us watch some of you do this. Good. Blow yourselves up again slowly, slowly; all of you do it in such different ways and all are very good. Keep blowing up larger and larger. Can you make your large balloon shape go moving quietly all around the room as if the balloon were floating in the air? Keep it floating lightly all over the room. Here is some music that gives us the feeling of floating. [Let them continue in the patterns they choose.]

"Rest for a moment and watch what happens when I let the balloon go-- see, it goes every which way because the air is coming out of it quickly and sends it zooming all over the room. What are some words you know that describe what you saw the balloon do?

"In small groups of three imagine that the air is coming out of you in

the same way. See if you can capture the quality of the zooming balloon.
Here you go, first three. [You may want to use a drum to get this fast and
percussive quality. Notice that you did not tell the children to "be a balloon," but that you asked them to watch its movement and try to capture the
quality of its movement. After all of the class has tried it you could review the whole idea again quickly or finish class with a new idea such as a
goodbye dance, letting each child do whatever he wishes before going home.]"

MINI-LESSON FIVE

Elements concerned: Exploring force involving sustained movement and percussive movement. Ideational stimuli are light plastic material for the light,
sustained quality and pieces of long, heavier plastic, requiring a lot of
energy to use, for percussive quality.

"Children, come over here by the phonograph for just a minute and listen
to this special music. [Use recorded music with a floating, sustained
quality.] What words can you think of that describe this music? [Hopefully
they come up with descriptions such as light, floating, soft.] Yes, it does
have that kind of quality. How would just one arm go dancing to this music?
Good! How could your whole body go dancing to this music? Show me. That
was pretty good, but I think if we use these small pieces of plastic material
to go with us and imagine they are made of the finest fabric--like a spider's
delicate web, or cotton candy thread--then maybe you would even be more careful to move slowly and gently. Try it and go in your own delicate way. Sometimes you might want to just stop and hold the plastic in an interesting
manner. Try it.
"Sit down on the floor now wherever you are and I will gather up the
plastic while you are listening to another kind of music on the phonograph.
[This time it should be very strong, maybe percussive, but definitely a contrast to the first.] Does it make you feel the same as the first record you
heard? No? Why? Okay, it is stronger and faster. Will it take more energy
to move to this music, do you think? Let us find out. Here is a long piece
of heavy plastic. I would like you to move it fast in the air, making all
kinds of shapes as if a strong wind were blowing it very hard. Never let the
plastic touch the ground. Always keep it moving fast and furiously in the
air. Here we go.
"Rest! What differences did you feel between the light and the strong
plastic? Did you get tired? All right, you were using a lot of force and
energy. Now you decide which one you would like to do the most, and each of
you may dance alone to the music of his choice."

MINI-LESSON SIX

Elements concerned: Locomotor steps, force as involved in the swing, and
space as involved in focus. This is an idea taught by Laurinda Beecher based
around a story. It has not been fully developed here, but a teacher could
do this according to desire.

"How many of you know the story of the Wizard of Oz? How many have seen
the movie? Let us imagine that we are on the yellow brick road that Dorothy
followed. [You may need to review the story for them.] Follow me. Skip and

skip and skip and skip and follow the yellow brick road. [Repeat, singing if you wish.] Swing your arms and lift your knees up; follow the yellow brick road. Swing your arms and point your toes if you can; follow the yellow brick road. [Stop suddenly.] Look over there in the cornfield. What do you see? Yes, it's the Scarecrow. Do you know how he is hanging there? Yes, on a pole. Who can tell me why scarecrows need to be tied up? [Let them answer.] Yes, they are stuffed with straw. If you were tied just like the Scarecrow, show me how you would move the part of your arm that is not tied down. [Swing or move your arm from the elbow on down.] Swing one arm; then swing both in different ways. If someone took away the pole our arms are tied to, we should be able to swing our whole arm. Doesn't it feel good to be free and able to make big swings with your whole arm? Try little swings too or one arm at a time; then swing both arms in different directions. [You could use swinging music as an additional stimulus.]

"If your back and waist were still tied to the pole to hold you up, but someone untied your legs, could you find some interesting ways to swing your legs, now that they are free to move? Show me how. [Point out good ways and have everyone try them.]

"If someone untied your back and left only your waist tied around the pole, you would drop over from the waist, because if you were a scarecrow all you would have inside would be straw. Stay there now. Did everything drop? Remember, the Scarecrow didn't have a brain because his head was filled with straw; so let your head drop clear down too. Good! Now I see some real floppy scarecrows. Now, just as if someone had tied strings to your head and arms and were pulling them, lift up and up and up until you are as high as you can possibly be. Drop again, lift again, drop, and lift. We have had a lot of fun swinging our arms and legs like floppy scarecrows."

Some Further Ideas

The story of the Wizard of Oz, like any story, lends itself to further development of movement which could be done a little at a time each day for several days if a teacher would want to. Here are some ideas on how it could be developed.

Hurricane: High energy movements, turns, spirals, exploration of levels in space, and accelerating tempos.

Waking up in Oz surrounded by Munchkins: Stretches, quick darting movements with the feet in locomotor patterns. Discuss what they think Munchkins are, how they would move; then explore their ideas.

Appearance of the Good Fairy, who gives the magic shoes to Dorothy: Exploration of what steps the magic shoes could do and where they could take one.

Setting out to find the Wizard of Oz: Skips or other locomotor steps on the yellow brick road. Students could make up their own combinations.

Meeting the Scarecrow: Floppy patterns and maybe swings.

Entering the forest and finding the Tin Man: Percussive movements and isolation of body parts as each joint is oiled and can move again.

Meeting the Cowardly Lion: Exploration of movements the body can do to express the shy and cowardly quality, such as pulling in and turning away with the whole body.

Running across the field of poppies and becoming drowsy: Stretches and slow falls to the floor in sleeping shapes. Work with decreasing tempos as students get more and more sleepy.

Entering the Emerald City of Oz: Exploration of ideas from the children's imaginations of what one would find in the wonderful city.

Approaching the Wizard: A shaking or vibratory quality as if frightened.

Setting out to find the Wicked Witch of the West: Exploration of witch shapes--gnarled, twisted, crooked, and angular shapes.

Melting the Witch: Exploration of melting patterns from high to low, ending in different shapes on the floor.

Celebration, departure of Dorothy for home: A happy dance with lively jumps, turns, and so on.

Other stories that could be used are "The Three Little Pigs," "Three Billy Goats Gruff," "The Three Bears," " Jack and the Beanstalk," "Hansel and Gretel," and "Peter Rabbit." Almost any children's story will do if the teacher uses plenty of imagination. Poems are also very good stimuli and should be used whenever possible.

R E F E R E N C E S

1. Educational Policies Commission, Policies of Education in American Democracy (Washington, D.C.: National Education Association of the U.S.), p. 186.

2. Rockefeller Panel Report, The Performing Arts, Problems and Prospects--The Future of Theatre, Dance, and Music in America (New York: McGraw & Hill Book Co., 1965).

3. Mary Joyce, First Steps in Teaching Creative Dance (Palo Alto, Calif.: National Press Books, 1973), p. 5.

4. Geraldine Diamondstein, Children Dance in the Classroom (New York: Macmillan Co., 1971).

5. Gladys Andrews, Creative Rhythmic Movement for Children (Englewood Cliffs, N.J.: Prentice Hall, Inc., 1954), p. 38.

6. As categorized by Elizabeth R. Hayes of the University of Utah.

BIBLIOGRAPHY OF CHILDREN'S DANCE BOOKS

Andrews, Gladys. Creative Rhythmic Movement for Children, Englewood Cliffs, N.J.: Prentice Hall, 1954.

Boorman, Joyce. Creative Dance in the First Three Grades. Don Mills, Ont.: Longsman Canada Limited, 1969.

_____. Creative Dance in Grades Four to Six. Don Mills, Ont.: Longsman Canada Limited, 1971.

Diamondstein, Geraldine. Children Dance in the Classroom. New York: Macmillan Co., 1971.

Murray, Ruth Lovell. Dance in Elementary Education. 3rd ed. New York: Harper and Row, 1975.

APPENDIX

<u>M E T H O D S   O F   W R I T I N G   D A N C E S</u>

Many record companies that record dance music also write instructions for dances. Here are five different samples of methods or techniques of writing dances. In case you ever have occasion to buy a record with instructions, you should become acquainted with all forms of writing.

P O L L Y   W O L L Y   W I G G L E R

Here is a dance as written by the Windsor Record Company. These instructions come with the records.

Starting Position: A "team" or two couples facing each other, one couple facing counterclockwise around room, women on men's right side, partners have inside hands joined. Teams arranged in a circle around the room.

Footwork: Identical footwork throughout the dance for men and women.

MEAS   VERSE

1-4   BALANCE LEFT; BALANCE; SLIDE LEFT, TWO; THREE, SWING;
Step to left side on left foot, touch right toe beside left foot, step to right side on right foot, touch left toe beside right foot; start left foot and do three slide steps to left side, then swing right foot across in front of left (the couple in each team facing counterclockwise has moved toward center and the other couple has moved toward wall);

5-8   BALANCE RIGHT; BALANCE LEFT; SLIDE RIGHT, TWO; THREE, SWING;
Repeat action of measures 1-4 except to start on right foot and move to right side, ending in starting position with couples facing each other; then all make a right-hand star in center;

9-12   STAR, TWO; THREE, FOUR; FIVE, SIX; STRAIGHTEN OUT;
In a right-hand star position and starting left foot, walk clockwise one full turn around with eight steps using the last two steps to straighten out to starting position, couples facing each other squarely, partners joining inside hands;

13-16   BALANCE FORWARD; BALANCE BACK; TWO-STEP THROUGH; ON TO THE NEXT;
Step forward on left foot, touch right toe beside left foot; step backward on right foot, touch left toe beside right foot; release joined hands, start left foot and take two steps forward passing opposite person right shoulders and progressing on to a new approaching couple. The new "team" all join hands.

MEAS	CHORUS

1-4   CIRCLE LEFT, TWO; THREE, FOUR; FIVE, SIX; SEVEN, TURN;
        Start left foot and all circle left (clockwise) one full turn around
        in eight steps, using eighth step to change direction in preparation
        to circling right;

5-8   CIRCLE RIGHT, TWO; THREE, FOUR; FIVE, SIX; STRAIGHTEN, OUT;
        Circle right (counterclockwise) one full turn around with eight steps
        starting left foot, using last two steps to face other couple squarely
        as in starting position, breaking circle and partners joining inside
        hands, ready to repeat the dance;

        PERFORM THE ENTIRE DANCE A TOTAL OF
        FIVE TIMES, ENDING WITH PARTNERS
        BOWING.

G O I N G   H O M E

Here is a different method of writing round dances that may be found accom-
panying professional records.

Position: Open for introduction
Footwork: Opposite throughout

MEAS	CALL	INSTRUCTIONS
	WAIT; WAIT	Bal Apt, Tch, -; Step Tog, Tch (To SC Pos). In semi-closed Pos do two Fwd two-steps to end in CP M's Bk to COH; Step to side in LOD on L hold 1 Ct, Close R to L, hold 1 Ct; Step to side on L, in place on R, then in place on L, hold 1 Ct;
1-4	FWD TWO-STEP; FWD TWO-STEP (To face): SLIDE -, CLOSE, -' SIDE STEP, STEP,;	
5-8	ROCK BACK, RECOVER, SIDE CLOSE, CROSS (Through), TURN TWO-STEP; TURN TWO-STEP	
9-16	TURN AWAY TWO-STEP; AROUND TWO-STEP; AROUND TWO-STEP; TOGETHER TWO-STEP; Arch to girl ahead	Turn away from partner in 4 two-steps (M-LF) (G-R) describing a circle, assume loose closed Pos, M back COH.

H A W A I I A N   M I X E R

The Los Angeles school district uses the following method in writing dances.

Prepared by: David G. Rumbaugh, Supervisor
              physical education

Approved by: Herbert M. Cadwell,
           Assistant Superintendent

Record: "Hawaiian Charms" Windsor #4684
Formation: Double circle, one couple facing another couple. Partners side
            by side, inside hands joined. Directions are for boy; girl does
            counterpart.

1. Balance forward on left foot. Balance back on right foot. Repeat.

2. Couples separate. Each boy steps sideways to his left with a step-close-
    step.

3. Each boy steps sideways to his right with a step-close-step.

4. Repeat no. 2 and no. 3.

5. Couples progress forward with four walking steps, passing right shoulder
    of opposite person.

6. Greet a new couple with an "aloha" and repeat entire dance.

P O P C O R N

This method of writing dances is occasionally used by the youth organizations
of The Church of Jesus Christ of Latter-day Saints.

Music: Modern pop
Formation: Lines. Up, down pulse. Bend knees on each music count.

SEQ.	COUNT	CALL	DETAIL
Side Pull			
1-2	1)2	Pull L	Stretch arms out L with loose fists. Pull arms toward body, bending knees. Repeat pull and knee bend.
3-4	3-4	Pull R	Stretch arms out to R and pull toward body (bend knees). Repeat pull and knee bend.
Push Pull			
5-6	2)2	Push	Push L hand toward floor, palm down (R hand hip-bone high, palm down; L knee straight, R knee bent). Push R hand down as you pull L hand up to hip-bone level (R knee straight, L knee bent).
Clap			
7-8	3-4	Clap	Clap hands behind back. Clap hands in front of body.
Hitch			
0-10	3)2	Hitch R	Point R thumb over R shoulder as if hitching

SEQ.	COUNT	CALL	DETAIL
			a ride; at the same time bend knees. Repeat R hitch and knee bend.
11-12	3-4	Hitch L	Repeat hitch with L thumb over L shoulder and knee bends twice.

Push, Pull, and Clap

SEQ.	COUNT	CALL	DETAIL
13-16	4)234		Repeat 5-8.

MIDTERM TESTS

ROUND DANCE TEST

DEFINITIONS

Define and give one example of each of the following terms.

1. Directional call--

2. Counting call--

3. Rhythm call--

4. Chanting call--

5. Prompting call--

TERMS

1. Name four words that indicate the following.

    A. Weight changes--
    1.   2.   3.   4.

    B. No weight change--
    1.   2.   3.   4.

2. Name four different periods mentioned in the history of dance.
    1.   2.   3.   4.

3. Before a fun dance is demonstrated, the name of the dance should be given.
    Name three other items of necessary information in their proper order.
    1.   2.   3.

STEPS

Write down nine basic dance steps with a counting call, using one measure or
four counts for each step. Call two beats ahead. Example: 1 2 chug now
    1.   4.   7.

    2.   5.   8.

    3.   6.   9.

WRITE DANCES

Write a double circle fun dance 4 measures long, using a <u>rhythm</u> call.

D A N C E   Q U I Z

Fill in the blank spaces with all the information required to understand and teach this dance correctly.

Formation: Double circle
Position: Two-hand
Footwork: Opposite (man L, lady R)

Music: Own choice
Record: Own choice
Rhythm: 4/4, 8 meas

MEAS	1	2	3	4	INSTRUCTIONS
	(music count)				
	now	let's	GRAPEVINE	4	Grapevine:
1	(write rhythm call)				
2	now	let's	two-'step'	forward	Two-step:
3	(write chanting call)				
4	now	let's	CHUG		Chug: Man step side L. Weight should be on L foot with R foot touching floor just long enough to push body sideward. Close R to L. Repeat 3 times. Touch R to L and repeat all to R.
5	(write counting call)				
6	now	let's	SLIDE		Slide: Man step side L and close R to L. Repeat 3 times. Repeat all to R.
7	(write directional call)				
8	now	start	over	grapevine	Repeat entire dance.

On the back, write the 7 items of introductory information in the order that you would call them.

364

FOLK DANCE TEST

MATCHING

Match the dance with the country of its origin. (Countries may be used more than once.)

_____ Korobushka
_____ Oslo Waltz
_____ Doudlebska Polka
_____ Hier Ek Weer
_____ Hora
_____ Misirlou
_____ Makazice
_____ Vayiven Uziyahu
_____ Huki-Lau

a. South Africa
b. Czechoslovakia
c. England
d. Russia
e. Serbia
f. Israel
g. Denmark
h. Hawaii
i. Greece

MULTIPLE CHOICE

_____ 1. An example of a snake dance is (a) Korobushka, (b) Misirlou, (c) Hora.

_____ 2. Couples can go anywhere on the floor in (a) Doudlebska Polka, (b) Oslo Waltz, (c) Vayiven Uziyahu.

_____ 3. The walk is the basic step in (a) Hier Ek Weer, (b) Hora, (c) Ve' David.

ARRANGE SEQUENCE

Number the step patterns on the right in proper sequence.

1. Doudlebska Polka

Men clap, women polka cw.
Men star L, singing tra-la-la.
All polka anywhere.

2. Misirlou

Grapevine R.
Two-step back ccw.
Step R, point L.
Two-step fwd cw.

3. Tant' Hessie

Do-si-do (pass L shoulders).
Walk fwd 4 (L shoulders together).
Turn for 16 steps in shoulder-waist
     position.
Walk fwd 4 (R shoulders together).
Do-si-do (Pass R shoulders).

FILL IN

Write the starting formation of each dance.

1. Misirlou--

2. Hier Ek Weer--

3. Korobushka--

365

CREATIVE DANCE TEST

TRUE/FALSE

_____ 1. Creativity is discouraged when spontaneity is inhibited.

_____ 2. Anxiety about subjects to be covered and checked on makes some teachers crowd out creativity in their teaching.

_____ 3. A teacher should love children if she/he plans to teach.

_____ 4. In teaching children, the teacher needs to use words the children will understand and needs to talk down to them.

_____ 5. The skip is the only locomotor step with uneven (long-short) rhythm.

_____ 6. Planning units and lessons in creative dance is not really essential.

_____ 7. Self-expression is a basic need of life.

_____ 8. Creative dance offers opportunities for physical growth and development as well as fostering aesthetic sensibilities in children.

_____ 9. Creative teaching encourages continuous growth in the teacher.

_____ 10. An important objective of creative dance is the building of a healthy self-concept.

SHORT ANSWER

1. Define and describe the differences between locomotor movements and fixed/axial movements. List all the basic locomotor steps.

2. Rhythm is in everything. Explain.

3. List the types of sensory stimuli a teacher could use and give four examples of each.

4. Discuss what creative dance can offer a child.

5. List and define the qualities of force.

6. Outline three lesson ideas that could be used in teaching creative dance (central idea or theme, development of the idea, culmination of the lesson, other possible lessons developing from the idea).